PROPERTY MATTERS

How Property Rights Are
Under Assault—And Why
You Should Care

JAMES V. DELONG

THE FREE PRESS

New York   London   Toronto   Sydney   Singapore

THE FREE PRESS
A Division of Simon & Schuster Inc.
1230 Avenue of the Americas
New York, NY 10020

THE FREE PRESS and colophon are trademarks
of Simon & Schuster Inc.

Designed by Carla Bolte

Manufactured in the United States of America

10   9   8   7   6   5   4   3   2   1

Library of Congress Cataloging-in-Publication Data

DeLong, James V., 1938–
    Property matters: how property rights are under assault—and why
you should care / James V. DeLong.
        p.   cm.
    Includes bibliographical references and index.
    1. Right of property—United States.   2. Land use—Law and
legislation—United States.   I. Title.
    KF562.D4   1997
    346.7304—dc21   96-48280
                                                           CIP
    ISBN 0-684-87437-7

To my children, who have always been my best teachers

Contents

PART IV. LARCENY, GRAND AND PETTY

PART V. SHAPES IN THE MIST

Acknowledgments

In the course of writing this book, I have accumulated more debts than I can possibly pay. My thanks go to the many people who generously shared their information, time, and thought, especially Jonathan Adler, Ronald Bailey, Martha Beauchamp, James Bovard, Roger Brown, James Burling, Clark Collins, Benjamin Cone, Jr., Christopher DeLong, J. Bradford DeLong, Michelle DeLong, W. Bradford DeLong, James Earnest, Richard Epstein, Paul Feldman, Bernard Goode, Robert Hahn, Philip Harter, Dale Jenkins, Paul Kamenar, John Kester, Julia Mahoney, Paul Mahoney, Ann Marie Marciarille, Nancy Marzulla, Garry McCauley, James Mietus, Frank Murray, William Myers, Robert Nelson, John Nicholson, William Niskanen, William O'Keefe, Roger Pillon, Margaret Ann Reigle, Michael Rostand, R. Neil Sampson, Ali Sevin, Benjamin Sharp, Jane Shaw, Julian Simon, Fred Smith, R. J. Smith, Richard Stroup, Ike Sugg, Steven Swanson, Jerry Taylor, Jonathan Tolman, William Tucker, Bruce Whiting, Steve Williams, Harold Wylie, Jr., Bruce Yandle, and many others. None of them should be held responsible for my errors, of course. I owe particular thanks to Dianne Dunlop Wyss, both for her personal support and for introducing me to the glories of the West; to David Bernstein of the Free Press for his faith in the project; to Beverly Miller for her careful and reflective editing; and to Loretta Denner and Jennifer Weidman, also of the Free Press, for their persistence in getting things right.

Finally, my profound appreciation goes to all the sources on a long list of references for making the work fascinating and to all the people involved in these battles for making it worthwhile.

PART I

LAYING THE FOUNDATION

Chapter 1

Stage Setting

Convince me I should care about property rights even if I am not a farmer or a lumber company

As any casual follower of the news knows, property rights is a hot-button issue. Pick up the newspaper. On the front page is a story about selling off factories and other assets in Eastern Europe or Russia, creating a system of private property where none has existed for half a century or more. Buried at the end of the first section are accounts of murderous conflicts over land rights in Mexico, South Africa, and Brazil. Turn to the business page, and read about intellectual property and negotiations with China or Japan over protection of patents and copyrights. Next to this story is a column on creating property rights in material on the Internet.

The local news section details zoning disputes and fights over historic preservation, and the national news tells of the latest assaults on the Endangered Species Act mounted by landowners who think the government is seizing their property. Nearby is a report of a cabinet officer's speech describing the administration's latest proposal to get pension funds to invest in areas the government regards as socially desirable. Alongside it are descriptions of the latest Supreme Court cases on wetlands regulations and the assets of savings and loan associations.

If you drop the paper and wander down the street, you might find the headquarters of a local group devoted to the defense of property rights. Some people estimate that five hundred different advocacy groups have sprung up, ranging from mighty coalitions to one person with a newsletter. Judging by the pile of material in my files, I could not prove to the contrary. In their offices are letters from people concerned about wetlands, endangered species, zoning, water, access to government timber, historic preservation, and a dozen other issues. Most of them ask for help: someone is doing something that devalues their property, and they do not know what to do. This is a true grass-roots movement, not—as its enemies would have you believe—a corporate front, and property rights was one of the powder kegs that blew the Democrats out of their congressional majority in 1994. Since then the prominence of the issue has continued to expand.

We usually associate property rights with land, and certainly land is crucial. Until quite recently, it was far and away the dominant form of productive property. For tens of thousands of years people have cooperated to use it to create wealth and civilization. For just as long, they have killed each other for it. Sometimes the cause is almost mystical, as when whole peoples struggle over an ancestral home. More often the conflict is over wealth—over the land's capacity to grow food or graze animals, its minerals, its water, its access to the sea and the riches of trade, or its strategic position as a defender of other land. Throughout history, land's importance has made it the fount of most thinking about property rights and the focus of most conflict. Who owns what, and how do you know, and what happens if A's use of his property conflicts with B's use of his?

ENGLAND, 1995

In a contemporary instance of a situation arising in one form or another for ten thousand years, a British rock star moves to the country. He is amazed, and outraged, to discover a neighbor fertilizing his fields with pungent pig manure. The aroma permeates the area. The star complains to the local council. This body, somewhat baffled by the star's view that his right to use his property means they should shut down an entire rural way of life, says, more or less, in a polite British way, "So what does he expect in farm country, perfume?"[1]

Despite the continuing importance of land, the industrial revolution of the nineteenth century and the information revolution of the twentieth changed the nature of property profoundly. Property is also the machinery to produce goods or the pool of money needed to buy both land and machinery. It can be a franchise, the right to ply a particular trade. The goodwill of a brand name known to billions of people is a kind of property, as is having one's name in the address books of a roster of blue-chip clients. So is a patent or copyright. Education and training of all sorts are property, known to economists as human capital, and U.S. workers and proprietors collect about three-quarters of the gross national income each year, largely as a return on investment in their own human capital. One of the best forms of property to have, though few think of it as such, is a tenured chair at a university. This provides reasonable and secure income and a platform to lecture about the evils of greed.

New kinds of property are invented constantly. The tax laws lead to the boxes in the air called condominiums, because home owners can deduct mortgage interest and real estate taxes while renters cannot. Ergo, renters are transmogrified into owners with a stroke of a legal wand. Another instance: The computer makes possible records of almost any degree of complexity, so Wall Street invents ways of slicing ownership of securities and other financial interests into infinite degrees of complexity. The huge market in complex derivatives could not exist without the computer.

In an advanced industrial-information society like the United States, land may no longer be the predominant producer of wealth, but make no mistake: this change will not tamp the conflicts over the nature of property rights. Because of its crucial role in fostering the wealth and the very survival of individuals and human societies, land has always aroused great passions, mostly greed, fear, pride, and rage. The potential for violence, combined with the workaday need to promote its efficient use, have made it a preoccupation of both law and custom. The new kinds of property excite all the same passions as the old, and many, though by no means all, of the principles and conflicts remain constant even as the nature of property changes. The safest of bets is that the expansion in the nature of property is making the conflicts more convoluted, not eliminating them. If you do not think people feel passionately about property rights in their computer software, you are not clicking on the right discussion groups.

To illustrate the continuity between land and other types of property, look at a progression of questions. If the government thinks it important to preserve an endangered species, can it order you to leave your property in a natural state to provide a home for it? If information on the effects of a drug is important to the protection of health, should a pharmaceutical company be told to publish the results of its research in a newspaper? If the Internal Revenue Service wants to study compliance patterns, can it order 153,000 randomly chosen taxpayers to take leave from their jobs to spend weeks on an audit from hell wherein they justify every penny of income and expense? Does the IRS have the right to appropriate your time this way, especially if you are a professional who bills by the hour?

After answering these, consider whether the needs of homeless people allow the government to order you to devote your second, vacation home to sheltering them. Next question: If poor people need legal counsel and medical care, should lawyers and doctors be required to devote 10 percent of their human capital to providing services gratis? If the government thinks everyone should have access to computers, can it tell you to allow any member of the public to use the home computer in your bedroom between the hours of 9:00 A.M. and noon each day? Suppose you write a piece of computer software. Can you be told to provide it free to all groups that perform public service, perhaps as defined by the United Fund? If you said yes to the first questions on the list, then bailed out at some point, where did you stop, and why?

This book is about property rights, and the current political, legal, and intellectual struggles swirling around them. It focuses on the immediate conflicts, where political passion is at its peak: land and natural resources. Over the long term, land may not be the most interesting area, but it remains the basis for our thinking about these issues. If a society does not get its principles right in the context of land, it is not likely to get them right for other forms of property either.

WASHINGTON, D.C., 1996

The Federal Communications Commission issues six hundred pages of regulations on the Telecommunications Act of 1996. Several telephone companies charge that the rules require them to sell their services at a price below actual cost and that this violates the protections of the U.S. Constitution by taking their property for public use without compensating them.[2]

This book concludes that some property owners are being treated badly and that their rights deserve more protection. This is a matter of great importance for the sake of both justice and national economic health. It is also, perhaps counterintuitively, crucial to the long-run success of the causes creating many of the collisions, such as environment protection, historic preservation, and even the production of software. This protection is also, again perhaps counterintuitively, vital to the interests of knowledge workers and urban professionals who think they are far removed from anything so basic as concern about the soil.

Its basic orientation does not make the book a polemic in defense of property though. The issues are often exquisitely difficult, and an abstract dedication to property rights does not answer concrete questions.

LITTLE ROCK, ARKANSAS, 1993–1995

During the 1993 Christmas season Jennings Osborne puts 3.2 million Christmas lights on his home, turning it into a tourist attraction that draws thousands of people. The neighbors sue. People labeling themselves advocates of property rights react in opposed ways. Some are distressed that the neighbors are trying to limit a person's right to do as he pleases with his own home. Others are equally appalled at his affront to the right of the neighbors to enjoy their property.

I find Little Rock an easy case (I'm for the neighbors), but the issues can get tougher. What if Osborne puts up only 1,000 lights, or he puts up blue lights when the neighbors like red? In real life, the neighbors win, and in 1995 Osborne is allowed to put up only 12,000 lights. But he wins too. The original exhibit is moved to Disney World in Florida, where it becomes the hit of the holiday season.[3]

MINNESOTA, 1995

An ongoing dispute pits an alliance of landowners and land users against the Mille Lacs tribe, which claims hunting and fishing rights under the Treaties of 1837 and 1855, untrammeled by state game laws, over large chunks of the state. Landowners, hunters, and fishermen are outraged, viewing this assault on state game and fish limits as an attack on their right to use the land, their property rights, and their livelihoods, which depend on the dollars spent by sporting tourists. They belong to the Alliance for America, the largest of the pro–property rights coalitions. As the Mille Lacs see it, they are only asking for the return of property stripped from them in the past, so they too could claim membership in a property rights defense coalition.

Given that I am all for property rights, who do I root for?[4]

Such dilemmas are common, and people end up in surprising positions. While Minnesotans want to promote effective state regulation as a means of safeguarding their property rights, in other places landowners regard government regulations as a serious impingement on their rights. Westerners staunchly defend the sanctity of property but protest when the federal government, as owner of a piece of land, acts like a landowner and raises grazing fees or limits access. To some people, the crisis over property rights is the local industrial plant's or pig farm's release of contaminants that migrate to their land. To others, the crisis is government restrictions on their historic right to emit contaminants in the course of using the land.

The list of surprising positions can be extended. Political conservatives who lecture on the need for people to exercise self-reliance and bear their own risks sometimes seem bent on protecting landowners from the vicissitudes of the real estate market. They want "to socialize losses while privatizing gains," a societal trend roundly damned in conservative journals when it arises in other contexts, such as welfare. To chide the other end of the political spectrum, many liberals who never meet a victim of social injustice they do not like are amazingly callous toward the pain of landowners being ground in the mills of wetlands or endangered species law. These mills grind exceeding small, and the number of horror stories is multiplying.

Yet another layer of complexity is created by the complicated nature of the various specific programs. Zoning is not the same as wetlands, and neither duplicates historic preservation. The West has a unique history and presents a series of unique problems. Getting rid of a panoply of outrageous government subsidies, a need about which liberals and conservatives agree in principle, is made difficult by the investments people have made in reliance on their continuation and by the capitalization of the subsidies into land values. Applying doctrines about rights developed in the context of real estate to intellectual property or to the switching equipment used in telecommunications introduces more difficulties. The basic themes remain the same, but each new twist raises its own set of problems.

The property rights controversy connects to many major trends in politics and society. The shift in the nature of wealth caused by the industrial and information revolutions has changed the political muscle of various contestants, reducing the power of landowners in relation to other groups and opening land up to raids. By one view, the holders of new forms of property, financial assets and intellectual capital in particular, are expropriating the wealth of landowners. Another dominating factor is the government's budget crunch, which encourages Congress, states, and cities to distribute largess by giving favored constituencies power to take wealth from other private citizens instead of giving them money out of federal tax dollars. Still other megatrends include the extraordinary expansion in the use of criminal sanctions during the past two decades, the multiplying failings of the legal system and legal profession, the rise of single-value government agencies devoted to a remorseless pursuit of their own narrow vision of the public good, and the increasing influence of scientific theories of dubious validity.

These linkages present both a problem and an opportunity. The problem is that they complicate analysis of the property rights. The opportunity is that they make the story more entertaining and important. Property rights is not only an interesting battle in its own right, it is a fine vehicle for examining fundamental issues that are perplexing the American public.

The linkages between property rights and these megatrends make another important point. Many knowledge workers and urban professionals do not see themselves as involved in these disputes. To them, property rights is a problem for farmers or loggers. Knowledge workers may obsess about the worth of their houses or condominiums, but real estate is not their important property. Their true estate lies in their professional degrees, connections, and civil service job protections, possessions shielded from appropriation by governments, and in the financial assets produced by these resources.

They are less shielded than they think. If the government gets into the habit of dealing cavalierly with land and resources, it will treat other forms of property and their fruits in similar fashion. What is the distinction between "regulating" land to protect wetlands and "regulating" to require a lawyer to spend 10 percent of her time on designated environmental causes, or "regulating" to require a telephone company to provide free switching services, or a writer of software to make the product available free to people designated as worthy by some government agency? If the Department of the Interior can direct the devotion of private land to habitat for a species of animal, regardless of the impact on the owner, because this is *pro bono publico*, then explain why the Department of Labor cannot require pension fund assets to be devoted to "socially useful" purposes, as defined by itself.

In *A Man for All Seasons*, Robert Bolt's great play about the sixteenth-century conflict between King Henry VIII and Archbishop Thomas More, More's son-in-law says he would be willing to cut down all the laws of England if necessary to get the Devil. More rejoins: "And when the last law was down, and the Devil turned round on you—where would you hide . . . the laws all being flat? This country's planted thick with laws from coast to coast . . . and if you cut them down . . . d'you really think you could stand upright in the winds that would blow then? Yes, I'd give the Devil the benefit of law, for my own safety's sake."[5]

Even inveterate urbanites should care if the principles protecting farmers, loggers, and other landowners are cut down. If these go, where will they themselves stand for protection against the political winds that then will blow?

Chapter 2

Some Stories

Yes, there is a real problem out there; many people are being treated quite shabbily, and they are getting mad as hell and do not want to take it any more

Anyone who went to camp as a kid sat around the fire late at night listening to the counselors tell horror stories. For any counselers reading this book, here are some additions to your stock in trade. True, these lack the usual cast of ghosts and ghouls, but they are guaranteed to terrify anyone who believes in the importance of the public's right to own and use property, free of either arbitrary interference by the government or appropriation by any band of fellow citizens that musters greater political clout. The stories represent the mere tip of a titanic iceberg. Hundreds more can be trotted out, and in the course of the book you will read a number of them. The purpose of detailing a few here at the start is to furnish evidence that there are real problems out there and to provide a sense of the variety of the contexts in which they arise. This provides a basis for the next chapters, which delve into the fundamental reasons rights to property are so important and make the case that every citizen should regard any assault on them with alarm.

FREDONIA, ARIZONA, 1994

Fredonia is a town of twelve hundred people north of the Grand Canyon, about four miles south of the Utah border. Settled in 1885 by Mormons, it has always been a timber town, processing the trees harvested in the nearby Kaibab National Forest. Such symbiosis between federal land and private labor and enterprise is a common pattern in Arizona, where 47 percent of the land, and a higher proportion of the valuable natural resources, belong to the federal government. Indeed, it is the pattern throughout the West.

Now, Bruce Whiting is telling his employees that the family sawmill, started fifty years ago and the last one in town, must close. The loggers and mill workers are out of luck. Regulations protecting the northern goshawk and the Mexican spotted owl and a string of environmentalist lawsuits against the U.S. Forest Service's timber sale plans have ended government sales. The mill has nothing to cut, and without the Kaibab wood, it has no prospects. On the videotape, you see that Whiting is not crying, barely. He says:

"You know, there's lots of words and emotions that have been going through my mind the last few days and weeks. Some of these are, unfortunately, anger, disappointment, frustration—trying to figure out was there any way not to make this decision. . . . It's the hardest decision my Dad and I ever made. . . . I can't think of anything we did wrong. We had good employees, we have a good product, we gave good service, . . . we did everything that you learn you're supposed to do in school. . . . And not one time did anyone ever say to me, your government might put you out of business because they don't like your industry any more. And that's just what's happened. We did nothing wrong. You did nothing wrong. . . . Our management has lobbied, we have tried to pass legislation, we have filed lawsuits, we have defended lawsuits, all thinking that, no, reason will prevail. Rationality will prevail. Rational people will understand that what's good for people, what's good for communities, what's good for forests is the right thing to do. Well, there are people who, I guess, are not rational or reasonable. Most of the people who made the decision I don't think have ever worked a day in their lives. They don't go to work and they don't get sweaty and they don't get bloody and they probably don't shed tears either.

"It's not fair to you, and it's not fair to your families, and it's not fair to Fredonia and Kaibab and the other communities. It's not fair to the citizens of the United States. It's not fair to that forest for us not to be up there and to let it just sit there and probably burn or rot."[1]

RIVERSIDE COUNTY, CALIFORNIA, 1993

Cindy Domenigoni, angry and articulate, is glad to tell her story. Regulations under the Endangered Species Act say that landowners cannot disturb the habitat of a member of a listed species that resides on their land. The Domenigonis have a 3,000-acre ranch in Riverside County that has been in the family since 1879. In 1988, the Fish and Wildlife Service (FWS) lists the Stevens kangaroo rat as an endangered species. In 1990, FWS tells the Domenigonis that 800 of their acres are habitat for the rats and cannot be cultivated or disturbed in any other way. By 1994 the total cost of the restrictions is up to $400,000 in lost income and direct expenses. Property taxes are still paid on the unusable land.

In the early 1990s California undergoes severe drought. In 1992 the FWS denies applications by the Domenigonis and others to create fire-breaks in their fields. Cultivation of the 800 acres is still forbidden, and the underbrush thickens steadily. In 1993, devastating fires char 25,000 acres and destroy twenty-nine homes. The Domenigoni home escapes, but the 800 acres are burned over. In the aftermath, the restricted area is reevaluated as a rat habitat. There is no sign of any rats. In fact, the rats all left before the fire because the brush grew thick, and they do not like thick brush. The measures taken to protect the rats not only cost the Domenigonis dearly and let the fires get out of control, they also created a habitat unsuitable for the animals.

So the restrictions are now lifted. But of course the logic of the situation is that farming will clear the brush, which the rats will like, so they will come back, so the restrictions will be reimposed until the brush grows thick and the rats leave, and so on, in a mad cycle.

The Domenigoni story has a second part, illustrating the bitterness of the current struggle over property rights. The tale is good media fodder and gets picked up by press, radio, and television. This is bad for the government because it makes Fish and Wildlife look both stupid and overbearing. Besides, people like rats about as much as they like lawyers, so any law that gets tagged as a rat protection program is automatically in trouble. Advocates of property rights are delighted. Problems with the endangered species program are aired to a national audience.

Then comes a counterattack. Congressmen sympathetic to the program ask the U.S. General Accounting Office (GAO) to investigate the contentions. In June 1994, GAO reports that firebreaks would not have stopped the fire: the winds were too high, and the fire jumped such breaks as roads and canals. Now the environmentalist community is delighted. A press release brands the claim that the law caused the destruction as a part of a "selfish agenda" to "spread lies."[2]

This triggers a counter-counterattack. As a conclusion, GAO's result is a bit of a headscratcher. Its investigation is perfunctory, and some of its quotes from local fire officials do not check out. Also, the argument has two parts. First, creating firebreaks keeps a fire from spreading. Second, cultivation generally, and creating firebreaks in particular, reduces the buildup of underbrush and decreases the intensity of any fire that does occur. The GAO addresses only the first of these issues, the firebreaks, and ducks the second. It focuses on the high wind that helped the fire jump natural breaks, not on the possible contribution of the buildup of underbrush to this wind. As a fire grows more intense, it sucks in air from around the fire zone, sometimes at hurricane force.

The Competitive Enterprise Institute, a Washington, D.C., free-market, property-rights-oriented research group, publishes a monograph, *Rats, Lies, and the GAO,* making the case that the GAO report is wrong.[3] Here the matter rests, with two contradictory versions of the story circulating, and each side convinced that the other is both malicious and mendacious.[4]

BUFFALO, NEW YORK, 1996

A small college in Buffalo buys an old rectory, planning to raze it to create room for parking. Community groups petition the city to designate the building as a landmark, and thus untouchable. The preservation board recommends denial of the petition, but is overruled by the Buffalo City Council. The rectory assumes landmark status. The college asks for compensation on the ground that the city has taken its property and must, under the Constitution, pay for it. The city refuses, and the court upholds the denial on the grounds that under the applicable legal criteria, the property is not "taken," even if it is now worthless to the college.[5] The local groups now have the benefit of the use (or non-use) of the land without the inconvenience of paying for it, and the college now owns a certified white elephant.

MONTGOMERY COUNTY, MARYLAND, 1994

Montgomery County is a bedroom community for Washington, D.C. The old Stabler place, now called Sunnyside, sits in its northern part, in an area that was once farming country but is now devoted to housing developments. The house is wood frame, growing decrepit. Built in 1866, it was designed for utility rather than aesthetic value, and haphazard additions by whimsical owners have not given it architectural unity. The inside is a maze of odd rooms. Outside, where it once overlooked amber waves of grain, the house now overlooks fields of red brick suburban homes, and these neighbors do not regard it with favor. Maintenance costs have become excessive, and the owners want to pull the place down and build anew.

A county ordinance provides for the preservation of anything that the Historic Preservation Commission (HPC) classifies as a historic or architectural resource. Heretofore unbeknown to the owners, the house is listed in the county's historical atlas, which means they cannot touch it until the HPC makes a formal assessment. The standards are a bit loose. A site qualifies as a historic resource if it "is identified with a . . . group of persons who influenced society." In case this definition is insufficiently broad, the ordinance contains three alternative criteria of equal imprecision. The definition of "architectural resource" has five categories, phrased in the same abstract terms.

If a property is designated, the commission must approve any changes. The goal is to protect the property "from unsympathetic alteration and insensitive redevelopment." The commission can also "prevent the demolition of historic buildings through neglect." In sum, if your property is designated, Congratulations! You now own a white elephant!

The commission decides that the old Stabler place qualifies. It is associated with the family that introduced the use of bat guano fertilizer to Montgomery County, and it "illustrates the changes in architectural taste and sophistication in Montgomery County during the nineteenth century." Other values of similar weight are cited.

The decision must be approved by the county planning board, but this is usually a rubber stamp; the commission is rarely reversed. The owners are now in serious financial jeopardy. Real estate agents and mortgage lenders say the house is unsalable because of structural deterioration and termite damage. An engineer says that saving it will require that a new foundation be poured within the old one, new footings installed, exterior walls replaced, and the entire house supported with new beams—none of this cheap. The owners lay this information before the planning board, arguing that listing will deprive them of the total value of their property. ("Deprivation of total value" is important from a legal point of view. If the county deprives them of 90 percent of the value, the owners are stuck. If the county deprives them of 100 percent, the county might have to pay.) The owners also point out that twenty-five other houses are also associated with the Stabler family and theirs is one of the least important. Faced with this evidence and with a real threat of litigation that might jeopardize their power in more important cases, the board overrules the commission and allows demolition.[6]

MARYLAND, 1990

William Ellen, an environmental engineer, is hired in 1987 to construct duck ponds on 3,200 acres on the Paul Tudor Jones II estate on Maryland's Eastern Shore. He obtains thirty-eight different permits. He also obtains assurances from an Army Corps of Engineers employee that one action that clearly affects wetlands is allowed by Corps rules. In 1989, the Corps changes its definition of wetlands. Acreage in the county that is classified as wetland goes from 84,000 acres to 259,000 acres. Acting under the new definition, the Corps orders Ellen to stop.

Ellen disputes the coverage, even under the new definition. At one point a representative of the Soil Conservation Service of the Department of Agriculture comes out to look over the work and tells Ellen he is all right; he has avoided the wetlands. A few days later, an official of the Corps (a different one) appears with the SCS guy in tow. This Corps representative says Ellen *is* filling in wetlands and should cease immediately. Ellen is outraged. He protests that the government's own expert, standing right there, told him just the opposite, that contractors are on-site and will collect hefty penalties if work ceases, and that he, Ellen, will be damned if he'll stop. The Corps representative threatens to call Jane Barrett, renowned as an avenging angel federal prosecutor. Ellen bows and halts the work.

Nonetheless, the government indicts Ellen, charging that wetlands have been altered illegally. At this point, the case is shaping up as a big one. It could be a fundamental challenge to Corps authority to redefine wetlands and then prosecute retroactively. However, the Corps learns that after Ellen received the cease-and-desist order he allowed workers to move two truckloads of dirt from one spot on the property to another. They've got him! Moving dirt is contaminating a wetland, and violating a cease-and-desist order is itself an offense. Ellen goes to jail for six months. Jones, his employer, avoids trial by paying a $1 million fine and making a $1 million contribution to the National Fish and Wildlife Foundation.[7]

In the court of appeals opinion upholding Ellen's conviction, the sequence of events is described in this way: "When Ellen refused to comply with their order to stop work, the Corps officials contacted the subcontractors directly, and only then did work cease."[8] The Corps employee who reassured Ellen about the legality of his actions cannot be found to testify at trial.

BUFFALO, WYOMING, 1995

Buffalo is in the high plains, hardly swamp country. Nonetheless, on a summer evening, Tom Rule can sit on his porch and watch the rising water wash away his livelihood. Rule is a third-generation rancher who bought a 2,132-acre ranch in 1989, of which 1,527 acres are potentially productive farmland. Irrigation ditches were cut on the ranch in 1883 to supply water to a hay meadow. The land slopes down, and a return ditch was built at the bottom edge. The ditch silts up and must be cleaned out regularly. Even when the ditch is maintained, water tends to collect at the bottom edge of the meadow, forming a swampy patch.

In the 1960s, Exxon bought the land as a possible source of coal. It leased out the property for ranching while it waited for the market to develop. This did not happen, and in 1989, with coal prices down, Exxon got out. During Exxon's tenure, the renters, having no long-term interest in the land, did not pay to clean out the ditch, and Exxon, having no interest in ranching, did not notice. The swamp, which comes out of the productive part of the ranch, not the waste, grew from 65 acres in 1935 to 127 acres in 1980 to 300 acres in 1994. When Rule bought the place, he assumed that he could clean out the ditch, only to be informed that federal law forbids the destruction of wetlands, anything that is flooded is a wetland, and if Rule cleans the ditch and thus drains the land, he can go to jail, despite the long history of irrigation.

The loss of the use of the land is costing Rule $150 per acre—$45,000 per year. He is investing $400,000 in sprinkler irrigation in the hope that this will cut the drainage. The benefits of having a swamp in the middle of the high plains are nonexistent. The Wyoming Fish and Game Department declines the opportunity to buy it for a wildlife refuge.[9] Rule is stuck.

MARIN COUNTY, CALIFORNIA, 1968–1987

In 1968, Donald Agins buys 5 acres of raw land on a ridge in Tiburon, a rich suburb 7 miles north of San Francisco. Land within 100 yards is already developed, at a density that will allow construction of about twenty homes on Agins's property. Soon after his purchase, the city becomes concerned about preserving open space, and in 1972 it sells $1.25 million in bonds to finance the purchase of the ridge, including Agins's land. Because land values are beginning to escalate, the parties cannot reach agreement on a price, so in 1973 the city downzones the ridge to permit housing only at a much lower density. The exact level allowable is not specified but is clearly less than one house per acre, and a subsequent building moratorium stops all development at least through 1987. Agins's property is not quite a park, since he can still exclude people from it, but it certainly qualifies as a general open space benefiting the city as a whole, and its value is cut to a pittance. Tiburon's action is upheld by the courts, including the U.S. Supreme Court.[10]

PACIFIC GROVE, CALIFORNIA, 1991–1994

The owner of a 1.1-acre lot on the Monterey Peninsula wants to build a house. Getting approval of the plans requires twenty public hearings and the nod from the Architectural Review Board, the Planning Commission, the City Council, and the California Coastal Commission. The process takes three and a half years and costs over $600,000 for carrying costs, lawyers, and studies. During one hearing, an Architectural Review Board member says, "In my former life as a seagull, I was flying up and down the California coastline and saw your house built shaped as a seashell." She votes against approving the plans for a non-seashell-shaped house.[11]

NEW YORK CITY, 1983–1994

Fordham University needs to build a new 480-foot tower for its non-commercial radio station due to a change in federal broadcasting regulations, and in 1983 it files an application for a building permit.

Eventually, the New York City Buildings Department grants it, deciding that the tower is an accessory to the university's main function of education and can thus be built as a matter of right. It also rules that the lattice-steel tower will not block light and air and thus does not need to be set back from the street. By mid-1994 construction reaches the 260-foot mark, and Fordham has spent over $1 million of a planned $1.3 million.

The nearby New York Botanical Garden now objects, arguing that the tower is ugly, visible from the garden, and will discourage visitors and contributors. In 1994 the Buildings Department withdraws its approval and decides that the tower must be set back 25 feet. This would mean writing off much of the money already spent, and the Botanical Garden still objects to any tower on the site, so the matter goes to the New York Board of Standards and Appeals. The board upholds Fordham's basic right to build but says the tower must be moved 25 feet or limited to 380 feet in height. Both sides go to court, where a state trial judge upholds Fordham's basic right to build with the comment, "There is no perceivable injury [to neighbors] unless it is some unredressable, speculative and unspecified chimera lost in the multiple variants of aesthetics." The Botanical Garden is appealing this decision, still arguing against any tower. Fordham has not decided what to do. It has already looked at twenty-five alternative locations without finding a better one.[12]

CULVER CITY, CALIFORNIA, 1995

Richard Ehrlich owns the site of a former private tennis club that went belly up economically. He wants to build thirty town houses. At first the city says no. Period. Once a site is used for recreation, only other recreational uses are allowed. After a round of threats and fights, the city says he can build if he pays a $280,000 "mitigation fee" to compensate the city for the loss of recreational facilities, a $30,000 "park fee," and a $33,220 "art fee" to buy public art to be displayed on Ehrlich's property. The California courts uphold the exactions. Thereafter, the U.S. Supreme Court decides an important case on the topic, and Ehrlich's case is now being reconsidered. Preliminary indications are that he will lose again.[13]

PRINCE GEORGE'S COUNTY, MARYLAND, 1995

Fourteen families live on half-acre lots near Broad Creek, a tributary of the Potomac River, which flows into Chesapeake Bay. They own jointly a 1.5-acre plot on the creek on which they build a community swimming pool. Pool maintenance costs go up, and the group wants to sell off half an acre of the pool lot for a home site so that they can devote the money to upkeep. The value of the lot is around $50,000. Virginia and Maryland have a Chesapeake Bay Critical Area program, which is designed to prevent further harm to the bay, and any action affecting land within 1,000 feet of any tributary of the Chesapeake requires a permit. To get a permit, a property owner does not simply guarantee that he is doing nothing to pollute the bay. He must do a complete survey of the land, examining for endangered species, topographic characteristics, trees, and all other features. Then the owner must sign an open-ended mitigation agreement with the county promising to do anything the county requires, with no limit on cost and no certain nexus between the Chesapeake, which is the ostensible basis of the requirement, and the county's demand. (In a conversation with the appropriate government department, one group member is told that cutting a tree he planted on his property long ago would require a permit and mitigation.) Fearing that the costs of the deal will exceed the value of the lot, the group decides not to try to sell it.[14]

NEW YORK CITY, 1983–1995

In 1983, Joan Dawson buys a three-unit brownstone in Harlem and moves in with her two grown children, two foster children, and a grandchild. Two of the units are renter occupied and covered by rent control, but the law allows an owner to take an apartment for family use. This is what Dawson plans. In 1984, the city changes the law so that tenants who have lived in an apartment for twenty years cannot be evicted under the owner-occupancy clause. Dawson sues, arguing that the change in the law took her property. She loses. The court notes that she should have known better than to rely on existing law since laws can always be changed. In 1994 she more or less buys her house again, paying the tenants to leave.[15]

WASHINGTON, D.C., 1992

A twenty-two-year-old soldier is driving his Honda in downtown Washington. He is waved to the curb by a woman. Actually, it is a male police officer in drag: over six feet tall, 220 pounds, dressed in a black dress, red wig, and red flats. The cop says the soldier said he was looking for a date. The soldier says that the cop offered him sexual services for twenty dollars, that he responded, "Yeah, okay," and then drove away. He was stopped by other police and arrested. The police drop the charge of solicitation of prostitution, for unexplained reasons, but they keep the car, arguing that it is forfeit under a recent law providing for seizure of vehicles used to solicit prostitution. The "Yeah, okay" (which some of us might interpret as the equivalent of "Riiiiiight!") is enough to establish probable cause that an offense was committed. Probable cause is all that is needed to justify the forfeiture. On the night that the law went into effect, the police seized three cars and a mountain bike.

As a general rule, a law enforcement agency gets to keep a large portion of forfeited property for its own use. Sometimes this principle gets extended even further. In 1993, members of the Los Angeles County Sheriff's Department were convicted of falsifying reports to show probable cause for seizures of cash and of stealing about $60 million.[16]

SNOHOMISH, WASHINGTON, 1995

This outrage jumps off the paper. In 1974, the writer buys a 4-acre plot that includes a two-thirds-acre pond through which flows a pure, clear creek. The pond and creek are home to waterfowl and birds, trout, frogs, and crayfish. In 1990 a commercial nursery buys 8 acres of mostly wetland half a mile up the creek. The owner begins filling in the wetlands, without permits, and ignores restraining orders. By 1995, the pond is one to two feet shallower, and it fills with silt after a storm. The trout are gone, only one-third as many waterfowl appear, and the creek does not flow in the summer. The nurseryman has joined various property rights defense groups. He believes that if Washington passes pending property rights protection legislation, he will be compensated if he is required to put in a retention pond to mitigate his actions.[17]

PORTLAND, OREGON, 1989

United Employer Benefit Corporation, (UEBC) markets health and disability insurance. It bundles small employers in the Portland area into like-kind groups and places the business with an Oregon health insurance company. By contract with the insurer, UEBC retains the title to its database on its customers. In 1989, the insurer goes bankrupt. The state's Department of Insurance and Finance (DIF) takes over and sells the insurer's Portland business to another company. The new company and UEBC cannot reach agreement on the terms of their relationship, and UEBC decides to transfer its customers to another insurer. DIF steps in and tells everyone connected with UEBC that if they help with such a transfer, they will be held in contempt of the orders of the bankruptcy court. They fold, the transfer does not occur, and UEBC goes broke.

UEBC sues the state, arguing that DIF "took" the customer list and that compensation is due under the Constitution. It loses.

On the surface, the case is a standard contract-property dispute. Who owns a customer: the company that performs the services or the finder who flushes a live bird out of the bushes? Ordinarily such arguments are settled through civil suits under established state law. The thumb of the state government on the scale turns this into a case involving a taking of property rights. No private party could short-circuit the normal channels of dispute resolution by threatening to put anyone dealing with UEBC in jail. It is hard to know if UEBC can sue the new insurance company for stealing its customers, since the basic problem is that it has no contractual relationship with the new people. Oregon, in the form of the DIF, has marched into what used to be a standard commercial situation and distorted it beyond the comprehension of conventional legal doctrine.[18]

THE UNITED STATES, 1995

About seventeen thousand corneal transplants and twenty-five hundred heart transplants occur in the United States each year. A lively trade has sprung up in harvesting organs from the recently deceased. For corneas, at least, states are passing negative-option laws saying that removal is legal unless the family denies consent, and a hospital need not ask for the consent. In some cases family refusals are ignored and organs removed anyway.

Federal law makes it a crime to sell human organs for transplant purposes. Exempt from the definition of a sale are any reasonable payments associated with the removal and processing (medical costs, in other words) and any payments to a donor for expenses incurred in connection with the donation. Current market acquisition costs are close to $1,200 for a cornea and $20,000 on up for a heart. A shadowy market exists whereby people with access to organs, such as morgue attendants and pathologists, harvest and sell them, avoiding the ban on sale by charging for the process, not for the organ itself. The result is that the only person not allowed to make money out of the system is a prospective decedent. He cannot arrange to sell his organs and leave the money to his family, nor can the family accept money in exchange for consent. But the doctor who removes the organ, the hospital that provides the facilities, and everyone else involved can charge what the market, or the insurer, will bear.

Joyce Carter, medical examiner for the District of Columbia, says: "They're getting organs from poor people here to give to wealthy people elsewhere. They say they don't make a profit, but there's a lot of money involved."[19] She has a point. If you are the prospective decedent, the system seems unfair. Twenty thousand could buy a year or two of education for your kin or help finance a small business, so if you are through using your organs, why shouldn't you trade them in? Where does the federal government get the right to forbid you to make a deal and improve the lot of your family? If someone has $10 million and a bad heart and you have no dollars and a working heart, why is it fair for the government to dictate that he end up with $10 million and the heart and your family get nothing?

Chapter 3

A Primer on Property

How we came to believe "property doesn't have rights, but people have rights, including a right to property," and why we are right about this and why it is terribly important

HOW IT BEGAN

Some young professionals living in New York City during the late 1960s grow tired of the shallowness of their urban lifestyle and its obsession with getting and spending. Following the maxim of the sixties, they tune in, turn on, drop out, and begin a communal existence in a remote rural area, where they can be free of domination by property. During their first year, after a summer of loving cultivation, their garden plot of marijuana is harvested and the crop carried away by persons unknown. Outraged at this appropriation of what was *theirs*, they resolve the next patch will be better protected, perhaps with a good fence. What is the point of investing all that effort only to see its fruits go to someone else?

These hippies are the spiritual heirs of the seventeenth-century English philosopher John Locke, whose ideas about the protection of private property and other rights underlie the Declaration of Independence and the Constitution of the United States. This might not surprise them. It would startle and deeply unsettle them to learn that they are also the darlings of generations of market-oriented economists, who have built the theory that the institution of private property is the best route to both justice and economic wealth. About ten thousand years of social development and five hundred years of theory are wrapped up in that little plot of grass.

In the beginning is the question, What do we mean by *property* or *property rights?* How are the terms defined? In 1995, a congressional panel asked a group of experts for some definitions. The experts agreed that property is an embarrassingly murky concept. "I know it when I see it, but don't ask me to define it" applies here. Nonetheless, some definition is necessary, and although the meaning of property gets murky at the edges, the core is clear enough.

To start, property encompasses real estate, such as land and buildings. It also includes the various special rights in real estate, such as leases, mineral rights, or the right to put a railroad track or a power line across somebody else's land. Property includes natural resources, such as game, water, wood, and ore, and all kinds of personal possessions, such as dishware and cars, and business assets ranging from airplanes to machinery.

Property does not necessarily have physical solidity. Money is property. This is most obvious when it is a wad of cash in the pocket, but an entry of accounts in a set of electronic ledgers is property too. Another large category is intellectual property, such as patents, trademarks, and copyrights. Permissions to use intellectual property are a kind of property. When you buy a computer software program, you purchase not just the physical disk but a license to use the program, and most definitely not a right to distribute it further.

Government payments create a curious kind of hybrid. No one thinks of social security payments as property in the same sense as houses or cars, but they are, in the sense that the government must grant a hearing before it cuts off the payments, and someone who steals your social security check has surely taken your property. We do not usually define social security as property because the right is inherently limited. You cannot transfer it to anyone else, and the government reserves the power to end or change the program at any time. These are limits on the property right, but what remains is still property.

Society is shot through with other kinds of sort-of-property rights. If you go to a beach on a summer day and put down your towel, that is now your spot, your property, and you expect people to respect your right. They do too. Have you ever seen someone's beach towel picked up and the spot expropriated? But there is a limit. If you leave your towel on the beach overnight, you would not expect your claim to the place to be honored the next morning. By social custom, beach rights end at sundown.

Pressed to give a definition, I would say property consists of anything that can be used, physically or mentally, so as to provide value of some kind. In our society we would exclude human beings, of course, but this is by no means universal as a matter of history. Much of the property law of ancient Rome developed around slaves, a significant source of labor. Yet this definition is incomplete because it lacks the final step of a transition to the idea of ownership. A thing can be used, but it is not really property until you say, "This is mine, [yours, hers, his, ours, or theirs]." An ocean can be put to productive use, but we do not think of it as property. A bucket of seawater is.

This is the point at which the scholars at the 1995 congressional hearing threw up their hands, because supplying this added step of ownership is very much a product of culture, not an inherent condition of nature. According to legend, nineteenth-century American Indians were often puzzled at the idea that someone might own the land. Thus they cheerfully sold it to Europeans and were then flabbergasted that they were now expected to keep off it. To them, land was too plentiful to be "owned." At the same time, recent scholarship has shown that the Indian cultures had well-developed concepts of property rights with respect to weapons and other personal possessions, captured game, and specific fishing and hunting sites. The basic rule seems to be that when something becomes scarce or requires labor to acquire, then people develop concepts of property.[1]

For prehistoric times we can only conjecture, though. Real knowledge of property begins only when civilizations began keeping written records, starting with the half-mythical Middle Eastern kingdoms of Ur and Uruk in the fourth millennium B.C. These had a simple concept of property: everything belonged to the Goddess, who parceled out the right to use it, as interpreted through the medium of a priesthood.

For most of history, the pattern of Ur and Uruk has prevailed in some fashion. The Romans had a system of property law that approaches ours, but in most times and places, important property, which was land, was held by the gods or the king. The person we would call the owner had a right to use it, but this was contingent on something. In Ur, it depended on piety. In medieval Europe, the right to land was linked to the duty to bear arms for your lord or to farm his land. In England before the Norman conquest in 1066, a few farmers held land that did not belong to the king or to any superior lord. Within a hundred years after the conquest, the Normans wiped out this form of tenure. All land was brought into the great feudal chain wherein the king held from God, barons and other great nobles held of the king, lesser nobles held of them, and so on down the line to the peasantry.

In feudal Europe, none of these people owned their land. They were seised of it, which means they had a right to possess it, and a transfer was not a sale but livery of seisin. The conditions governing transfer were tricky. Because holding the land was contingent on the performance of feudal duties, the king or the baron had a strong incentive to control transfers. He did not want some stout knight to transfer land to someone unable to bear arms.

How do you transfer land in a society in which almost no one is literate? For a horse or a cart, simple change of possession may be enough, but this does not always work for land. Possession may remain in the hands of a subtenant, or the new owner might be off to do his forty days of annual service in arms for the king. You might get a deed written out by a local monk, since the church has a virtual monopoly on writing, but this is not a complete answer. A monk is not always handy when you need one, and the church will want to be paid for the service. Ecclesiastics are also known to forge charters deeding land to themselves. A deed cannot be signed by the transferor, who is unlettered (even if he is the local duke), nor can a deed alone establish the new title in the minds of the also-illiterate neighbors and tenants. Besides, although a deed shows that the *transferor* wants to make the deal, land has its obligations as well as its rights, and it is important the *recipient* signal his acceptance of these.

A logical answer evolves. First, you make a physical transfer of some symbol of ownership, such as a clod of earth, and accompany it with verbal announcements of transfer and acceptance. Second, you do it in front of witnesses who will be able to testify to the fact of the transaction. The preferred witnesses are young boys, since they will outlive the adults. It is best to use several, because mortality is high. Third, you give the boys enough of a beating to make the event memorable.[2]

This feudal structure of land for service lasted for centuries, but in some important ways it was unstable. A system in which a knight owes forty days per year service and then goes home is a chancy way to raise an army. Problems of discipline and coordination are formidable. Most kings and lords eventually saw that a permanent professional force was better than a feudal levy. A professional army costs money, and the best way to obtain money was from the nobles. The mechanism was called *scutage;* the knight paid to be relieved of his duty to serve, and his feudal superior used the money to hire full-time soldiers. Other feudal duties, such as duties to labor in the lord's fields or to work on the roads, were also transmuted into monetary obligations over the centuries, and for the same general reasons. If someone does not want to perform a particular duty, it is always to the benefit of all parties involved to let him buy his way out and then use the money to hire someone who is happy to do it.

Introducing cash into the feudal structure changed the nature of property in two important ways. The first was a shift in who could hold it. As long as the right to hold property depended on the ability to fulfill feudal duties, the kinds of people who could hold it were limited to those who could perform the duties. Thus, the widow or orphan of a deceased noble could not do service in arms, nor could a wealthy merchant. At the lower levels of society, the holder of land must be able to provide the necessary labor to farm the lord's property. In both cases, the limitation was not only to adult males, but to adult males with particular skills. No women, children, merchants, or craftsmen need apply.

Converting feudal duty into a cash payment broadens the possibilities because the category of people who might have money is more inclusive than the category of fighting men or sturdy peasants. If the land produces a cash return, then anyone—widow, orphan, merchant, or anyone else—can meet a monetary obligation. Over time, cash eroded the feudal bond as the basis for landholding.

Money eroded the bond in a second way. Payment in lieu of services can start out as an annual obligation, like the services themselves, but cash introduces new options. The holder of land can make a large single payment in permanent discharge of the feudal obligation. Since kings and barons were often broke, this idea appealed to them, and many feudal obligations were commuted forever in exchange for quick cash. After a few decades passed, it became harder to remember that the land was in theory held in feudal tenure, given that no duties were ever due. It came to look as if the possessor owned in his own right rather than as a vassal.

The erosion of feudal land systems was also fostered by the spread of literacy. The system of passing a clod of earth and boxing the ears of the witnesses lacks subtlety. It cannot capture partial estates, such as terms of years, or limitations on use, such as the right to dig ore but not to farm, or any other complex mix of ownership. As writing spread, it became possible to record complexities. In turn, the opportunities for more efficient use of the land created by these new combinations increased their use. (Note the analogy to the contemporary spread of the computer and the opportunities it creates for new types of property rights.)

Even as the ideas and institutions of ownership evolved, one right that we regard as fundamental lagged behind: the right to sell. Until the sixteenth century, at least, in Europe, and even longer in other parts of the world, land was regarded as a possession of the family and could not be alienated outside it. Devious ways around this existed as early as the twelfth century, but the principle remained an important part of the structure of property. It took centuries for the champions of the right to alienate land to prevail in theory as well as in practice.[3]

The exact date varies from one country to another, but by the seventeenth century in Europe, the idea evolved that you own your land and do not hold it of any higher power. Ownership includes a number of rights over the land that are referred to as the "Blackstonian Bundle," named after the English jurist who summarized much of the law in his eighteenth-century *Commentaries*. The Blackstonian Bundle includes the idea that a single entity owns the whole thing, in perpetuity. The property has physical boundaries, and these are defined in some identifiable way. In the historic bundle, before the age of the airplane, the motto was that possession extends from the center of the earth to the heavens. The owner has the absolute right to exclude anyone or anything, and the right to use or abuse the property. He is entitled to receive all income derived from it and to sell its resources. There are some differences by place. In England and the United States, mineral rights belong to the owner; in the rest of the world, subsurface rights belong to the sovereign. Finally, the owner has the right to transfer all or any part of the estate.

Lawyers call this the "bundle of sticks" theory of property. This means that you do not "own property"; you own certain rights in property, such as the right to harvest crops, or to build, or to exclude others, or to cut trees, and so on. If you own all the sticks without exception, the legal term is that you own the "fee simple."

Human ingenuity being what it is, people have invented ways of splitting the property bundle into sticks and even twigs and transferring them. The time-share condominium is a fine example. You own a fragment of a building and a share of its common space for a week or two each year. Even finer distinctions are possible for intellectual property. You can have a license to manufacture under a patent that is limited to a prescribed number of units, or for sale in designated geographic areas, or for a set time, or all of the above. You can have a right to perform a piece of music once, or only over the radio, or for a single recording, or without limit.

Property rights evolved a long way from feudal seisin toward ownership well before John Locke, the English philosopher of the seventeenth century, but Locke made some important additions to the philosophy of property. Given the feudal origins of land tenure, the increasing freedom of landholding created a problem. If the right to land comes from the king, then what keeps him from taking it back on whim? If the right to land does *not* come from the king, then whence does it come? Locke's view, adopted with enthusiasm by the rising middle classes, was that the right to property, along with the rights to life and liberty, is a natural one. It comes not from a temporal power but from God—and not from God as a kind of surrogate feudal lord but from the very nature of justice in a universe governed by rational principles. The opening lines of the U.S. Declaration of Independence are pure Locke: "We hold these Truths to be self-evident, that all Men are created equal, that they are endowed by their Creator with certain unalienable rights, that among these are Life, Liberty, and the Pursuit of Happiness."

Locke is most famous for the next phrase of the Declaration: "That to secure these Rights, Governments are instituted among Men, deriving their just Powers from the Consent of the Governed." It was this concept of government as the creation of consent and compact among the people, not as a product of the divine right of kings or any other authority of a limited governing caste, and as founded precisely to protect these great natural rights, that created the order of liberal democracies governed by elections that we inhabit today.

To attribute all this to one scribbler would be misleading. Locke codified ideas that developed over half a millennium and that were in the air by the 1680s. Writings of John Winthrop, the first governor of Massachusetts, dating from the 1620s are permeated with Lockean concepts. In 1624 England enacted the first patent law, a recognition of a property right in the fruit of creative thought.[4] It is convenient to use the shorthand term of "Lockean philosophy," but it was in truth a broad social movement, not just a single sacred text. Hair-splitting distinctions about what is or is not found in Locke's own corpus of work are beside the point.

Among philosophers, explaining and criticizing John Locke is a serious industry, partly because his discussion of property is so maddeningly sketchy that it leaves great room for dispute over what he really meant. One expert refers to the "quite controversial question" of whether Locke was an "uncharitable apologist for capitalism or a leveling social revolutionary, a radical voluntarist and libertarian or a social welfare theorist, a secular humanist or theological ethicist."[5] Economist William Fischel, in a fine analysis of land use issues, says that "reference to Locke is . . . an invitation to fruitless debate. Locke has been cited by scholars dedicated to full compensation . . . and by scholars dedicated to nationalization without compensation."[6] Despite these cautions, referring to "Lockean ideas" is a useful shorthand, as long as it is clearly understood that the reference is to a general mode of thought, not to the explicit statements of one person.

THE ARGUMENT FROM JUSTICE

For purposes of this primer on property, five crucial implications of these Lockean ideas about property can be isolated. We will name these the Argument from Justice in favor of a regime of private property. After these, we will develop some other families of arguments.

The first important Lockean idea abolished the feudal chain. To Locke, property still came from God, but it did not come from God to king to noble and so on. It came directly to its owner. The basis of government is not a feudal hierarchy but a compact among the governed, designed to protect their natural rights, including the rights to property.

The second crucial point is that there is no such thing as "property rights." Property does not have rights. People have rights, including the right to hold property. Efforts to draw a distinction between "personal" rights or "human" rights and "property" rights produce mischief.

The third point concerns the mechanism by which property is created initially. In Locke's system, this happens when someone mixes labor with the natural bounty of God in a way that makes the resource useful. Property is given to all people in common, but anyone can appropriate a share by putting it to use. Once reduced to private ownership by this action, the property becomes transferable, and the new owner takes the same natural rights to it as the first appropriator.

Point four is that most of the value of things comes from labor. Raw materials and raw land are worth little until human labor is added, and to take someone's property is to take his labor, and thus himself.

WASHINGTON, D.C., 1996

It is the Great Blizzard of '96. My car is parked on the public street. I shovel it out of two feet of snow and drive off, after putting a garbage can in the cleared space to mark it as mine. I have claimed it by labor. I keep doing this for a week, until the snow melts, and no one violates the claim. Throughout the city, spaces are marked with cans, lawn furniture, boxes, or whatever else is at hand.

Parking is sometimes tight on my street. Could I make this claim as a matter of routine, turning the fifteen feet of curb in front of my house into my personal space? My neighbors might acquiesce, at least as long as they could find alternative slots. But they certainly would not regard this as a legitimate action on my part, and they probably would not obey if it became a nuisance to them. The labor is crucial.

The fifth point is access to resources. A person is entitled to use her labor to convert nature's bounty into her own property, but this moral right is dependent on "enough and as good" being left for others to appropriate with their labor. The idea that large tracts of land could be declared off limits and left unused would have been anathema to Locke. John Winthrop wrote that enclosing land was permissible as long as enough was left for the use of the Indians, "there being more than enough for them and for us."[7]

Locke is vague on what happens when all the good resources are already appropriated. What are later generations to do? Certainly the rise of Lockean philosophy in England, where by Locke's time there were few unclaimed resources, did not result in any redistribution. It could be, though the scholars are not agreed, that Locke was concerned with defending the distribution of property that had evolved by the late seventeenth century, and with justifying the subordination of the Crown to

Parliament that was embodied as a part of England's Glorious Revolution (1688), not with attacking the status quo. It could also be that Lockean philosophy might apply to England only as a metaphor, going back to some mythical time when resources were there for the taking, and that Locke never quite worked out how to extend the metaphor to the real world. In another part of the world outside Europe, there was no problem in making the metaphor real because the state of nature was not mythical but real. This place was America, a paradigm of the Lockean initial state of nature. Locke himself said: "Thus in the beginning all the World was America."[8]

Contemporaries of Locke regarded the American Indians as primitives who lived off the land without appropriating it by means of their labor. They were wrong, because Indians had been sculpting the terrain to their purposes for centuries, but the colonists did not know this.[9] From their point of view, the New World was an unappropriated Eden, full of resources that were of little value if left alone. Only when mixed with labor did the resources become valuable. For the 150 years of the colonial period, America remained more or less in this Lockean state. Resources were abundant, but the labor needed to give them value was scarce. English colonial policy sought to get labor into the colonies by inducements of land grants, duressed migration of religious minorities, transportation of convicts, slavery, indentured servitude, and the compulsions of crop failure or draft evasion. It was accompanied by the suppression of the Indians, who often annoyed the colonists by their refusal to turn into good slaves. Like most history, the story is not for the squeamish.

The point that labor was the source of value is easily illustrated. In colonial times and throughout the nineteenth century, raw land could be had cheaply. In 1796 the government held a sale of land in Pennsylvania and Ohio and found few takers at $2 per acre. At the time a year of unskilled labor could be bought for $150 plus room and board, and a strong man with a good axe could clear about 17 acres of land in a year, so the cost of clearing was at least $10 an acre. The prices for cleared land reflected this hard arithmetic. The pioneers who kept clearing land and moving west were more independent sellers of labor than they were land speculators or farmers. They made their profit by the sweat of their brows.[10] Given this situation and history, it is not surprising that Lockeanism took deep root in America. To the colonists, Locke's view of property, with its labor theory of value, was not a theory; it was the reality of their lives.

THE NORTHWEST TERRITORY, 1785

The Northwest Territory—the land between the Appalachian Mountains and the Mississippi River north of the Ohio that was ceded to the new United States by Great Britain as part of the treaty that ended the Revolution in 1783—became the states of Ohio, Indiana, Illinois, Michigan, and Wisconsin. In 1785 it had no government and no laws, and the Congress was anxious to ensure that its development was orderly. Thus it barred settlement until the territory could be organized.

My father once ran across a resolution passed by the Continental Congress sometime around 1785. It stated that certain ruffians had crossed the Ohio River and were illegally settling the territory, and called upon said ruffians to remove themselves forthwith. It then listed the names, including one Simon DeLong.

Congress's effort to control the land did not work, for Simon or for thousands of others. My grandfather was born ninety years later in southern Ohio, probably the descendant of these ruffians. In the end, Congress had to accept, here and across the West, that the squatters believed that their labor earned them the right to land. Land speculators displaced them at their peril, and squatters' rights were repeatedly formalized into the laws governing the disposition of the public lands.

The settlers did not believe that they held their land of any sovereign, and one of the themes of the westward movement in the United States is the repeated efforts of eastern authorities to control the land and the equally repetitive foiling of these efforts by squatters. The settlers were appropriating resources that would otherwise lie fallow, and the value with which they imbued these came from labor. They regarded efforts to block access to resources as illegitimate assertions of outmoded privilege by an effete upper class.

THE ARGUMENT FROM ECONOMIC EFFICIENCY

The Lockean view of property turned out to have a benefit besides abolishing the remnants of feudalism and absolute monarchy and providing justification for hard-working seventeenth-century Puritans and their spiritual successors, the American immigrants of the eighteenth, nineteenth, and twentieth centuries. Lockeanism turned out to be a great engine of economic growth and development. Nobel Prize–winning economist Douglass North says that the explosion of useful technology that began in the eighteenth century was touched off by the development of rules of property that increased the incentives for innovation.[11]

Some flavor of this can be found in Locke's own writings, but the real theoretical underpinnings had to wait until the development of systematic economic thought in the nineteenth and twentieth centuries.[12] The arguments may seem elementary to anyone raised in a liberal market society; nonetheless, they are worth recounting. They are less obvious than they may appear to us, as demonstrated by the fact that through history relatively few societies have managed to attain continuing economic growth. The per capita income in Rome of the second century A.D. was probably as high as that of any other society until the nineteenth century.[13] Humankind's capacity to get things wrong is enormous. In particular, the tendency of governments to choke off economic improvement is a constant factor in human affairs, from the Ur of 3500 B.C. to the Soviet Union of the 1980s.

Communist governments are particularly good at suppressing productivity and economic development. As one economic historian puts it, "Depending on how you count, between two-thirds and seven-eighths of the potential material production and prosperity of a country was annihilated if it fell under Communist rule" during the twentieth century.[14] Communism is not the sole culprit, though. In 1900, Argentina was a First World nation, about as well off as Norway. It has progressed; its per capita output is about thrice its 1900 level. But Norwegian per capita output is nine times its 1900 level, so Argentina functions at a level that is, at best, only one-third of its potential. The cause lies in its political choices.

If Locke developed the Argument from Justice for property, economists have developed the Argument from Economic Efficiency.

First off, people work harder, more efficiently, and with greater ingenuity when they work for themselves. Throughout history, idealists have thought it would be a kinder, gentler world if people were more generous and if they contributed according to the Marxist idea of from each according to his ability and to each according to his need. It may work in small, tightly knit religious communities, where the communitarian nature of the enterprise is usually enforced by bloodcurdling sanctions of ostracism and shame on earth and damnation in the hereafter. It has failed to work for any extended period of time anywhere else. The irony is that even in religious communities, people work for themselves, but the coin is salvation rather than money. Rewards that depend on a pure sense of altruism are not successful.

SAN JUAN Y MARTÍNEZ, CUBA, 1995

The *Washington Post* reports that Cuba is discovering capitalism. "For the first time in the thirty-six years of Cuba's socialist economy, Jorge Aguilar has a reason beyond revolutionary zeal to work hard in the nation's famous tobacco fields: The more he works, the more dollars he gets." The paper goes on to quote Aguilar: "'To be honest, often before we did not really care about how we worked, because those that worked got paid the same as those who did not. . . . Now, if I work hard I get dollars, not pesos, and with dollars I can buy . . . things.'" This is a change from the revolutionary fervor of 1959, "when President Fidel Castro talked enthusiastically about creating a society with a 'new man' who would rely on 'moral incentives,' not material ones, to work for the common good."[15]

This is not some exotic foreign problem. Right here in the United States, land held by the Bureau of Indian Affairs in trust for American Indian tribes is at least 50 percent less productive than equivalent land that is owned privately.[16] The American colonists in Jamestown and Plymouth started out with a communal system of farming and almost starved. Contemporary observers commented on the high level of sloth at Jamestown at a time when the colony was desperately short of food. The fundamental problem is that each worker gets only a small share of the increase in production caused by his efforts. He bears all of the costs of the unpleasantness of hard physical labor and gets all of the benefits of idleness. Furthermore, a communal system is vulnerable to a domino effect. If anyone defects and shirks, then the incentives for others increase too. Each addition to the pool of shirkers increases the pressure on the others to do likewise. Who wants to be the only one working? The Soviet Union of the late 1980s embodied the end result, where a common description of the situation was that the workers pretended to work and the government pretended to pay them. Jamestown and Plymouth soon privatized their land, and prospered.

This introduces the second major Efficiency argument for property rights as the great generator of economic well-being: the concept of investment. Few productive assets maintain themselves automatically. It takes money and work—investment—to make and keep them productive. In Jamestown or Plymouth, land had to be cleared. No one would do it unless he could get the benefit over time, since one year's crop would not repay the effort. Farmland in general must be drained, fertilized, and fallowed, and encouraging these activities requires that the doer get the benefits of the effort. The same holds true for other types of productive assets, ranging from the simplest shovel to a complex machine or an intricate piece of software. Production and maintenance take time and effort, and giving ownership to its maker is the most direct way to provide the proper incentives.

Ownership in perpetuity encourages not just investment but long-term investment. Giving people ownership of assets over time encourages them to think for the long rather than the short term. If you have the right to use property for only a limited time, you will make only those investments that will bear fruit during your term. You will not plant trees on a woodlot that will reach maturity only after your lease is up, for example. You are also likely to waste resources. You will cut immature trees that would be more valuable in a few years because you get the value of trees cut now, but not the value of those cut in the future. Property rights are a means of conserving resources. If the trees are yours forever, then you will calculate more shrewdly. What can you get now, and what can you get in a year or two?

THE PACIFIC NORTHWEST AND WASHINGTON, D.C., 1913

The U.S. Bureau of Corporations has a grievance against the Big Three logging companies of the Pacific Northwest: They are conserving timber. The time-honored approach in the industry has been to clear-cut and move on. This technique deforested the Midwest and the South, but now, with no "on" left to move to, the companies are worried about their future. Instead of clear-cutting, they are working up theories of sustainable forestry and are making long-term investments in transportation and processing facilities. The bureau accuses them of tying up natural resources for purposes of private gain, refusing to cut now in the hope that the timber will be worth more in the future.[17]

The advantage of title in perpetuity is that the owner captures the value of improvements, or of deferred harvesting, by adding the benefits of these actions into the price of the land. If I own the land, then I will plant trees that will mature in forty years because doing so raises the price of the land on the market. I will not harvest immature trees when I can get more for land with mature plants. People who plan to trade their houses or cars next year still improve or maintain them so as to increase the resale value.

This idea of preserving resources for future use is an important dimension of the Argument from Efficiency. In political discussion, it is often pointed out that future generations do not vote in present elections, which tempts current politicians to ignore their interests. The point is well taken. But future generations do have a powerful representative in the present: the owner who calculates that they will make it worth his while, or worth the while of his progeny, if he preserves resources for their use. The much-maligned speculator actually compensates for a serious flaw in the workings of the political system.

Ownership also encourages exploration and development. No one will undertake the expense and risk of seeking developable resources if they do not get the rewards of success. Furthermore, if the chance of success is low, then the rewards when it is achieved must be unusually high. The winning hands must generate enough profits to pay for the losers.

THE ATLANTIC OCEAN, OFF THE SOUTH CAROLINA COAST, 1857 AND 1995

The SS *Central America,* bound for New York out of San Francisco, carries about $1.2 million in 1859 prices in gold coin from the San Francisco mint, plus an uncalculated amount of wealth in the hands of individual passengers. Estimates range up to a billion dollars, at 1995 prices. The ship sinks in a storm, beyond the reach of 1850s discovery or salvage techniques. Various insurance companies pay off, and the other losers take their lumps.

In 1988, the Columbus America Discovery Group, a speculative salvage operation, finds the ship and starts recovering the gold. The insurance companies, last heard from in 1859, pop up, claiming that they paid for this gold and it is their property. Who should have it? The shipping company? The insurance companies? The descendants of the drowned miners? Columbus America? The government, or possibly the United Nations, as proprietor of the ocean bed?[18]

John Locke would probably say that the gold on the *Central America* returned to a state of nature and belongs to whoever appropriates it through labor. A modern economist would agree. The salvage company's efforts represented "a paradigm of American initiative, ingenuity, and determination," according to the court that heard the case. If it does not get the gold, then in the future few will waste time and money inventing new methods of salvage and gambling that their efforts will succeed. Gold will remain at the bottom of the ocean, useless to all. You might argue that the heirs or the companies have incentives to recover it, but it is difficult for them to get together and develop new means of salvage. They are unlikely ever to do it. For proof, look at the fact that they never moved a finger except to file suit against the people who did the work of recovery.

Allowing different types of interests in the same piece of property to be split up and sold separately also contributes mightily to economic efficiency. The amount of land needed for various individual purposes varies greatly. If I go to college, I do not want to build a dormitory. I want a single room. The college, on the other hand, cannot build a room at a time; it erects a dorm and rents out pieces of it to individual students. But it cannot have nothing but a dormitory. It must have enough land for football fields, beer halls, and perhaps a classroom or two. So it buys a lot of land, and then splits off part of it to rent to students, or perhaps it simply sells the land to private parties who will take care of building dormitories.

The ability to subdivide property interests is crucial to economic activity. If I have a 160-acre farm sitting on top of a coal seam, it will not be practical for me to start a coal company to exploit the deposit. I might band together with my neighbors and form a coal company, but we are farmers, not miners. Besides, coal might best be exploited by a large company that already has mines, equipment, coal cars, docks, sales contracts, and all the other components of a coal business. But a coal company has no interest in farming my land, so we split the estate:

I retain the surface and the right to farm and sell them the right to mine. Or the process can be reversed: the coal company can buy the whole estate and then split off and sell to me the right to use the surface. Either way, we better agree on who takes priority if our respective uses come into conflict.

SCRANTON, PENNSYLVANIA, 1910–1923

Scranton is in the Pennsylvania belt of anthracite, a type of hard coal that burns cleanly and was in great demand for residential use in the days of coal-burning furnaces. Scranton, like many other coal towns, sits on top of the seam. The belt is big, and locating the town out of range would lengthen commutes to the mine to an inconvenient degree, so the Pennsylvania Coal Company bought the land and then sold off rights to the surface to people who wanted to build houses. Most of these people worked for Penn Coal. (Who else would live on top of a coal mine?)

When it sold the surface rights, the company clearly reserved the right to mine the coal even if doing so damaged the houses on the surface. As of the 1910s, this chicken came home to roost. The company's practice had been to leave pillars of coal underground to support the surface. In the boom times around World War I, the price of anthracite went up, the company began to whittle away at the support pillars, and chunks of Scranton were in danger of falling into the mine. Pennsylvania passed a law prohibiting coal mining that would cause surface subsidence. The company sued on the ground that the law violated the clause of the U.S. Constitution that says that private property cannot be taken without compensation. Who should win? (This is one of the great cases on the meaning of the Fifth Amendment's prohibition against taking private property for public use without compensation, *Pennsylvania Coal v. Mahon,* and it will come up again in Chapter 14.) The short answer is "the company." The Supreme Court held this was indeed a taking, and started seventy years of confusion over the issue. The long answer is that everyone won. It turned out that the company's practice had always been to repair any damage caused by subsidence at its own expense. After all, everybody who lived there worked for the mine, and this included most of the managers. The company kept right on doing this after the case.[19] It just did not want to be forced to buy up every house where subsidence might occur.

> In 1987 the Supreme Court decides an identical case in precisely the opposite way, without mentioning the conflict.[20]

The ability to split the Blackstonian Bundle into pieces tailored to particular needs is one of the great inventions of our legal system. Ownership can be divided so that different activities needing different amounts of property can buy only what they need, and several of them can use a single piece of property simultaneously. This idea has made an immeasurable contribution to economic progress and individual welfare.

Consider a modern example: licensing computer software. Every time you buy a program, you are buying a property right—usually a right to use the program on one machine but not to sell it or duplicate it. The total ownership of the software is split into many estates. We take this method of doing business totally for granted, but think of the inefficiency, and the consequences for the computer age, if either legal or technical reasons inhibited this practice. Each user would have to buy or develop its own program for every application. As a result the only companies able to afford computer programs (such as word processing) would be those large enough so that their cost savings offset the total costs of developing the software. Because those costs are high, such an inhibition would compel a massive trend toward the creation of large companies in every field of endeavor. These would be the only companies that could use computers.

Take another example of estate splitting, from an entirely different angle. A fundamental property right is the right to be free of intrusive noise. You cannot build a boiler factory next to my house and drive me crazy with the din. The logical implication is that every boiler factory, and every other industrial plant, should buy a huge buffer zone to keep its noise from bothering other landowners.

This, like my hypothetical inhibition on licensing software, would be silly. It would require every noisy industry to buy excessive tracts of land that would then lie idle, unused even by those who care nothing about the noise. The solution is obvious: group noisy activities together so as to reduce the amount of land required by each. Each owner gives up its right to quiet in exchange for reciprocal concessions from its neighbors. Nowadays, this result is usually achieved through zoning, but given the economic logic of the situation, it could be reached by contract. For each of the companies, the ability to split up its bundle of sticks and to sell off the stick of its right to quiet reduces its investment substantially.

BOZEMAN, MONTANA, 1995

Friends own a house in Bozeman with a view of the surrounding mountains. Their place adjoins a vacant lot, and a house built on the back half of this lot would block the view. To prevent this, they buy an interest in the lot from its present owner. The interest, called an easement, gives them the right to a clear view across the property. No future house can block the mountains, and this prohibition "runs with the land," which means it is recorded in the official county records as part of the chain of title and restricts any future owner as well. It also runs with the land belonging to my friends, and any subsequent purchaser of their house gets the benefit of the easement on the neighboring lot as well. Everyone is happy. My friends secure their view and enhance the value of their house. The lot owner gives up little, because he can still build on the lot with no loss of utility, and he gets some extra cash for accepting a restriction that does not really cost him anything.

Relations between the holders of different interests in the same property are seldom simple. The law books are full of disputes between landlord and lessee, or between life tenant and the remainderman who takes the land after the tenant's death, and these relations are usually governed by careful contracts about who has the right to do what. Anyone who has lived in a college town knows that the conflict of student and landlord is one of those timeless classics. Students have a limited time interest in their property. They are also highly mobile and will soon be beyond the reach of any suit for damages. The result is restrictive leases with prohibitions on such deeds as pounding nails in the wall and practically everything else, generous damage deposits, and high rents. If students bought their apartments and resold them at the end of the academic year, none of these provisions would be necessary.

We have not exhausted the Argument from Economic Efficiency. The next point is that allowing property to be transferred allows it to gravitate toward its most productive use. Let's go back to my farm on top of the coal seam, only this time suppose that you must choose between mining and farming; you cannot do both at once. If demand for coal is high and the price is also high, it is worthwhile for a company in the mining business to offer me more for the land than I can make out of farming. The land then moves from farming to the higher, more productive use of coal production. Everyone is happy: me, the coal company, and the people who need coal to burn.

Now suppose I am not allowed to sell. I am not a coal company, so I must keep on farming for a living. Now everyone is unhappy. I am busting my back on the farm instead of living on the proceeds of selling the land, the coal company is making no money, and the potential users of anthracite are either freezing or burning bituminous coal and polluting the atmosphere.

If this example seems far afield from current issues of property, examine how the principle affects a topic dear to the hearts of millions of Americans: housing and property values. The much-maligned real estate developer is like the coal company. It is possible to dig your own coal. It is also possible to build a single house, and many people do, but it is more expensive than buying one from a developer. Just as the coal company brings economies of scale and efficiencies of organization into the coal mining process. Similarly, it is cheaper to buy a large tract of land; subdivide it; install water, sewers, streets, and landscaping; buy materials, labor, and professional services in bulk; and build many housing units than it would be to build the same number of houses one by one. In a competitive economic system, the home buyer gets the savings. We nondevelopers should encourage developers for the same reason we encourage coal companies: developers save us money.

Lumber companies are subject to the same calculus. For example, the issue whether timber should be harvested from government lands in the West is often treated as inquiry into whether Weyerhaeuser Corporation and its ilk should get this favor. Again, think it through. If you want some boards and have time on your hands, you can go to the woods, find and cut a tree, haul it back to your house, and cut it into lengthwise planks with axe and saw. Our ancestors did exactly this 150 years ago. It took a good axeman 17 years of effort to clear the trees from a 160-acre farm. This is a dreary way to spend your life. If I want to build a house, I would rather not spend the years it would take me to split enough planks. I go to a lumber yard and buy wood, or send a developer to the sawmill to buy it for me, as cheaply as possible. Then I can spend the time I save doing something more interesting to me than laboring with an axe. I care not a whit about Weyerhaeuser or its stockholders. I care about me, and as a citizen I am a stakeholder in these government lands and have some claim to the use of the timber. From my perspective, Weyerhaeuser is merely the instrumentality through which I turn my claim into a reality.

A basic tenet of economics is that in a free market resources will be bid into their most productive use. A person who can make more money out of using the resource than can the present owner can afford to pay enough to lure it away. This system can work only if the property can be sold though. If alienation (the right to sell) is restricted, then uses become frozen into unproductive patterns. Again, when applied to land, this ties in with the economics of scale that come with development. The builder who can achieve superior efficiency can make more out of the land than can someone else, and will bid it away from alternative uses.

The right to alienate is also crucial to finance. If I have the power to sell property, then I can mortgage it for cash, sell pieces of it, sell easements, or in some other way use it to raise money. In other words, ownership makes land and other nonmonetary assets more liquid—more like cash. This aids economic growth by easing the transfer of resources into more productive uses. At my farm on the coal seam, if I do choose to mine the land myself, I need money to dig the mine, buy the equipment, and support myself until I get revenue from sales of coal. If all I have is the land, I am at an impasse. Only if I can mortgage the land can I get the capital to start the mine, and my ability to do this depends on my ability to promise to give someone who has money title to the land if I default.

This discussion of transfers (otherwise known as restraints on alienation) may sound highly theoretical, but it is of great practical importance. Restraints supposed to help some favored group or inhibit some villain are mostly demagoguery. In the nineteenth century, the Homestead Act imposed a 160-acre limit on the land that could be claimed. In the arid West, it was not possible to make a living on 160 acres. The only possible value of the land to the homesteader was to sell it to someone who was trying to put together a workable-size parcel. Luckily, the restraints were porous and easily avoided, but ever since historians have been bemoaning the "land fraud" of the era. In the twentieth century, the government keeps considering allowing people to maintain individual retirement accounts. This money would be inalienable, except under hefty tax penalty. Exemptions to the penalty would be made for college expenses, medical costs, or first-time home buyers. (No exemption to buy a computer, start a business, or take a year off work to write a symphony.) Do you think this pattern of restraints is really designed to help the IRA owner? Or is it due to the political clout of the education, medical, and real estate industries, which are already absorbing a disproportionate share of the stock of national investment capital?

The final Argument from Economic Efficiency concerns decision making and information. Someone who owns a resource free and clear and accountable to no one can make decisions with dispatch. The more that the use of a resource is restricted in various ways, the more decision making about it becomes decision by committee. We all know about committees and their tendency to take forever to agree, and then reach only the lowest common denominator.

This dispatch can be attained only if property rights are well defined. If I have a right to mine coal, do I or do I not have the right to ignore what happens on the surface? If it is clear either way, then decision making can proceed quickly because I can calculate the potential of the project. It may well be that the mine is profitable if I can ignore the surface owners but not if I have to pay for any damage. The law says I have to pay them. So be it. Either pay them off or do not dig coal. It is when the lines are blurry that decisions are slowed. If I might have to pay, but then again I might not, then how do I decide whether to dig? I cannot even begin to negotiate with the surface owners if none of us knows what we own.

The effect of ownership in fostering good decisions goes still deeper. The quality of my decisions about a piece of property depends on the quality of the information and attention I bring to bear. Ownership provides me with incentive to get the right amount of information and to take it seriously. Should I turn my farm into a coal mine? How should I know, until I look at the markets for the different types of products, determine the long-term effects on the land and its uses, and consider how all of these will affect the way my family will live? Ownership gives me the motive to collect the information on these points.

Now ask me if a parcel in the next state should be a coal mine or a farm. Again, I do not know, only now I will not bother to find out either. The effort required to get the information will produce no return, so why should I make it? If you tell me that I must make a decision anyway, I will shrug and flip a coin, or decide on whim. I saw a movie about a coal mine once, and the work was dirty and, besides, those miners had a hard life. No coal mine! Let's get more contemporary. Ask me if trees in Oregon should be cut for timber or left standing as homes for spotted owls. This is a complex question involving lots of deep information, and even more misinformation, about forestry, biology, and economics. Why should I spend time sorting it out? Owls are cute. I saw a logger once, and he was ugly. Up with owls!

It is good to have decision makers bear the consequences of their own actions. It forces them to acquire the necessary information, focuses their minds, and prevents decision by wishful thinking. Life requires a recognition of the limits of possibility and the need for trade-offs and choices. Private property and its concomitant, the free market, are instruments for inserting reality into these calculations.

ARGUMENTS FROM POLITICAL FREEDOM

Another pillar of support for property rights consists of a series of Arguments from Political Freedom. The philosophers and statesmen of the seventeenth and eighteenth centuries thought hard about the conditions necessary to avoid a tyrannical state. Absolutism had been the lot of humankind forever and was only slowly being shoved back, and creating the prerequisites for the stability of representative government was much on their minds.

One bulwark against tyranny is for property to be in the hands of individuals, rather than doled out by the government. Any book of quotations is filled with epigrams worrying over the tendency of any government or governing class to abuse its power. The institution of private property is an important check on this tendency. People with an independent basis of economic support are able to stand up, speak freely, and oppose government. People whose income can be cut off by government must be much more careful.

Again, the Soviet Union provides an example. Material benefits of all sorts—apartments, access to consumer goods, cars, vacations, everything—were disposed of by the state according to political criteria. To criticize the ruling class could result in loss of everything. Some heroic dissidents did it anyway, but this grip on the allocation of the means of survival helped keep the party in power for a long time. The Soviets were not unique in discovering the effectiveness of threats of financial ruin as a means of social control either. Queen Elizabeth's government in sixteenth-century England fined people brutally for failure to attend services at the newly established Protestant churches, with the direct intent of breaking the stubborn Catholic dissenters.[21]

The second prong of the Arguments from Political Freedom is that widely held private property is necessary for the stability of a nation. If the founders worried about tyranny, they also worried about mob rule. The conventional wisdom of the time was that a democratic government could not work because it would turn into rule by a rabble that, being envious of all who were better off in intellect, property, or breeding, would wreak havoc. One solution, in the mind of Thomas Jefferson particularly, was widespread dissemination of private property. In the eighteenth century, this meant land. Jefferson was the champion of the ideal of a nation of yeoman farmers. Such men, and their families, would have a stake in stability and order and would make the considered judgments characteristic of people who have something to lose. They could never be a mob or an aristocracy, and would remain as a bulwark of government of, by, and for the people.

The industrial revolution belied Jefferson's immediate vision of yeoman farmers. In the intervening 200 years we moved from a nation with 95 percent of its people in rural areas to one with only 25 percent there. Almost none of these are yeoman farmers. It did not belie the fundamental concept underlying this vision, though. It remains true that democratic government needs an electorate with a stake in the society, one with something to lose if politics runs off the rails. The types of stakes that fill this bill have expanded beyond those available to the eighteenth century to include suburban homes, retirement accounts, Ph.D.s, copyrights and trademarks, stocks and bonds, job tenure, and other things. The principle remains constant: widespread distribution of private property, of a material stake in the orderly operation of the society, is essential to the long-term survival of democratic government.

One of the Arguments from Economic Efficiency is that private property fosters realism in economic affairs, discouraging decision making by wishful thinking and whim. The current point is a clone, translated into the political context. For political decisions, as for economic, private property encourages the investigation, accumulation of information, and sober calculation of people who know that a wrong decision can cost them. The more widespread the holdings of property, the greater the number of such people, and the more secure the polity.

THE ARGUMENT FROM PERSONAL AUTONOMY

The Argument from Personal Autonomy extends part of the Argument from Political Freedom to the need for freedom from the big institutions that now dominate both the public and private sectors. Large public and private bureaucracies so pervade the lives of Americans now that we forget that the big organization, particularly the large business enterprise, is a recent innovation. With some exceptions (e.g., armies, churches, early civil services, a few trading companies), large hierarchical enterprises, with "large" meaning anything over about ten people in any one place, came to dominate the industrial world only between 1850 and 1920.

Most people inhabiting these behemoths have a love-hate relationship with them. They acknowledge the power of organization and the economics of scale that often go with large size, but they tire of the internal politics and the whims of superiors. Even more, as a generation of middle managers who thought they had lifetime employment are learning in the current mania for downsizing, these organizations are not dependable. Thousands of people are deciding that they would rather be independent contractors making and selling products or services to whoever appreciates what they offer than be locked into crazy hierarchies. They are learning that if corporate employees cannot depend on the organization, then the only road to autonomy and security is property and the right to use it how they will.

This argument takes an extended view of property. It counts a woodlot that can be cut or an apartment unit that can be rented to finance your retirement. It also counts investment in human capital, because any skill others want to buy is a form of property. So is having your name on a lot of computerized address books. These are investments in reputation, and they are immensely important.

Attaining autonomy requires investment—whether in material goods or human capital—and investment always creates property of a sort. If autonomy is necessary to enable people to live as other than casual day laborers, however glorified, then the investment that creates it must be secure, a condition achieved only when property rights exist and are respected.

This argument can take an even deeper form. One of the basic needs of the human personality is to pursue craftsmanship and productivity, to seek a sense of satisfaction in interacting with and shaping the material world. Craftsmanship requires raw materials—whether ideas and ink for a writer or tools and trees for a logger. Using these resources requires a concept of property. Our sense of identity gets bound up in our ability to pursue this need, and depriving us of the material basis for the pursuit can be a fundamental attack not just on livelihood but on personal identity.

COMBINING THE ARGUMENTS

Now think about a situation that wraps Justice, Economic Efficiency, Political Freedom, and Personal Autonomy into one package. The example is an area that at first glance might not seem to concern property rights at all: airline overbooking.

The time for this scenario is sometime before 1978. Suppose I am an airline agent for a flight due to leave. It has ninety-nine seats, but we sold one hundred tickets, so someone must be bumped. I must decide who, and I am charged with making a decision that is just and fair. Clearly this will not be easy. I must interview all one hundred passengers to determine their individual reasons for traveling and decide whose need is least worthy. Some of the passengers may lie to me, so I need to investigate suspicious stories. Perhaps each deserves a chance to investigate the stories of all the others and to introduce evidence of lying, or to bring in witnesses as to the urgency of his or her journey. We will have hearings! They can hire lawyers! This could take a while, but who can object to delays in the name of Justice? And I am not going anywhere.

Real-life airlines are interested in quick departures rather than perfect Justice, so their approach to bumping was more direct. As the agent, I would pick someone and say, "Sorry." Randomness might seem fair, but there were other considerations. The prosperous-looking woman with the expensive briefcase might complain to the airline president and cost me my job. She was not in the draw for the black ball. The tough-looking gent picking his teeth with a bowie knife might impose other kinds of costs on me personally, so let's not bump him. Airline agents were instructed in the art of choosing victims. Elderly people were regarded as less likely to make trouble, so they were a preferred category. The one certainty was that the chosen sacrifice would be angry. In an effort to avoid inflicting this pain on passengers and on themselves, the airlines tried to underbook, allowing an ample safety margin for no-shows. Often the planes took off with empty seats that could have been filled. This cost the airlines money and raised ticket prices.

This system changed in 1978 through an act of creative government. The Civil Aeronautics Board, acting at the prodding of economist Julian Simon, required airlines to institute a "voluntary bumping" system. This meant that they were required to offer to pay bumpees. The procedure is simple. If the airline sells too many tickets, it offers money to anyone who will give up her seat on the next flight out. If not enough takers appear, the offer is raised until a sufficient number of passengers volunteer. The underlying structure of the deal is that the airline gives each ticketed passenger a property right in his seat, and if it overbooks, it buys this right back at a price satisfactory to the passenger.[22]

The results please everyone. Almost 700,000 passengers profited from a buy-back payment in 1993. By definition, they are happy because they wanted the money more than they wanted the seat on that flight. They were also spared the ignominy of having their fate decided by the whim of airline passenger agents without knowledge of individual needs. All the people not bumped are happy, or would be if they knew of their escape. The airlines are able to increase overbooking, which raises their load factors. This makes their stockholders happy indeed. Fares have gone down, to the joy of the traveling public. Ticket agents do not get grief from bumpees, which improves their lives. Particularly vulnerable people have ceased to be special targets for bumping. No one has claimed damage from the system. The net result is that the new system of making an airline seat into property is an improvement on the old system of random bumping in every possible dimension—Justice, Economic Efficiency, Political Freedom, and Personal Autonomy—and it all results from creating a property right. Who, given the choice, would substitute a system where a passenger agent, however capable and earnest, is charged with finding "Justice"?

In case you think this airline example is far afield from current real-life property rights issues, let us look at an example of replacing the allocation of land through property rights and market exchange with a search for perfect justice through government administration.

HAWAII, 1921–1995

Under a 1921 law, native Hawaiians are to be offered special opportunities to lease land for agriculture, aquaculture, and grazing. In determining whether and how much to award, the government is to consider individual characteristics and needs. It is also to consider the needs of all applicants on the waiting list and all competing demands for land for use as residences, agricultural homesteads, and commercial ranching. As of the late 1980s, only forty-eight people have gotten land, and a group of potential beneficiaries sues the state in 1989. Resolution of preliminary procedural issues takes until 1995, when the matter is sent back to the lower courts for further action on the substantive issues. The name of the plaintiffs' group is "The Aged Hawaiians."[23] The irony inherent in the name is appropriate. These plaintiffs could spend their whole lives waiting for their airplane to take off.

Chapter 4

Complexities

The Tragedy of the Commons, spillovers, technological change, and
other difficulties

I f each piece of property existed in isolation, you could state the case
for private property as the great engine of Justice, Economic Efficiency, Political Freedom, and Personal Autonomy, and stop there.
However, not much property of any type meets this description. Rather,
private property is embedded in a complex web of property belonging to
other individuals and property used by many people in common. Land
depends on access and the availability of transportation, for example.
And one person's use of his property often impinges on others, as when
the English farmers applied manure near the rock star's home, or when
your factory discharges pollutants upstream of my water intake. The
value of new types of property also depends on a network. A bank
check presupposes a financial system. A piece of software assumes the
existence of computers.

These interdependencies raise two types of complexities. First, a respectable chunk of the worth of any individual property comes from its
place in the web, from the *network value*. Second, a society has to figure
out how to resolve the inevitable conflicts. If smoke from my chimney
drifts onto your land, do I have a property right to discharge smoke—or
do you have a property right to be free of it? If you have fished in a particular public lake for years and the fish are getting scarce because of an
influx of new anglers, do you have a property right to exclude the new
people, or do you have to share?

The complexities can be divided into five overlapping families:

1. *Public facilities*—things built and operated by the government, such as courthouses, parks, arsenals, office buildings, and wildlife refuges.
2. *Transportation and other infrastructure*—a category that includes roads, rivers, canals, railroads, stations, and so on. It also covers utility and communication lines.
3. *Various types of commons*—resources used by many people at a time or even by humanity at large. Oceans and rivers are here, and so are parks and most transportation facilities. The term covers a sprawling and diverse collection of assets.
4. *Spillovers*—the effects that my use of property has on yours. Pollution is the obvious one, but there are many others.
5. *Technological change*—which encompasses the impact on property rights of changes in what is technically possible and feasible.

These categories are not totally separable, and some things, such as a transportation facility, can involve all five of them. A road is usually a public facility. It is also a commons, and it generates spillovers. Transportation is subject to constant technological change. Nevertheless, despite this overlap, it is convenient to consider the categories separately because they present different types of problems for society and government. Dealing with spillovers from a road is a different problem from dealing with the consequences of its nature as a commons or with the impact of access on land values.

The efforts of private actors or governments to deal with these complexities are an integral part of the Lockean system. The right to use a commons is worth little if inexorable incentives for overuse lead the users collectively to destroy it. Dealing with spillovers is crucial to the value and enjoyment of property and its fruits. Property is worth nothing without access and transportation, and the steady expansion from oxcart to railroad to truck to airplane has been accompanied by a vast increase in wealth. The same process is occurring for intellectual property as the expansion in access called the information superhighway proceeds apace. A Lockean government, as a principal part of its function of protecting people's right to property, must figure out how to deal with these complexities.

PUBLIC FACILITIES

At first glance, this category seems trivial. Governments need court-houses, prisons, forts, offices, and other physical facilities. These sit on land and use many other kinds of property, ranging from furniture to computer software. Ergo, title to some property must be lodged in the government, which becomes like a private owner.

The practice now is for governments to buy necessary property on the open market, like anyone else. The governments of the United States and of every state also reserve the power of eminent domain—the right to take property by compulsion—but use of this power is conditioned on payment of just compensation. The requirement of compensation is codified in the words of the Fifth Amendment to the U.S. Constitution: "nor shall private property be taken for public use without just compensation." State constitutions impose similar conditions on the power of eminent domain, and even if they did not the federal protection covers takings by states as well as by the federal government.

The underlying principle is obvious: everyone benefits from property used for public facilities, so it would not be fair to require any individual to pay for them. The formulation used by the Supreme Court is that we do not "forc[e] some people alone to bear the burdens which, in all fairness and justice, should be borne by the public as a whole."[1]

To anyone raised with twentieth-century concepts of fairness and justice, this requirement that government pay for what it takes seems self-evident. It was not always so clear, though, and history indicates that our modern assumption is shallow-rooted. In earlier times, English governments sometimes simply took property, on the theory that everything belonged to the king anyway, and he was simply asserting his reversionary right. American colonists objected when English functionaries marked the best and straightest trees, necessary to provide masts to the navy, as belonging to the king. In the eighteenth century troops were quartered in private homes, with "quartering" including food as well as housing. The practice was important enough, and distasteful enough, to induce the drafters of the Bill of Rights to give it an amendment all its own. Amendment III says that troops cannot be quartered during peacetime without the consent of the owner. (They *can* be quartered in time of war, by the way.)

TRANSPORTATION AND INFRASTRUCTURE

No personal property is worth anything if it cannot be moved to where it can be used, and no land is worth much if its fruits cannot be moved. To a tremendous degree, the worth of any piece of property depends on the quality of the transportation that serves it. In contemporary urban America, you can extend this to other infrastructure, such as sewers, water, and utility lines.

As with public facilities, we of twentieth-century America tend to think that *of course* the government provides transportation facilities. No single property owner can afford to build a network connecting a town, country, or world. The cost is out of proportion to the value of his property.

This assumption is less obvious than it might appear on the surface. Until the canal and railroad, major transportation rights-of-way simply existed, in the form of rivers and oceans. Vehicles were privately operated on these natural rights-of-way, though a government might build some docks and do some dredging. Some road construction took place, but it was not a major activity. Enough for local needs was performed at a local level, and long-distance travel consisted of using one local network after another. The concept of the National Post Road, a limited net maintained by the central government for purposes of internal communication, developed, but these were not heavy duty roads for trade. In the nineteenth century United States, the first grants of federal land to encourage the construction of transportation facilities went to the builders of wagon roads.

Property law was concerned with water transportation in one important way. Rivers existed naturally, but landowners along the banks could certainly block them. Piers for vessels might be built, dams and water wheels for milling, or toll gates to collect from passing vessels. Rules developed making waterways subject to a navigational servitude, which meant that no one could block them for purposes of their own. Owning the bed or bank of a river did not and does not allow you to use it in a way that interferes with shipping. To this day, this remains true. You cannot interfere with the use of water as an artery of transportation.

Historians are not too sure how colonial America acquired land for rural roads. It may have been paid for, but evidence indicates that sometimes it was not. Improved and unimproved land may have been treated differently in some places, with the former paid for and the latter not. In a society where access to a road was an important part of the value of the land, unimproved land was reasonably plentiful, improvements cost great effort, and the labor for improvements had to be supplied mostly by the inhabitants, the issue of payment was probably not too important as long as policy was uniform. You would expect people to squawk about losing laboriously cleared land for public roads, but not at losing raw land, as long as their neighbors were in the same position.

In the United States, the growth of cities and the transportation revolution of the eighteenth and nineteenth centuries converted the production of transportation facilities into a property rights problem. Land needed for urban streets, intercity railroads, and, later, streetcar tracks was already valuable, and so was the land used for airports in the twentieth. In the country, canals, railroads, and heavy-duty wagons took more land than had been needed for rural cart tracks, and as the country became more settled, this property was also more valuable. Governments, controlled by constitutional provisions, had to pay for it.

The main issue that arose was not whether the land had been taken for the public use of building transportation, because it clearly had been. The issue was valuation. Governments took the view that transportation facilities enhanced the value of a landowner's adjoining, untaken property, and that this enhancement should be deducted from any payment for the property that had been taken. Landowners protested that the facilities also enhanced the worth of neighbors' land without requiring them to give up anything and that it was unfair to put the entire burden on the owner unlucky enough to have the right-of-way go through his property rather than next to it.

This issue, named the *offset-benefit rule,* bounced back and forth in the courts for years. The dominant view was that the enhanced value of a landowner's remaining property would not be deducted from the amount paid to him, unless he received some special benefit not available to his neighbors.[2]

An underlying issue has never been solved. Construction of transportation facilities confers immense benefits on the parcels of land most immediately served. There is something asymmetrical about a system in which anyone who loses out when a right-of-way is built at public expense is fully compensated, albeit at the preimprovement value of the land, while anyone whose land increases in value as a direct result of the road gets to keep the increment. The asymmetry is handled in various ways. The most common is to ignore it, letting the chips and the cash fall where they may. This system makes the job of selecting highway or rail routes or locating airports powerful and often quite lucrative. Millions can be made by anyone who controls these routes or can get advance knowledge of their locations.

A second way to deal with the issue is to integrate the land and the transportation facilities. This principle was followed in building the railroads across the West in the nineteenth century. Western land remote from transportation was worth nothing. The railroad made it valuable because crops and cattle could be moved to market. The railroads were granted large tracts of land from the public domain in exchange for building the line, on the theory that they could sell the now-productive land for enough to cover the costs of construction, and then make money by hauling the produce.

You can also integrate transportation and landownership by putting the cost of building transportation on the landowners who will benefit. This was done in the nineteenth century in the form of assessments for street repairs levied on owners of abutting property, a practice still followed sometimes. In recent years, it has become common to put the burden of paying for new local streets on real estate developers. No Happy Acres is built on streets paid for with public funds. The developer puts them in, sometimes dedicating them to the city and making them public roads that are now maintained at public expense. Increasingly, though, title is retained in a home owners' association, a gate is erected, and control of the streets becomes another marketing point for selling the houses.

The idea of making the landowner-beneficiary pay has spread to subways. The Washington-area Metro just announced that a new subway station will be paid for by the owner of the large tract at which it will be built. This will be, Metro says, the first public subway station ever built in the United States with private funds.[3] New York City sometimes requires a developer to dedicate land for a subway stop, but it has not gone so far as to tell him to build it himself.

THE COMMONS

Our next category is the commons, a resource used by many people at a time or even by humanity at large. Some things cannot be reduced to ownership. It is physically impossible to control all the oceans, so they are treated as a giant commons, which all can use to harvest fish or for transportation. Where it is possible to control access, nations do so, reserving the controllable part for their own citizens. Other things, such as forests or mountains or grazing land, can be reduced to ownership by excluding interlopers, but the cost can overwhelm the value of the property. When this is the case, the assets are usually held as common assets of a community. Groups of families may pasture animals on a village green. Forests and other homes for wild animals may be held in common, with each participant taking what he can capture. Rivers, lakes, and groundwater are usually treated as a kind of commons. No one "owns" water until he actually captures and removes it from the common pool.

Commons come in many shapes and sizes, not all of them obvious. The capacity of air or water to absorb pollution without degrading public health or aesthetics is a kind of commons. An underground pool of oil or water is another commons. Anyone on the surface can drill into it and extract the resource. Other commons consist of spaces that produce pleasure, such as parks, beaches, and village squares. Anything occasionally useful to large numbers of people is likely to be held as public property open to use by all. Some of these are among the high points of civilization, such as New York's Central Park, Chicago's lakefront and Grant Park, or Washington's monuments and green space.

Transportation facilities are a commons. Everyone has a legal right to use them. The government cannot forbid anyone to use the road network or let some citizens and not others use the waterways. This idea that transportation must be broadly available is extended even to private rights-of-way, such as railroads. They are called *common carriers,* which means they must accept anyone willing to pay the fare. The same common carrier status applies to buses and ships. As technology has advanced, the principle has been extended to telecommunications companies.

You can find complex economic discussions of the various types of commons, but in general it is useful to think of the following progression. Property rights will not be established when it is not worth anyone's while to try to exclude others. A small group living next to a large forest does not even think about "owning" the forest. Even if these people could control it, there is no point. At low population densities, there is enough wood and game for all, so no benefit comes from spending effort on establishing and defending property rights. Similarly, assets that are worthless will be unowned. No one will defend rights to a barrens.

If the balance begins to shift so that the forest does not provide resources enough for all or oil is found in the barrens, then groups will create principles of ownership—typically first in the form of group ownership. The resource will be a commons as far as members of the tribe are concerned, but outsiders will be excluded. As long as the resource can meet the needs of the in-group, it is improbable that ownership beyond the simple one-of-us or one-of-them will be established. American Indians had a strong sense of tribal land even if they did not think in terms of individual ownership.

The next stage in the progression comes when the resource becomes insufficient to meet the demands placed on it by the insiders. Now we begin to get into the phenomenon known as the Tragedy of the Commons. This phrase was made famous by environmentalist Garret Hardin in 1968, but the concept has been around in the literature of the economics profession for decades. The Tragedy of the Commons is that each individual has an incentive to use as much of the resource as possible before it is used by others. As everyone responds to this incentive, the resource is overused and destroyed.[4]

Think of a sheep pasture with sufficient fodder to support a thousand animals on a sustainable long-term basis, and perhaps three hundred more for a season or two. It is surrounded by twenty families. Absent any agreement, each family has an incentive to put as many sheep as possible on the land, to the point where the grass is eaten to the dirt and the land can support no sheep at all. The reason is straightforward. Any family that adds sheep will get the entire benefit produced by their animals. The costs they impose will be split among all the families. Furthermore, any family that restrains itself will simply make room available for a less scrupulous family. It cannot reap the reward for its good sense. You may know that putting another sheep on the land will hasten the day when there are no sheep at all, but if you do it you will get at least a short-term benefit. If you do not, someone else will, and you will lose your sheep while getting no benefit.

This incentive structure applies to the pollution commons. A municipality, farmer, factory operator, or other producer of contaminants gets all the economic benefits of releasing them into the air or water. The contamination disperses so that the releaser pays only a small share of the costs it imposes. Furthermore, any individual polluter who decided to spend large sums to avoid releasing contaminants would be foolish. He would be providing a general benefit to everyone using the commons, but would capture only a small portion of that benefit. This action would be like a sheep herder fertilizing an entire range when it runs only a small percentage of the sheep. Given these forces, in the absence of some means of overall control we would expect commons of air and water to be overexploited and degraded by polluters, and we would be dead right. This is what happens.

Oil is subject to the Tragedy of the Commons. A surface owner who rations his consumption does not help himself. He just leaves more for others to take. And the act of grabbing can destroy the resource, like a pasture eaten down to the roots. Rapid pumping can also reduce the overall capacity of an oil field, leaving large pools untapped when they could be removed by more careful methods. Groundwater is subject to the same calculus.

Roads too are subject to the Tragedy of the Commons. The next time you are in your car on a parking lot called an interstate highway at rush hour, soothe yourself by musing on the reason for your predicament. Each driver gets the entire benefit of his use of the road but pays none of the costs he imposes on other drivers. The result is overuse and congestion, to the point where the overall carrying capacity of the highway is greatly reduced.

Human societies have been dealing with commons problems for thousands of years, and a number of techniques have evolved. Small, closely knit groups can solve their commons problems by excluding outsiders and keeping tabs on each other. They can impose sanctions on those who violate the code, ranging from physical punishment to social ostracism to religious damnation. The system in Ur, where land belonged to the Goddess and its use was conditioned on piety, makes sense as a solution to a commons problem. In most of the semiarid Middle East, agriculture required large-scale irrigation systems. These could be produced and maintained only by communal rather than individual efforts. In other words, the irrigation system was a commons benefiting all individual farm plots. If shirking irritated the Goddess, then making the right to use property dependent on her judgment, as interpreted by the priests, would ensure that each farmer did his bit to keep the irrigation system functioning. If the right to farm a particular plot of land were absolute, then each would have an incentive to skimp on his share of the work needed to maintain the common irrigation system and devote more time to his personal plot.

Commons problems in larger groups are harder to resolve. The overuse of the commons becomes more inexorable as costs of exclusion and monitoring become higher. There are a series of problems that interfere with the use of private agreements to allocate the use of commons and avoid overuse. These go by the names of transaction costs, holdouts, moral hazards, and free riders. They are the subject of a huge academic literature, but they all boil down to the proposition that it is difficult to get a group of people to agree on anything, even when it is in their own interest. It takes a lot of time and effort simply to explain things to everyone and talk it out. Someone will always refuse to attend the meetings and then vote no because he does not understand it. Somebody else will angle to get more than his share, and a third person will want to pay less than hers. Anyone who has ever tried to set up a lunch involving more than five people will immediately grasp the problems.

Despite all these barriers, groups often do manage commons problems on a voluntary basis, but it is not easy. An important function of government is to take over this function, because governments have controls of sanctions and rewards that are not available to private groups. In fact, governments are created among people precisely because compulsion is needed to organize the use of the commons.

Thus, the twenty families surrounding the sheep pasture may get together and either divide up the commons into individual plots or agree on sheep quotas. However, quarrels over quotas can become difficult because the just allocation is not clear. One family holds out for straight pro rata per family: 5 percent each. Another thinks this unfair because it has five people able to herd while the first family has only one. Another family has only one herder, but she has unusual prowess at fighting wolves and demands a bigger cut.

This is the kind of problem that leads to government. If the families cannot agree, they may simply appoint one person to be king (or he will appoint himself), empowered to decide all sheep quota issues. The likely result, given some time for the system to develop, is that the king will get about five hundred sheep, four of the toughest herdsmen will become barons with about one hundred each, and the fifteen remaining families will divide the last one hundred. But seven sheep are better than nothing, which is what the fifteen families (now called the peasantry) will get if there is no order.

A HISTORICAL DIGRESSION

Students of political science will recognize this example as the Hobbesian view of life. Thomas Hobbes was the seventeenth-century philosopher who described life in a state of nature as "nasty, brutish, and short," and as a "war of all against all." His point was that people would embrace government, however tyrannical, rather than endure disorder. The logical outcome was that the governors would leave the populace enough sustenance for life but would take anything over that for themselves as the price of maintaining order. At the time Hobbes wrote, this allocation was accepted as right. To put it in the terms of the time, God had appointed kings and barons to keep order and to rule.

John Locke, writing after Hobbes, placed government on a different basis. It operated by the consent of the people and as their surrogate. Thus the governors had no right to the surplus above a subsistence level. It was for the precise purpose of protecting this surplus—this property—that governments are instituted among people, deriving their just powers from the consent of the governed.[5] In Locke's philosophy, the purpose of government is to keep any set of kings and barons from appropriating the use of the commons, guaranteeing to each of the twenty families its full share. In this context, Lockean philosophy is a justification for allocating the fruits of order to the people as a whole rather than to their rulers.

Whether implemented by private agreement or by government, four basic ways of controlling commons problems are available. In the first, a single authority exploits the commons and divides the proceeds among those who have the rights to use it. This solution avoids destruction through overuse but does not solve the basic issue of how to divide the proceeds. All the sheep quota issues are still there. As another example, how do you divide the take from a unitized oil field? Is it allocated by acreage of surface area over the field, number of wells, level of investment, or some other factor? For that matter, should it have any relationship at all to ownership of the land over the pool? Can a slant driller participate?

A second method for controlling a commons is by pure regulation. This technique is used to control pollution. People releasing contaminants are subjected to a variety of detailed requirements. Sometimes they are given specific quotas of allowable levels of pollutants. Sometimes they are told to install a certain type of technology, and the society accepts whatever this produces. The regulatory approach is used in many other contexts as well. Anyone may be allowed to fish a stream, but the catch is limited. Cattle ranchers using the public domain are subjected to elaborate rules on the numbers of cows and the conditions of use.

A third method is handicapping. People are allowed to use the commons, but their methods are limited. Crabbers in Maryland can work only a limited number of days per week, for example. Other fishermen can be limited in the types of nets used or in the capacity of their ships. This solution makes sense when the object is control of a sport, such as hunting or fishing. It makes little sense in a commercial context, where it creates incentives for people to invest more and more money in equipment that can be used with less and less efficiency. The paradigm of the approach is seen in subsidized agriculture, where farmers subject to acreage limits spend heavily on fertilizer and equipment to make those acres produce as much as possible.

The fourth approach is to create property rights in the commons. The most obvious example, and perhaps the most important in the United States, is water law in the western states. Whoever first appropriates water from a stream gets a right to continue to appropriate that quantity of water. The right is valid against all later comers. Other forms of property rights in commons are also used. The government, as the administrator of the commons called the public lands, auctions off the right to cut timber or to graze. The buyer now has a property right, just as if he purchased from a private landowner.

Property rights in the form of transferable quotas are sometimes used. Fishermen can be given catch limits but be allowed to transfer them to others for money. The right to release pollutants can be made the subject of a system of transferable quotas. The advantage of this approach is that it promotes economic efficiency and cost reduction, for the same reason that allowing private property in general to be transferred encourages the migration of resources to their highest and best use. In the most sophisticated systems, quotas can be bought and retired by people who think the activity should not be conducted at all. For example, those opposed to whaling can buy up a whaler's quota and retire it. Those opposed to logging in a national forest can bid at the timber sale and not cut the timber if they win.

The Electromagnetic Spectrum (EMS), used for television, radio, cellular telephones, and other methods of communication, is a commons in transition. It cannot be left uncontrolled, or the various users will interfere hopelessly with each other, reducing its value to zero. Historically, the government allocated the spectrum through hearings that approximated my earlier hypothetical example about fairness in airline seat allocations. It held comparative hearings about who was best qualified to receive channels. The lucky recipient then had a property right. It could freely transfer its station, and its license, to anyone without further approval. Now the government is moving to a system of auctions whereby the highest bidder gets the license and can transfer it. The system still contains a lot of restrictions designed to bless the politically favored, though.

Developing a system of property rights in a commons usually raises three distinct types of problems. First, you must decide who is eligible to be in the pool. Who has the right to catch crabs in Chesapeake Bay, for example, once it becomes clear that the total catch must be limited? Can any citizen claim a share? Do you hold a lottery among those interested? Do you grandfather in those who were in the crabbing business when the need for restrictions became clear? What about the capacity of the bay to absorb pollutants? Can you build on your lot, then forbid me to build on mine on the ground that you have appropriated as a property right the ability of the bay to absorb the runoff from homes?

The second problem is how to allocate shares in the commons once you decide who should be in the pool. Does each individual get a quota? Each family? Do you sell shares, or assign shares according to level of investment? Do you auction off the rights, limiting the bidders to those in a special pool of eligibles?

The third problem is development over time. Rules governing commons must be able to evolve as the pressure on the commons increases. People seem to have an instinctive acceptance of this. Fishermen, foresters, and other users of a commons do not seem to feel that their rights are immutable. They seem to make an instinctive decision between their property, such as a fishing boat or a house over which they have absolute dominion, and property rights in a common, which are somewhat fluid. They may feel that they have a right to fish, not to be shut out entirely, but they seem to recognize that the details of this right are subject to adjustment over time.

OLD RAG MOUNTAIN, SHENANDOAH NATIONAL PARK, VIRGINIA, 1995

Old Rag is one of the most popular spots in the park, 100,000 hikers visit it each year, with as many as 900 on the trails on a typical weekend day. The crowding is irritating everyone—rangers, nearby residents, and hikers themselves—so the Park Service has started limiting the number of hikers allowed on at a time to those carried in the two hundred cars that can get into the parking lot. Additionally, fees will be charged, with the proceeds devoted to maintenance. Most hikers endorse the changes.[6]

SPILLOVERS

This family of complications is called spillover effects, or, in the formal language of economics, externalities. It is impossible to contain the impact of uses of property completely within the property. No matter what you do, other people will see, hear, smell, taste, or feel it. Even if they cannot sense it physically, what you do may affect the value of their property, so they may have an interest in your actions.

Property law and practice constantly address the conflicts over spillovers. This is the area of the law called nuisance, and it covers a host of day-to-day minor and serious frictions among property owners. Suppose my land lies uphill from yours, and water runs off mine and washes away your prize tomato plants. Is this my fault? Am I supposed to have stopped the water? The usual answer of common law courts was that I was not responsible as long as the land was in its natural state. If I dug it up or built on it and the water ran off as a result of my changes, then I was liable.

A famous legal scholar once wrote, "There is no more impenetrable jungle in the law than the area of nuisance." Lawyers are fond of quoting this line. In particular, government lawyers like to use it when arguing that whatever agency they work for needs more power. Unfortunately, the line is not right. The country has a lot of land, a lot of fact situations have arisen, and a lot of legal cases have been decided, not always consistently. Despite the complications, the basic principles on nuisance were distilled by Chicago professor Richard Epstein in his classic work, *Takings*, in 1985, and they represent a solid, commonsense view. The starting point is that I cannot physically occupy your property. I cannot put a house on it, or build my house so that the roof overhangs your land, or dig a tunnel under your surface. I cannot occupy your land even temporarily, by walking across it without permission. Does this mean that I can sit there and watch you build a house that extends one foot over my property line, then tell you to tear it down, unless you pay me many dollars? No. The law is not quite that dumb, and doctrines dealing with such traps evolved long ago. Also, a minor and accidental physical invasion might result in an order to pay damages, not to tear down the house.

I also have the right to expect you not to change the natural state of your property in a way that damages mine physically. You cannot dig up your property in a way that diverts water onto mine, for example. I also have a right to lateral support from the soil on your land.

ANY URBAN CONSTRUCTION SITE, 1997

Look along the property line where the soil has been removed to put in the foundation. You see a retaining wall of some sort, strong enough to prevent any cave-in of the adjoining property. This is the responsibility of the owner of the construction site, and everyone knows it. If the wall fails, he pays. It is rare for a wall to fail, given the cost of error and the well-developed technology of its construction.

At the other end of the spectrum, you have no control over anything I do on my land that has no physical effect on yours. You have no right to keep me from building because you like the view across my property or dislike my taste in architecture. Nor can you interfere with my use of the property on the ground that you prefer that my property be put to some other use. If I want to build a shopping center, for example, you cannot object on the grounds that my property should become a wildlife refuge for the black-footed ferret. You cannot claim spillover unless my action directly affects your personal physical being or your *property*—not your interest in historical preservation, or your concern about the architectural aesthetics, or your desire to save the spotted owl, but your person or your property.

BACK TO BOZEMAN

My Bozeman friends' purchase of the easement is a win-win situation in which all parties are left better off. Less benign situations are also possible. What if my neighbor builds a house that blocks my view when he could perfectly well (in my opinion) have built one just as good that leaves the view open? What if he builds a thirty-foot-high fence across his backyard that (again in my opinion) serves no purpose except to cut off my view, and says he will take it down only if I pay him $5,000? You think people would not do that to their neighbors? In the late nineteenth century, Massachusetts required municipal permits for the construction of fences over six feet high precisely because too many "spite fences" were being built and the quarrels endangered the public peace.[7]

In between the ends of the spectrum, when there is a physical effect on person or property but no total physical invasion, things become less certain. Noise, smells, and contamination are judged on a more pragmatic standard. The line is uncertain, and generations of lawyers have argued over when a physical effect is so great as to be tantamount to a physical invasion. The general principles are sketched out by Epstein and others:

• *Live and let live.* Minor frictions should be ignored. Questions of degree always exist, of course, but occasionally barking dogs, decorative lights at Christmas, the occasional aroma of fertilizer, and so on are part of the give-and-take of life in a community.

• *Look for local practice.* In deciding the boundaries of live and let live, the nature of the area matters. A nail factory seeking to stop the noise from an adjoining foundry would not succeed, nor would a cow rancher who objected to the smell of sheep manure. On the other hand, putting either facility down in the middle of a residential area is inappropriate.

• *Look for quid pro quos.* Restrictions on the use of property are likely to be upheld if each owner gets the benefit from comparable restrictions imposed on everybody else. The importance of this concept of mutual restrictions can hardly be overstated. Zoning started in New York in 1916 and swept the country during the 1920s as people devised ways to protect newly purchased homes from any threat to real estate values. If zoning through public law is not sufficient, Americans love to set up home owner associations to ensure that no one comes into the neighborhood with a mobile home or some outlandish piece of architecture and upsets property values. They also like to zone out uses that would cause their property taxes to rise.[8] In 1962 the nation had about 500 home owners' associations acting as private governments, regulating the use of land and the design of buildings. By 1992, it had an estimated 150,000 such associations, governing 32 million people.[9]

These are commonly created when a developer buys a large tract of land and then sells it off with conditions governing spillovers attached. People opt in to the system when they purchase property. Anyone who does not like the rules does not have to join, and no hard feelings. Most people are reassured by having limitations on land use that bind their neighbors, and the existence of these private governments has become a powerful selling tool.

• *Look for equality, and look at the general versus the specific.* If a neighbor's use of property puts a special burden on my property that it does not put on anyone else, then I am more likely to collect damages than if it creates some sort of generalized nuisance. The general nuisance is more likely to be enjoined though.

• *Look at whether a land use has a negative spillover or simply removes a positive spillover.* Land use guru Robert Ellickson of Yale makes an important distinction between positive and negative spillovers.[10] He posits that in most situations there is a sort of baseline of normal land use for an area. These tend to have a constant and acceptable type and level of spillover effects on their neighbors. Single-family homes on large lots, for example, or commercial development but not industrial, are common patterns. Many disputes over land use erupt when someone wants to use property for a different use that has more spillovers. An effort to put town houses into an area of freestanding residences is a common problem; the existing residents feel that the newcomers will downgrade the neighborhood aesthetically and bring in more traffic.

Sometimes, though, someone is using property in a way that confers a benefit on the neighborhood—a positive spillover, in the jargon of the trade. A buildable tract may remain vacant, giving the residents the benefit of open space, less traffic, and a de facto park. Or a historic building may lend tone to an area. An effort to change a positive use is also likely to generate intense opposition. People who live across from a vacant tract or a historic building tend to regard the situation as their right. Give them a legal lever for the exercise of opportunism and a rough rationale to salve their consciences, and they will appropriate the current positive spillover as their own, forever.

Ellickson's point is that you can see this distinction running through the legal cases, though it is not spelled out in quite this way. The rule that the courts seem to grope for is that the neighbors can prevent a downgrading in use that will cause negative spillovers. They do not have the right to the continuation of a positive spillover. They should not be allowed to prevent their neighbor from using his property in the same fashion as everyone else unless they are willing to pay for it. If I have a historic house in a residential neighborhood, I should be able to tear it down and build a regular house, but maybe I cannot put in an apartment building.

It is not surprising that spillover effects provide the stuff of numerous law school courses. Some the problems are hard, but they are not as hard as people asserting the need for government regulation would have you believe. In many instances, the old adage applies that the substance of a rule is not as important as its clarity. Take the idea that I cannot disturb my land in a way that drains the water off it and onto yours. It can be argued that putting the responsibility on you would be fairer. After all, is it my fault that you live downhill? Maybe we need a case-by-case inquiry each time, with a full examination of the relative ability of each of us to bear the burden, and so on. Obviously this is the road to perdition, like the example of seeking perfect fairness in airline bumping. Building a drainage ditch will cost about the same no matter who pays. If we each know where the responsibility lies, we can plan accordingly and pay appropriate prices for our parcels. If the rule is unclear, then the transaction costs generated by the uncertainty will eat up more than the cost of the ditch.

TECHNOLOGICAL CHANGE

Property rights get defined within a particular technological context, and they are subject to rethinking when the context changes. During the nineteenth century, title to land went to the top of the heavens. No one bothered to insert a reservation saying, "But if anyone ever invents something called an airplane, you have to let it fly over your property." Nonetheless, when the airplane came along, property rights got limited this way; otherwise, air travel could not exist. Your title is supposed to go to the center of the earth, too, but if anyone ever invents a machine that tunnels through the earth at a depth of 1,000 feet without disturbing the surface, you will learn that this is not really true either.

Take a nineteenth-century example. Ramming railroads through cities to terminals was immensely disruptive. These were steam engines, emitting dense smoke, dust, dirt, sparks, and cinders, and the effects were not limited to the immediate right-of-way.

WASHINGTON, D.C., 1913

Richards owns a house sited 100 feet from the south portal of the railroad tunnel that leads under the Capitol and into Union Station. About thirty trains go by every day. Some of them delay outside the tunnel entrance, waiting and belching. The ventilation system in the tunnel also takes all the smoke and gas emitted while trains are in the tunnel and pumps it out the south portal. The house has also been damaged by vibrations, and overall the value of the property has declined about 20 percent.

Richards sues the railroad on the theory that the tunnel is a nuisance. He both wins and loses. The Supreme Court's first conclusion is that Congress immunized the railroad from paying for damages that are "shared generally by property owners whose land lies within the range of inconveniences necessarily incident to proximity to a railroad." The judges note that the rule can impose heavy loss on property owners, but they bow to necessity. Without it, railroads are not possible, and considering the extreme importance of the railroad, such an outcome would be inconceivable. Thus the railroad does not pay for the damage from vibration or from the smoke and fumes emitted as trains approach or exit the tunnel.

But this immunity is sharply limited. Congress did not shield the railroad from paying special damages borne by Richards alone and not by the general class of property owners. Indeed, Congress could not do so, because this would be a taking of Richards's property—his right of action for nuisance—and if Congress took it, Richards would have to receive just compensation. Thus the railroad must pay for damages caused by the smoke pumped out of the tunnel by the ventilating system, because these are not inflicted on property owners generally.[11]

If you do not like what the Court did, then think about it in the following context. In a scene in the movie *Clueless*, multiple members of a group of California Valley Girls in a physical education class pull out cellular telephones and begin dialing up various friends and each other. It is a funny touch, but there is a hitch: cellular phones need 150-foot-tall antennas on monopoles—about 100,000 of them nationwide and costing up to $10 billion. Valley Girls and their parents may love their phones, but they do not love the antennas. Where tall commercial structures exist, siting monopoles is easy, but in residential areas the NIMBY (Not-In-My-Backyard) problem is getting serious. Fairfax County, Virginia, received forty-nine applications to build poles in 1994 and forty-one through the first ten months of 1995. A local high school got $25,000 up front and $10,000 per year in rent for providing a home for a monopole. This kind of money is persuasive for a landowner. Any cellular company that wants my address should give me a call. For that kind of money I will put a pole in my backyard and call it art. The problem is that my neighbors might object, because they get the view of the pole without the money, and my right to inflict this on them is a little unclear. Some people are also concerned about the supposed health risk from electromagnetic radiation. In 1996, the U.S. postmaster general decided to reap millions of dollars by leasing out tower sites at post offices all over the nation, taking advantage of the federal government's power to cut through municipal restrictions. Many local officials are not happy, and the deal is far from settled.[12]

So suppose Richards's descendants now occupy a house in the suburbs of Washington. They sue to prevent construction of a cellular telephone monopole sited a block away, arguing that it is ugly and will cast a shadow on their patio. Monopole construction is inconceivable if the phone company has to litigate and pay for every alleged decline in subjective aesthetic value that results from its facilities. Should Valley Girls be deprived of their cellular telephones so that the Richards can have a sunny patio and be free of a fear of electromagnetic radiation? Even as we speak, the issue is being fought out, city by city.

Given the necessities and the economics, the technology of the railroad shrank the Richards's property rights. Technology can also give them back though. The engines involved in the *Richards* case were coal-burning steam engines. Within the next few decades, diesel and electric locomotives came in, and the coal burner disappeared, first from cities and then from the railroad generally. If electric locomotives had existed in 1913, it is almost certain that the Court would not have allowed the railroad to impose the costs on Richards. The intrusion ceased to be necessary. Pollution control technologies always affect our ideas of who has a right to what. Smoke or noise that is tolerated when it is an unavoidable part of an important industrial process becomes unacceptable when new technology makes it controllable.

Technological change also has a heavy influence on our treatment of the commons. As technology makes better monitoring and control possible, it will become possible to create property rights in various commons. One reason roads or hiking trails are commons is that it has not been feasible to monitor use and charge people accordingly. Electronics is making monitoring possible, thus creating new possibilities for property rights and for market approaches to financing facilities that have long been treated as public responsibilities. The result will be both more efficient, as people vote on quantities desired with their dollars, and fairer, as the freight is paid by the people who actually use the facilities.

There you have it—enough complexity to delight a nation of lawyers, even in a society wholeheartedly devoted to the basic idea of property rights. Sorting out the complexities presented by public facilities, transportation networks, commons, spillovers, and technological change is a difficult task for any society. The questions are intricate and the passions strong. It is, nonetheless, an essential function, and performing it fairly and competently is a fundamental duty of government.

Chapter 5

Political Legitimacy

Prologue to the battle, OR, *if you think "they can't do this to me!" just watch them*

The justifications for a system of private property described in the last two chapters can fairly be called the Lockean tradition. Using the term takes liberties because the description contains much that was unknown to Locke. He never heard of network values, externalities, or the commons, and did not need to face problems posed by train tunnels, let alone telecommunications. The argument based on the need for autonomy from large private organizations would sound alien to Locke's ears. Few existed in 1681. There is also little unenclosed land left to acquire these days, and the concept of ownership through work is no longer tied tightly to specific chunks of land. It is a general concept holding that you have a moral right to property you obtain through your own legitimate efforts.

It is also possible to overdo the idea of labor as the source of value. As society has grown more complex technically and socially, so have ideas of economic value. You must take a broad view of labor to make the theory work at all—one that encompasses intellectual contributions, entrepreneurship, and management—and you also must recognize that the arguments from Economic Efficiency do not really rest on labor. Property rights are necessary to the efficient use of resources, whatever the source of the original title.

On all these points, rich refinements have been added to Locke by subsequent thinkers. Nonetheless, calling this description the Lockean

73

tradition is fair because the basic attitude and approach remain recognizable, and the thread of continuity from the seventeenth century to the present is clearly visible. Locke's name is attached to a universe of beliefs and attitudes, and to a great tide of social change extending far beyond the work of his own hand.

U.S. laws, customs, and attitudes toward property are deeply rooted in this tradition, including all the great arguments that buttress it. This does not mean that people stand around at cocktail parties arguing over the tensions between the Argument from Justice and the Argument from Economic Efficiency, or discussing Thomas Jefferson's emphasis on the Argument from Political Freedom or the growing weight of the Argument from Personal Autonomy in a world of large conglomerates. It means that the validity of these arguments is generally accepted without much explicit discussion as an organizing principle of our personal lives and as a basic premise of the political system. Knowledge workers who sneer at "property rights" still obsess about the worth of their suburban homes. They also protect fiercely other types of property, such as financial assets, professional degrees, and intellectual inventions. Their denigration of property applies to commercial real estate and housing developments, not to any types of property they themselves own. When it counts, they are Lockean to the bone.

CONFERENCE ON INTELLECTUAL PROPERTY, 1991

A group of scholars meets to discuss current "societal constructs" of intellectual property. The U.S. registrar of copyrights appears at one of the sessions. Harvard professor William Alford describes the scene: "Participants paused in the midst of three days of strenuous attacks on the idea of authorship and the notion of copyright to pepper [him] with a stream of questions concerned, in large measure, with how they might secure fuller protection for their work under current copyright law."[1]

This gut-level acceptance of the tradition of property rights has helped make the people of the United States free and rich, and it holds great promise of letting them continue and improve this happy state. The basic reason is simple: the arguments that constitute the tradition are right. Or to phrase this point more modestly, they have never been refuted, and no alternative system has ever produced comparable results. We reject them only at great peril.

Nonetheless, over the past thirty years this tradition has come under increasing assault from governments at the national, state, and local levels. Of course, not everything sometimes branded an assault on property rights should qualify for the label. Property issues have always been complex. Problems of public use, transportation and network value, commons, externalities, and technologies have produced a huge body of law and practice. In 1988, a noted scholar finished a new edition of his treatise on land law. It takes up eight fat volumes. In preparing it, the author read every one of the more than ten thousand property cases published in the legal reports up to that date. Afterwards, under the impact of environmentalism, the number of reported cases exploded beyond the absorbent capacity of any single brain, and he read only the most important ones.[2] And this covered only property in the form of land. Adding other categories would explode the numbers even further. The fine points of intellectual property, an issue now moving to the forefront of the consciousness of the nation's professional and business classes, show promise of exhibiting the same intricacy.

The losers in these contests want to cast the issue as a fundamental dispute over property rights rather than as the latest in the interminable history of quarrels among landowners. If local law says that you cannot fill in a wetland in a way that floods your neighbor's land, you can yell "property rights." Who knows? Maybe someone will let you fill it in without paying to install drainage, and land that you bought for a song because it was a swamp will increase in value. Suppose I live in the backcountry and set up a rifle range in my backyard. The neighborhood fills up, and new residents object to lead flying around their houses. I claim: "You are stopping a previously legal activity! A taking! Fifth Amendment!" Maybe a judge will agree and let me keep shooting, and thus let me appropriate a portion of my neighbors' property. Not all claims that basic property rights are being diluted should be taken at face value.

Now add a caveat from the opposite point of view. Fundamental assaults on property rights are often garbed as conventional quarrels. Anyone trying to grab some of a neighbor's property rights will mask the intent by casting the issue in terms of spillovers or saving the commons. If you do not like your neighbor's taste in architects, you call his house design a "nuisance," or "aesthetic pollution," or "an appropriation of the visual commons." You do not say, "I want to look at a house of a certain shape, and I want you to pay for it." If you want to turn someone else's land into a birdwatching sanctuary, you talk of "her duty as a citizen and a landowner not to eradicate a species," not about any duty of yours to help pay to provide the habitat.

The effects of these caveats make claims difficult and often tedious to sift through. A further complication is that most of the programs involved in the attack on property rights have more than one dimension. To a degree, and often to a large degree, they are valid mechanisms for dealing with one of the basic complexities. Only when pushed too far or abused do they cross the line and become part of the assault on property rights. Zoning, for example, can be a game in which everybody wins. It can also turn into a competition as to who can steal from whom. Historic preservation can represent a laudable cooperative effort to preserve history and protect property, or it can be blatant expropriation.

A major component of the contemporary assault on property rights, and a major cause of the current political controversy, lies in the double-edged nature of these programs. Too many legislators, bureaucrats, and judges approach decisions not in the spirit of "How do we deal with the complexities so as to make this Lockean system work?" but with the question, "How can we get the use of this property without paying for it?" They are encouraged by private interests with something to gain from the government action. For example, later in this book you will meet cattle ranchers who think the government should reserve federal range land for grazing, excluding any other use, and their foes, environmentalists who want the government to prohibit grazing. Neither side thinks in terms of the Lockean tradition, which would be, "How do we administer this resource so as to create property rights, and then let the genius of our civilization and our people work itself out?"

This sort of private behavior—called "rent seeking" in the literature of political science—is more addictive than drugs. As the government responds, private actors pour more money and effort into seeking government favors and less into productive activity. The government responds to these efforts with more actions transferring property, and so on in an accelerating downward spiral. To escape this vortex of destruction requires clear limits on the role of government, a clear demarcation of forbidden territory. This demarcation is made by the concept called political legitimacy, and it is the last great building block of the Lockean tradition that must be put in place before turning to specific controversies.

Given that the government has a strong role to play in an economic and political system based on private property, what defines this role, and what marks out its limits? What gives a particular form of government and a particular group of governors the right to make decisions? When do even the losers in specific controversies accept decisions about property as reasonable, and when do they feel ill used, possibly even rebellious?

ENGLAND, 1154, AND MASSACHUSETTS, 1957

Samuel Beer, professor of Government at Harvard University, is cramming some subtleties of political analysis into his class. The historical context he selects is England in 1154, when Henry II becomes king. This is far from twentieth-century America, but Beer is a maestro of the lecture hall with a point to make about the concept of political legitimacy. He wants to demonstrate the general applicability of his analysis, so he starts with a civilization nearly as remote from his listeners as an alien planet in a science-fiction novel.

When Henry Plantagenet arrives from his French home, England has been riven by twenty years of anarchic conflict between rival claimants to the throne. Order has broken down, barons are conducting private wars against each other, and the royal writ runs nowhere, even if anyone knew whose writ was royal. Henry, whose right to be king is good, but not perfect, under the rules of feudal inheritance, takes over. Within a year the baronial wars stop, unlicensed castles are pulled down, the royal writ runs everywhere, and the nation is at what passes for peace in the twelfth century.

Beer's question is: Why? Henry will prove a forceful king, but in 1154 he is twenty years old, untried, and unknown in England. He is dealing with a fractious nobility that has disobeyed everyone for twenty years and that can, if it wishes, drive him out and maintain its independence. Given all the forces for chaos, why does the country come to order?

Beer uses this question to explore the basis of Henry's authority. It does not rest mainly on force. Certainly Henry can hire force for money, but so can the others. Most of his force exists because barons rally to him. His real power base is that to everyone from baron to churl he has legitimacy—the right to rule. His claim is good enough so that to a baron deciding which way to go, Henry is *the king,* and to go against him is to go against a deeply felt sense of duty and propriety. Even a particular baron who weighs this duty lightly, as many do, or discounts the validity of Henry's claim to the crown knows that others take it seriously. A sober calculation of personal advantage tells him that others will obey the king, which means that rebellion would be lonely, and maybe fatal. Henry's real power is that everyone thinks he is the legitimate ruler and thinks further that everyone else thinks so, too, and that he has the right to bring the country to order.

This concern with the legitimacy of the exercise of power echoes through the centuries. It permeates analysis of the English Revolutions of 1642 and 1688, the French Revolution of 1789, the American Civil War, the Russian Revolutions of 1917 and 1989, and the fall of the Berlin Wall. Beer's injunction is that in any situation of political turmoil, whether a society is coming together or falling apart, you must look at the nature and sources of legitimacy. Who do people believe possesses the right to exercise what powers, why do they believe it, and what do they think everybody else believes about these questions? How is legitimacy gained, and how is it lost? The concept is as important to twenty-first-century America as it was to twelfth-century England, and it is crucial to understanding the current controversy over property rights.

What are the sources of legitimacy in the United States today? This is not a legal question but a political and social one, so this chapter focuses first on the sources of legitimacy in the popular mind. Many of our current woes over property are due to the belief of lawyers that legitimacy *is* a purely legal issue. They are baffled and indignant when the citizenry does not accept their conclusions.

The starting point is easy. United States political theory and practice stems from England, so we start with Henry and his fellow royalty. Thereafter, the history of Anglo-American government is a story of the slow development of limits on sovereign power and the rise of the legislative assembly as the legitimate repository of power. Fast-forward through the six hundred years between 1154 and 1787 (pausing briefly for John Locke in the 1680s), and we find the fundamental conclusions on the nature of legitimacy embodied in the Constitution. For the United States, this is the anchor of any analysis.

The broad Constitution of the popular imagination includes the whole set of ideas surrounding the Revolution, including, most explicitly, the Declaration of Independence in 1776. Both the Constitution and the Declaration contain the Lockean concept that the sovereignty being exercised belongs to the people as a whole, which delegates it to a government formed under the Constitution and subject to its limits. This is the most fundamental of American political concepts and the touchstone for popular views of legitimacy. In twelfth-century England, the legitimacy of a particular government was based on the concept that this king was anointed by God. In our time and place, it lies in the concept that people have delegated their sovereignty to this government.

This idea is stated more strongly in the Declaration than in the Constitution itself. The Declaration was an act of rebellion. It focused on the fundamental nature of legitimacy because it needed to explain why the king had lost it. The answer is from Locke. Because any particular government is the creature and servant of the people, when it becomes destructive of the inalienable rights of life, liberty, and the pursuit of happiness, the people have a right to alter it. George III is accused of a long list of grievances, as a result of which "these United Colonies are and of right ought to be Free and Independent States." King George is guilty of ignoring the needs of his sovereign, the people, and is therefore removed from office. It is a neat switch on a system in which the king, as sovereign, removes ministers who displease him.

The Constitution is more businesslike, omitting the rhetoric. By 1787 the revolution is over, the Articles of Confederation are in need of major repairs, and it is time to get on with the business of creating a government, not jettisoning one. Rhetoric is not required. But the Constitution still makes clear where the ultimate sovereignty lies by its opening words that it is the creation of "We, the people of the United States," not of any king, legislature, or group of delegates.

Leaving aside what lawyers or justices say about the terms and conditions on which the Constitution delegates this sovereignty to the government, what do people *think* is in there? If you convened a focus group of representative citizens to describe the Constitution, what would they come up with? I suggest that a few minutes of introspection will produce a pretty good list of the factors that most people would regard as defining the legitimacy of the way the government deals with private property or with anything else. People often say that the Constitution of the United States is written while the constitution of England is unwritten, but in fact the United States also has an unwritten constitution, and it is extremely important.

A bedrock principle of legitimacy is that the government is not entitled to do anything at all unless its officials were chosen by the means prescribed in the Constitution, through free and open elections. Power in the United States can come only from the choice of the people, and democratic processes are crucial to the American sense of legitimacy. Laws must be passed in proper form by bodies duly authorized to enact them. Furthermore, these bodies must not be corrupt or overly self-interested, within reason. The citizenry must have a rough confidence that the lawmakers are acting for the weal of the public, not for the benefit of themselves or of their own in-group.

If this sense of disinterest is lacking, then the areas with which the governors can deal become circumscribed. If the government must do something, then people do not seem to mind when politics, or even graft, determines who gets the side benefits of the activity. If military bases must be built, they might as well be put in the districts of the chairs of the congressional committees on the armed services. If somebody must repave the city streets, the contract can go to friends of the mayor, as long as they do the job. When the causation is reversed, things get troublesome. That is, if the streets are repaved unnecessarily so that a particular contractor can get the business, or if an unneeded aircraft carrier is built so that the chairman's district gets the work, then a line of legitimacy is crossed. To take it a step further, the capture of government by special interests that then use its power to interfere with other people's property and livelihood goes beyond the bounds of acceptance.

Concerns about limits and controls become more important as authority is delegated down the chain of government. Legislators have freedom to delve into whatever needs to be addressed. Executive branch officials are expected to use their powers only to further the legitimate functions of their offices. People get nervous when officials begin using their formal powers to make this a better world in ways unrelated to their jobs. A few years ago, some fire marshals began aggressively using their power to control smoking in public places—to ban it even when no fire risk existed. These rules were clearly within their formal powers. Equally clearly, the agenda was not fire prevention but health. This bothers people. A court of appeals once commented caustically that the Federal Communications Commission's power was limited to things that would promote broadcasting. It did not have roving authority to issue a rule just because it was "a Good Idea [that] would lead to a Better World."[3] Having legions of officials acting as knights errant to slay anything that looks like a dragon to them is a prescription for chaos.

Officials are also supposed to be boxed in by the specific limits imposed on them by the Constitution and by law. Most people are not legal scholars, and their concept of these limits is fairly rough and ready, based mostly on ideas of "fairness" inculcated from childhood. Keeping the focus on property, most people probably think the government has substantial power to protect and promote the value and utility of their property. Insofar as this involves land, the national love affair with public and private zoning is strong. So is support for efforts to deal with the five great complexities of a regime of private property: spillovers, commons, transportation, public facilities, and technology. Insofar as this involves other types of assets, the growing nerd classes expect the government to promote intellectual property by rationalizing the rules and defending it against all piracy, foreign and domestic. Protection of intellectual property has become a source of considerable friction between the United States and China.

Popular views of legitimacy also place limits on these powers. We do not think the government can seize property summarily; the prohibition against taking is deeply ingrained. For lesser actions, those that fall short of a total taking, we do not think the government has a right to keep us from doing something on our property that does not bother anyone else. Nor do we think it right for the government to impose a servitude on us for the benefit of our neighbors, unless the principle on which this is done is ancient and well known, which means more or less within the familiar bounds of the pentagon of spillovers, commons, transportation, public facilities, and adaptation to technology. For example, we would not think it right for a government to announce a new rule that an owner cannot build anything if a neighbor objects. We also assume that there should be a direct relationship between the burdens that government imposes and the public ends that are being served.

We assume that change should be evolutionary, not sudden, and that settled rules should not be reversed. On many, many issues, you can argue cogently for rule A or for rule B. In the end, it does not matter much as long as society picks one so people can make their decisions and calculate their actions and investments. For instance, storm water runs off my land and floods yours. Do I have to control it or do you? Which rule is adopted might not matter in the long run. If I must control, the value of my land is reduced by the price of digging a ditch. If you must control, the cost comes out of your hide. If the state has a rule on the issue going back a century, the cost of the ditch has been factored into the decision of every person who ever owned either of the properties. If the state suddenly changes the rule, it is changing the values of both our properties, transferring money from one of us to the other.

No, we expect our lawmakers to trust our civilization and its history. Most new rules should be limited to filling in the gaps and gray areas, to handling the tough fact situations that arise because of the infinite variations in human affairs. Major changes should be made only in response to genuine crises or genuinely new problems raised by technological change. Even these should draw heavily on our collective experience. Furthermore, when rules are changed, retroactivity is disfavored. If you made a decision based on a particular law, then you should know that this law will continue to apply to your situation even if the rule is changed for future transactions.

The principle that burdens should not be imposed on one person when they should be borne by all is also deeply felt. So is the more general idea of equal treatment. Rules that single out one or a few people are not regarded as fair unless there is a good reason for the difference.

When the laws are applied, the great ideal of due process becomes crucial. You have a right to be heard by an honest and impartial arbiter, to introduce evidence, and to try to rebut the evidence against you. You have a right to a speedy resolution of your case. The government should also aim at producing speedy justice in an efficient manner. It should not try to wear you down with procedural minutiae and lawyers' fees so that it can impose its will on you regardless of right or law.

Another component of legitimacy is important, though not codified in any statute and never mentioned in the legal literature: competence. We do not regard the exercise of power as legitimate unless its wielders know what they are doing. We do not expect rules to be based on false data or junk theories. The legislature that micromanages in areas about which it is ignorant eventually loses the respect of the people. We expect a city building department to understand buildings, and to be able to process applications expeditiously, on pain of becoming a butt of humor. This area is tricky, because habit carries things a long way. For years, people can believe that a government or a part of it is not very competent, but they still regard it as having a legitimate right to enact laws that must be obeyed, even if these laws are silly. Eventually this feeling erodes, and the commands cease to have moral force simply because the commanders, whatever their formal authority, are incompetent. This phenomenon is accelerated when the legislative or administrative process gets frozen so that errors become uncorrectable. Everyone knows that mistakes get made, and an important part of legitimacy is an ability to respond to feedback. The lack of this capacity is more seriously undermining than the original error.

A part of this need for competence is to expect governmental power to be exercised at the appropriate level. We do not expect Washington to worry about trash collection or the city council to dabble in foreign affairs. The old saw, "Well, let's not make a federal case of it," expresses well the concept that we do not expect the national government to be concerned with local matters. When governments get out of their proper roles, the usual reaction is puzzlement: "What do *they* know about *that?*"

This list of popular expectations is our unwritten constitution. It seems pretty reasonable. If anyone wants to take any item on it and stand up for the proposition that the citizens of a rich, literate, and long-established democracy should *not* expect this from their government, I will be interested in hearing the argument. It all sounds like a Fourth of July speech, right after the part about motherhood and apple pie. *Of course* this is what the Constitution says.

There is a problem, however. This catalog of characteristics that define political legitimacy was not drawn out of thin air or pure introspection. It is basically a list of the complaints made by people who believe their rights to property are being trampled. They think the government is acting illegitimately. These people are saying something very serious, and they deserve serious attention.

WASHINGTON, D.C., 1995

The scene is a forum on enforcement of environmental laws. The participants are a mixture of members of Congress, foundation types, and business executives. Congressman Nathan Deal (Georgia—once D, now R) speaks: "The only thing that keeps [a democracy] together is the confidence of the American people in the elected system of government. . . . All [the horror stories] are cumulatively . . . undermining the confidence of the American people in their system of government. . . . If we in the name of the government allow injustice to be perpetrated on the American public and those who we must depend on to sustain that government and do nothing about it, then I think it comes to the point that it will ultimately undermine that confidence that holds us all together."[4]

An important reason that people not immediately involved in these property issues tend to assume that the complaints about illegitimacy must be invalid is that they share the popular conception of what is in the Constitution. They too regard the catalog as motherhood and apple pie. *Of course* the Constitution contains these protections. Therefore, the government cannot be ignoring these rights and expectations; if it were, the courts would stop it.

It is not so, at least at the federal level. The legal view of legitimate governmental power is much more expansive than the popular view. It is startling and sobering, and ominous, to realize the degree to which judicial inquiry into the legitimacy of government action has come unmoored from popular conceptions, to realize the extent of the gulf between our written and unwritten constitutions. Some state courts are more protective, but at the federal level the gulf is a chasm. This matters. The most crucial programs are federal, and thus beyond the reach of state courts.

The law, like popular opinion, starts with the Constitution, but this is a rather different document from the unwritten constitution of popular image. It does not include the Declaration, which is incorporated only on the rare occasions when judges give it heed in the course of interpreting the words of the Constitution. As a result, the Constitution is missing the ringing reminders that ultimate sovereignty is in the people. These are present only in the Ninth and Tenth Amendments, which are interpreted by the courts as meaningless verbiage, having almost no practical effect.[5] (The Ninth says: "The enumeration in the Constitution, of certain rights, shall not be construed to deny or disparage others retained by the people." The Tenth: "The powers not delegated to the United States by the Constitution, nor prohibited by it to the States, are reserved to the States respectively, or to the people.")

Future justice Oliver Wendell Holmes, in the most famous quotation in American legal history, wrote, "The life of the law has not been logic: it has been experience. The felt necessities of the time, the prevalent moral and political theories, intuitions of public policy, avowed or unconscious, even the prejudices which judges share with their fellowmen, have had a good deal more to do than the syllogism in determining the rules by which men should be governed."[6] Periodically the Constitution gets reinterpreted in major ways because an old view no longer reflects a national consensus on the "felt necessities of the time." In the course of a series of these reinterpretations, most notably during the crisis of the Great Depression, the Constitution of the legal profession lost its protections for property.

At the same time that the courts were expanding the boundaries of Congress's authority, they were withdrawing from the business of inquiring into the rationality of laws governing property passed by either state or federal legislatures. All that is needed is a "rational basis," which means that a law stands as long as its defenders can invent a hypothesis under which the law is not totally crazy. This is not a stringent requirement.

It is also difficult to find any check on the power of individual agencies. Congress can delegate its legislative authority to agencies, which then make rules necessary to carry out the statutes. The agency must not act beyond the bounds of the law, but Congress is often vague and incomplete, and the agency's lawmaking power is considerable. Further, it is the agency itself, not a court, that decides just how far its power goes under any law. As long as its interpretation of the statute is "permissible," which means as long as it does not clearly contradict the terms of the statute, the agency view stands. Most statutes these days are drafted so badly and ambiguously that it is impossible to find any interpretation that can be called contradictory. Once upon a time there was a constitutional doctrine that forbade overvagueness, but the Supreme Court got rid of that one too.

People in general do not know that agencies have this immense lawmaking power and are not happy when they find out. They are even less happy when they learn that this power is little controlled by courts. They are under the illusion that courts are the arbiters of the meaning of regulatory statutes, a proposition that is true only at the extreme.

This doctrine is a prescription for abuse. Many federal agencies have a single mission, such as protecting wetlands or endangered species. They are not charged with concern over the costs of this mission or with finding the point at which the benefits of a particular rule are no longer justified by the costs. As a result, they interpret their charters as broadly as possible. Many of the problems caused by endangered species and wetlands protection have arisen precisely because of aggressive interpretations of statutes by agencies determined to extend the reach of their programs. A newspaper piece on the late Mollie Beattie, the head of the U.S. Fish and Wildlife Service, said that she viewed the Endangered Species Act "less as an act of civil legislation than divine ordination."[7] The comment was meant as a tribute. In fact, it is a quite damning thing to say about a high government official charged with implementing a civil statute having tremendous impact on millions of people, including Bruce Whiting and his former employees at the Fredonia sawmill. Her oath of office was to the Constitution and the laws, not to any personal interpretation of divine ordination.

In the programs discussed in the balance of this book, one thing that stands out is how often the principles of legitimacy are violated. Property is conscripted for public use as a wildlife refuge or environmental buffer. Federal legislatures are exercising power over matters of local concern, without competence or knowledge of local conditions. Property owners are subjected to incredible procedural shuffles. Burdens are put on one person or a few that should properly be borne by all. Officials are using authority to promote one set of purposes as a roving commission to foster others. Retroactivity has become a standard practice, as new obligations are imposed or old rules changed. Mistakes are never corrected. Appeals and objections are decided by the same agency and even the same people who made the original decision. And so on, right down the list. Practically every popular concept of legitimate government is getting a thorough roughing up.

By this point in the narrative, any lawyers who are reading will be hopping up and down wanting to tell me that I am blurring an important distinction. In legal theory, to say that something is constitutional does not mean that it is wise or good. Legislators have broad powers to do silly things. Pursuing this line, to say that a government action is constitutional does not necessarily mean it is legitimate; it means only that a court will not invalidate it. If the people regard it as illegitimate, their remedy is the ballot box.

As a legal matter, this approach is correct. It was reiterated recently by Justice Clarence Thomas when he said, "This case is ultimately a reminder that the Federal Constitution does not prohibit everything that is intensely undesirable."[8] But it misses an important part of the problem. Voting is a very blunt instrument for preventing abuses of power that affect only limited numbers of people. Granted, courts are not always good instruments. But this means that it is incumbent on a government that wishes to maintain its legitimacy to set up better instruments of control over itself. If I think the government has illegitimately taken my property and given it to two other citizens, just how can my right be vindicated at the ballot box? They outvote me. The courts do not consider such a remedy adequate in dealing with such areas as freedom of speech or freedom of religion. Why is it adequate for property, where the immediate incentives for citizens to abuse their fellows may be even stronger? Part of the current crisis of legitimacy is the courts' solemn insistence that citizens must rely on a remedy that is palpably inadequate. In the long run, of course, if enough citizens are offended, then the critical mass necessary to become a political movement is achieved, and redress at the ballot box becomes feasible. But this can take a long time, and the price of creating a society in which change can occur only through political convulsion is high.

To sum up, in the area of protection of property, a chasm has developed between the unwritten constitution of popular credence and the formal Constitution of the Supreme Court and the legal system. Most people are surprised when they learn how little the Constitution protects their property. Federal judge Douglas Ginsburg wryly refers to the various provisions that once served this purpose as "the Constitution-in-exile," which were "banished for standing in opposition to unlimited government." Their memory "is kept alive by a few scholars who labor on in the hope of a restoration."[9] This Constitution-in-exile also exists in the population at large, judging by the refrain of shock and disbelief that runs through the reactions of people confronted with the reality of the breadth and depth of governmental power. The shock is intensified when the power is exercised by agencies or their individual minions rather than by legislatures.

The result of these forces is that the people's assumptions about the limits of legitimate government action and the actual limits enforced by the legal system are significantly different. Political institutions may fill the gap eventually, but in the meantime much harm can be done. This harm is being exacerbated by the tendency of government officials to equate legitimacy with constitutionality. They are pushing their power to the constitutional limits, assuming anything legal is legitimate. This is putting them seriously at odds with the unwritten constitution.

For all of this, the people who feel aggrieved find no effective remedy. The federal courts have withdrawn from protection of property, except for occasional unpredictable interventions in some of the most egregious situations. In response, the aggrieved have coalesced into a political movement. This may ultimately prove effective, but it consumes a lot of time and energy in the process, and many people must suffer to provide the vivid examples necessary to move the process. Political movements also tend toward overkill, and the results are likely to be dicey indeed.

PART II

MARCHING AS TO WAR

Environmentalism as Religion and Property as Heresy

Chapter 6

Endangered Species

How to create a monster that causes peasants carrying torches and pitchforks to storm your castle

T he Endangered Species Act (ESA) is one of two federal programs particularly responsible for stoking outrage over violations of people's right to property. The other is federal control of wetlands. Without these, many problems would arise under many state and federal laws, but wetlands and ESA are heating the boiler to the bursting point. Federal agencies are rigging safety valves, but the solutions are more sound bite than substance. In any event, the problems are too fundamental for palliatives. The conflict will grow hotter.

Endangered species and wetlands protection have a lot in common. Each program responds to a problem serious enough to justify concern and action. In each case, the response is to conscript private property to national environmental causes with no compensation. In each, some of the most troublesome aspects were not enacted by Congress; they were added later by agencies and courts through aggressive interpretation of ambiguous statutory language. Congress has since squirmed and evaded, claiming credit or denying responsibility according to the immediate political winds. Both programs are run by federal agencies on a mission, with no sympathy for any values, such as economic efficiency or individual economic pain, in conflict with their goals. Neither program exhibits any sense of trade-offs or limits; each claims absolute priority for its purposes over all other possible uses of the land. The agencies give as little ground as possible, and only under intense political pressure. Each program grows steadily more intrusive, and each resists reform.

ESA is based on a combination of science crossed with religious fervor. The people whose property gets swallowed by the program do not believe much of the science and do not subscribe to the religion. Wetlands has the same characteristics, though perhaps not painted in colors quite so bold. Proponents of both programs also use them as levers to promote ends far beyond their formal purposes. These proponents are not just pro-species or pro-wetlands. They are anti-industrial society and its accoutrements, and the programs are handy tools in the service of this obsession. Both also rely on the stick of commands, prohibitions, and punishments rather than the carrot of incentives and rewards, and both have made enemies out of the people whose cooperation is most needed. Criminal penalties can be imposed even on landowners who have no reason to think they are violating the law. Although this power is rarely pushed to this extreme, its existence makes those who inadvertently offend very tractable in negotiations. Each program raises in stark form fundamental issues of government legitimacy, and every government institution—agencies, Congress, courts—involved with either is undermining its own legitimacy in the eyes of the public.

A final family resemblance is important: both programs are administered through rules of numbing complexity, and the complexity is in each case a source of legal and political power for the agency running the programs, its allies, and its constituents. This contention may seem dubious. Because the point is counterintuitive and because it is very important and will come up again, it is worth pausing over.

The principle involved, called rational ignorance, is one of the fundamental axioms of modern political analysis. Rational ignorance is a simple idea. My resources of time and concentration are limited, so I ignore many topics, including some of great importance. Foreign policy receives little of my attention. My decision to remain ignorant in this area is highly rational, even though U.S. successes or debacles overseas can greatly affect my life. I do not influence foreign policy. It would make little sense to spend time and energy on an area remote from my livelihood and not subject to my influence that I do not find entertaining, even though it is important.

Pundits often bemoan the ignorance of the public about some issue or other and tout the need for a well-informed public. This is mostly wrong. "Being well informed" is not an achievable state. There are too many different areas, and trying to master them all is impossible. Most people are too sensible to try to be well informed on things outside their ambit of immediate concern and influence. They are aware of the main lines of argument but not of the details.

If policy for my children's school is made at a local PTA meeting or by a local school principal I can visit, then it is rational for me to invest time and energy to understand and influence it. If the governing body is a city-wide school board, it is worth some effort, but not as much. If the policy is made by the federal Department of Education, it is worth none of my time because no matter how knowledgeable I become, my chances of influence are small. To have an impact would require me to devote serious time and energy to organizing a political movement of like-minded people. Short of this, my best strategy is to accept school policy as a black box beyond my control, and keep my children in the school if I like its policies or find a private school if I do not.

Rational ignorance poses a major dilemma for democratic government. The larger the number of areas in which the government is active, and the more removed these are from the individual citizen's ability to affect them, the lower will be the overall level of public knowledge. As the number of policy areas escalated to a federal level increases, the general level of rational ignorance among the citizenry about any one of them increases—a paradox perhaps, but the logic is ironclad.

On the other hand, special interests, including the beneficiaries and government operators of programs, find it rational to remain well informed, and this is how they spend their daily working lives. They influence the system through campaign contributions, direct contact with legislators and regulators, and the ability to mobilize ignorant constituents. It is worth considerable effort on their part to master the system.

These groups also find advantage in promoting rational ignorance on the part of the public because the more it costs other people to become informed, the greater is their own influence. Complexity in a program raises the costs of becoming informed, and the public, which is probably not as cynical as it should be, becomes subject to the argument that the ends of the program are good, the whole thing is too complicated to explain to laypeople, and people just need to trust the program's operators. Politics becomes more and more the product of general impressions, sound bites, symbolism, and manipulation. In 1995, an assistant secretary of the interior happily told Congress that polls show citizen support for the Endangered Species Act by a margin of two to one, and 71 percent agree the law is effective.[1] There is not the remotest possibility the average citizen understands the real workings of this law well enough to have a legitimate opinion on these questions. But the margin of support, which is based on sound bites, is an important political fact.

NEW YORK, 1996

The front page of the *New York Times* reports on something the environmentalists call "greenscamming"—picking a name that makes a corporate lobby sound like a tree hugger. The latest is Northwesterners for More Fish, a coalition of utilities and other companies under attack for depleting the salmon population of the Pacific Northwest. A staffer of an environmental association calls the new federation "an ersatz organization" and "a Styrofoam dummy." Environmentalists give the *Times* a planning memorandum heisted from the new group. It says: "While the public can and should be swayed by having the facts on the issue, the message must also appeal at a gut, emotional level. Too often, those who advocate a more rational approach to such issues fail because they compete against a well-orchestrated public relations campaign that tugs at the heart strings."

A few days after the *Times* story the environmentalists report with glee that the picture chosen as a logo by the Northwesterners for More Fish is not really a salmon at all. It is a squawfish, a bottom feeder that eats young salmon.[2]

The environmentalists' assessment is correct: these groups are taking advantage of the public's fuzzily favorable attitude toward environmental protection and are relying on the principle of rational ignorance. They assume people will not make the effort to dig beneath the name. On the other hand, the coalition's planning memo is also dead right. Environmentalist groups like to surf the waves of the polls showing that two-thirds of Americans regard themselves as "environmentalists." They too cultivate rational ignorance, encouraging people to ignore the deep problems involved in reconciling environmental values with the needs of an industrial society and its people. The groups also circulate outrageous scare stories—apples and Alar, asbestos in schools, radon in homes, for example—and minimize the extent to which environmentalism serves the self-interest of their own contributors and staff members, in league with a growing industrial sector of cleanup contractors. Environmentalism itself is now a big business, involving money, power, access to resources, and interesting travel. Its practitioners are often greenscammers of another kind.

Rational ignorance is crucial to the endangered species and wetlands programs. The basic goal of increased protection of the environment deserves the high level of public support indicated by the polls. The United States is a wealthy nation, and it makes sense to divert increasing resources to environmental amenities. Personally I would rather have cleaner air and water and more nearby parkland than a more expensive car or any number of other personal goods. I enjoy visiting Civil War battlefields and using the bicycle trails built on abandoned railroad rights-of-way. Old buildings and historic districts are interesting, and I like them preserved. Yellowstone and Yosemite National Parks are national jewels. If a pollster asked me if I were an environmentalist, I would be among the two-thirds answering yes. I doubt many members of the Sierra Club would agree with my self-characterization. The difference between me and most of the environmental groups is that I think industrial society is a wonderful thing and want to foster its development and spread its benefits. Within this context, I want a large dose of environment protection, but I am not willing to give the environmental status quo absolute priority over human activities or to pursue the will-o'-the-wisp of eliminating all risk of all harm. Nor do I regard any change in any ecosystem as a matter for grief. I also know that the best road to increasing the level of protection of the environment is through better definition and enforcement of property rights. To many of the environmental groups, this set of values makes me an enemy.

I suspect most people responding to the polls are in my camp, and their favorable answers reflect this general goal of environmental protection within the framework of a growing industrial society. They assume environmental programs are administered in this spirit. However, general goals can be popular and desirable while the programs that purport to attain them are highly imperfect. If the imperfections can be hidden behind a veil of complexity, then rational ignorance on the part

of the public will translate into political strength for the program operators and clientele. This is the state of the endangered species program.
(Wetlands, too.) The public supports the stated goals but does not
make the investment necessary to understand the details of the implementation.

Naturally, those hurt by the programs no longer regard ignorance as
rational. They investigate and learn the details, especially the imperfections, of the program. Thereafter, they become frustrated and outraged when a program doing them great harm cannot be reformed
because of an alliance between government officials and direct beneficiaries, supported by a rationally ignorant public dependent on sound
bites.

The problem of governance in a democratic society is not to find
ways to eliminate rational ignorance—this cannot be done—but to devise ways to make democratic government work despite rational ignorance. A very bad form of government is to settle every issue by a
plebiscite in which those with a stake in the matter and those without,
those who are informed and those who are ignorant, each have an
equal voice. Property rights is one of the devices for avoiding such
plebiscites, thus making democracy possible. By creating rights, we give
people an incentive to become rationally informed about matters impinging on them. We also give them a defense against outsiders who are
rationally ignorant. When you cut down rights in property, as when you
cut down the laws in *A Man for All Seasons*, the winds that then do blow
are in large part the winds of rational ignorance.

With this as background, we can now plunge into the thickets of the
Endangered Species Act, explaining why it arouses intense opposition
even from many people who are sympathetic to its basic purposes. You
already heard Bruce Whiting closing down the Fredonia sawmill. That
is not an isolated incident.

PENDER COUNTY, NORTH CAROLINA, 1930–1996

In the 1930s, Ben Cone's father buys 8,000 acres of cut-over timberland
as a place to hunt and fish. He names it Cone's Folly, in response to
friends who call him a fool for buying such worthless land, and makes it
a pine forest. The land is managed primarily for game, such as turkey,
quail, deer, and bear. Timber is cut and sold every six or seven years,

usually through selective thinning. Timbering is limited to the amount necessary to show a profit on the land and maintain tax advantages. The forest is also thinned by fire, essential for good ecological management of pine. As a direct result of the management practices, the red-cockaded woodpecker finds Cone's Folly an agreeable place.

Ben Cone inherits the property in 1982. In 1991, he plans a timber sale. His consulting forester says there are signs of woodpeckers, which are now listed as endangered. Cone must pay for more surveys. These find twenty-nine woodpeckers in twelve colonies. The Fish and Wildlife Service of the Department of the Interior, which administers the act, says this means that 1,121 acres must be exempted from any future timber cutting. The immediate loss of value to Cone is $1.4 million. Furthermore, the rest of his land is now in danger. If the woodpeckers expand their range, he will lose that as well. This is a real risk, especially because he is now forbidden to manage the 1,121 acres of woodpecker habitat properly. The tract will become steadily less attractive to the birds, so they may move to the better-managed part of the property. Cone tells FWS that he has no choice except to begin clear-cutting his remaining land. Since the story of Cone's Folly is receiving lots of media attention, this, like the Domenigoni rat incident, will make FWS look pretty stupid. Cone also files a lawsuit that raises the stakes by putting the whole habitat protection program on the table.

Faced with these threats, FWS reaches an agreement with Cone. The essence is that he pays $45,000 in ransom in the form of creation of habitat, and in exchange he regains control of his land.[3]

SANGRE DE CRISTO MOUNTAINS, NEW MEXICO, 1995

Since 1750, villagers in thirty-eight poor Hispanic hamlets in the Sangre de Cristo mountains have collected firewood for cooking and heating from an area that is now national forest. In August 1995, a court enjoins the practice because the Mexican spotted owl, which is on the endangered species list, feeds on the rodents that live in the dead or downed wood.

The Forest Service has spent eight years and $1.5 million in research without finding any owls within one hundred miles. The environmentalists who brought the lawsuit argue that the protection is still necessary because owls might migrate into the area.[4]

AUSTIN, TEXAS, 1973–1994

Thinking ahead to retirement, in 1973 Margaret Rector buys 15 acres of land on a busy highway west of Austin. In 1990 the golden-cheeked warbler is listed as endangered, and FWS says her property is suitable habitat. The land, in the fastest-growing part of the county, is now unusable. Its assessed value falls from $831,000 in 1991 to $30,000 in 1992. FWS says she might be able to get a permit to develop, but this would require her to finance extensive studies and to mitigate any impact on the warbler. She regards this as a tool that is available only to large corporations engaging in multimillion-dollar developments.[5]

NORTH COAST OF CALIFORNIA, 1995

This is timber country. Mary Fattig, a former Outreach consultant for schools, makes a statement to a committee of the U.S. House of Representatives. She is joined by the director of social services of Humboldt County and the superintendent of schools of Trinity County.

The problem is the northern spotted owl, which is listed as threatened. U.S. Forest Service timber sales are at zero, though some private timber is still being cut. The picture is one of growing economic depression. From 1987 to 1993, timber cuts have declined by 41 percent. In 1987 the two counties had seven working sawmills and plywood mills. Now there are none. About 2,000 direct jobs have been lost, and every one of these costs another 1.5 jobs. Trinity County's unemployment rate is 19 percent, Humboldt's is 9 percent. The high school dropout rate is about 50 percent. In one school, 100 percent of the children are on the free lunch program, and rates in others are 68 to 84 percent. Government receipts are plunging. Private timber interests pay 30 percent of all property taxes, and if they cannot harvest, then the value of their holdings drops, and so must taxes. The federal government does not pay taxes, but it pays the county a share of timber receipts in lieu thereof. These payments are also plunging. Reports of child abuse and neglect are up 67 percent in two years.[6]

These situations, and many others, are consequences of the Endangered Species Act of 1973.

During the 1960s, as concern about the possible extinction of species grew, a Department of the Interior report said eighty-three species of domestic fish and wildlife might be endangered, so the task of protection did not appear overwhelming,[7] and Congress took some tentative steps in that direction. By 1973, just the right balance of forces existed. The issue of endangered species had become large enough to provide political energy to get something passed but not so large as to cause a lot of people in the Congress or the White House to look closely at what they were passing. No organized opposition existed to force a close scrutiny. At the same time, the occupants of crucial staff positions knew exactly what they were doing and stuck in some time bombs. These might or might not have amounted to anything, but the pro-species forces were riding the wave, and the resources of power they inserted could be exploited later when their forces were stronger. Over the next decade, the law was amended several times, always in the direction of more protection for species, but 1973 was the watershed year when the basic structure was put in place.

The 1973 law passed without a single negative vote in the Senate and with only four in the House. Unanimity in major legislation is a virtually infallible sign Congress does not know what it is doing. Charles Mann and Mark Plummer, in a fine book on endangered species issues, *Noah's Choice*, comment that the director of Fish and Wildlife, who did know what was involved, approached implementation "with caution that verged on terror." He knew, for example, that most protected species are insects, plants, and fungi. This fact, he also knew, "would come as a surprise to Capitol Hill," which was "thinking of huge grizzly bears and bald eagles and stately monarchs of the air," not of "dung beetles."[8]

Ultimately many problems would stem from the law, but for most of the 1970s these were dormant. The heavy machinery begins to move only when species are listed, and FWS did not list the first species that can be found on the U.S. mainland until 1975. Even then the enterprise proceeded cautiously, and the immediate impact was small. It grows as the number of species listed increases. Far from the 83 that formed the estimate on which the law was passed, as of February 1996, 430 species of animals are on the list as either endangered or threatened, and another 138 are well on their way to inclusion; 526 plants are listed, and 280 are in the pipeline. The impact of the law can only expand.

The act charged the Department of the Interior with maintaining a list of "endangered" species—those in immediate danger of extinction through all or a significant portion of their range. It also told Interior to maintain a list of "threatened" species—those likely to become endangered within the foreseeable future. The act allows Interior to extend the full protections of the law to threatened species, and Interior has done so. The two listings are now for most purposes equivalent. The Code of Federal Regulations contains unified lists, one each for animals and plants, with the individual entries distinguished only by an E or a T to show the difference in status.[9]

The most fundamental provision of the law makes it illegal to "take" a member of an endangered animal species, even on private property. "Take," in the context of wild animals, means to kill or capture. This caused no outcry. In terms of our Lockean categories, wild animals are a kind of commons, and regulating their hunting is a legitimate function of government. In the United States, game laws go back to the seventeenth century. Prohibiting any taking of endangered creatures was generally regarded as a reasonable extension of this rule. Besides, hunting these animals is not a major commercial or recreational activity in the United States, and owning land for the purpose of selling the shooting rights is very rare. The prohibition impinged on few people.

Other provisions of the law extend the protections further. They cover both federal land and private land, but not in the same ways. Three major distinctions must be made.

On federal land, no federal action can go forward if it is likely to jeopardize the continued existence of any listed species, nor can any action go forward if it will adversely modify any habitat that Interior has formally dedicated as critical to the species. (Endangered fish are protected by the National Marine Fisheries Service of the Department of Commerce. Its authority parallels that of Interior's Fish and Wildlife Service, and the two agencies work in harness. This discussion deals only with FWS, to keep the level of complexity under control.) In addition, no federal action can go forward that will adversely affect habitat in a way that harms the species, whether or not the habitat has been designated as critical. This is the provision of the law that stopped the sale of wood from the Kaibab Forest and the collection of firewood in the Sangre de Cristo mountains.

These same limitations restrict any federal permits necessary for private actions on private land. If I need a federal permit of any kind, the agency operates under the same restrictions that apply to federal land.

For example, a permit that would normally be granted routinely as a matter of wetlands law will not be granted if my activity on my own land would affect habitat designated as critical by FWS.

The third impact of the law is on private land not subject to any federal permit requirements. On its face, the law imposes no obligation on purely private activities besides the fundamental one of not deliberately killing or capturing any member of the species. However, the law also contains a standard provision allowing the Department of the Interior to make regulations necessary to implement the law. As of the 1970s, not many species were on the lists, and the law was having minimal impact. FWS took advantage of this low-key state of affairs to put in place a definition that revolutionized the statute, changing it from an instruction to federal agencies about administering the federal lands to a program of nationwide control over the use of all private land in the United States.

All three of these categories are having important impacts. The balance of this chapter, though, will concentrate on the habitat protection rules. These provide a good context in which to illustrate the problems of complexity and the impact of rational ignorance, and to discuss the problems of morality and legitimacy raised by the Endangered Species Act. The first set of problems, the use of federal lands, is returned to later in the book, in the chapters in Part III. The second set, the limits on federal permits, is important but hard to analyze. No data exist, and the problems gets buried in information on other programs. To some degree, it is taken up in the next chapter, on wetlands, the program on which the rule has the biggest impact.

Now let us return to problem number three, the protection of habitat on private land. The terms of the Endangered Species Act make it illegal to "take" an endangered species. The term "to take" is defined as meaning "to harass, harm, pursue, wound, kill, trap, capture, or collect, or to attempt to engage in any such conduct." Interior's 1975 rules plucked the word *harm* out of the definition of *take* and expanded it by declaring that *harm* includes any modification of habitat that injures wildlife by "significantly impairing essential behavioral patterns, including feeding, breeding, or sheltering." This makes it a crime for private landowners to modify the habitat of an endangered or threatened species located on their own property. Knowledge is not required. Habitat modification is criminal even if you do not know that the creature is there, that it is on the lists, or that your patch of ground is its natural habitat. It may even be criminal if the creature is not there. It is possible to interpret the rule as meaning that you cannot modify habitat if a member of the species might want to come there at some future date even if none is there now. FWS is coy about whether it might take this view, but it has used the habitat restriction rule as the basis for a suit to prevent logging on private property over 1.5 miles from any owls.[10]

These threats are not illusions. Ben Cone was forced to end his forest management practice of burning over the woods periodically because FWS told him that if a fire got out of hand and destroyed a woodpecker, he would probably be prosecuted. A California farmer was threatened with criminal indictment because his disker killed a kangaroo rat. An Arizona arts center paid a fine because cars using its driveway ran over a couple of desert tortoises. The Domenigonis, whose story is told in Chapter 2, faced certain prosecution if they did not let their land lie idle.

Surely, you might think, FWS cannot expand the law this way. Surely the courts will say no. To uphold this rule would require a court to say that in 1973 Congress gave the secretary of the interior the power to control every acre of ground in the United States and to "impose unfairness to the point of ruin . . . upon the simplest farmer who finds his land conscripted to the national zoological use," and no one noticed or objected. Can anyone believe a law granting such power could pass unnoticed and be approved by Congress with only four no votes in the House and none in the Senate? Well, there is bad news. In 1995, a majority of the Supreme Court, in the *Sweet Home* case, said this is precisely what Congress meant to do, and upheld the rule.[11]

This scope of Interior's rule turned out to be far-reaching, but in 1975 it caused little stir. Interior used a technique familiar to connoisseurs of bureaucratic power: it made a revolutionary claim at a time when making it had minor impact. Throughout the 1980s, the agency did not move against landowners, who remained oblivious to the rule and modified habitat with unconcern. The first significant legal article on the whole issue appeared only in 1990,[12] and *Sweet Home* was not decided for another five years. The usual next step of this approach to power is to start enforcing eventually and express bewilderment when people object, saying: "But we settled that point years ago. Why didn't you say anything then?"

Eventually other groups with other agendas found the ESA a wonderful tool. The statute provides for private lawsuits. Anyone who thinks a landowner is destroying habitat can sue. If they win, they can collect attorneys' fees from the landowner or, if the government is the defendant, from the government. By 1994, the Sierra Club Legal Defense Fund had reaped $1.8 million litigating over the spotted owl, collecting at billing rates of up to $205 per hour.[13] Anyone who opposes any kind of development, out of dislike of development in general or dislike of a particular project, can brandish the ESA.

As the 1980s wore on, more species were listed, more people learned of the law's value as a weapon, and the impacts grew. The stories began to multiply. The desert tortoise, the northern spotted owl, the Mexican spotted owl, the Florida gnatcatcher, the black-capped vireo, the golden-cheeked warbler, the California gnatcatcher, the marbled murrelet, the Alabama beach mouse, the red-cockaded woodpecker. The screws on individuals tightened, though no statistics are kept that would provide a fix on the total effect.

The impact on habitat for endangered species and for wildlife generally is also severe, but not quite in the way the framers of the law intended. The program sets up terrible incentives for landowners. If a species is found in your neighborhood, massive habitat destruction is the wisest course. If a member of the species migrates to your land, you will lose control of your property. If you want to retain the option to build on your land someday or to sell it, farm it, log it, mine it, or anything else, you are foolish to allow it to remain attractive as habitat. The economically rational course of action is to scorch the earth. In the late 1980s, as the golden-cheeked warbler moved toward listing, a wave of habitat destruction swept through the area around Austin, Texas. As long as members of the species are not yet listed, anyone can destroy habitat. After a species is listed, you can destroy habitat that would be attractive to it, as long as it is not actually present. (At least, this is how most people interpret the law, though FWS might take a different view, saying destruction of potential habitat is illegal even when the species is not in residence.) Ergo, Texans got out the chain saws, and down came the oak and juniper.[14]

You are also foolish to investigate whether any members of the species are already on your land. FWS says you are responsible if scorching the earth harms species there unbeknown to you. FWS may be right, as a matter of law. Ignorance is not a defense, and deliberate ignorance is even worse than innocent ignorance. But if the habitat is destroyed, the animals leave, which makes it difficult for FWS to establish that they were there in the first place. If you hire a biologist to check the property, then he is one of the same biologists who also does work for or at least knows the staff at FWS, and if he finds any species you are stuck.

Because of these incentives, landowners fight to preserve their state of ignorance. In 1993, Interior wanted to establish the National Biological Survey to assess species populations across the nation. The proposal was killed in Congress after bitter opposition from landowners, who feared a survey would cause them to lose the use of their land by finding endangered species. Landowners resisted entry onto their land by the FWS employees. The feds were threatened by prosecution under state laws against trespass in some cases and by shotguns in others. In November 1993, Interior Secretary Bruce Babbitt created the National Biological Service by administrative decree, but it cannot initiate formal surveys on private land without written permission from the owner and cannot undertake any work without permission from the occupant.

The rule against habitat destruction also prevents private landowners from managing property in a way that encourages the presence of wildlife generally. Imagine you own a tract in California, where 161 species are listed and another 158 are on a conveyor belt heading there. To retain any ability to use your land in the future, you must make it unattractive to every possible species. Who knows, who can keep track of, what species might be present or what habitat might be attractive to some species of which you are unaware? The protections given the spotted owl in the Northwest after 1990 led to panic cutting, especially by small landowners who, while not immediately affected, owned forest land to which the owls might migrate. As in Texas, out came the chain saws.[15]

The need to scorch the earth to prevent confiscation goes deeply against the human grain. No landowner likes doing it, and it is particular anathema to people raised on the land and inculcated with an intense relationship to it. It is a testament to the strength of this feeling that only a small proportion of people in jeopardy from endangered species seem to be following their economic self-interest. Those who do destroy habitat look on the destruction as yet another grievance chalked up against the government and resent deeply the government's role in compelling them to perform such an act. They would rather nurture nature, but they cannot afford to expose themselves to serious economic damage.

Nor is destruction limited to habitat. It extends to actual animals. Landowners are well aware that finding an endangered species is a disaster. The species, not you, now owns the property. The shorthand description of a common outcome is "shoot, shovel, and shut up." Again, the people who shoot a spotted owl do not hate the owl. They hate the government for putting them in a position where they feel they must shoot it.

Property rights advocates like to point out how different things could be if the incentives facing landowners worked the other way. What if the government paid a bounty for every species found on your land? Owners would compete to make their property attractive so as to lure species. If one landowner found it more profitable to develop the land, it would not matter. This would open a market niche for a neighbor, who could make money by providing an environmental niche for the species.

Faced with these problems, Fish and Wildlife has turned the habitat modification rule into the equivalent of a protection racket. You are allowed to use your land as long as you pay off the government. The mechanism is something called the Incidental Take Permit. Fish and Wildlife issues permits allowing people to "take" members of endangered species in the course of some other activity, such as property development, farming, and so on. You must prepare a plan showing how you will minimize the impact and agree to anything else FWS thinks necessary to protect the species. Part of the price may be action to protect species not yet listed. Getting the permit requires lots of money and paperwork, and the Incidental Take Permit has been institutionalized into Habitat Conservation Planning. The *Preliminary Draft Handbook for Habitat Conservation Planning and Incidental Take Permit Processing*, dated September 15, 1994, is eighty-eight single-spaced pages long, with another 150 pages or so of appendixes containing regulations, templates for contracts and letters, government forms, examples of permits, and the rest of the paperwork surrounding the program.

The conditions FWS will put into a Habitat Conservation Plan depend on the particular circumstances, your own status, and your plans.

There really is no clear limit on what can be extorted from you. To build a seaside cottage in the habitat of the Alabama beach mouse, you must agree to conditions on the placement of the house, construct walkovers, and forgo pets, landscaping, and outdoor lighting. A developer wanting a permit covering 22 acres of Alabama beach also chipped in $60,000 to acquire habitat elsewhere. A 17-acre development and golf course in Palos Verdes, California, home of the California gnatcatcher, came steeper: FWS extracted conservation easements, an open space preserve, predator control, revegetation, and perpetual funding of habitat management.

The government of Clark County, Nevada, wanted land for public and private development. The desert tortoise was there. The resulting plan covers 113,900 acres and costs $1.3 million per year in mitigation fees, plus a development fee of $550 per acre, which multiplies out to $62.5 million. To harvest timber on 60 acres in Oregon, a company agreed to take measures to minimize the impact and to donate 49 acres to the U.S. Forest Service. The City of Bakersfield, California, wanted to build sewers on 88 acres. It bought 80 other acres as a home for the blunt-nosed lizard and deeded them to the state fish and game department, and it agreed to cash mitigation payments. Weyerhaeuser, a big forest products company, met the American burying beetle in Arizona and Oklahoma. To operate on 40,000 acres, it agreed to a comprehensive conservation plan. The draft plan for the Stephens kangaroo rat in California would impose a $1,950 per acre fee on any landowner within a 520,000-acre area (812 square miles) who wants to modify habitat on his own property.[16]

A Habitat Conservation Plan presents many problems aside from their financial costs. The paperwork is interminable and the processing time long, especially when many landowners are affected. Perhaps most important, plans are not final. If you agree to donate property to protect the gnatcatcher, and tomorrow they find the kit fox on your land, or list some entirely new species, you are back to square one. You now have to negotiate a new plan for the kit fox or the new species, and nothing you did for the gnatcatcher counts. Furthermore, FWS usually insists on some weasel words in a plan to allow reopening at the option of the agency. Not surprisingly, by 1993 only about a dozen plans had become final.[17] The pace has picked up since then. From June 1994 through

January 1996, 135 Habitat Conservation Plans started working their way through to approval. Of these, 56 are $1,500 contributions to the Balcones County, Texas, Conservation Fund in exchange for permissions to build single-family residences in the terrain of the golden-cheeked warbler, so the overall numbers are not impressive.

FWS has announced a couple of reform plans with great fanfare, and its standard answer when anyone raises any of these examples is to claim that these reforms have fixed everything. Do not believe it. In mid-1995, FWS proposed to exempt activities associated with single-family homes on less than 5 acres of land from the habitat modification rules. The proposal starts by laying out the supporting reasons, such as the minimal effect on threatened species of activities on small parcels and the negative incentives created by existing rules.[18] Then it starts adding qualifications. The policy will apply only to *threatened* species, not to *endangered* ones. And it will not apply to any species already on the threatened list, only to those added in the future. And, oh, the policy will not apply to any species already in the middle of the listing process. For these, FWS will decide case by case, but the default presumption will be *against* the new policy. So the policy will apply only to species proposed for listing in the future, and even then it will apply only as a default assumption. FWS can declare it inapplicable for any species for any reason it chooses. By the way, the new policy does not apply if the "cumulative impact" from many small adjacent landowners might be severe. Finally, the policy, watery as it is, is only proposed. It may never be final. But proposing it lets the administration talk about its reforms of the Endangered Species Act before the 1996 election, and rational ignorance does the rest.

When you parse the actual language of another much-trumpeted reform called "No Surprises," which purports to be a program guaranteeing landowners who sign conservation plans against arbitrary change, you find the same pattern of extravagant up-front promises followed by shifty language. The government guarantees not to change unless it feels like it.

The moral basis for imposing these burdens on private landowners is as dubious as the legal underpinnings. The concept of species was invented during the 1700s to describe life forms. The ladder of classification has seven major steps, plus a couple of minor ones. These are illustrated by the example of your faithful dog, which belongs to: King-dom—Animalia; Phylum—Chodata; Class—Mammalia; Order—Car-nivora; Family—Canidae; Genus—Canis; Species—familiaris.

All dogs, from Great Danes to Pekinese, are members of *Canis famil-iaris*. The basic test is whether they will interbreed. Great Danes and Pekinese will, though perhaps not easily. Therefore, the different breeds of dog are subspecies. However, this rule is not always held to, and an element of arbitrariness enters into classification of species. Wolves, dogs, and coyotes are all different species, but they can interbreed and you hear of wolf dogs from time to time. In the judgment of biologists, cross-breeding does not happen often enough for the three to be grouped together, and they remain genetically distinct.[19]

Approximately 1.4 million species of organisms have been discov-ered and named. The total number of species on the earth is usually es-timated at 3 to 30 million, but some respected biologists think the number may be as high as 100 million.[20]

Any species, including the human one, is careless of other life forms. The ancestors of the American Indians crossed to North America from Asia about twelve thousand years ago. A few hundred years of hunting wiped out mammoths, sloths, horses, camels, eagles, tapirs, giant wolves, saber-toothed tigers—at least thirty-three kinds of creatures in all.[21] The same thing happened in New Zealand and throughout the South Seas when Polynesian hunters arrived, and later the rats and cats trav-eling with European sailors did in still more species. The fates of the passenger pigeon (extinct) and the American buffalo (barely saved) in the nineteenth century are well known.

One widely repeated estimate is that humans eliminated 75 species of mammals and birds between the years 1600 and 1900 and another 75 in the century since.[22] Even when we humans are not hunting species into extinction for food or sport, we can crowd others by our voracious presence. The World Conservation Monitoring Center in London esti-mates that since the year 1600, extinction has overtaken at least 583 species and subspecies of animals—20 reptiles and amphibians, 33 fishes, 103 birds, 63 mammals, and 364 invertebrates—and 654 species and subspecies of plants. Not all these losses are due to human activity, but the rate of extinction has climbed since the explosion of the human population from about 600 million in 1700 to 5.7 billion in 1995. The inference of a causal link is strong.

The center maintains a "Red List" of 169 amphibians, 316 reptiles, 741 mammals, 970 birds, 979 fishes, 2,754 invertebrates, and 26,333 plants. Between 10 and 33 percent of the entries for each class are regarded as endangered, which means they are in immediate danger of extinction. The rest are regarded as vulnerable.[23]

To be even, human activity also creates new niches enabling species to flourish. The American Indians hunted some animals to extinction, but they also managed the forest, largely through fire, in a way that made much of North America into "a vast and exceedingly well managed game farm."[24] By doing this, they fostered not only the game animals they valued but such other creatures as the Karner Blue butterfly, which, since the end of Indian management practices, has dwindled to the point where it is now on the endangered list. Artillery practice and tank maneuvers at Fort Hood, Texas, create terrain suitable for the black-capped vireo, which likes the edges of the open trails created by the tanks and the brush growing up in the wake of the fires set by exploding shells.

The trend line of extinctions is less clear. A school of analysis argues that the London center's figures are deceptively conservative and that we are in the middle of an "extinction crisis" in which the world will lose millions of species of plants and animals as humankind compresses their habitats. This view is fostered by conservation biologists, who regard action to stop extinctions as imperative and are exerting great influence over government policy.

The alarmist case is not proved in any scientific sense. The scientific way to establish that extinctions are indeed occurring is by observation. If we know a species existed at some time in the past and it has ceased to exist, then we know it has become extinct. This is the standard applied by the World Conservation Monitoring Center, and no empirical evidence demonstrates the disappearance, unknown to it, of any significant number of species. The more extreme estimates are based on assumptions concerning changes in habitat. For example, they assume that a decrease of a given percentage in habitat will result in the extinction of a calculable number of species. The assumptions are not supported by experience. From the beginning of European settlement in North America until the end of the nineteenth century, forestland in the mainland United States declined from about 950 million acres (about half of the total land area) to 614 million acres in 1920. (It has since come back to about 737 million acres.)[25] If the extinction crisis theories are correct, the shrinkage, especially the massive deforestation that occurred in the eastern half of the United States, should have caused massive die-off. It did not happen. Only three species of forest birds are known through observation to have become extinct. Because people do look at and record the existence of birds, it is improbable many species could have disappeared without notice.[26]

Debate over the extinction issue is extensive and vitriolic, but, on balance, go with the skeptics. The argument that an extinction crisis is occurring depends on dubious techniques for extrapolating from either bad data or no data. Furthermore, my work on environmental issues has taken me into too many other areas where the predictions of disaster are based on bad information, faulty analysis, and the benefits the predictors will derive from a state of public alarm. Government agencies and their dependents manufacture crises with the same predictability with which Ford makes automobiles. This is the business they are in, and this is what they are going to do. Crises are necessary to provide national and international bureaucracies with money, power, status, and interesting travel.

The only firm conclusion to be drawn from the data is that since 1600 human activity has contributed to the extinction of some number of species. Most of these were exotics developed in long isolation in a narrow range of habitat. Beyond this, little can be said, as a matter of science, about what happened in the past or will happen in the future.

The deeper question is why we should care about extinctions. Most people feel a sentimental admiration for buffaloes, bald eagles, whooping cranes, and grizzly bears and would rather they did not disappear. These are called the poster species of the protection movement. The issue becomes tougher when you get to the snail darter, a small fish distinguished from other darters in quite minor ways, or the North American burying beetle, or the black-capped vireo. We might not go out of our way to harm a species, and we might take moderate steps to preserve it, but it is far from clear whence comes any moral duty to preserve it at all costs. Individual species evolve to fill niches on the planet. Thousands and millions of them have disappeared over time when their niches closed for natural reasons. If the niche closes because of human activity, it is not clear why this is a catastrophe.

Nonetheless, many people do regard the loss of a species as a catastrophe. Obviously, I would not be their chosen spokesperson, and for a fuller explanation you must consult other books.[27] Nonetheless, let me lay out the bones of their arguments, together with the reasons they seem unpersuasive to me.

The case comes in two forms: the prudential and the ethical. The prudential case argues that each species contains unique genetic information that might at some point be useful to humans—for example, quinine used to treat malaria, taxol used to treat ovarian cancer, and cannabis used to prevent nausea from chemotherapy. All of these, and thousands of other drugs, come from natural sources. Researchers are now looking at bloodsucking creatures—leeches, mosquitoes, ticks, hookworms—to find anticoagulants useful in treating human beings.[28] If a species is wiped out, then the possibility of discovering some beneficial use is forever gone.

At a theoretical level, this concept of preserving possibly useful information has appeal—but also defects. Not many individual species are so unusual that their loss would result in the disappearance of genetic information available absolutely nowhere else. Subspecies and even distinct populations, both protected by the ESA, are even less genetically distinct. Also, the chances of finding unique benefits from any particular species are small. Humans have been looking for tens of thousands of years, and science rarely turns up a useful plant not already known to the wisdom of our species. Research projects screening plants and animals at random have produced little, and are not regarded as promising ventures even by people who stand to make pots of money if they hit on something. Considering the millions of species that will not become extinct that have never been closely examined, the idea that we will lose irreparably as a result of extinction is improbable. Charles Mann and Mark Plummer put their finger on it in *Noah's Choice*, when they say biodiversity is important, but individual species are not.

The prudential argument is, at bottom, an economic argument that it is worthwhile to maintain all the information contained in the genetic "library" of all species, at any cost. As an economic argument, this is a bust. People are always making choices about what information to keep and what to discard. We cannot, as individuals or as a society, decide to keep everything.[29] Periodically, news accounts tell of some eccentric who discards nothing and whose home fills up with old newspapers, magazines, letters, and other junk. Eventually the occupant lives huddled in a corner, imprisoned by his own mania. To argue that we humans cannot afford the loss of a single piece of genetic information, regardless of the impact of its preservation on our living space, is to argue that the whole world must be turned into a home for mad magazine savers.

The ethical case argues that humans do not have the right to eliminate another species. To do so is to usurp the functions of God or nature, and to sin. No one is immune to the pull of this argument. The nineteenth-century sportsmen who rode the rails through the Dakota plains shooting buffalo as fast as they could load their rifles seem appalling. So do the sailors who in 1844 clubbed to death the last two known great auks for no reason recorded by history. The real question is why we find this behavior appalling. Is it worse to club an auk to death for fun if it is the last auk, or nearly the last, than otherwise? If so, why? Is it because the clubber is depriving future humans of the chance to see the auk, or do we have some sense of an offense against an abstract category of "aukness"? Every couple of years, as many cattle are slaughtered for meat as the number of buffalo killed in the 1870s. Every year, hunters in Maryland kill 50,000 to 62,000 deer out of a state population of 220,000 animals.[30] If this did not happen, the state would be forced to cull the herd, or the deer would destroy their forage base and starve. I am more troubled by killing the last auk than I am by killing of a plentiful species like deer, but it is hard to explain why. Similarly, I react to the buffalo but not the cattle.

The advocates of the ESA take their argument a step further. They say not only should a species not be eliminated directly, but individual humans have a duty to ensure that their activities do not eliminate any environmental niche occupied by any species.

AUSTIN, TEXAS, 1983–1988

Fred Purcell leads a group of real estate investors in Austin, which is growing rapidly. Many people find it a pleasant city, and they need homes, shops, and work sites. Purcell's group buys a former ranch, planning a mixed development of housing, light industry, and a supermarket. A major reason for their choice of a site is that the selected parcel is the only piece in western Travis County listed by the city as free of all environmental constraints on development.

The land where the supermarket parking lot is to go contains a cave just below the surface, about forty feet in diameter, five feet high. Travis County has lots of these caves, and builders have been plugging them up for years. The caves are the home of troglobites, underground invertebrates that do not leave their home caves. As a result of the isolation, the inhabitants of different caves evolve differently, and Purcell's cave has a spider, a beetle, and a scorpion not found elsewhere.

Members of the environmental group Earth First! conduct a sit-in in the cave to get across the message that "all creatures are created equal." The troglobites are listed by FWS as endangered, and in the end Purcell agrees to develop a protection plan for them and donate the land around the cave to a state agency. He is not happy. "I have nothing against parks, or endangered species, or even endangered bugs. But . . . if they're so good, then why doesn't the whole country pay me to protect them? Why should I get stuck with the bill for it all?"[31]

It is at the level of niche preservation that most people, including me, part company with the ethical argument. Like Fred Purcell, we ask, Why is this my duty? In fact, why is it a duty of humans collectively? Since the beginning of time, bioforms have come and gone with changes in available environmental niches. The existence of humans is one of the features of the planet that affects the available niches. Why is it our responsibility to try to pretend we are not here or to try to replicate the conditions that would exist if we were not here?

Furthermore, it is not even clear that you can fairly say human activity "causes" the extinction. If a specialized species with a narrow range becomes extinct, is the extinction "caused" by filling in the cave or by the troglobites' limited survival capabilities? Sometimes blaming the victim seems perfectly appropriate. If the needs of a species become impossible to meet because of conflict with the needs of other species, including humans, and the species cannot survive, has humanity destroyed it, or is it simply one of evolution's losers?

The weakness of the moral argument that all species must be preserved becomes even more obvious once you understand the looseness of the standards for making the list. The ambiguity surrounding the meaning of the term *species* only begins the problems created by the listing process. The act allows listing of subspecies and even distinct population segments as well as species. (The provision on subspecies applies to plants, fish, and wildlife. The protection of population segments extends only to vertebrate fish or wildlife. You were rationally ignorant of this, and will be again about five minutes after reading it. But it is crucial to people affected by the program.)

The scientists' criteria for defining subspecies are exceedingly unclear. Anyone can see a Great Dane is not a Pekinese, but the basic genetic distinctions are small, and no barriers prevent reproduction. The most common reason a subspecies disappears is interbreeding with another subspecies and merger into that population. Nonetheless, the listing of separate subspecies has a powerful impact on human activities.

Look on the list under "owl" and you find listed as threatened (*not* endangered) the northern spotted owl, the subspecies causing the anguish in Humboldt and Trinity counties described earlier. These counties are unlucky. If they were south of the Pit River, then the owls would be California spotted owls, which are not on the list. Still farther south, the same basic creature becomes the Mexican spotted owl, also threatened, and the reason the poor residents of the Sangre de Cristos can no longer pick up downed timber for firewood. The species is spotted owl, otherwise known as *Strix* (the genus) *occidentalis* (the species). Northern, California, and Mexican are all subspecies. There is no genetic variation between the two coastal subspecies (northern and California). There is some variation between these two and the Mexican, caused by the isolation of the latter.[32] In reality, spotted owls as a species are not endangered or even threatened, and all the trauma of the West is unnecessary for their survival.

Another oddity in the theory underlying the endangered species program is that populations often turn into distinct subspecies and species because of isolation. Isolation also causes inbreeding, which has never been regarded as a sign of genetic robustness, let alone moral virtue. In the merciless tournament of Darwinian evolution, inbreeding is associated with weakness and vulnerability. The Florida panther, which is endangered, shows severe effects from inbreeding, and biologists have introduced panthers from Texas to improve the gene pool. This raises a question about the whole enterprise of the program: How do you "preserve" a species by crossing it with a different one? Just what is it you are trying to save? The ESA makes no distinction between species that are interestingly well adapted to conditions and those that are simply freak products of isolation. The act imposes on humankind a duty to reverse Darwin and ensure the survival of everything, strong or weak, with a particular obligation to the least robust of evolution's creations.

The decision to list is, in theory, based totally on "scientific" criteria. The northern spotted owl is listed, despite its similarity to the California and Mexican spotted owls and the devastating impact on large numbers of humans, because the American Ornithological Union (AOU) separates the three subspecies. As far as FWS is concerned, this ends the matter. There is no inquiry into whether the AOU's criteria bear in any way on any human purpose, or relate in any way to the underlying purposes of the act. Economic factors are not to be considered in a listing decision.

Finally, a single species or subspecies can be divided into distinct population segments, any of which can be listed. This decision is not scientific at all. It is a malleable concept giving FWS total discretion. The ocelot is listed because its hold on its South Texas range is tenuous. But Texas is the northern extreme of the range, and 100,000 or more ocelots roam Central and South America. The ocelot is not in danger of extinction, whatever happens in Texas. FWS has issued a policy statement on the use of this power, saying in essence that any island of a species population can be listed as endangered if FWS feels like listing it.

Under these amorphous definitions, the numbers of listed species, subspecies, and population segments are growing like weeds. Once the decision to list is made, a species is entitled to total protection. Congress has created an entitlement whereby the listed species has an absolute right to habitat regardless of the impact on anything else. Costs or consequences to humans play no role.

An earlier chapter referred to the religious fervor brought to the Endangered Species Act by the late Mollie Beatty. Bruce Babbitt, secretary of the interior, keeps circling closer to putting the Endangered Species Act on an explicitly religious foundation. In 1995 he rejected the concept that the Endangered Species Act should take costs into consideration or that some priorities among species should be recognized. His reason was that Noah, in Genesis, was commanded to save two of everything, not just two of species that are useful.[33]

Babbitt's views include an almost religious reverence for the natural world. One of his arguments for excluding all oil exploration from the

Alaska National Wildlife Refuge is that caribou around humans become used to human contact and "tame," and thus are somehow less worthy than wild caribou. Also, wolves and grizzly bears would not be found anywhere near exploration equipment, so they and the caribou would not be "interacting naturally." One can only wonder what the caribou think about their natural interactions with wolves and grizzlies. It isn't *The Lion King,* with all the creatures of the wild cavorting happily together. A realistic TV show about interactions at ANWR would not be fare for five year olds.

ISLE ROYALE, MICHIGAN, 1996

Isle Royale is 210 square miles in Lake Superior, about 20 miles from the mainland. Around 1900, moose first arrive—perhaps by swimming, perhaps across an ice bridge. They find lots of balsam fir for winter food and no predators, and the population explodes into the thousands. By 1935 the balsam fir is eaten close to extinction, and only a few hundred moose are left, starving. A fire in 1936 burns 40 square miles, allows a new forest to grow up, and the population recovers. The island is made a national park in 1940.

The winter of 1949 is bitter cold, and a pair of wolves crosses the ice to the island. Like the earlier moose, they find Eden: lots of food (the moose) and no enemies. The wolf population expands. Isle Royale is now a paradise for naturalists as well, since it provides an unparalleled opportunity to study the predator-prey relationship. What they study is classic "nature, red in tooth and claw." The moose tend to overeat their forage base, and the calves and the old die when winter is harsh. After long expansion, the moose population drops from 2,400 in early 1995 to 1,200 a year later. If it drops to about 700, then major forest regeneration can occur, and the herd will grow again. This is likely to happen because the loss of the calves causes reproductive rates to drop after a couple of years.

The wolves also cull the moose herd, eating like, well, like starving wolves, and concentrating on the old and the young. When the moose population declines, the number of the wolves also declines, lagging the decline in moose by a few years. The wolf population fluctuates between 13 and 50 and now stands at 22. "The balance of nature is a dynamic process" and the relationship between balsam fir, moose, and wolves "a constantly changing kaleidoscope of events."[34]

Isle Royale is an interesting place, worth preserving for its scientific and educational value. But the argument for some religious imperative to make all or even large parts of the United States into a giant Isle Royale out of reverence for this forage-prey-predator relationship escapes me.

Robert Nelson, a former economist at the Department of the Interior and current professor at the University of Maryland, has written extensively about the religious foundations of much contemporary environmentalism.[35] Practitioners describe the human race as a cancer, or as "the AIDS of the earth." As Nelson says, "Such dark visions hark back to the Calvinist and Puritan conception of a depraved world of human beings infected with sin." These people go onto exceedingly treacherous ground with this foray into religion. For one thing, although biblical arguments are out of favor with America's urban upper middle class, they are much in favor in other parts of society. It is easy to find such arguments. See, for example, the biblical Parable of the Talents, which makes the point that the wealth given to the world by God is to be used, and that refusing to use it is offensive to its Creator. In this line of thought, locking up the natural resources of the world is a form of paganism that should not be tolerated.

For another thing, elevating something into a religious duty does not give you license to stamp on my rights under secular law. This is a part of the separation of church and state, and very important it is, too. If a more obvious religion than environmentalism asserted the right to confiscate property for purposes of worship, we would have no trouble telling its adherents to buy space, like everyone else. Once you start saying that self-defined religious duties trump secular rights, you open the door to bitter conflicts. Someone could start a church with a tenet that all vulnerable species should be eliminated to make more space for humans. This church could then tell its members to enter your land and club your great auks to death. Hey! Religious duty overrides property rights, you know! What's your problem, bub? This is my religion! Watch out, or I might add human sacrifice, and guess who goes first!

Separation of church and state is necessary if people with diverse religious views are to live together in peace. This requires separation of church and property rights. Those who would make the ESA into a religious war better be careful what they ask for. "When the gods wish to punish us they answer our prayers."[36]

In the end, I do not belong to the biopreservationists' church, and their arguments are as lost on me as would be an appeal to the basic principles of Zoroastrianism. For the sake of the general principle of bio-diversity and out of deference to my many fellow citizens who care more than I about preservation of individual species, I am happy to support the idea of large nature preserves designed to give as many species as possible a good shot at survival. I am not willing to accept as a moral imperative the preservation of every niche for every species, especially at the expense of the private property rights that are so essential to social progress and harmony.

The biopreservationists will not persuade me of the correctness of their view unless they produce better evidence than they have mustered so far. On the other hand, I will never convince them of the validity of my views, either. Differences are part of life, and some cannot be reconciled. Differences can be mediated and muted, though, and the best mechanism for this is property rights and the market economy. If you believe preservation of each species is crucial, then buy the land. If you insist on placing the duty on the landowner, the result will be continuing bitter conflict, especially when you, who are imposing the duty, evade all the costs. This practice also puts your good faith in question. People who insist their own ideas of virtue be financed by others as a sacred duty become targets for deserved mockery.

Respectable elements of the environmentalist community recognize the need to introduce money back into the program. Land trusts are growing rapidly. These are nonprofit organizations that buy land or easement restrictions for the sake of species preservation, wetlands, open space, or other environmental purposes. Much of it is donated by landowners. Restrictive easements are often welcomed by owners, especially when their neighbors agree to similar conditions. Use of such mechanisms leaves everyone happy.

In the eyes of those bearing the brunt of the ESA, the law not only lacks moral legitimacy. It also lacks political legitimacy, when judged by the criteria spelled out in the last chapter. ESA is a confiscation of land to provide the public facility of wildlife refuges. If you want to use the concept of the commons, then it is a confiscation to convert property into a national zoological commons. Affected landowners also think ESA is invoked for purposes having little to do with species. They believe the agenda of the environmentalists is to stop building, logging, agriculture, and other uses of land and that the species are of secondary importance. In 1988 an environmentalist spokesman commented, "The northern spotted owl is the wildlife species of choice to act as a surrogate for old-growth forest protection. Thank goodness the spotted owl evolved in the Pacific Northwest, for if it hadn't, we'd have to genetically engineer it."[37] This is quoted repeatedly as confirmation that the owl is actually a tool, not an end. Many landowners believe the government has been captured by special interests—people who want to maintain untrammeled access to property for their own use and enjoyment without the responsibility of managing it or paying taxes on it. Communities in the Northwest affected by the spotted owl decisions are particularly bitter. They characterize the environmental activists as a bunch of pot-smoking freeloaders who live on welfare and have nothing to do except interfere with hard-working loggers. (I merely pass this on, admitted into evidence, as the lawyers say, as proof of state of mind, not as proof of the facts alleged. I have not been there. I do not know the truth of the matter.)

That the law is retroactive is obvious. It imposes new duties out of the blue, not fine-tuning of a system rooted in history. The federal government has taken over minute decisions about land use at the local level. The program puts on randomly chosen landowners responsibility for species preservation, an action that benefits society as a whole. Also, as the victimized landowners are quick to point out, the main cause of any need to protect existing habitat is the destruction of habitat in other places. Now the people who benefited from destruction are putting all the burden for solving the problem they created on others.

Many questions about the competence and the honesty of the science are also raised. Much of the original research triggering the listing of the northern spotted owl has since been thrown into question, and it is clear that the original research was extremely dubious. Demands for better science are a constant refrain, especially considering the loose nature of the decisions about subspecies and distinct population segments. The government shows no inclination to correct its errors.

All classes of landowners believe the government wears them down with paperwork and regulatory minutiae. They do not believe the soothing noises about working together, and they do not think the government is genuinely interested in minimizing the burdens placed on them. They regard Habitat Conservation Plans and other proposed reforms as political exercises designed to make FWS look responsive while actually retaining as many roadblocks as possible. As illustrated by the 5-acre exemption, reforms are more show than substance.

As further evidence of the government's bad faith, landowners point to the position it is asserting in a pending lawsuit over the legal doctrine of "standing to sue" under the Endangered Species Act. The government argues that the law is a one-way street: anyone who thinks the Fish and Wildlife Service has not done enough to protect a species *can* sue, while anyone who thinks it has done too much *cannot*. As this book was going to press, the matter was argued before the Supreme Court.[38]

The biggest problem is the one taken up in the discussion of *Sweet Home*: delegation of power. By definition, the regulatory power exercised by the secretary of the interior under the ESA is constitutional. The Supreme Court said so, and that is the end of it. But no one subject to this power agrees that the exercise of the power is right, and the Court has set up an ominous split between the legal and the popular concepts of legitimacy.

The issue presented to the Court was not whether the regulations governing habitat modification "take" property within the meaning of the Fifth Amendment to the Constitution. The issue was whether the statute gives the secretary of the interior the authority to impose the regulations in the first place. Could Interior use a law prohibiting the "taking" of a species to enact a rule prohibiting any action affecting the habitat of a member of the species? The Court upheld the agency's power, after engaging in the standard lawyers' autopsy on the "intent" of the Congress based on the minutiae of committee reports, last-minute language modifications, and floor comments.

Dissenting justice Antonin Scalia identified the weakness in the agency's logic. The statute does not forbid "harm" to a species. It forbids "taking," a term with longs roots in both common usage and law that means to capture, dead or alive. The term *harm* is subsidiary, used only to define *take*. Rather obviously, the list of words (including *harm*) used by the law in the definition of *take* are intended to cover the various things that can happen when you try to capture or kill an animal. The drafters of the statute did not want a malefactor to squirm loose because his shot only broke the eagle's wing or missed entirely and he failed in his attempt to "take." The real question was whether Interior could legitimately define *take* as forbidding habitat modification if the word *harm* were not in the law. The answer is rather clearly no. This is not what *take* means, as a matter of English usage, no matter how far you stretch it. As a matter of legal usage and logic, you cannot expand a word in a definition to sweep in situations far outside the meaning of the original word to which the definition is anchored.

As Scalia showed, the legal reasoning of the majority in *Sweet Home* is anemic. Even if it were strong, though, it is divorced from the realities of the situation. The Court tied itself up in the minutiae of subsection X and regulatory proposal Y, and committee report Z, treating a matter crucial to hundreds of thousands of people and profoundly important for the proper functioning of democratic government as a legal trivia quiz. Only Scalia's exasperated dissent notices that important problems of governance and legitimacy are involved.

Whether the obligation of habitat protection upheld by *Sweet Home* is good or bad, just or unjust, it is too important a policy to be made by stealth and upheld by pedantry. The result of the case is to undermine respect for every institution responsible for the outcome, and rightly so. Each has acted shabbily. If Congress meant to enact such a doctrine, acting by stealth brings Congress itself into contempt. If Congress did not intend the result, then why is it too supine to rein in Interior? Either way, Congress looks—because it is—shifty, weak, or both. Interior is also damaged. It is not a representative institution, and in the popular mind it has no legitimate right to impose such a heavy burden based on so tenuous an authority, whatever loopholes its lawyers find in formal legal doctrine on the delegation of rulemaking power. To anyone injured by the law, the agency is abusing its power. The legitimacy of the Supreme Court also suffers. For anyone familiar with the stakes involved in the case, the word that comes to mind while reading the majority opinion is "shallow"; it reads like something written by a precocious but unsophisticated law student. If Professor Beer were still teaching his course, he could take up the Endangered Species Act as a case study in how governments fritter away legitimacy.

MONTANA AND OREGON, 1995

Some stories are about things that do not happen. Dr. David Cameron is a retired professor of biology and genetics who lives in Montana. He is also a third generation livestockman from a family with a tradition of promoting wildlife. Dr. Cameron's father reintroduced pronghorn antelope in the 1950s, and he himself wants to revive the Montana grayling, a native fish that has all but disappeared. He learns that the grayling is under consideration for listing as endangered. His plans must be shelved. If the fish were listed, reintroducing it could cost the Camerons the right to graze their pastures, and the risk is too great. He asks a congressional committee: "How many times has my story been repeated? How often has the ESA impeded biological restoration? I think more often than you want to believe. Reasonable property owners are frightened and angry at you, the government, for managing with brick bats. Why does the hosting of a rare and troubled creature have to be a threat to their livelihood rather than a source of pride and pleasure? It *doesn't.* It is clearly unfair to make a few individuals both the scapegoats and the bearers of stress because of forces beyond their control and perpetrated by society at large."[39]

Terri Moffet of Oregon testifies before the same committee. The Moffets own 60 acres of farm and 120 acres of forest that has been in the family 138 years. The timber was treated as a rainy day college fund, and they invested in forest improvements and maintenance. Now, predictability and confidence are gone, and investment has ceased. Moffet protests that landowners are viewed as radicals if they voice their concerns. "Even the suggestion of a scientific peer review [of ESA] receives responses like 'we want to gut the act.'" She suggests that members of Congress, before imposing any more uncompensated requirements, ask themselves if they would be willing to donate a bedroom for use as a shelter for the homeless.[40]

Chapter 7

Wetlands

More villagers carrying torches and pitchforks

FENWICK ISLAND, DELAWARE, 1992–1995

In 1992, the Turners buy a run-down forty-year-old beach house in a 1.9-acre wetland. The state tells them that they can renovate as long as they stay within the existing footprint of the house, and they start applying for the required permits. The state denies them permission to install a new roof because its six-inch eaves will cast a shadow on the wetland. It denies permission to build a deck because sunning and viewing are not water-dependent activities, and thus the deck is not a proper structure for a wetland. New stairs are forbidden because the landing would be a "fill" of wetlands. The same theory is used to reject a proposal that an elevated walkway be built to the pier to minimize foot traffic on the wetland; the pilings would be fill. The Turners cannot park on a previously filled area where the previous owner parked for forty years. In the meantime, the county government tells them to get cracking on the renovation or the house will be condemned.

The Turners get help from a respected advocacy group in Washington, the Defenders of Property Rights, and in the summer of 1995 they receive the state permit. Now they can start working to get the necessary federal approvals.[1]

Once upon a time, no one would say a good word for wetlands. Whether called swamps, marshes, bogs, mires, sloughs, or fens, they were worthless as real estate and feared as breeding grounds "of malarial and malignant fevers." The popular attitude was that the power of the state "is never more legitimately exercised than in removing such nuisances."[2] In the nineteenth century, the federal government gave away public wetlands to states in exchange for a promise to drain them.

Wetland could often be transformed into prime agricultural land, sometimes through the relatively simple process of digging a network of ditches and allowing water to drain. In colonial Virginia wetlands were the richest soil. In the Midwest lots of prime farmland was created out of wetlands during the early part of this century. Iowa does not look like a swamp, but between 1906 and 1925, Iowans formed 3,000 drainage districts and converted between 1 and 2 million acres of swamp (3 to 6 percent of the state) into farmland.[3] These early districts were and are paid for by farmers on the basis of hard cost-benefit calculations. Later, the federal government, with its usual overenthusiasm for aiding farmers, started subsidizing conversions that could not pass a market test, a practice that continued until 1985.

These attitudes resulted in the draining of a lot of wetlands over the years. The mainland United States had about 215 million acres of wetlands at the beginning of European settlement, which is about 11 percent of the total land area of the nation. By the mid-1970s this was down to about 99 million acres.[4] A caution is necessary, though. These estimates about the decline of wetlands acreage are tossed about constantly, but the definition of wetlands being used is exceedingly unclear. Thus, it is not really clear how much wetland existed originally. Nor is it clear how much remains. Nor do we really know whether what remains is too much, not enough, just right, or a matter of indifference.

Converted wetlands went overwhelmingly for farms. Between just the mid-1950s and the mid-1970s, 9 million acres of wetlands disappeared, 87 percent of it into agriculture.[5] Much of this conversion was subsidized and would not have occurred otherwise. Some was multipurpose. Wetlands disappeared in the orgy of dam building and flood control that occurred in the decades after 1930. Some wetland was wet because it was floodplain, and when the rivers were hemmed in the land dried out. The land was converted to farming, but flood control was the moving force. A high proportion of wetlands conversion was caused by the federal government, which is now making many people do heavy penance to expiate its own sins.

This domination of agricultural uses is not surprising. Where simple drainage is not enough because land needs filling in or building up, converting wetlands to other uses is not worth the expense unless the going rate for local real estate is high. Only wetlands near population centers or prime recreational areas are serious targets for development. Of the 9 million acres of wetlands that vanished in the twenty years before the mid-1970s, only about 1,125 square miles went for urban development. Scattered over a nationwide mainland land mass of about 3 million square miles, and covering a period of twenty years of rollicking economic growth, the figure is not impressive. Another 700 square miles of wetlands went for "other development"—roads, bridges, recreation, and other nonurban uses.[6]

We must screen out the current drumfire of propaganda that views converting wetlands to other purposes as inherently evil. There are excellent reasons to change wetlands over to other purposes. Before the age of DDT and other pesticides, the last thing you wanted anywhere near you was a swamp. People may not have known that mosquitoes carried disease until the dawn of the twentieth century, but they knew that cities near swamps were not healthy places. Cannibalizing swamps for urban building is also an old and honorable practice. Any entrepreneur willing to gamble the money to convert wetlands into useful real estate was regarded as a public benefactor. A map of Boston during the Revolutionary War shows major differences from the city of today. Now-fashionable Back Bay was once part of the bay—a mud flat. Political commentators often note that Washington, D.C., was built on top of a swamp, usually drawing an analogy to the capital's current status as a moral and intellectual morass.

Wetlands near rivers and lakes were also logical candidates for development, especially during the prerailroad and pretruck era when water transport was the only economical way to move bulk goods. Land with good access to transportation was too valuable to lie idle as a swamp. Furthermore, people like to live near water, and riparian land has always commanded a premium for residential use.

Despite all the conversion, the United States still has a lot of wetlands of various types. A lot of them are in river valleys. The rivers of the southeastern United States are surrounded by deltas, including the greatest of them all, the Mississippi alluvial plain, which extends for 600 miles from Cairo, Illinois, down to New Orleans, covering 26 million acres in seven states. At one time, the delta had about 24 million acres of bottomland hardwood forest wetland. This wetland is now about 5.2 million acres. Most of the rest of the delta is now agricultural.

Nebraska has the Rainwater Basin, a 4,200-square-mile area dotted with patches where subsurface clay keeps rainwater from penetrating. The result was 4,000 individual wetlands totaling 95,000 acres. For the most part, they are unconnected to any surface water. Some are temporary, some seasonal, some more or less permanent. They serve as a rest stop for migrating waterfowl. These wetlands are fairly easy to drain, and only about 34,000 acres remain.

Some parts of the country are covered with swamps. The Everglades of Florida is the best known of these, followed by Okefenokee in Georgia. Minnesota has a lot of swampland in its northern half. So does Michigan. The West has riparian wetlands, areas of saturation adjoining rivers and creeks. North Carolina has 695,000 acres of natural-state pocosins, which are "nutrient-poor, forested or shrub wetlands that evolved . . . due to blocked drainage and peat accumulation."[7] North Carolina is a pretty boggy place in general. It is the home of a large part of the Great Dismal Swamp, 40 miles long and 10 miles wide. Of the state's 31.2 million acres of land surface, fully 11.1 million acres were originally wetlands. About 5 million acres of these remain.

One of the largest wetlands areas is the coast of Louisiana, which has 2.9 million acres of coastal wetlands—about 40 percent of all coastal marshes in the United States. These are constantly changing from the natural action of the ocean. Alarmist estimates of the rate of wetlands loss in the United States usually forget to mention that much of the loss expected over the next few years is due to this natural action in Louisiana and that the same forces will result in the creation of wetlands somewhere else.

The United States is dotted as well with minor patches unconnected to any surface water. According to U.S. Army Corps of Engineers figures, the mainland United States, excluding Alaska, has 8.3 million individual isolated wetlands of less than a half-acre each.[8] Many of these are in the prairie pothole region of the Dakotas, Iowa, Minnesota, Montana, and Canada. These are isolated depressions that fill with water from snowmelt, spring rains, or groundwater seepage. They are often ephemeral, disappearing as the wet season ends. The Dakotas alone have 2.3 million of them.[9]

Wetlands have always been a concern of the law. If you fill in your land so water drains off it or cannot flood it in the first place, then the water must go somewhere else, and that somewhere else may belong to me. The legal issues have been around for centuries: Who bears the cost if you fill in your property and flood mine, or clear your land and expose mine to uncontrolled runoff following rainstorms, or dig a ditch that carries water off your place and dumps it onto mine? The usual answer of the common law is that changing the natural state of land in a way that diverts water to a neighbor makes you liable for the harm.

Applying this basic rule is not simple. Water being water, it usually goes where it wants, and where this is is not always obvious. If you fill in your land on the headwaters of the creek, the impact may show up miles downstream. Reclaiming land for agriculture in Iowa can cause floods in Mississippi. Cumulative effects are also important. Filling in one lot may not matter, while filling in a hundred is noticeable and filling in a thousand is a major act. Domino effects matter. If upstream land is filled in, dry downstream property might flood. Its owners then put in levees or fill, which shifts the flooding farther downstream, and so on. The area has generated a lot of legal work over the years.

Starting in the 1960s, attitudes toward wetlands began to change under the impact of the environmental movement. The perception grew that they possess a variety of values. Wetlands are home to animals and plants of many types. Some of these need the aquatic environment; some simply flourish in areas inhospitable to human use. Wetlands protection is closely tied in with preservation of endangered species, and within the government the administrators of the two programs are hand in glove. The first thing you see on exiting the elevator at the offices of the section of the Fish and Wildlife Service responsible for Habitat Conservation Plans is a giant map showing the wetlands of the United States. FWS is the agency responsible for the National Wetlands Inventory, a project to map the wetlands of the United States with infrared aerial photography. It is important to know that the conflict over wetlands is largely the conflict over endangered species transferred to a new arena.

Wetlands have environmental values beyond endangered species habitat. Tidal wetlands provide sustenance for important commercial types of marine life. River valley wetlands provide reservoir space that tamps down the effects of flooding. Wetlands serve as sinks for pollution, cleaning metals, pesticides, and other pollutants out of the water before it ultimately flows downstream. Scientists are on the trail of genetically engineering plants that will absorb metals even more efficiently than natural ones. In a recent lab test, 1 acre of engineered mustard plants cleaned up mercury at a rate of over a ton per week.[10]

Wetlands were brought under federal regulation by aggressive interpretation of a law enacted for other purposes. This bastardized origin is crucial to understanding the problems created by the program. As often happens in such cases, twisting a law to serve novel ends has created a Frankenstein monster that smashes anyone unlucky enough to come within its reach, a monster too strong to resist and too brainless to reason with. So here is the story.

Since time out of mind, governments have kept navigable waters free of obstructions. This maintenance of the transportation net is a classic government function within the Lockean tradition. As a part of its power to control interstate commerce, Congress regulated the navigable waters of the United States. Their improvement is and has always been a major function of the Army Corps of Engineers, and as a natural corollary of this power, the Corps is charged with preventing other people from obstructing them. The Rivers and Harbors Act of 1890 tells the Corps to regulate dredging and filling operations, and in 1899 Congress added a ban on private deposit of refuse into navigable waters unless the Corps issues a permit. Standard canons of property law allow the owner of land on a body of navigable water to build a dock, but this does not mean you can extend it out into the channel.

In 1972, Congress seized on this ancient concept of navigable waters as the basis for its assault on industrial water pollution. As long ago established by the Supreme Court, the "commerce" that Congress can regulate under the commerce clause of the Constitution is not limited to commercial transactions. It includes intercourse of all kinds. The Mann Act, for example, criminalizes the transportation of a woman across state lines for immoral purposes. No one doubts the authority of Congress to control pollution of water that flows among the states. Still, if Congress wants to attack *contamination* of water, it is a bit anomalous to cast the jurisdiction in terms of *navigation*. Whether water is navigable is only slightly related to any theory underlying action against pollution. In fact, to get at pollution, control must extend way upstream to cover not just waters that are themselves navigable but waters that affect waters that are navigable. Storm sewers in Arlington, Virginia, bear signs saying "Chesapeake Bay Drainage" to remind residents not to throw their crud down there. Few people quarrel with the breadth of the federal government's assertion of control over water pollution, though, because if the river is to be clean all sources must be controlled.

The mechanisms of the Clean Water Act that carry out this control over contaminants are incredibly complicated, but the basic structure of the law is simple. It is illegal to discharge a pollutant unless you have gotten a permit from the government okaying the discharge. The definitions in the law explain what is meant by "discharge" and what is meant by "pollutant." To discharge is to put a pollutant into navigable waters. "Pollutant" is defined as "dredged spoil, solid waste, incinerator residue, sewage, garbage, sewage sludge, munitions, chemical wastes, biological materials, radioactive materials, heat, wrecked or discarded equipment, rock, sand, cellar dirt and industrial, municipal, and agricultural waste." (*Cellar dirt?* Why did it ever occur to Congress to make cellar dirt equal to these other categories? There must be a story here somewhere.)

Congress did not have preservation of wetlands in mind when it wrote this definition. Rather, it combined the old Corps authority to protect navigation with the new Environmental Protection Agency (EPA) authority to prevent contamination. It bundled them both under the concept of pollution. Unfortunately, the two goals do not fit together very well. Protecting navigation requires power to keep people from dumping rocks and dirt into the channels, but it does not require control over every tributary. Controlling pollution is only slightly concerned with rocks and dirt, but it must extend far upstream. By bundling these two different purposes into one definition, the law wound up saying you need a permit to put a rock into a creek. (Yes, children skipping stones in the stream behind your house are violating the law.)

A BAR ASSOCIATION MEETING, MID-1970s

Senator Edwin Muskie of Maine, a prime architect of the Clean Water Act, is speaking. To illustrate the toughness of the law, he holds up a glass of scotch and water. He says that if you mix the drink by pouring

the water into the glass first and then adding the scotch, you have contaminated the water and thus violated the law.

Muskie was right. You probably have broken the law if you add
the scotch to the water rather than the water to the scotch—which
means that Congress did not bother to think through the lines between what it really wanted to control and what it did not. It said, in
effect, "Everything is forbidden, and we'll let the agencies decide
when we really mean it." It enacted a mess and delegated to agencies
the job of sorting it out, a practice that has become a habit on Capitol
Hill.

The Muskie story is also troubling because it suggests perfect, disinterested administration of the law. It would be absurd for an agency to
attack scotch drinkers. But as the song says, "It Ain't Necessarily So."
If the Army Engineers or EPA is taken over by the bourbon interests,
they may well go after the scotch drinkers. If the program is captured
by the modern equivalent of Carry Nation, the nineteenth-century
temperance champion who broke up saloons with a hatchet, then all
the distillers are in trouble. Unlimited authority, once created, lies
around like a sharpened axe, ready for any hand that grasps it. This
hand can use it for any purposes, including some not in accord with
what most congressmen had in mind or with the public understanding
at the time.

So it was with the Clean Water Act. The breadth of the definitions
did not really matter in 1972. The Corps knew its job (protect navigation), and EPA knew its job (prevent contamination), and nobody worried about putting rocks in creeks or filling in a swamp or two.
Nonetheless, the axe was honed, and eventually the environmental
movement and activist judges swung it.

In the division of authority between the Corps and EPA, EPA's main
function is to control releases of industrial, commercial, and agricultural wastes from specific "point sources." Since all discharges into
water are forbidden unless specifically authorized, this involves an immense and comprehensive effort of setting standards, writing permits,
and enforcement, called the National Pollution Discharge Elimination
System (NPDES).

For the Corps to carry out its role of fostering and protecting navigation, it needs to control dredging spoil, dirt, and fill, but it does not

need to reach very far upstream. You can argue that building a house in Harpers Ferry, West Virginia, can release dirt into the Potomac River, which will flow 100 miles downstream and silt up the channel below Washington, D.C., but the argument is pretty strained. No one would claim with a straight face that the Corps should have a veto on all home construction because otherwise a channel hundreds of miles away might silt up infinitesimally. (Note that I said, "with a straight face." Government lawyers routinely make such claims, but this does not count because they had their smile muscles removed during the first year of law school.)

The mechanism of the Corps program is set up by section 404 of the 1972 law, which looks on its face like a routine bit of government business. It says the Corps can issue permits for the disposal of dredge and fill materials into navigable waters. The Environmental Protection Agency and the Corps are to develop guidelines on acceptable sites. EPA alone can ban the use of any site where disposal would have an adverse impact on wildlife, recreation, water supplies, or other uses of the water. True to the principle that Congress loves farmers, the law exempts routine farm activities from 404.

In the mid-1970s, the Corps reacted to section 404 quite sensibly. It defined the scope of its program to require permits only when disposal would be into waters traditionally recognized as navigable—those subject to the tide, those used for transportation, and natural river meanders. Excluded were most wetlands and shallow or isolated waters where fill would not affect boats.

Environmentalists sued, arguing that Congress intended to assert its full constitutional authority and to control not just the navigable parts of waters but all waters that might affect these navigable parts, such as streams and wetlands. The point is true enough for chemical contaminants. It is not true for dredging and filling, but Congress did not distinguish among the different types of pollutants. It lumped dirt together with chemicals. The courts upheld the environmentalists, and the Corps eventually bowed. It redefined its jurisdiction to include all streams, mud flats, prairie potholes, or ponds "the use, degradation or destruction of which could affect interstate commerce." This is an unlimited extension. For a time, the regulators were troubled by isolated ponds that lack any connection with commerce, but they finally hit on the solution. In 1985, the general counsel of EPA signed off on a guidance letter known as the "glancing goose" letter. It says that a migrating bird flying across state lines might see one of these isolated wetlands and decide to stop at it. Therefore they affect interstate commerce. Besides, hunters cross state lines to shoot the migrating birds.

The new, broad definitions were upheld by the Supreme Court in 1985. There is still a lingering doubt about control of the wholly unconnected ponds, but the courts of appeal for the most part have upheld federal control of even these, and the Supreme Court refused to take up the issue. As of now, the situation is that putting a piece of dirt into a wetland, any wetland, without a federal permit violates the law. It is, like most other environmental laws, a criminal statute.

PENNSYLVANIA, TEXAS, AND FLORIDA, 1988–1994

John Pozgai and Ocie Mills have something in common with William Ellen, whose story was told in Chapter 2: they go to jail for violating wetlands regulations. Pozgai gets thirty-three months, the longest term ever given an environmental offender of any sort up to that time. Marinus Van Leuzen avoids joining them only by agreeing to a modern version of the public pillory: he pays to erect a billboard apologizing for his offense and spends thousands of dollars to create a mudhole around his house.

Surely, you think, these people must be doing something dreadful—perhaps filling in the entire Everglades. Actually Pozgai cleans up a vacant lot that is full of old tires and trash. Then he puts fill on it to make it usable. Mills bought his lot from a relative, who had been told by the Corps of Engineers that it was a wetland. It does not look like a wetland to Mills, so he gets Florida's Department of Environmental Services (DES) to do a wetlands survey. The state team puts up flags dividing upland from wetland, and Mills begins to put sand on the upland side. The Corps tells him to stop. Its letter gives a telephone number to call if he has questions, and the number is that of the Florida DES, so Mills calls it and DES says there is no problem. Mills writes the Corps about this, waits a year and hears nothing, assumes the problem is solved, and begins to put more sand on the upland side of the flags. The Corps again tells him to stop, in a letter that gives him a number to call if he has questions, and the number is, again, that of the Florida DES. Mills writes back to the Corps. In the words of his lawyer, he "suggest[s] to the Corps that it get its act together and get a more competent authority such as a court to straighten the matter out." He waits six months, hears nothing, puts more sand on his lot, and is sent to jail for twenty-one months.[11]

Marinus Van Leuzen is the most hardened entry in this rogues' gallery. He owns a bait camp on a 0.4-acre plot in the middle of a flat, ugly hunk of Texas along Route 87 near Galveston Bay, surrounded by developed land containing commercial structures. No question that it is a wetland, though; the "before" pictures show the shack housing the bait store smack dab next to a large mud puddle. He starts to build a house without bothering to find out the environmental requirements. When he is almost done, the Corps of Engineers comes and tells him that he needs permits, so he stops work and goes to find out what is what. Informed that six different agencies would have to approve, he decides this is ridiculous. Van Leuzen, who is seventy-four and fled Holland ahead of the Nazi invasion during World War II to serve with the U.S. forces, is known to his neighbors as a "hard-headed Dutchman." So he finishes his house. To nail him, four employees of the Corps spend a full day staked out across the street with a video camera. He is ordered to erect a 10-foot by 20-foot billboard with a message of apology, to pay $350 per month fine for twelve years, to dig a 2-foot deep moat around his house and create a wetland managed by professional biologists at his own expense, and, after eight years, to remove the house.[12]

These cases, like Ellen's, are causes célèbres among property rights defense groups. The rejoinder by the U.S. Army Corps of Engineers is that in each case, the victim was told that what he was doing was illegal, and he did it anyway. None can claim unfair surprise. This is the truth, but it is not the whole truth. In each case, the requirement violated is a creation of an agency stretching its authority a very long way, not a clear statutory command of the Congress. In each instance, the government takes an extreme position, and the property owner is incredulous, finding it impossible to believe that the Corps is correctly stating the law. In each, he has the choice of acquiescence or defiance and chooses defiance. Pozgai, Mills, and Van Leuzen, along with Ellen, are not really punished for harming wetlands. They are punished for offending the *amour propre* of the U.S. government.

Understanding wetlands issues requires an inquiry into two big questions. First, just what is a wetland anyway? You may think you know, but you do not, as you are about to learn. For example, you, being rationally ignorant, probably think that a wetland must be wet. How silly of you. The second question is, How do you get a permit?

First things first. What is a wetland? "Wetlands" is not a clear concept. Most land sits on top of groundwater, located anywhere from a few inches to hundreds of feet down. Most land exhibits some degree of dampness after rain, with the rate at which it dries out dependent on soil characteristics, total rainfall, groundwater depth, and topography. Some land is flooded by rising waters, on a schedule that can range from annually to every century. Water that transforms a parcel into a wetland need not come from the surface or from precipitation. It can bubble up from springs or arise from a shallow groundwater table. There is no sharp dividing line. Instead, there is a series of gradations from surface water at one extreme to dry land at the other. Classifiers of the hardwood forest wetlands of the southeastern United States recognize five zones between "open water" at one end and "uplands" at the other. Prairie potholes are divided into seven different classes, ranging from permanent fens to occasional puddles.[13]

In short, defining a legally controlled wetland is a judgment call. In the words of a Corps official, "for regulatory purposes, a wetland is whatever we decide it is."[14] It is also a moving target. Between 1986 and 1994, the basic definition of wetlands used by the government changed at least six times. To explore this question fully would require an explanation of the *Corps of Engineers Manual* of 1987, the 1989 revision, the 1991 compromise, the congressional action blocking the use of the 1989 revision and mandating a return to the 1987 version, the National Research Council Report of 1995, and several memoranda of agreement between the Corps and EPA. You might even want to start with the Swamp Act of 1850 and work your way forward through the 1956 Fish and Wildlife Service definition, the 1979 Cowardin Report, and other primary sources. You will need to examine Circular 39, which contains the definition of wetlands used by the Department of Agriculture and the definition used for coastal wetlands by the National Oceanographic and Atmospheric Administration of the Department of Commerce in its Coastal Change Analysis Program.

For a short-cut, call the Environmental Law Institute in Washington, D.C., and buy its *Wetlands Deskbook*, published in 1993. This lays out the field: 661 pages of fine print of explanation, analysis, statutes, regulations, guidance letters, interagency agreements, and other documents.

Then get its 1996 articles updating the explanations in the 1993 work. (Things change fast.) Add a few *Federal Register* notices published in the last three years, the 1995 National Research Council report on wetlands, some congressional hearings, and you will be ready to go.

If you are a landowner thinking of doing something with your property, you better make this investment or hire someone who has already made it. This will cost you a thousand dollars a day on up. If part of your property is wetland, then delineating its boundaries so that you can tell where your property ends and that belonging to the Corps of Engineers (for all practical purposes) begins will take a few days and several thousand dollars. You can ask the Corps to make the determination; they may or may not do it. This is low priority for them, so it is easier to put the burden on you. Standard practice is to tell you that you have wetlands and that it is up to you to hire a consultant to delineate their extent. The Corps does not necessarily accept your expert's conclusions, of course. It can disagree, and then you can pay more thousands while the experts argue—or you can build and then go to jail if your expert fails to convince the Corps.

For regulatory purposes, though, a line must be drawn. On one side is regulated wetland; on the other is not. A useful way of describing the boundary is to distinguish between wetlands and wet lands. The Corps, since it saw the light of the wetlands faith in the 1970s, and EPA consistently push the line toward the dry land end of the continuum, bringing in what most people would call "wet land" or perhaps even "formerly or occasionally wet land" rather than real "wetlands." In 1995, Bernard Goode, ex-chief of the Corps' Regulatory Branch and current wetlands consultant, told Congress: "Twenty years ago the government was generally delineating swamps, marshes, and bogs rather than depressions in corn fields, hundred-year floodplains, pastures and meadows, dry woods, weed-covered vacant lots, moist tundra, winter-wet grassland depressions, pine-palmetto flatlands, and dry desert washes."

NEVADA, 1996

The Double Diamond Ranch is 2,425 acres. As ranchland, it is not worth much. The area averages 7 inches of rainfall per year and depends on irrigation. However, Double Diamond is very close to Reno, which is expanding rapidly. The land is zoned for commercial and residential uses and sold for $20 million in late 1988. Current estimates put the value at $50 million or more. In 1988 a Corps of Engineers report identifies twenty-eight acres around a natural spring, and nothing else, as wetland, a conclusion that contributed mightily to the present owners' decision to buy. In 1991, pushed by forces opposed to development, the Corps re-assesses the property and decides that 281 of the most valuable acres are wetlands. The basis of the decision is that wetlands-type plants grow there. This is true, but only because of the irrigation. The wetness is artificial. If the owners stopped buying irrigation water, the land would return to its natural state: bone dry. So the owners are now required to keep buy-ing water to maintain as wetlands the property that they are forbidden to use because it is supposedly an ecologically invaluable wetland.[15]

This theme is common. The Defenders of Property Rights or the Na-tional Association of Home Builders or some other group will be glad to send you photographs of properties classified as wetlands that look as if they were taken in the middle of the Gobi Desert. William Ellen had pictures of workers wearing masks to protect them from dust stirred up by their work on "wetlands." To identify a wetland, according to the National Academy of Sciences, requires a "knowledge of plant taxon-omy, botany, soil science, surface water hydrology, general ecology, wetland (or aquatic) ecology, sampling methodology, . . . plant mor-phology, . . . ground water hydrology, geology, plant physiology, and per-haps other disciplines."[16] As Bernard Goode says, it sounds as if they are building a space station.

The government has not prepared maps showing where the wetlands are because the effort would take 14 million maps and cost $500 mil-lion.[17] The costs that the lack of maps imposes on landowners do not seem to be a matter of governmental concern. The Fish and Wildlife Service is engaged in a congressionally-mandated National Wetlands Inventory mapping project. Relying on aerial infrared photography to identify wetlands, so far it has produced 38,000 maps covering 75 per-cent of the United States at a scale of 1:24,000.[18] These maps cannot be relied on for regulatory purposes. They are not binding on the gov-ernment, and the congruence between them and on-site surveys is far from perfect. Besides, it all depends on which agency's definition is used. There is substantial disagreement when these definitions are tested on wetlands, so no single map would do. Also, the maps may show things that are not wetlands. Anything damp looks like wetlands to an overflying camera. A landowner was cited for violating wetlands law when he removed a watering trough.

Just in case you think you now understand this stuff, let me introduce a few more complications. The comment that the Corps has authority over wetlands and EPA authority over contaminants is the truth but not quite the whole truth. The environmentalists have always preferred control by EPA to control by the Corps. After years of interagency cat fights, responsibility was divided: the Corps makes most individual determinations about the presence of wetlands, but EPA can take over any specific case if it chooses. In administering the program, EPA has power to issue binding guidance about interpretation and enforcement. The Corps makes the decisions about granting or denying individual permits, based on EPA guidance. EPA can summarily veto any individual decision by the Corps to grant a permit. Denial by the Corps is final.

This only begins the roster of interested agencies. The Fish and Wildlife Service is particularly important. Remember that a federal permit cannot be granted for activity on private land if it would modify habitat of an endangered or threatened species. Wetlands permits are where it bites. FWS can also veto use of wetlands on general wildlife protection grounds, even if the species involved are not endangered. Wetlands consultants say more permits are refused because of wildlife issues than because of water quality concerns.

The roster is not done. Because wetlands on agricultural land are under special rules, the Department of Agriculture, especially its Soil Conservation Service and its Agricultural Stabilization and Conservation Service, comes into the act. The Forest Service, also part of Agriculture, administers the national forests. Other agencies are involved too. The Department of Commerce administers programs relating to the coastal zone and to marine fisheries. These intertwine with wetlands. The Department of the Interior controls national parks (the National Park Service), grazing lands (the Bureau of Land Management), and wildlife refuges (Fish and Wildlife Service). The United States has 470 wildlife refuges with 90 million acres, about 32 million of them wetlands.[19] All of these agencies have a voice in determining what is a wetland. Some of them, like FWS in the course of protecting habitat, have a strong interest in expanding the definition as far as possible.

In addition, almost every state now has its own wetlands program.

This may or may not use the same definitions or even the same maps as the various federal agencies. It is perfectly possible for a landowner to deal with three or four different bureaucratic entities, each with a different definition and information base, over the question, "Is this a wetland?" Since the Corps makes over thirty-five thousand jurisdictional determinations per year, and any or all of these other agencies can be involved in any or all of them, the possibilities for confusion and delay are monumental.

The wetlands protection program is causing problems and anger even when it is applied to property that is absolutely sodden—property clearly wetland by any definition. The confusion over the definition, and the agencies' aggressive efforts to extend it to all wet land, is an independent cause of outrage among landowners. These efforts have been highly successful too. In 1995, reforms were proposed to require that nothing be classified as a wetland unless it was truly wet: the standard would be that the land be wet for twenty-one consecutive days at some time during the growing season. Loud protests were lodged on the ground that this would remove protection from 60 to 80 percent of the lands covered under the present definition. Thus it appears that up to 80 percent of protected wetlands would not be perceived as such by the ordinary person.

Furthermore, you act at your peril when you deal with these wetlands. If you dump a shovelful of dirt onto wetland, you have committed a criminal offense, even if there are no obvious indicia that it is wetland. Your government would not prosecute you for this, of course; as long as you undo whatever you did, no matter what the expense, and tug the forelock, you will stay out of jail. You might, as the price of staying at liberty, be forced to get an "after-the-fact" permit. This would allow you to do what you did, but first you would have to undo it, removing whatever fill you put in. Then you might be allowed to put the fill back in. Ransom, in the form of creating wetlands somewhere nearby, would also be required. If you say, "What are you people? Nuts?" then you have a problem. You, too, could wind up in jail.

By now you should be convinced to take all this seriously. You want to know how to get permission to put your shovelful of dirt onto wetland. It is not easy. In 1988, George Bush made a campaign promise that "no net loss of wetlands" should occur; ever since, this has been the official policy of the U.S. government. This puts pressure on the permitting agencies not to grant them. Nonetheless, there are three routes, and they are so different that they amount to distinct systems.

The first way is to be a farmer. Because Congress loves farmers, it exempted from permit requirements a long list of activities necessary for routine agriculture. No permit is needed if these affect wetlands a little bit. However, because Congress does not love farmers to excess, and EPA, the Corps, and the courts love them not at all, these exemptions are limited. They allow incidental impact on wetlands but do not exempt anything that would bring new wetlands under the plow. Also, EPA is zealous to recapture wetlands that were converted to cropland over the past two hundred years. Several lawsuits have dealt with a situation in which a drainage ditch was dug around 1900 but subsequently silted up and let water spread over the land. Farmers now want to clean out the ditch. Is this normal maintenance, and thus exempt? Or is it a new ditch, and thus a criminal activity? The government usually claims that the ditch was "abandoned," a legal term of art, and cannot be refurbished. The level of complexity here is incredible. If the farmer stops farming the converted wetland, it reverts to wetland status and cannot again be farmed—unless it was left fallow as part of normal crop rotation, in which case it is still cropland and can be farmed. But what if it was converted from wetland to upland, and then back to wetland crops? Can it be converted back to upland crops? Or is it now irrevocably wetland? What if it was originally upland but was artificially made into wetland? Can it go back to upland? On each of these points, you will find rules, guidance documents, and lawsuits. The whole business sounds funny from a distance, like something out of a particularly awful Soviet government central planning manual, but the stakes are hundreds of thousands of dollars and criminal convictions. The players see no humor in it. Remember the story of Tom Rule, the Wyoming rancher who has to stand by while a swamp created by irrigation engulfs his ranch.

Agriculture is made even more complex because the government used to pay farmers to destroy wetlands. In 1985, a program called Swampbuster, which despite its name is designed to preserve rather than bust swamps, removed the incentive for farmers to destroy wetlands by eliminating subsidies for crops grown there. (This applies if the wetlands were converted to cropland after 1985. If the conversion occurred earlier, subsidy programs still apply. A whole legal and consulting specialty now revolves around the definition of "prior converted wet-land.") Another Agriculture program is the Wetlands Reserve, which pays farmers for making or preserving wetlands.

Swampbuster and Wetlands Reserve are interpreted by the Department of Agriculture. The exemptions from section 404 are determined by the Army Corps of Engineers and EPA, not by Agriculture. All agencies rely on the same basic factors to define a wetland, but Agriculture uses a different field manual from the Corps and EPA, so the results sometimes vary. It is possible for the Agriculture to decide that farmland is not wetland, and thus that crops grown on it are eligible for agricultural subsidies, while the Corps and EPA rule that the same land is wetland, and the farmer who tills it should have his subsidy check sent to him at the jail.

The second way to get permission to use a wetland is to get a Nationwide Permit. For many activities with minor impact, all you do is tell the Corps, perhaps delineate the wetland affected (which will cost you some dollars for consultants), and as long as the Corps, EPA, Fish and Wildlife Service, and perhaps a few other agencies do not object within a set period of time, go ahead. Some of these permits do not even require notification. Altogether the program covers thirty-seven different activities.

In the five years between 1988 and 1993, almost 92,000 activities were conducted under nationwide permits. Various Corps regions have also set up general permit programs, and these issued another 14,000 permits. An unknown number of actions are taken that do not require notification to the Corps. The Corps says only about 5 percent of the requests for permits are denied. This is not a reliable index, because the Corps encourages "preapplication" consultation, and no one knows how many applications are aborted at this informal stage.

Comments on the wetlands program sometimes say that the Nationwide Permits allow you to fill in wetlands. This is not really so. No permit is available for activity in any part of the Wild and Scenic River system. None can be used if the activity would adversely modify habitat of an endangered species or affect historic properties. Discharges into wetlands must be minimized to the maximum extent practicable. The Corps district engineer can veto any permit if it will result in "more than minimal" adverse environmental effects or if it would "be contrary to the public interest."[20] In sum, the district engineer is God. Until

1995, the Corps did not even have a procedure by which a landowner could appeal a district engineer's decision within the organization itself. If you felt aggrieved, see you in court, where your chances of overturning an agency decision are exceedingly dismal. Courts are very deferential.

The rules also require that any impact on wetlands be minimized, insofar as this can be done consistent with the project. In other words, the Nationwide Permit program is designed to allow some minimal impact on wetlands to occur in the course of carrying out some other activity, such as maintaining existing structures, continuing already-authorized oil and gas and mining activities, building small boat ramps, reconfiguring existing marinas, and similar activities.

The most important of the Nationwide Permits may be Number 26, which allows a landowner to have an impact on up to 10 acres of isolated wetlands or headwaters, which are upstream of the point where the flow of water averages 5 cubic yards per second. Until 1992, landowners could split their property and then take advantage of Number 26 for each part. No more, and the "no more" is retroactive to subdivisions erected after 1984. Another commonly used permit applies to discharge of less than 25 cubic yards that causes a loss of no more than 0.1 acre of wetlands.

A permit created in 1995 allows construction of a single-family residence on less than 0.5 acre. It is designed to mollify an angry, and vocal, constituency of owners of homesites made unusable by wetlands regulations. This permit is much trumpeted by the administration, but it is actually laden with restrictions. It applies only to nontidal areas; no oceanfront homes allowed. Advance notice must be given to the Corps, so the action can still be vetoed by the Corps or any other agency. The change applies only to lots in existence as of 1991. This limits it to people who already own their homesite, or to someone who purchases an existing site, which makes it a tool for the rich. The price of grandfathered-in homesites will go up because no more can be created. Corporations and other business entities cannot use it, which means no builders. This increases the tilt toward the rich because only someone who can afford to custom-build a house will be able to take advantage of the permit. Someone who is not rich and who wants a waterfront home needs the services of a builder. The builder buys land at wholesale and puts in the infrastructure of roads, sewers, and utilities, getting economics of scale by building multiple units. By excluding builders from the benefits of this NWP, the government excludes anyone who cannot afford to buy a grandfathered-in site, hire an architect, install infrastructure, and pay a contractor to erect a one-off house in a remote area. The reform is more sound bite than substance and is, in effect, a land grab by the rich.

The last way to get permission to put your shovelful of dirt into a wetland is by an individual permit. This is sought when no Nationwide Permit covers the activity. The numbers that follow, like the earlier numbers on general permits, were put together in a 1994 report by Bernard Goode and Washington lawyer Virginia Albrecht.[21] Since the information had to be extracted from the Corps district by district at considerable cost in time and effort, the product is unique, and everyone who toils in this field is indebted to the authors.

For individual permit applications, the Corps again encourages advance consultation, which means that an unknown number of anticipated applications never materialize. From 1988 to 1993, 26,761 individual applications were submitted. Of these, 10,499 were granted, 1,312 denied, and 14,950 withdrawn. Over half of the withdrawals are really denials; the application is withdrawn by the Corps because of 'insufficient information" or "inadequate response to objection." In another third of the withdrawals, the application is pulled back under some type of duress, such as an enforcement action or a decision to move the project out of the wetland. Only about 12 percent of the withdrawals are for reasons that would allow the project to go forward, such as eligibility for one of the Nationwide Permits. So the best surmise is that 88 percent of withdrawals are denials in disguise.

The application process takes a long time: 256 days for permits eventually issued, 483 days for denial with prejudice (which means "don't bother us with this turkey again"), 133 days for denial without prejudice, and 390 days for a withdrawal. These times do not include the time an applicant needs to gather information and put the paper together, which can be considerable. Albrecht and Goode reckon it at about seven months. Nor does the time clock start until the Corps agrees that the application contains sufficient information. Public notice of an application is required, and any member of the public can request a hearing. There is no way to make the process speedy, and the more complex or controversial the project is the more likely it is that the neighbors or other federal agencies will weigh in, and the smaller the chance is of success for the applicant.

The review process is strongly biased against approving any project that is not trivial. It starts with the premise that no discharge should be allowed unless there is no practicable alternative. The rules are silent on what constitutes an adequate demonstration of the lack of an alternative, except to say that it takes into account cost, existing technology, and logistics in the light of overall project purposes. If the project is not absolutely dependent on proximity to water, then such alternatives are presumed to exist "unless clearly demonstrated otherwise." The fact that you do not own any other land does not constitute the necessary demonstration. You could buy some.[22] In no event will any discharge be allowed to cause significant degradation of the wetland or water, regardless of the availability of alternatives. The interpretation of "significant degradation" seems to be pretty much up to the discretion of the Corps.

So how do you get a project approved under an individual permit? Mostly, you keep it small. Albrecht and Goode extracted from the Corps a pile of about 400 individual decision files for 1992 that contained enough data to be useful for analysis. Of these, 303 had information on acreage affected. Only 3 applicants even tried to affect more than 100 acres, and only 50 dealt with more than 10 acres. Of the three big projects, two were by other government units, and succeeded. The other was private, and failed. Seventy-four involved less than a quarter-acre. The smallest came from a construction company wanting to fill in 25 square feet of wetlands created by a leaking pipe in downtown Boise, Idaho. It was withdrawn after 450 days.[23]

Getting a permit also requires payment of ransom. Suppose you can assure the government that you have considered less damaging alternatives, and none meets the needs of the project. You have minimized the impact of your work on wetlands. To get your permit you must offer to pay for creating or restoring some other wetlands. Applicants generally agree to finance about 2 acres of mitigation for every 1 acre of wetlands affected by their activity. As an alternative, you might contribute to a conservation group so that it can engage in mitigation. In notifying the Corps of your intention to act under one of the Nationwide Permits, you can also attach mitigation offers if you want to try to sway the district engineer's view of the "public interest."

Mitigation is not cheap. To restore one-time wetland in the Midwest might cost you $10,000 per acre, but in most of the places the bill is higher. In the East, the cost can be $50,000 to $100,000 or even more per acre. One knowledgeable observer suggests a rule of thumb of $60,000 per acre plus land acquisition costs. Also, not just any old wetland will count toward mitigation. It has to be in the same water system, and maybe in the same subsystem. You cannot get approval for filling in wetlands near the Potomac by creating new ones on the Ohio.

Government numbers on permits paint a rosier picture than do Goode and Albrecht. This is sound-bite politics again. The government lumps together applications for individual permits and applications for Nationwide Permits. It does not analyze the withdrawals or classify them as denials. Its numbers lack detail on individual cases. Perhaps most important, they ignore the effects of the preapplication consultation process, which surely culls most applications that would be denied if formally submitted. Considering the expense in preparing an application, no sensible person will file after being told he has no chance.

Anger over the program is accentuated by some procedural quirks. If the Corps decides your property is not a wetland, your neighbor, who enjoys gazing out over your undeveloped acres, can immediately go to court to get a review of this decision. If the Corps decides that it *is* a wetland, you *cannot* go to court. You have two choices. The first is to build anyway, wait until you are prosecuted criminally or assessed a civil penalty of up to $25,000 per day, and appeal the jurisdictional determination then. Most people find this gamble unattractive, especially because it is hard to prove that something is *not* a wetland, given the fuzziness of the definition. The second option is to request a permit, even if your chances of approval are zero. You must hire a wetlands delineator, prepare a plan, and in general go to a lot of expense. Once the permit is denied, you can sue, saying it is not a wetland. Of course, it is possible for a permit never to be denied. More information can always be requested. Or the application can be denied without prejudice, which means that maybe something else would be approved, and you still cannot sue because the agency has not made a final decision. You can get jerked around for a long time. If your investment in the land is substantial, the carrying costs go through the roof.

At this point, any contemporary knowledge worker who worships nature (from the windows of a high-rise condo while working on a computer, of course), should be feeling a little uncomfortable. Surely there is one redeeming feature. The program is saving wetlands, isn't it? Even if it is inefficient and unfair, it must at least be accomplishing this purpose.

This turns out to be a bit of a mystery. Puzzling out basic trends in wetlands is hard. The administrator of EPA said in 1993 that the nation is losing wetlands at the rate of 300,000 acres per year, and this figure is frequently repeated in sound bites. Her motive was to show that even more stringent measures are necessary, though you could also interpret this as meaning that the program is not very effective. However, worrying over what spin to put on the statement is unnecessary. The number is nonsense. Jonathan Tolman is the wetlands expert for the Competitive Enterprise Institute in Washington, a free-market think tank. He points out that Browner's figure was based on aerial photographs taken between 1974 and 1983, when the government was providing maximum incentives for filling in wetlands.[24] Later analyses indicate the rate of conversion of wetlands to other purposes has declined sharply and probably stands at about 100,000 acres per year.

Even this figure is deceptive. It includes conversions *from* wetlands but not conversions *to* wetlands. Tolman notes that several private-government cooperatives are in the business of creating wetlands. In 1994, Partners for Wildlife made 32,000 acres, the North American Waterfowl Management Plan 50,000, the Wetland Reserve Program 75,000, and various mitigation efforts conducted to obtain permits created 15,000 acres—a total of 172,000 acres of new wetlands. In 1995, these same groups created 254,000 acres. Based on these numbers alone, in 1994 the nation gained at least 70,000 acres of wetlands rather than losing 290,000. The true net gain is even larger because this estimate does not include the 33,120 acres restored by the Fish and Wildlife Service in the National Wildlife Refuge System. Nor does it include the tens of thousands of acres of wetland created by private organizations, such as the Nature Conservancy, the Conservation Fund, and the Trust for Public Land.[25]

A final puzzle remains. How are 100,000 acres a year converted for development, given the stringency of the permitting requirements? And if conversions are still possible, why are landowners complaining so bitterly? Tolman's view is that the decline in the rate of wetlands acreage lost is primarily a decline in agricultural conversion, triggered by long-term trends in productivity and the decline in the subsidies that promoted conversion.

This argument has a lot of force. In 1992, the nation had 822 million acres in farmland, worth an average of $849 per acre (that includes the buildings as well).[26] Converting wetlands has to be cheap, or subsidized, to be worthwhile. It does not pay an individual to spend large sums to bring marginal land into production. Sometimes the subsidies are indirect, of course. Massive flood control projects removed hundreds of thousands of floodplain acres from the rolls of wetlands. Subsidized insurance encouraged building in floodplains and tidal areas that would not have been economically feasible in a free-market regime. Today's landowners are being asked to bear the brunt of the no-net-loss-of-wetlands policy that was created in reponse to misguided federal actions. The people who profited from these actions bear none of the burden.

Tolman points out that conversion for development remains fairly constant at about 90,000 acres per year despite the hurdles. He attributes this to the fact that there is enough slack in the 404 system to allow wetlands to leak out. Nationwide Permits allow minor conversions that individually do not amount to much but nevertheless add up. In addition, the developers' bag of tricks is not empty. It is possible to ditch an upland in a way that drains a wetland: dig it deep and let the water flow downhill. It is also possible to divert a creek only a little but enough to change its flood pattern away from a large tract of land, which then ceases to be wetland.

Also, a good application writer can do a lot for a developer. For legal reasons, the Corps is reluctant to deprive a developer of all use of its property. It wants to let the property be used in some fashion so that the owner cannot argue that it has been "taken" as a matter of constitutional law. This need to avoid total takings gives developers scope for ingenuity. For example, the rules say a developer must demonstrate a lack of any practicable alternatives that would meet the project objectives and at the same time avoid any effect on wetlands. This places a premium on stating the project purposes in a way that narrows available geographic options. A developer wanting to fill 97 acres of New Jersey wetlands stated its objective as the construction of a large-scale (3,301 units) housing project within a particular area designated by the local planning commission. The Corps bridled at this and bounced it back for more work. Maybe 2,500 units would be enough. The decision documents in this matter get into such absurdities as the Corps' trying to assess the need for low- and moderate-income housing in a particular part of New Jersey and examining the economic feasibility of real estate development.[27] Nonetheless, a large project was eventually built. The developer's goal is to phrase its application so that no other piece of property would be suitable. Its next step is to show that it is minimizing the impact on wetlands. Finally, the developer must agree to mitigate by replacing wetlands destroyed. This is a matter of money. As Tolman points out, the government talks about losses of wetlands, not gains, so the mitigation does not show up in the sound bites.

Tolman suggests that all the confusion and pain of the wetlands program has accomplished little. In places where developing wetlands is economically worthwhile, people often find a way to do it eventually. Section 404 steers development from one wetland to another, albeit arbitrarily, traps some unlucky or unwary landowners, raises everyone's costs significantly, and delays projects. It hurts small landowners who cannot afford the transaction costs and helps the rich. Its mitigation requirements contribute to preventing the net loss of wetlands, though other, voluntary programs of wetlands creation are far more important. Otherwise the program has no overall impact. A program of making new wetlands to replace any that are converted would accomplish the same thing without the harmful side effects.

Now step back and look at the wetlands issue in long-term perspective. Clearly it is impossible to avoid some conflict over wetlands. The rise in environmentalism and the shift in attitudes was certain to reshape thinking about them and to reshape property rights. Even if the reach of the Clean Water Act had not been extended, difficulties would have arisen. A lot of property value had been created by two centuries of government programs designed to eradicate swamps. A change in this pattern would have unsettled a lot of existing arrangements.

However, the Clean Water Act and the stealth techniques used to extend regulation over wetlands greatly poisoned the situation. To this day, neither environmentalists nor government officials seem to understand the anger of the landowners, so far as I can tell from reading piles of testimony on proposed wetlands reform bills. One statement after another jumps from the premise that wetlands are valuable to the conclusion that therefore the government can do whatever it damn well pleases. The equivalent would be for an admiral to say that because the United States needs a navy, the government can take your land for a dockyard without paying you.

To get the flavor, consider the testimony the government submits to Congress on the various environmental and property rights reform bills. From these, you would conclude that the wetlands program has a few minor technical glitches undergoing reform by a wise government and that the people who object to going to jail or having their land appropriated are a bunch of greedy environmental looters. Anyone engaged in productive activity, ranging from land development to logging, is treated as an enemy. There is no hint that achieving the most minor changes, such as establishing an appeal process within the Corps so as to reduce the costs of contesting a determination, has taken more than a decade of bitter struggle and occurred finally only because 1996 was an election year. A competent government should make such concessions to fairness on its own initiative as a matter of routine. Reform should not occur only when extracted by mounting public militancy.

The wetlands mess is like the habitat protection provisions of the Endangered Species Act. It was decided, some years after the fact, that in 1972 Congress enacted a law appropriating all wetlands, plus millions of acres that no one thought of as wetlands, turning them into a new kind of commons, and no one noticed this or objected to it at the time. (Observe the artful use of the passive voice in the last sentence: "It was decided." Who decided? Who do I vote against? Hard to tell.) The owners of affected property do not accept the legitimacy of this action. As with habitat protection, legislation by stealth is an unfortunate approach to government. The rage it creates is deepened when the legislation is followed by years and years during which Congress rants about out-of-control agencies while bureaucrats talk unctuously of their humble role as mere tools of congressional intent.

To go back to first principles, wetlands have environmental values, but so do all other types of terrain. As you read about other environmental issues, you come to statements similar to the hymns found in the descriptions of wetlands. Deserts are uniquely fragile and home to unusual wildlife. Ditto for old-growth forests. The prairies of the Midwest have unique grasses and life forms replicated nowhere else. Mountains, of course, have special properties, and these differ between the western Rockies and the eastern Appalachians. All types of environments have their special values and beauties. That is one of the interesting things about the world. On this scale of values, I do not know that wetlands are "uniquer" than anything else. Maybe the wetlands PR machine just got cranked up sooner.

The various types of terrain also have other uses besides the environmental. They are good for agriculture, lumber, mining, commercial or industrial activities, recreation, and residing. All of these are good and worthy activities for humans to pursue, not acts of rape against nature. There is no moral superiority in living like pre–stone age people in an untouched natural world in a style described by Thomas Hobbes: "No arts; no letters; no society; . . . continual fear and danger of violent death; and the life of man, solitary, poor, nasty, brutish, and short."

The key is balance and trade-offs. Some land that is wetland might be better used for some other activity. Some would not. It really depends on which use of a particular parcel is the best, according to our standards of value. There is no one-size-fits-all approach. A parcel of land in the middle of a city is probably best used for commercial activity, not as a wildlife refuge or a flood reservoir. A tidal wetland in remote area might be used as a nature preserve rather than a marina. A wetland with resources of oil or ore might be mined, while wetland functions are left to one that cannot serve these purposes. It all depends.

The U.S. legislative process has many flaws, but at least it is somewhat open. Major problems with legislation can usually be identified. Because the wetlands protection program was not really enacted by Congress, its problems never received a true airing. Instead agency interpretations created a system that says, in essence, that any use of wetlands for an environmental purpose, however minor the contribution to that purpose, is superior to any use of the wetland for human activity, no matter how valuable that activity. Balance and trade-offs are not quite forbidden, because permits can be granted, but balance is heavily tilted in favor of the wetlands and against all other activities. The only reason permits are granted at all is the government's fear of the takings clause.

There is a difference between respecting wetlands and worshiping them. The defenses offered for wetlands certainly justify respect. They do not justify worship. For example, the argument that wetlands are home to wildlife is certainly true, but it does not lead logically to the conclusion that wetlands acreage should be expanded without end.

Any type of land left undeveloped becomes home to wildlife. The return of eastern farmland to forest over the past seventy years has caused an explosion of the deer population. No one, except maybe hunters, says that because we like Bambi, all uses of land except forest should be forbidden or that no one should be allowed to touch a tree.

The chapter on the endangered species habitat protection program opened with a sermon on the impact of rational ignorance on property rights and government. This one, on wetlands, closes with a sermon on a related topic: the problem of the single-mission agency.

Government agencies are created to carry out missions—process social security applications and mail out checks, for example, or provide for the national defense. The recurrent problem is how to impose appropriate limits on an agency once it is given one of these missions. How much is enough? Sometimes this can be determined without undue difficulty. Standard techniques for analyzing industrial operations can tell you, roughly, the level of resources necessary to handle the social security program. Sometimes there is no real answer because the mission could soak up as many resources as the agency can get its hands on. The question, "How much defense is enough?" has no clear answer.

To deal with such problems, the government developed the budget process. Congress decides how much money should be devoted to the mission after a long, partly rational, partly political, partly indescribable process of analysis and infighting. Defense gets to spend what Congress decides it should spend. So does the Department of Housing and Urban Development. The agencies have no authority to levy on the wealth of the nation except as authorized by the budget. We would regard it as absurd to give the secretary of defense the power to commandeer "such resources as shall be necessary to provide for the defense of the United States." A military given such open-ended power would always find some further need that must be met to ensure that the United States is truly defended. There would be no stopping point, and we would have a tank in every garage.

When it created the environmental protection agencies, Congress adopted a different approach to funding. EPA and the others receive some money through the budget process for personnel, contracts, and so on, but most of the resources devoted to protection of the environment are obtained from society by means of regulations. EPA requires that the private sector spend money to meet a particular standard.

This approach has a philosophical base in economic analysis and in our Lockean system. Pollution is regarded as an external, a spillover. It would make little sense—politically, morally, or economically—for the government to pay people not to produce harmful externalities or for the government to fund that part of an industrial plant devoted to waste control. These expenditures should be factored into investment decisions. However, this lack of limits creates a problem. Because the budget process does not serve as a limit on the resources devoted to the mission, the environmental agencies do not face any logical stopping points to their efforts. It is always possible to argue that some additional step, and probably many additional steps, are necessary before the environment can be regarded as truly protected. Since EPA and the Corps are spending other people's money and are not responsible for the financial health of either the people they regulate or the country as a whole, they lack any incentive to decline to take these additional steps. The single mission is the environment. Why should they listen to arguments that they should stop short of perfection? Why should they not insist on the environmental equivalent of a tank in every garage?

The moral is simple: it is not wise to give an agency like EPA, which has the single mission of protecting the environment, the authority and responsibility to determine when the environment is now officially protected, and it is time to think about other, possibly conflicting values. It will never reach this point.

For most environmental laws, Congress sought substitutes for the budget process. It tried to invent mechanisms to force balance and trade-offs between environmental protection and other social goals, such as economic viability, so that the regulatory process would not go totally out of control. For the most part, the mechanisms chosen involve limits on the level of risk that EPA can regulate or on the types of control technology it can require. The pollution-control side of the Clean Water Act, for example, is a jungle of standards. It is loaded with permissible contaminant levels, distinctions between "available" technology and "practicable" technology, and similar devices.

How well these devices work is a story all its own. They have clearly produced significant improvements in the environment, probably at a price that was several times what society really needed to pay. For purposes of the wetlands program, and for the endangered species program, the point is that even these rough techniques are not used. Because Congress never enacted the programs, it never thought about imposing any stopping points on EPA or the Corps. Furthermore, because these programs do *not* involve external effects that the landowner is imposing on others, there is no logical stopping point except total control over the land. There is not even a point at which you can say, "Now we can stop because the externalities are eliminated." As a result, there are no limits except those the agencies impose on themselves. The result is the imperial program that wetlands has become.

Looking at the problem through this lens of how to control a single-value agency highlights the importance of property rights. In particular, it highlights the importance of forcing an agency to pay for the economic value it appropriates. There is simply no other way to force the agency to think about where to stop in its pursuit of the good, the true, and the beautiful.

Author's Note: As this book was going to press in December 1996, the Corps of Engineers announced its intent to tighten up the Nationwide Permit program, effective immediately. NWP 26, the most important single permit, will be entirely eliminated over a period of two years. Environmentalist organizations expressed satisfaction, arguing that NWP 26 is an illegal violation of the Clean Water Act. Builders, farmers, and other groups are, predictably, not happy. (See Joby Warrick, "Government to Tighten Wetlands Regulations; Army Corps of Engineers Will Phase Out Controversial Permit," *Washington Post,* December 6, 1996, p. A1.) So much for recent EPA and Corps of Engineers statements that they are accommodating the concerns of the landowners and trying to achieve balance in the program. Now that such soothing soundbites have served their purpose of muting opposition until after the election, these single-mission agencies can abandon the pretense of reasonableness and resume their true identities.

PART III

EMPIRES OF THE WEST

Chapter 8

The National Commons

Some history and geography, OR, all hell needs is water and a good system of property rights

Much of the energy fueling the defense of people's right to property comes from the West. To an eastern mind-set, this is puzzling. Almost half the West is owned by the federal government, so the movement seems to be staking a claim to the lands and natural resources owned by all the people of the United States. Surely, the rationally ignorant assume, the claim must be ridiculous. Greedy cattle, timber, mining, and water barons have raped the West for 150 years, have they not? Isn't this just more of the same?

The conflict in the West is indeed mostly over the use of the public domain, but this does not mean the westerners' claims can be dismissed out of hand. Their case is rooted deep in the history of federal policy toward the region. The conflict involves a complicated mixture of concerns over grazing, timber, mining, and several types of recreation, and water. Some of the claims are legitimate, and some are covers for good old-fashioned land grabs.

Starting in the nineteenth century the federal government saddled the West with a system that makes everyone's right to use property ambiguous and insecure. "Ownership" became and remains vague and fragmented, and resources are allocated by political rather than market mechanisms. This makes it impossible for people to make the bargains that smooth the shift of resources to new uses. As is always the case when vague and insecure property rights are up for political grabs, this system favors the rich and powerful. They can buy political power, both to get and to protect.

WASHINGTON, D.C., 1880 AND 1996

Federal law allows railroads building track through public lands to cut timber for construction purposes along the right-of-way. In 1880, the railroads get a friendly secretary of the interior to define "along the right-of-way" as extending fifty miles on each side, as well as fifty miles in advance of the head of track. A railroad with a generous definition of "construction purposes" can lay rails into the middle of government forest, take out the timber, and sell it without paying the government a dime. In 1996, when Congress decides to give away chunks of the electromagnetic spectrum worth $35 to $70 billion, it does not dial up the Little Sisters of the Poor. The booty goes to large, powerful corporations with the money and control over publicity to influence campaigns.[1] As the French say, "The more things change, the more they remain the same.

The result of the ambiguity over property rights to the West is misuse of resources, conflict, inflexibility, and continuing environmental harm, lasting down to the present day. What the West really needs is not, as is often stated, an end to "cowboy culture" and a shift to more communal decision making. It needs a good dose of property rights. If these are to serve as the great engines of justice, economic efficiency, political freedom, and personal autonomy, they must, in a formula coined by Richard Stroup of the Political Economy Research Center in Bozeman, Montana, meet the test of the "three D's": they must be (1) *defined* clearly so as to reside with a specific person or entity; (2) *defended* easily against nonowners who might wish to use or steal the asset; and (3) *divestible*, or transferable, by the owner to others on whatever terms are mutually satisfactory to buyer and seller.[2] Three-D property rights are the prescription for what ails the West.

The West is an empire in size. The territory beyond the one hundredth meridian, which runs through western Kansas and Nebraska and marks off the eastern boundary of the Texas Panhandle, contains 40 percent of the United States. (Here, and throughout the rest of this chapter, numbers do not include Alaska and Hawaii. They are special cases of everything, and Alaska is so big that lumping it with other states distorts understanding.) The discussion here leaves out the rumps of the prairie states and concentrates on the Mountain West— Montana, Wyoming, Idaho, Colorado, Nevada, Utah, Arizona, and New Mexico—plus the Pacific West—California, Oregon, and Washington. These states contain 753 million acres, 1 million square miles, which is over 33 percent of the United States.

The West is awesomely rugged, an empire of mountains and scenic grandeur—and also an empire of desert. The one hundredth meridian is regarded as the boundary marking the beginning of "the West" because of rainfall. Beyond it, rainfall is less than 20 inches per year, not enough to farm. There are only two belts of good rainfall: one in western Montana/northern Idaho, and one in northern California and along the Oregon-Washington coast.

The West is also an empire of grazing land for cattle and sheep. Over 401 million acres are classified as rangeland and another 12 million acres as pasture. This is 55 percent of its total area. It is an empire of forestland: 62 million acres of federally owned commercial-grade forests and 60 million acres of private forest. It is an empire of metals, coal, oil, and, where water can be brought to bear, some rich soil. Much of it, including its millions of acres of wasteland, is an empire of scenic grandeur and of opportunities for recreation with territory aplenty suited to fishing, hunting, boating, snowmobiling, riding, hiking, camping, climbing, four-wheeling, skiing, bicycling, and just sitting.

The West is an empire of the federal government, which owns 48 percent of the Mountain West, ranging from 28 percent of Montana to 83 percent of Nevada. The government also owns a surprising 45 percent of California and 52 percent of Oregon. It does not own any significant part of Texas, which is why this state is usually excluded from the discussions of the problems of "the West." Most of these problems are intertwined with federal ownership. All told, the federal domain in the Mountain and Pacific West is 354 million acres. In square miles, this is 553,000 out of 1,176,000.

The plural *empires* also applies to this public domain. It is run by several agencies, each with its own sphere. The Bureau of Land Management (BLM) of the Department of the Interior has mostly grazing land but includes a little forest and lots of minerals. It also controls the minerals on 66 million acres sold off to private parties, with the mineral rights reserved for the government. The Forest Service of the Department of Agriculture has mostly forest but runs considerable grazing as well. The National Park Service (NPS) runs parks and National Monuments, and the Fish and Wildlife Service has wildlife refuges. Both NPS and FWS are part of Interior. The National Parks are also wildlife refuges, so FWS has some say in those. The cooperation among these agencies is spotty. The Park Service bookstore next to Old Faithful Geyser in Yellowstone Park does not sell Forest Service maps of the surrounding national forests, nor do the Forest Service bookstores sell Park Service maps.

These four agencies are not the only feds involved. The West is also an empire of dams and water resources projects, built by Interior's Bureau of Reclamation and the Army Corps of Engineers. The bureau builds for irrigation and produces flood control and hydroelectric power as a side benefit. It operates or oversees 238 projects, encompassing 355 storage dams and reservoirs, 52 hydroelectric power plants, 240 pumping plants, 300 recreation sites, 15,853 miles of canals, and 17,002 miles of drains. The Corps builds for flood control and power and produces some irrigation as a side benefit. Its empire includes 459 lakes covering almost 10 million acres, and 1.7 million acres of surrounding land, home to 4,329 recreation areas. The Corps oversees 383 major lakes and reservoirs storing 219 million acre-feet of water, including 68 used for irrigation water, and its hydropower plants make up 3 percent of total U.S. electrical power capacity. Other big landowners are the Departments of Defense and Energy. The West has some huge military reservations, and the Department of Energy runs laboratories and atomic production facilities.

Finally, the United States has more than 300 American Indian reservations, and over 90 percent of this territory is west of the hundredth meridian. This is not part of the public domain. It is hardly part of the United States for some purposes, because Indian tribes are sovereign nations, but title to this land is held by the secretary of the interior as a trustee for the tribes, and Indian rights contribute to the conflict over property rights in the West.

For those who like numbers on federal land in the eleven western states, here they are:

FEDERAL LAND: ELEVEN WESTERN STATES

Agency	Acres (millions)	Purpose
Bureau of Land Management	177 66	Grazing, some forest mineral rights only
Forest Service	141	Forest, some grazing, wilderness
National Park Service	17	Parks
Fish and Wildlife Service	6	Wildlife/Refuges
Department of Energy, Department of Defense, Bureau of Reclamation, Army Corps of Engineers	13	Energy facilities, defense, dams, recreation
Bureau of Indian Affairs	55	Indian reservations

The West may occupy one-third of the territory of the United States, but it is home to less than 20 percent of its population. Even this over-states the numbers. The California megalopolis running from Sacramento west to the coast, then south to the Mexican border, has a population of 26.4 million people. These people use the water and recreation of the West, but they do not really live in it. They are a separate civilization. The population of the Real West consists of the 28.8 million people in the Mountain and Pacific West, subtracting the California coast.

This West is surprisingly urbanized. Of its 28.8 million inhabitants, 14.8 million live in Portland, Seattle, Denver, Las Vegas, Phoenix, Salt Lake City, and the cities that serve the agricultural empire of California's Central Valley. This leaves only 14 million people in eleven states outside the non–big city West. It is a big, empty country.

Its remoteness is deceptive though. We associate the West with distance, isolation, loneliness, and self-sufficiency, yet it is and always has been tied tightly into national and international commodity markets. In the East, farmers could be basically self-sufficient, insulating themselves from the vagaries of broader markets. In the West, no such isolation is possible. If the local timber mill stops work, or the beef market crashes, or the transportation network is disrupted, or the water supply interdicted, you cannot put in a crop and wait for better times. You must move or die. Even the mountain trapper of the 1820s, deep in the Rockies and not seeing another human for months at a time, was yoked to a rage for beaver hats in London and Paris. Today you drive westward for miles across the thinly settled Snake River plain in Idaho, then suddenly a Micron chip plant looms and you are in Boise. The fortunes of that factory are tied more closely to events in Japan than to anything in the territory you just crossed, and its workers have more in common with their fellow techies in Silicon Valley or Phoenix than with the loggers and farmers of other parts of Idaho. One of the most crucial facts about the controversy over western land and water is that it is as much a civil war within the West as a "war on the West" by other parts of the country.

To understand the current conflict over these empires, you must know something about how the West came to be settled. It was different from the East, and thinking based on eastern patterns did not work then and does not work now.

The settlement of America was largely about the human hunger for property, for the means to make a living. To the immigrants of the seventeenth, eighteenth, and nineteenth centuries, this was a hunger for land, because farming was the means of existence for 90 percent of the population. (Many of the later immigrants who came after the industrial revolution got rolling became laborers, but in the beginning it was the land.) The history of the country is rich in conflict between the authorities, both colonial and English, who wanted to keep settlement concentrated, and the itch of the settlers to keep pushing west to where they could get land. It is also rich in other conflicts over access to land. One of the grievances of immigrants from Asia to the Pacific Coast was the effort to exclude them from landownership. One of the grievances of African Americans in the South was the failure of post–Civil War Reconstruction to give them a share of the land on which they had worked for generations. A continuing grievance of American Indians was the caucasian habit of entering into solemn treaties accepting Indian rights to land, then breaking them a couple of years later when the land turned out to be worth something. A grievance of women was the laws keeping them from owning property in their own names. The concept that is wrong for people to be denied access to the natural resources needed to make a living is deep in our bones. The denial is more than wrong. It is a cause to overthrow a sovereign. George III's effort to prevent settlement of the trans-Appalachian was included on the list of complaints in the Declaration of Independence: "He has endeavored to prevent the population of these states; for that purpose obstructing the laws for naturalization of foreigners; refusing to pass others to encourage their migrations further, and raising the conditions of new appropriations of lands."

All of America west of the original thirteen colonies was once part of the public domain. From the Revolution to the Civil War, Congress debated the best use of this national patrimony. It flipped back and forth between the idea that land should be made freely available to foster an independent yeomanry and the idea of selling it for cash. For most of the early nineteenth century, it got sold. While Congress dithered, unruly settlers like Simon DeLong kept pushing westward. Congress repeatedly revised the land sale laws, and each time it was forced to give squatters first dibs on land they had occupied illegally. The public domain between the Appalachians and the tier of states west of the Mississippi was disposed of to the citizenry as private property, and prospered. The land was fertile, and a farm of 80 acres or even less was adequate to support a family.

American settlement was also about timber. The forest was the great curse and the great blessing. It had to be cleared with backbreaking labor, which took about twenty workdays per acre. To hire it done cost fifty to seventy-five cents a day, depending on the state of the local labor market. If the stumps were pulled, this took another twelve workdays, plus the use of a team of oxen. A small eastern farm required 30 cleared acres, with 20 more left in woodlot, so developing a modest place represented almost three years of solid work, which was usually spread out over about ten years.[3] To clear 160 acres took about seventeen years of solid work. This was the curse. (A rough benchmark for assessing nineteenth-century prices is that in the years after the Civil

War, a farm laborer made about $0.50 per day, an unskilled industrial laborer about $1.50, and a skilled laborer about $2.50. Local shortages could push these wages up, of course. Prices were stable or slightly declining from 1865 to 1900. Then between 1900 and 1994, the consumer price index increased by a factor of almost 18, so the current value of these wage rates would equal $9.00, $27.00, and $45.00 per day, respectively.)

The blessing was that the wood was so useful. It built the house and provided furniture, fencing, and fuel. It also financed the clearing operation. A cord of wood sold in town for a dollar or two, and an acre of forest produced an average of twenty cords. This left a profit even if the farmer hired a drifter to cut it up ("cord it") for fifty cents a cord. The wood was an integral part of the mechanics and economics of frontier settlement.

As the nineteenth century wore on, the pattern changed. Logging became an industrial operation that fed the needs of the industrial and agricultural revolutions. Clearing land ceased to be the first activity of a new settler. Instead, the logging company did it, sold the timber, sold the now-clear land for agriculture, and moved on to new forests. Clear-cutting was the necessary first step in converting land to agriculture, not an offense against nature.

After land and timber, a third factor in the pattern of eastern settlement was water. Sometimes it was too abundant. The problem was draining the wetland. Securing a source of water was important but not a serious constraint. Folks settled on any of the innumerable creeks. Later they drilled wells, and water came. Water rights were not a serious source of conflict over property. The East adopted the old English concept of riparian rights: the owner of land next to a stream has the right to draw out as much as necessary for his own use. His only limit is that he must leave the flow essentially unimpaired for the use of the downstream users. It is a Lockean "enough and as good" situation, but it presented few problems in a land of abundant rainfall.

The final factor in settlement is transportation. This was a limiting factor on eastern settlement, and the issue of developing a transportation net was a preoccupation of nineteenth-century politics. The Erie Canal was finished in 1825, along the only sea-level route from the East Coast into the interior of the continent, and canal building was the rage for a time. All told, state and federal governments invested $160 million in it. Canals were also supported by federal land grants: 3 million acres in 1827 and 1828, and another 1.5 million acres later. Oceans and rivers were important too, but surprisingly little money was spent on river improvements until late in the nineteenth century. In the early part, people must have taken them as they came from nature. The Mississippi, of course, provided a highway for the agricultural goods of the Middle West to reach the East and Europe. Wagon roads were important, but no national numbers exist on these. Cartage was up against the same iron laws of economics it has always faced. Unless you have free feed for the horses, your range is limited. A four-horse supply wagon can haul about 1,200 pounds. Each horse needs 20 pounds of dry fodder per day, so the horses eat up the hauling capacity in fifteen days. If the fodder is wet, a horse needs 50 pounds of it in a day, and the maximum range for a round trip is three days out from home, allowing for no payload.[4] Starting in the 1840s, the East became linked by the railroads; 9,021 miles were built by 1850 and 30,626 by 1860.

The West had land, some of it fertile, but other vital ingredients were missing. When the edge of settlement reached the Great Plains, it hit a wall even before it got to the rainfall line of the hundredth meridian. It hit the end of the timber. This did not stop the tide of settlement, but it certainly changed things by increasing dependence on the transportation net. You could live on the Kansas or Montana plain in a sod hut while you kept warm by burning buffalo chips, but not well and not for long. You needed wood for fences, houses, stores, furniture, barns, tools, and other uses. Lots of wood grew in the great forests of Michigan and Wisconsin, but it had to be moved. You could not do it economically by wagon. In 1838 it cost over $50 (the equivalent of $700 in 1994 prices) just to haul 1,000 board feet of lumber from Chicago the 125 miles to Peoria.[5] This is not much wood either. Piled into a wagon, the load would be 8 feet long, 4 feet wide, and about 2½ feet high.

This might seem like a minor matter, but it changed the economics of settlement. You could not finance your first year by selling wood in town. In addition to cash for food and clothing, you needed it for wood for your house, barn, fences, and fuel, and you needed access to transportation to bring it in.

A little farther west, when settlement reached the hundredth meridian, it outran the water. Unlike the East, you cannot farm on 160 acres; you cannot even ranch on it. A cow and her calf, or five sheep, is called an *animal unit* in the language of the Bureau of Land Management, and needs about 800 pounds of grass per month.[6] In arid regions, 160 acres is enough to support about one animal unit for a year. In the driest territory, such as New Mexico, a full 640 acres—a square mile—is needed. The great explorer John Wesley Powell put the facts into his *Report on the Arid Region of the United States* in 1878, and they have been recounted many times since. Powell recommended homesteads of 2,640 acres—4 square miles. This was for families with thirty-five to fifty head of cattle, not for real ranches. He also wanted to lay out his proposed 2,640-acre farms so that each had access to water, in preference to the rigid grid pattern used in the East.

The need to ranch rather than farm reinforced the need for transportation. If you are growing cash crops, you need a market and a way to reach it. Given the lack of rivers in the West, this meant access to a railroad. And you needed a way to get your cash crop to the railhead. Even if you could grow crops, carting them by wagon is a serious problem. Livestock has a great advantage in a big country: it walks to market.

Around the mid-nineteenth century, as the settlement of the West began in earnest, people were well aware of the transportation problem. They knew that the West could not be settled unless it was furnished with a rail grid, and they set about to supply it.

This brings us to another point about political analysis to go with the earlier discussions of rational ignorance, complexity, and single-mission agencies. This one is particularly important to the West, only it does not have a name: it is the practice of projecting the values of the present back to the past, judging long-ago actions by current standards. "Presentism" is used sometimes, to parallel "racism" or "sexism," but it is not satisfactory. These terms are associated with politically correct, value-neutral thinking. Presentism implies that no reason exists to prefer our current values to those of the past. This is error. Our present respect for the environment is indeed better than the destruction of the past, given our circumstances. As a product of the 1990s, I am not value neutral when it comes to hydraulic mining or the disposal of toxic wastes or deforestation of whole mountain ranges. I am against them, and I think current values are better than those of the past. The mistake is to think that this makes us morally superior to the people of the past. We are not. We have the luxury of wealth, and therefore greater choice, largely because of what they did. They were more constrained, and their values reflected this.

Since no good word exists, the term *"time blur"* is used here to describe a blurring of present and past. Time blur has several components. It projects the values of the present onto the past. It assumes, often implicitly, that the material circumstances and constraints on people of the past were the same as now, so they must have been bad people not to demonstrate these values. It often includes another factor: a belief that the injustices and errors of the past justify punishment in the present, as if history can somehow be made just and all its books of account put in balance.

It is not only the size and multiplicity of its empires that make grasping the West hard. It is also the degree of time blur that permeates discussion. Much of this consists of talk about "giveaways" of land and natural resources—to railroads, mining companies, and ranchers, in particular—and of large-scale land fraud. Most of this is misleading. Certainly frauds and rascals abounded, in and out of government. So what else is new? (Columnist George Will defines the word *cynic* to mean "student of government and human nature."[7]) Giveaways there also were, later on, largely in the form of water, but for the most part the westerners of the nineteenth century deserve more respect. They were in a situation that was prototypically Lockean. Land, though not water, was abundant, and so were timber and minerals in some places. Labor and transportation were in short supply. The natural reaction was to give land to those who would add their labor to it. There was lots of illegality, but on inspection, its nature becomes much more ambiguous. It looks less like dishonesty and more like people on the spot trying to make the best of unrealistic government policies in the face of official incomprehension of the true state of affairs.

This point is important to current political debate. You see repeated references to the "plundered province," the "rape of the West," the "giveaway system," and the "Great American Barbecue." These are the products of time blur, and they misguide analyses of the current situation. Too many commentaries seem to take the view that anything done now to ranchers, railroads, timber companies, or miners is only fair because it balances the historical balance sheet. We'll teach those swine to cut the forest in 1880! Another misleading assumption is to draw a line between stupid, shortsighted corporations and wise, farsighted government. This formulation is half right. The corporations were indeed greedy, often stupid, and usually shortsighted. Again, what else is new? But these adjectives apply to organizations in general, not just to corporations, and the government matched them in spades. As is true for wetlands, the government is now forcing a lot of suffering onto other people to expiate its own sins.

Now, back to the railroads. The concept of time blur is introduced at this point because the most widely cited example of Western "giveaways" was the practice of making land grants to railroads in exchange for building the road. This practice continued an earlier policy of giving land in exchange for construction of canals, wagon roads, and river improvements. For railroads, land grants were made between 1847 and 1871. They ended as a result of scandals surrounding the construction of the transcontinental Union Pacific.

The conventional sour view of this program is silly. Land grants were a logical response to a chicken-and-egg problem. Building a railroad is expensive. No one will do it if there is no traffic. In the mid-nineteenth century, it made sense to lay rails between existing cities, transporting goods between them and picking up traffic from the farms and towns in between. It did not make sense to lay rails in frontier states like Illinois or Iowa, which were unsettled. On the other hand, these needed the railroad to become settled. So a railroad could not get built until the population was larger, and the population would not grow until the railroad got built.

Where public land had already been sold to speculators, the railroads could induce the owners to put up capital for construction. Land went up in value with the coming of the railroad.

ILLINOIS, 1851

James Barret owns 4,215 acres in Sangamon County. He agrees to buy thirty shares of the Alton & Sangamon Railroad, which is planning a route next to his land. The railroad then changes the route, bypassing him. Barret, enraged at this blow to his wallet, reneges on his stock purchase. The railroad sues him and wins, due largely to the painstaking efforts of its lawyer, Abraham Lincoln. The decision is cited in twenty-five other cases throughout the United States and puts Lincoln on the road to a career as one of the most prominent railroad attorneys in Illinois.[8]

Where the land still belonged to the government, the logical solution to the conundrum was to integrate the land and the transportation network, and this is what the government did. The government gave public land to the railroad, which then sold it or gave it away to settlers who would generate traffic. It worked too. The nation's rail network grew from 9,021 miles in 1850 to 74,096 in 1875. It kept growing after the land grants ended, to 166,703 miles in 1890, as the nation industrialized and as the agriculture of the plains became mechanized. For the land along the railroad retained by the government, the price was doubled, to $2.50 an acre. Giving half the land along the right-of-way to the railroad actually cost the government nothing. Its remaining half was now worth as much as the whole parcel had been before the road.

The value of the land was useful to the railroads but not overwhelming. They wound up with 180 million acres, which they sold over time for $495 million, or $2.75 per acre. This was enough to pay for one-third the cost of construction of all trackage west of the Mississippi up to the year 1882. Historians have fought for many years over the true value of the subsidy. The railroads agreed to carry government cargo at discounted prices, which offset some or all of the proceeds, but on the other hand they got timber and minerals and sold some of the land to their own subsidiaries, and so on, back and forth.[9] The crucial point is that frontier land was not very valuable, even with transportation, and it was virtually worthless without it.

OREGON, 1869–1916

The Oregon & California Railroad runs through prime Oregon forest. It has 2.9 million acres from a federal grant dating to 1869. The terms of the grant require the road to sell land to homesteaders for $2.50 an acre if asked. In the latter part of the century, the gold strike in the Klondike triggers a timber boom, so the O&C cheats: it logs land before transferring it, sells land to dummies, and finds other finagles to duck its obligations. President Teddy Roosevelt objects, and eventually, in 1916, Congress pays the O&C $2.50 an acre and takes the land back. Then the government tries to sell it to homesteaders for the same price. It fails. The terrain is too steep, the trees too big, the land too infertile, and the climate too wet. The government logs some of the land to clear it, but the farmers still will not take it. In the meantime, the local communities are screaming because the railroad used to pay property taxes but the government does not. Eventually the government goes into the logging business and splits the profits with the counties.[10]

The O&C tale is a good caution on the limited value of western lands. The land did not increase in value over a period of forty-five years. If the O&C had sold its land for $7.25 million in 1869 and let the interest compound in 2 percent bonds until 1916, it would have had $18 million. (The information does not tell how much it made from the logging though.) Also, just think: this is prime Oregon spotted owl habitat, and your great-great-grandparents could have bought it for a measly $2.50 an acre in 1916.

The real game was to foster settlement. Railroad land agents met the immigrant boats in New York. The Northern Pacific kept 800 agents in Europe trolling for settlers. The backers of the Great Northern, running from St. Paul, Minnesota, through the northern plains to Tacoma, were too late to get in on the land grants, but they did not regard free land as essential to success. They built slowly, putting out tendrils off the main line as they went along to encourage development of traffic-generating farms. When you think about it, why would a sensible and greedy railroad try to gouge its land buyers? It could make a lot more money selling land cheaply so as to increase the number of farms, and then using its monopoly power over freight rates to siphon off most of the value produced by the land. Railroad freight rates became one of the dominating issues of American politics for several decades in the late nineteenth century. The truck and the interstate highway muted its importance, but the issue still boils occasionally, as in the fight over the merger of the Union Pacific with the Southern Pacific in 1996.

One of the many lasting impacts of the railroad land grants on the West was the checkerboard pattern that resulted from giving the road every other section within a given distance of the track while the government kept the rest. The railroads sold much of their land to private owners over the years, while much of the government land remained in the public domain. To this day, in some places public and private lands alternate in this checkerboard pattern. When you speak of public land, you are not speaking of a large, contiguous range but of alternate square miles intertwined inextricably with privately owned property.

With this background, the next chapter turns to four specific areas of conflict in the West that are entangled in the dispute over property rights: grass, forests, ore, and water and their use as raw material for productive enterprise. They also involve the potential use of the same resources as raw materials for the new industry of recreation, and the conflict, as old as history, between the old and the new.

Chapter 9

Grass, Timber, Ore—and Backpackers

Homesteaders, cattlemen, loggers, miners, and other shootouts, OR, Go back, Shane!

E ncouraging railroads was the first great pillar of national policy toward the West, and a good idea it was too. Other dimensions of national policy were less sensible. The most important failure was the basic land policy, the Homestead Act, which may have worked fine on the prairie states but was a disaster in the Far West.

Under the law, a homesteader filed a claim on 160 acres of public land. If he was within the ambit of a railroad, the claim was limited to 80 acres, illustrating the government's opinion of the value of the transportation network. He then had to "prove up," which meant living on the claim and cultivating it for five years. He had an out after six months of residence, though. He could commute the five-year obligation and take immediate title by paying $1.25 per acre.

WYOMING, 1889

It is one of the great scenes of late night moviedom. Shane, the mysterious stranger, takes up the cause of Joe Starrett and the other homesteaders who have moved into the valley. To protect his range, the local cattle baron hires Wilson, a villain so dark that the saloon's mangy dog gets up and slinks out every time he enters. As the conflict builds toward its climax, the adversaries meet. The aging rancher, grizzled head back-lit by the western sky, speaks:

Rancher: Look, Starrett. When I came to this country you weren't much older than your boy there. We had rough times, me and the other men that are mostly dead now. . . . We made this country. Found it and we made it. With work, blood, and empty bellies.

. . . Some of us died doing it. . . . Then people move in who never had to rawhide it through the old days. They fence off my range. They fence me off from water. Some of them, like you, plow ditches. Take out irrigation water, and so the creek runs dry sometimes. I've got to move my stock because of it. And you say we have no right to the range. The men that did the work and ran the risk have no right? . . .

Starrett: You talk about rights. You think you've got the right to say that nobody else has got any. Well, that ain't the way the government looks at it.[1]

Despite our momentary pang of sympathy for the rancher, the tide of history cannot be stopped. Shane shoots the villains, including the old rancher (in self-defense, of course), and the West is made safe for the march of agriculture. Shane rides on, the classic example of a man with no place in the civilization he helped to make. We go to bed in a warm glow, musing on progress.

There is the problem: the old rancher was mostly right. The Homestead Act, which brought Starrett and his fellows into the valley with the promise of 160 acres of farmland, was absurdly ill suited to the arid conditions west of the hundredth meridian. You cannot make a living on 160 acres, which was only 6 percent of Powell's estimate of the amount of land needed for a modest homestead. Nor was Powell's conclusion unique. Other explorers had said the same thing, long before Congress passed the Act in 1862. They had no effect. Easterners assumed that if 160 acres was a good-sized farm in the East and Midwest, it was good in the West as well.

Powell's estimate also assumed access to water. Under the Homestead Act, the survey lines ran straight as a ruler, disregarding such features as creeks and mountains. Not many of the 160-acre quarter sections had water, and those that did were taken up first. In the West, rights to water could also be acquired separately from land by the first person to start using it. This too shut latecomers off from the water. One of the mysteries in *Shane* is how the old rancher was so careless as to let the homesteaders anywhere near the creek. The normal practice was to blanket both land and water with claims filed in the names of the family members, the cowboys, the passing gunfighter, and even the mangy dog.

The Homestead Act was a mainstay of western land policy until it was finally buried in 1934. Other land laws followed. Each tinkered with the system, trying to micromanage the affairs of the settlers in a way that did not suit the realities of the situation. This moment of conflict between Starrett and the old rancher is the prelude to historical tragedy, not triumph. The homesteaders will grow old young, and most will abandon their claims. The ranchers will go through boom and bust cycles, pressed to the wall by the combination of a fierce climate and an ignorant and cynical government. The grass of the range will become the textbook case of the Tragedy of a Commons overused to the point of destruction. Much later, the eminent historian Bernard DeVoto will describe the history of the West that grew from these events as "a history of experience failing to overcome in time our thinking, our illusions, our sentiments, and our expectations. The results were hardship, suffering, bankruptcy, tragedy, human waste—the overthrow of hope and belief to a degree almost incredible now."[2]

Historian and novelist Wallace Stegner summed up the results: "Despite incandescent enthusiasm for the Homestead Act at home and abroad, the forty years before 1900 saw no more than 400,000 families—about 2,000,000 people—homestead *and retain* government lands. Yet in that time the population of the United States grew by 45,000,000. . . . 43,000,000 potential home-seekers either could not take advantage of free land or failed to hold their claims."[3]

Since farming was not possible, sensible people for the most part used the West for raising stock, as God clearly intended. The 1860 census showed no cattle in Colorado, Wyoming, or Montana. By 1880, there were 1.8 million. A little later the sheep population exploded. Wyoming went from negligible in 1884 to 1 million in 1891, and Montana from a quarter million in 1881 to 6 million in 1900. Raising stock required units that made economic sense, and big money came in, from the East and from England, with the capital to put these together. An Idaho ranch ran 175,000 cattle in 1885, and the Swan Land & Cattle Company bought 456,778 acres of Wyoming land from the Union Pacific Railroad.[4] The Mormons put together some large operations in Utah.

Numerous smaller operations, large by eastern standards but just grubbing it out in the West, were created.

Contrary to much time-blurred commentary, big parcels for ranching could be put together legitimately. Civil War veterans got warrants for land and traded them on the open market. Eastern states got scrip for western land, which were sold so the proceeds could fund the land grant colleges. Western states got land to sell or lease and use the proceeds to support education systems. All told, 140 million acres went for schools. Congress was changing its Indian policy in the late nineteenth century, and 100 million acres of reservation land went on the market. The railroads sold land, naturally, often on good terms. Until 1891 the government would take cash for land that had been open for homesteading with no takers. There must have been plenty of this, because, to make the farmer-homesteader's prospects even more dismal, land within about 40 miles of a railroad could not be claimed until the railroad had made its land grant selections. This could take years, during which the homesteader had to go too far out to be within reasonable wagon range of the rails. When the final tally is added up, a billion acres of the public domain were disposed of, and only about one-fourth of it went for homesteads.

Of the homesteaded land, some unknown amount was actually acquired by large operations. If the $1.25 an acre required to commute the five-year obligation came from the local range lord, and the title was immediately transferred to him, all was perfectly legal. Modern writers tend to regard this as fraud, but the claim filer got $200 for his trouble, which was a good stake. Another legitimate way to increase holdings was to buy foreclosed property. Land forfeited by a busted sodbuster did not revert to the government if a bank held a mortgage taken out to pay for wood, stock, seed, and tools. It went to the bank, which recouped what it could by selling the place on the open market, usually to ranchers or speculators.[5] It is amazing that any of the land in the Mountain West went to farmers.

If these legitimate and quasi-legitimate means were not enough to put a reasonable spread together, an elastic conscience was indeed a help. Claims were proved up by outright fraud, and considerable ingenuity went into inventing systems for making fraudulent claims. These sometimes approached an assembly line. The California Redwood Company would regularly collect a batch of sailors from a San Francisco bawdy house, take them to file for citizenship, move them to the land office to file a claim, pay them off, and take them back to the boarding-house to wait for their ships. It is hard to prove fraudulent intent when the claimant is now across the Pacific.

Let us pause to consider a question. Do you think these people were wrong to engage in shifty dealing, including outright land fraud? Under the circumstances of the nineteenth century, with their liveli-hoods and even lives at stake, dealing with an uncomprehending, or uncaring Congress sitting fifteen hundred miles away and governing by the nineteenth-century equivalent of sound bites? Or do you think that the westerners, unable to make silly policy work, did what sensible peo-ple should do in such circumstances. Cheat. If you think they were wrong, what should they have done? It is an important question. Re-gional memories last, even in the mobile twentieth century, and the memories of the lack of realism of the land laws are deep in the collec-tive memory of the West.

If you said they should have been law abiding until they could get the law changed, here is another story for you.

NEW YORK CITY, 1974–1996

In 1974, New York tries to secure its place as a manufacturing center by banning any activity except manufacturing from over 20,000 acres—al-most 15 percent of the city. The project is a failure. As the *New York Times* says, "There was a vainglorious poignancy to the blanket declara-tion that the tides of time and industrial relocation should somehow be halted by whim of city bureaucracy." As of 1996, the zones are still in force even though two-thirds of the 800,000 manufacturing jobs are gone.

The zones have not become ghost towns, and in fact are home to a thriving new computer-media industry. They have also become the lo-cale for some new superstores. The salvation owes nothing to the plan-ners. It came about through massive violations of the zoning laws, some creative interpretations by zoning staff, budget cuts that reduced the number of inspectors, and screaming by landlords who cannot stand empty buildings. The city has never gotten around to repealing even the silliest of its rules. For example, a SoHo landlord must make an effort to get a manufacturing tenant and can be required to advertise for up to a year.

> One New York urban designer says proudly: "The city had one idea
> of how we were all supposed to live and function and it turned out to be
> a mismatch. Being practical, we don't obey."[6]

The Old West lives in SoHo, and you New Yorkers should rethink
your views on nineteenth-century land fraud.

Even with fraud, it can be hard to create an economically sized
ranch. It is tedious to accumulate land in 160-acre chunks when you
need thousands. Another way to get enough grazing land was to use the
public domain. Land not sold or homesteaded was called the open
range. Federal law said it was open to all, so you just used it. You did not
have to pay for it. The trick for a rancher was to keep anyone else from
using it, because the open range is a classic commons. If too many animals are put to graze, they eat the grass down to the roots, trample the
roots to dust, and destroy the carrying capacity. But no individual user
has any incentive for restraint. If he keeps his cattle off, someone else
will put his on.

As the country filled up, conflicts over the open range became a bigger and bigger problem. Fights over privately owned land grew as well,
especially since government and private lands were jumbled together.
Keeping others off your range was difficult. The cost of wooden fence
was high—about $1 per rod (16.5 feet) minimum. Posts and rails had to
be railroaded in from the East, wagoned to remote ranges, and laboriously nailed together. Miles and miles of fence were required, especially
where the rancher had to distinguish between his range, to which he
had exclusive rights, and the government range, which he could use but
from which he could not exclude anyone. Imagine the cost of marking
off all the miles of the individual sections of the checkerboard when it
cost $1,320 to fence each 680-acre section.[7]

In the 1870s, a solution came: barbed wire. It was cheap to make and
transport and easy to string. It made protecting land simple, and it
changed the West. Barbed wire allowed landowners to protect the
range they owned, but it could not solve the tragedy of the commons on
the open range belonging to the government. Ranchers tried a number
of approaches, all of them illegal. Some used barbed wire to enclose
public domain. The government responded with the Unlawful Enclo-
sures Act of 1885, and in 1887 the army was called in to help enforce it.
Other means of exclusion included associations of existing stockmen

formed to divide the range among themselves and keep out any new-comers. "Keep Out" notices were posted, violence threatened, and in a few cases herds of invading animals killed.

Nothing solved the problem. The herds expanded during the good years, like the 1870s, when rain fell and the winters were normal. Then the murderous winters of 1886–1887 wiped out a third of the cattle, perhaps 75 percent in some places. This was followed by the great drought, which lasted into the early 1890s. Then the weather moderated, the herds built up again, more people moved in, and by the early 1900s, far too many animals were using the range again. The process continued until the open range policy was ended for the BLM lands by the Taylor Grazing Act of 1934. Open range had been ended on Forest Service lands long before, in 1891.

The more important effect was to fasten on western stockmen a strange system whereby they would be forced to rely on the public rangeland for part of their grazing. The government restrained its own ability to sell the range, insisting that it go only to homesteaders. No homesteaders would take it, sensibly. So the government kept it rather than sell to the ranchers, who were the logical market. Then the government insisted that the public range remain an open commons. It resisted efforts made at the local level, and there were many, to develop rational commons management devices. This ensured that the range would be overused.

The legacy of the open range was set forth in a 1936 Forest Service report estimating that the carrying capacity of the range had been reduced by more than half. Range capable of supporting 22.5 million animal units was now capable of supporting only 10.8. Karl Hess, an astute commenter on the grazing issue, notes that the precision of this number is suspect but that it seems to agree generally with the opinions of most contemporary observers.[8]

In 1934 the Taylor Grazing Act finally ended the era of the open range and imposed the system that governs to this day. Individual ranchers are given permits to exclusive use of allotments of public grazing lands. The permits specify the number of animal units to be grazed and the fee, and each is good for ten years. In theory, the number of animal units is tailored to the condition of the specific land, but this is rough. Permits cannot be given to anyone except the owner of private ranchlands adjoining the public land, and once given, they cannot be revoked except for cause. In law, the permits are not property. However, if the private ranch to which permits are attached changes hands, so do the permits, and the government cannot refuse the transfer. The sale price of private land depends heavily on the permits attached to it. If the permit holder dies, his heirs pay estate tax on its value. Landowners can also trade permits to other local landowners but not to outsiders.

The permits are usually exclusive. Herds are not mingled on a particular piece of land, though the government is now experimenting with some joint permits. Permits are also use-it-or-lose-it. If the holder does not graze the maximum number of animals allowed, then some of this person's allotment can be removed and assigned to another rancher. This has a serious consequence. A rancher who thinks that a patch of public range is in bad shape dare not cut down on the number of animals to let it recover. He would be vulnerable to losing part of his allotment, and thus losing part of his ability to run stock in the future. He might also lose some of his water rights, which depend on putting the water to continuing beneficial use. It would depress the value of his ranch. The rule discourages good stewardship.

Grazing fees are set by a complicated formula that takes the year 1966 as a base and then adjusts according to current private lease rates, beef prices, and cost of production. For 1996 the fee was $1.35 per animal unit month, down from the $1.97 it reached five years ago. This is way below the average for private grazing rights, which is almost $10 per animal unit month. Interior keeps trying to get Congress to raise the fees, and the ranchers keep protesting that the yardstick of private land costs is not valid because the best land was taken up under the land laws and the public domain represents the dregs. They also say that the government has not nurtured the range. BLM, of course, denies these charges. The truth of the matter is not clear, although BLM numbers show that permit holders who sublease their grazing rights to others collect a premium over the government rate.

Considering the degree of heat generated by the permit system, the economic stakes are surprisingly paltry. In 1993, BLM grazing fees produced revenues of only $16.7 million. This land is supporting, on a full-year basis, about three-quarters of a million animal units. The total U.S. population of cattle in 1993 was 99.2 million, and sheep and lambs totaled 10.2 million. It is clear that the BLM lands provide less than 2 percent of the grazing for the livestock industry. Add the Forest Service grazing land, with its $11 million in revenue, to the BLM range, and the government is still supplying less than 3 percent. Toss the nation's 58.2 million hogs into the pot, all of them raised on private land, and the public domain is even less important to the livestock industry.

Nor is the number of ranchers in the system large. Only 27,000 families hold permits, and this covers Forest Service as well as BLM land—307 million acres in all. They are outnumbered by employees of the two agencies. The average permit holder pays about $1,026 per year for 552 animal unit months. Karl Hess points out that 43 percent of all public land cattle ranchers have fewer than 100 head, and 90 percent have fewer than 500.[9] The National Cattleman's Association estimates that 500 is the economic break-even point for a cattle operation, so the permit holders are not exactly plutocrats.

These bare numbers understate the importance of public lands grazing, though. Not many animals are on government land full time. In most ranching operations public and private land are integrated. The range may supply only 3 percent of the total grazing, but in several states, 75 percent of the stock grazes on public land part of the time. Partly this is geographical, a result of the checkerboard pattern; animals wander between public and private land. Partly the integration is temporal; the animals are put on BLM land in the spring, then moved to private land as the season goes along. When BLM tinkers with the system by cutting the number of animals allowed or shortening the season or changing the rules on rangeland improvements, it is not just dealing with government land; it is putting a spoke in the wheel of a complex operation.

For forty years after the Taylor Act, the chances that Interior would mess up a ranching operation were small. In 1935 the Grazing Service (BLM's predecessor) had only sixty employees. It relied on advisory councils of local ranchers, a practice that represents either a wise reliance on local knowledge or a corrupt capture of a government agency by a special interest (take your pick). In the 1970s, life changed. Environmental groups won a big case requiring the government to start doing environmental impact statements for grazing lands. Then Congress passed the Federal Land Policy and Management Act of 1976. This law officially rejected the idea that the public domain should be put into private hands. It also officially recognized that interests in the BLM lands other than grazing deserved recognition. It recognized the interests of recreation (BLM land contains 86,000 miles of fishable streams) and wildlife, as well as exploration and production of minerals, and it charged BLM with achieving a vague mission based on multiple use and sustainable yield. The advisory councils, theretofore limited to the cattlemen, were expanded to include other interests. An immense structure of planning requirements was imposed on the public lands, based on the theory that somewhere there is an optimum solution to the use of the land, and that if enough numbers are crunched and enough different interests reason together, it will be found.

This has not happened yet, nor does it appear likely to happen. As of 1997, Congress is thinking about laws that would perpetuate the primacy of grazing. This is the wrong way to go because it perpetuated the fundamental problem of the grazing lands: the lack of property rights. As the system has evolved, the ranchers have a bastardized form of property that is protected by the political rather than the legal system. It is both insecure and inalienable. Its nature keeps the West from adapting to changes in technology and taste and ensures that the land will not be put to its best use.

If the range with its grass was the first great source of conflict in the West, the bitterest current controversy centers on the forest more than on rangeland. The issue here is the withdrawal of government-owned forest land from logging and the broader effort to limit access to backpackers, excluding all permanent residences and all motorized transport.

These exclusionary goals are pursued by environmentalists through three major mechanisms. One is the Endangered Species Act, with its provisions limiting any use of federal land that might jeopardize a listed species or its habitat. The second is designation of forest as wilderness, which excludes its use for any purpose, as an antiquity, which excludes its use for most practical purposes, or for some other special purpose that limits its use. The third is litigation under the National Environmental Policy Act (NEPA), which requires the federal government to prepare environmental impact statements for every major and many minor actions. Given a sympathetic judge, it is easy to pick holes in these statements and force them to be redone repeatedly. This delays the proposed action and runs up the cost, making it less attractive to both the government and the private parties involved. Every proposed timber sale these days gets litigated, so even where logging is theoretically permitted, it can be brought to a halt.

The environmentalists have been highly successful in attaining these goals. In Idaho, the federal–owned national forests cover 16 million acres. Of this, 13.5 million acres are designated as wilderness or as roadless. In the Pacific Northwest as a whole, projected timber harvests in national forests are already down by 80 percent from historic levels, and even these targets are being about one-quarter met.[10]

The property rights movement is made of the people excluded from using the national forests by the environmentalist offensive. It includes the logging industry and its workers, who have the most at stake. People talk glibly of replacing timber jobs with tourist-centered work, but in Idaho, timber workers get $38,000 per year while servicing tourists pays $12,700.[11] The movement also encompasses a number of other interests, such as people who like to operate four-wheel drive or all-terrain vehicles on old logging roads, or those who simply want better access and facilities in semiwild areas. At present, there is little middle ground between the wall-to-wall humanity of the great national parks and the inaccessibility of wilderness areas.

Here is the story of where we are and how we got there.

In pre-Columbian times, half of what is now the United States was covered with forest—about 950 million acres of it. More than 750 million acres of this was in the eastern half, especially the territory east of the Mississippi, which was solid trees everywhere except in patches of Illinois and Florida. By 1920, the low point, the total forest was reduced to 614 million acres. By 1992, it was back up to 737 million acres, with 380 million in the eastern half and 357 million in the Rocky Mountains and the Northwest.[12]

After the Civil War, logging became industrialized. It was no longer a matter of an individual farmer clearing land for planting. An organized industry developed to supply the westward movement of agriculture across the plains to the hundredth meridian and to feed the maw of the industrial revolution. Economic pressures encouraged clear-cutting. Logging was a transportation-intensive industry. About three-quarters of the cost of manufacturing lumber was absorbed by the costs of moving the wood.[13] Once the investment was made in logging roads and rail facilities, it was important to wring out every last dollar. To our modern eyes, pictures of the cut-over Midwest logging sites that resulted are appalling.

As the forests of the Midwest and South were cut, timber operations began to intensify in the last great forest area, the Pacific Northwest. Several factors began to make people queasy about the continuation of old practices though. One of these was that the nature of the ground did not lend itself to farming. In the East and South, clear-cutting was part of the natural pattern of settlement. Land was logged; then the farmers moved in. Industrial-style operations were doing more efficiently a task that needed to be done anyway. In the Pacific Northwest, most of the timberland was not suitable for farming. It was too steep, too high, too infertile, and too wet. Relentless harvesting left a wasteland, not a farm. The land was worth nothing, not even the $2.50 per acre that the government charged for farmland. The resale of the land for farming had always been a vital part of the economics of timber operations, and the loss of this source of revenue forced reconsideration of the standard logging methods.

Other forces were also at work. Near the end of the nineteenth century, people grew concerned about the rate of cutting. As best they could tell, the original forests of the United States had contained about 1,139 billion cubic feet of timber. By the early 1900s, this was down to about 500 billion cubic feet. Annual growth was about 6 billion cubic feet, and cutting was about 26 billion cubic feet annually. At that rate, all the wood would be gone in twenty-five years. The Pacific Northwest was the last frontier, and when that was gone, there would be no more woods left to assault. They thought a timber famine loomed.

A modern sensibility might like to think that the industrial Paul Bunyans who leveled the Midwest and the South paused at the idea of denuding this last great forest area, with its majestic firs and redwoods. It is more likely they thought, "Hey, if there is going to be a timber famine, then the price of timber and timberland will go up! Why are we selling this wood cheaply today when we can get more tomorrow? And why cut half-grown trees? Maybe they will be worth enough more in ten years to pay for the decline in efficiency that goes with selective cutting." The companies began to think about the idea of sustainable yield, treating trees as a crop to be harvested steadily over time.

The forces of the Progressive era around the turn of the last century did not particularly trust the timber barons, and with good reason. The tales of fraud in connection with timberland rival, and perhaps exceed, the frauds of the Homestead Act. The tale of the railroads' cutting for "construction purposes" was recounted in the last chapter, but railroads were not the only villains. Under the Timber Culture Act of 1873, a claimant got government land in exchange for a promise to plant trees on it. He had four years to do the planting. He could, and people did, take land that already had timber, log it, graze it bare, then give up the claim and move on. Even less subtle forms of theft from the public lands were also commonplace: people went in and stole the trees, sometimes on an industrial scale.

As with the Homestead Act, interpreting these events is not as simple as it looks. The government had no mechanism for selling timber on the open market or for selling the timberland itself. It kept trying to allow special groups to cut wood in particular places for designated purposes. Like the Homestead Act, this approach did not fit the circumstances, so the legal requirements kept getting bent. The timber was needed for all kinds of purposes, but since timberland was not good farmland, these uses were not usually at the site of the cutting. The wood had to be moved, which required an industrial-scale operation. Again, was the local reaction, which was to ignore the laws, really fraud, or was it an intelligent response to rule by distant fools? In the end, local pressure grew irresistible, and Congress finally passed laws that gave away the wood to the inhabitants of the West. Like the open range policy, which created a commons open to the unlimited use of everyone, this policy threatened to destroy the remaining timber on public land.

A serious movement to preserve the greatest of the West's grandeur got under way during the last half of the nineteenth century. In 1872, 2 million acres were turned into Yellowstone National Park. Yosemite became a national park in 1890, and the system eventually expanded to its current 17 million acres. In the 1880s it was settled that parks were dedicated to park use alone. There would be no mining, logging, or other use.

Many interests also endorsed the creation of a national forest system. Some understood the Tragedy of the Commons being enacted before their eyes. Some feared a timber famine and wanted reserves. Some wanted pure preservation. Even some of the timber barons who owned the private forests were on board; they wanted to suppress competition from public timber. In 1891 the National Forest Act passed, and the first 13 million acres of forest reserves were designated.

The act did not answer one crucial question: Was this land to be set aside untouched until it might be needed someday, or was it to be harvested judiciously, according to the new theories of sustainable yield? At the outset, the question was left open, but no cutting was allowed. The issue came to a head in 1897, when 21 million more acres were designated. Communities that had enjoyed complete access under the Free Timber Act were suddenly cut off, a serious deprivation. The outcry from the West forced Congress to pass the Forest Management Act, which firmly passed the buck to the Secretary of the Interior. He could govern the national forests, providing for their improvement. He also had discretion to allow timber harvesting, grazing, generation of hydroelectric power, mining, and agriculture.

WASHINGTON, D.C., 1905–1910

The 1905 session of the American Forestry Conference is orchestrated by Gifford Pinchot, former forester for the Vanderbilts, renowned conservationist, intimate of President Theodore Roosevelt, advocate of the "wise use" of the public domain, young man on the make, and political operative extraordinaire. Four hundred delegates attend. The names "read like a rollcall of the prominent and influential, not only in forestry but also in the lumber industry, railroads, grazing, irrigation, and government."[14] Later that year the forest reserves are transferred away from the Department of the Interior and into Pinchot's Forestry Service in the Department of Agriculture.

Pinchot rallied foresters, western residents, congressmen, and corporations under his wise-use banner, arguing that the forests could be shared by all. He took a decidedly economic view. In 1904, a scheme by sportsmen's clubs for the development of game preserves was discouraged because it would interfere with livestock grazing on national forest lands. The next year the stockmen supported the transfer of the forests to Pinchot's jurisdiction.

The preservationists, headed by John Muir, founder of the Sierra Club, thought the forests should be extensions of the national park system and inviolate. They jumped off Pinchot's ship. With all the support he mustered, Pinchot did not need Muir and his ilk, nor could he have succeeded if he had adopted their platform. The movement to lock up the land was too small. Under Pinchot's leadership, the Forest Service was trusted by all the other interests, and by 1910 it had control of 168 million acres. It remains about this size today (still excluding Alaska).

The Forest Service, and forestry, prospered. By the 1920s a crucial shift in thinking was complete. Timber was no longer regarded as a mine, like a vein of ore to be dug and exhausted. To the pioneers, there was just so damn much of it, and it looked mostly like an incredible chore. (Remember those seventeen years of work with an axe to clear 160 acres.) They made railroad ties out of walnut, one of the rarest and most valuable of woods, if that was what was handy.[15] In the twentieth century, wood became a crop, to be produced on a sustainable basis. The big timber companies joined the movement, and the old days of ruthless clear-cutting were gone forever in the United States.

From the standpoint of property rights analysis, the end of the clear-cutting was the right result. It may be the most efficient way to log, but it can do too much damage to the watershed. Some restraint is necessary to protect the property rights of the neighbors and the downstream owners. Clear-cutting also involves one of the most complicated issues in environmental protection: the concept of *existence value*. As we have grown richer and as hacking a living out of the land has become less of a grim struggle, we were able to appreciate and want to conserve its beauty. We derive pleasure from knowing of the existence of great natural beauty, or forests, or deserts, even if we never lay our own eyes on them. In the circles of people who analyze issues of public policy, this is called existence value, and it is important. The owner of a redwood forest can get pleasure out of cutting the trees and spending the money. The rest of us get no pleasure out of this, and in fact the cutter deprives us of the pleasure that we get from thinking about or actually looking at the redwoods.

In theory, a system of private property takes care of such problems. Those who like to look at trees, or even think about them, buy the property from the logger. He gets the money, and they get the trees. The problems are free riders and transaction costs. How do you get all the people who enjoy the redwoods to contribute? Many will calculate that others will pay and they can free-ride. (The latest solicitation from my local public television station says that 1 million households watch it; only 145,000 contribute.) Even if everyone is honorable and willing to help, how do you collect small sums of money from millions of people without spending all your income on the collection?

The usual answer to this dilemma is "the government." The solution is rough but workable. The government collects taxes from everyone and supplies a variety of collective goods, of things that cannot be provided efficiently by the market. The standard portfolio should include parks and nature, libraries, assorted cultural events catering to different tastes, information services, and lots of economic infrastructure. Of course, the government is not allowed to appropriate the collective good. It cannot confiscate the redwoods or command a group of actors to perform a play or a publisher to give books to a library. It acts as the purchasing agent for the people, entering the market and buying. If the government is allowed to appropriate, whether by confiscation or regulation, with no financial check, then citizens whose hands are on the levers of power will develop an unlimited appetite for controlling private property in the name of existence value.

In the West, this unlimited appetite is apparent in the treatment of private timberlands. A lot of regulation is going on. Some of it is legitimate control on the external costs of some forestry practices; much of it is appropriation of property for the sake of existence value felt by powerful political constituencies. And it is often hard to tell which is which.

With respect to the government forests, the issue is rather different. The pioneer heritage was to regard them solely as a resource to be used in building a country. Starting in the late nineteenth century, and accelerating into the present day, a different type of interest began asserting a stake in the forest commons: people who valued the existence of the forest, not its utility as raw material.

There was no market mechanism through which this new constituency could assert its interest. The transaction cost and free-rider problems were too great. The government could not adopt the straightforward market solution of putting the land up for auction and letting people support with hard cash their assertion that they valued the existence of the forest. Instead, the government took on the role of manager of the commons, promising to mediate all the claims and be sure that none was ignored.

It is important to understand the context of the bargain Pinchot put together. The people of the time did not regard the public domain as the property of a landlord, the United States, that was graciously letting them use it. They regarded it as a commons, to which they had access as a matter of natural right. When they agreed that the government should keep it, not sell it off or continue to give it away, they were delegating to the government the function of managing a commons. When government land managers today write about the government as owner of the land with the right to do what it pleases, they are rewriting the old bargain unilaterally. This is not what the people of the West agreed to. Rather, they trusted the Forest Service to be the honest broker among the various interests in the commons.

As with the range land, the results of this bargain got woven into the West. Part of the weave is economic. It guaranteed access to the economic base of the forest. People live on private land but rely on this government land for their livelihood. Part of this weave is physical. Not only are government and private lands intermixed, but the boundaries of the forest sweep in considerable property that does not belong to the federal government. The total area within the forest boundaries is 207.2 million acres. (This includes the East but not Alaska.) Of this, 169.3 million acres are owned by the government and 37.9 million acres by other people, called "inholders." Part of the weave is spiritual. Author Alston Chase describes it as "cork boot fever," an identity as a logger doing good and useful work that benefits humanity.[16]

OROFINO, IDAHO, 1995

Orofino is about halfway up the state, near the point where Idaho, Oregon, and Washington come together. This is logging country, and the walls of Becky's restaurant are hung with old tools and photographs. One shows a grinning logger next to a tree that has been cut and loaded onto a railroad flatcar. A sign on the tree says "The White Pine King— 425 years old—207 feet tall—29,000 board feet."

Up the street from Becky's is the drugstore. It has a rack, measuring about 1 foot by 2.5 feet, devoted entirely to metal splints, rubber pads, and other devices to care for broken, crushed, and lacerated fingers. The drugstore near my office in effete Washington, D.C., has nothing remotely like it. Logging is not for wimps.

Part of the weave is social. The bargain guaranteed the people a degree of social stability. One of the problems of the timber industry was its short-term nature. Men moved in, cut everything, and moved on. It was a lonely life of isolated camps, hard work, bunkhouses, and booze, and equally lonely for the women left behind in the towns. The idea of sustainable logging, taking out the increase in a forest on a steady basis, promised a much better lifestyle. Economic and personal investments could be made for the long term, the same as if the people themselves owned the crucial resource, the timber.

This basic bargain was reaffirmed in theory by the Multiple Use, Sustained Yield Act of 1960 and in the National Forest Management Act of 1976. Nonetheless, as early as 1964, the bargain began to unravel. The Progressive era battle between Gifford Pinchot, the apostle of wise use, and John Muir, the prophet of pristine preservation, was only round one. Starting in the 1960s, their heirs fought again, and this time Muir won. The turning point was the 1964 Wilderness Act, under which Congress designates lands as wilderness on which humans are to be only temporary visitors. Similar other laws followed. By 1994, of the 341.6 million western acres controlled by the nondefense federal agencies, over 106 million were locked away. The categories include the 17.2 million acres in western national parks and the 6.1 million in western national wildlife areas, of course. They also include Wilderness, Wilderness Study Areas, Wild and Scenic Rivers, Areas of Critical Environmental Concern, National Conservation Areas, Antiquities, National Primitive Areas, National Recreation Areas, Research Natural Areas, National Game Refuges, National Scenic-Research Areas, National Monuments, and Other. Other is a catch-all sweeping in archeological, botanical, geological, and historical sites, plus trails.[17] Except for preexisting rights, the natural resources cannot be used. They are also closed to motorized recreational vehicles.

The figure of 106.1 million acres locked away probably understates the impact of the set-asides on logging. The Forest Service may have 169 million acres in the West, but only about 62 million acres of this is commercial-grade forest; 41.2 million acres of Forest Service land are designated as wilderness, and most of this is forest and most in the West.

This figure is also not quite the complete story. The General Accounting Office says that of the acreage not "managed for conservation," another 90 million acres are closed to mineral development, 77.3 million acres closed to oil and gas development, and 20.6 million acres closed to grazing. The biggest omission from this list is the Endangered Species Act. Chapter 8 looked at the explosive issue of habitat on private land, and the bitterness aroused by *Sweet Home*. The act has another dimension: it governs management of federal land, forbidding any activity that would disrupt a threatened or endangered species. In addition to areas declared off-limits to human economic activity through designation as park, wilderness, or wildlife refuge, millions of acres of federal land are locked up by the requirements of the ESA. The most important of these are the territories of the spotted owl in the Pacific West and the Southwest, and of the marbled murrelet, in California and Oregon. No one seems to know the exact acreage involved.

The basic themes of the ESA are replayed in the context of the public forest, as people dependent on the woods for their livelihoods, their communities, and their very identity see themselves driven out by an owl that is not actually endangered. No one believes the estimates about the numbers of existing owls dished out by the FWS or the environmentalists, largely because more owls keep appearing.

You can argue that the people of the United States own this land, and in their capacity of landlords they have the right to do whatever they want for any reason they want. You are probably right as a matter of the legalities, since the basic bargain of access to the commons was not recorded in any of the legislation. But it is not right as a matter of history, and it is asking a little much of the people whose lives are disrupted by being cut off from this commons to expect them to accept this without complaint, especially when they see it as a manifestation of an odd religion—the ESA—that they do not share. In fact, the religious element of contemporary environmentalism extends even beyond endangered species. It increasingly encompasses trees, as if humans had no moral right to cut them down and use them. This is not a position that people who grew up in logging country can fathom.

Think about the picture of the grinning logger on the wall at Becky's. Times change. Nowadays cut a tree that is 425 years old, and the only picture likely to be taken is for a "Wanted" poster. This modern attitude is not rational, though. Trees become old and stop growing. For a white pine, the books put the maximum age at between 200 and 500 years, so the White Pine King was getting pretty far down the trail. As trees grow old, they cease to be effective agents for absorbing carbon dioxide and giving off oxygen. After a few more years they die. This is, alas, the sylvan condition. Then they dry out and become potential fuel for fires that can destroy a forest for centuries. Eventually they rot, releasing carbon dioxide.

Why not cut the White Pine King and put it to use? The logger in the photo and his friends thought this way. They were proud of what they did. It mattered to them that the tree had 29,000 board feet of useful lumber. The photo looks like a spontaneous moment, not planned company propaganda. The happy logger has not just done a macho deed with his own hands, using only double-bitted axe and cross-cut saw. He has a sense of contributing to his society, and this too is a source of pride. He is building a civilization, not raping a land.

We are back to the distinction between respect and worship. The White Pine King deserves, and in the photograph it is getting, respect. It does not deserve worship. It is not some virgin god, to remain forever untouched. Nor is a forest as a whole. Current attitudes toward the forest have shifted in the direction of an animism that is difficult to understand. Thus the loggers call the environmentalists "tree huggers" and "Druids." So far the ESA and the trees have demanded the sacrifice of almost 300 sawmills, 30,000 forest industry jobs, and another 40,000 or so other jobs.

NEW YORK, 1996

The governments of New York, New Jersey, and the United States are dickering over Sterling Forest, a privately owned woodland that takes in about 30 square miles on the New York–New Jersey border. The states are trying to get Congress to put up $17.5 million of an estimated $50 million purchase price needed to turn it into a park. A group of western representatives tosses in an amendment to designate Sterling Forest as a wilderness area. This would require roads to be closed and power lines torn down. Easterners, and the administration, excoriate this as a silly idea.[18] Westerners ask why what is now routine in the West should be regarded as unthinkable in the East. If much of their land is locked up, why shouldn't the East play by the same rules?

The westerners' bitterness is heightened because treating the forest as untouchable is not good for it. The environmentalists assert that morality requires the forest to be left untouched. The westerners believe this morality is frighteningly wrong-headed and is in fact exceedingly immoral. Thus Bruce Whiting's comment, quoted in Chapter 2, that closing the mill in the Kaibab "is not fair to that forest."

Forestry is a difficult science. Arguments are constant and theories change. Some trees should be harvested by thinning, while others do not regenerate well if they must grow in the shade. These, such as Douglas fir, thrive on clear-cuts. No one really knows what an absolutely natural forest would be like because we have not had one since the Indians arrived on this continent more than ten thousand years ago. Nonetheless, the environmentalists favor doing nothing, and from their homes in New York and San Francisco, they are enforcing their views of proper forestry through lawsuits.

The role of fire is particularly controversial. For over half a century, the Forest Service strained every sinew to prevent forest fires. But this is not nature's way. Forests get burned over regularly due to lightning-caused fires. Before the European settlement, natural fires were augmented by the American Indians, who were adept at using fire as a tool to maintain forests as game preserves. Fire thins, keeps down brush, and improves forest health. Because not much fuel builds up between fires, no fire burns hot enough to kill most healthy trees. Suppressing these periodic fires can cause the number of trees and the volume of dead material to increase to the point where the inevitable eventual fire is a real killer. It can then take centuries for the forest to regenerate.

In the national forests, the goal for a century was to suppress all fires. As a result, fuel loadings have increased drastically, and when the inevitable fires occur, they are destructive indeed. People now advocate a return to nature's way of allowing periodic fires. How do you do this, when decades have passed without the normal fire incidence? The fuel loading is too high. At the same time, environmentalists oppose even salvaging dead timber so as to decrease the fuel load. The ultimate result, fear those who know something about forestry, will be catastrophic fires.

In Arizona, the density in some ponderosa pine forests has increased from historic averages of 25 to 60 stems per acre to 275 to 850 stems per acre. Spotted owls have moved into this habitat, so forest managers are now forbidden to reduce density. In 1994, a National Commission on Wildfire composed of forest experts says, "By leaving the forest in its unhealthy condition, managers must accept the fact that it now has an exceptionally high risk of a stand-consuming wildfire that will kill all the trees—and the owls."[19] In 1996, the ponderosa forests start to burn: 16,000 acres near Santa Fe, New Mexico, and 31,000 acres in Arizona. The Kaibab, the site of the Whiting sawmill, had the biggest fires in fifty years, but they were stopped short of catastrophe. All told, by the end of August 1996, 5.7 million acres of western forest had burned, the most in twenty years, and twenty-seven major fires involving 781,000 acres were still burning.[20]

Even if we reduced fuel loadings, it would not be possible to return to some earlier, pre-Columbian, pre-Indian day and allow fire to go un-checked. Decades of fire suppression have changed the nature of the forest. Professor Nancy Langston, who has taken a thoughtful look at the Oregon forest, gives an example. Frequent small fires burn off litter and keep the surface of the ground dry, so the roots of the ponderosa pines must go deep to find water. This keeps the roots safe from the fires. Where fires have been suppressed for decades, the ground is wet, trees find water near the surface, and the roots are shallow. Now small fires singe the roots and kill even huge trees. Langston draws the moral: "Each disturbance . . . represents a branch in the path of forest his-tory . . . and takes the forest in a slightly different direction. We cannot simply backtrack to a time before some particular decision we now re-gret, because so many additional changes have radiated out from that original action."[21]

The truth is that we are stuck with managing the forests, like it or not. There is no going back to an earlier day when humanity was not a presence on the earth, and there is no point in pretending that we can.

Grass and timber—and ore. Mining was the third great magnet of the West. Even the wiliest avoider of high school history has heard of the California Gold Rush, or at least of the San Francisco Forty-Niners. Not many people know that the third western state to come into the union was Nevada, in 1864. Its population was purely the result of mining. Las Vegas had not been invented. In the current day, mining in the West is as contentious as range and timber.

In the beginning, mining followed the classic Lockean pattern. The public domain was a commons, open to all. The value of its mineral re-sources was mostly in the labor needed to extract them, and anyone willing to invest the work got the title. The series of mining laws now commonly called the 1872 Mining Act was designed to settle relationships among the various claimants, not to establish the claims of the government as landlord. Most of the original act was based on the law of the mining camps as it had developed in California and Nevada. Everyone, except the lawyers, wanted to end a situation in which twenty cents of every dollar taken out of the earth was paid to lawyers to handle disputes over mining claims.[22]

The 1872 law allows unlimited exploration of the public domain, except in areas specifically withdrawn. If a mineral find is made, the finder can claim the land for a payment of $2.50 an acre. He must keep working it, and if he can show a commercially practical lode, he can get title to the land. The law is akin to the other land laws of the time, such as the Homestead Act or the timber laws, in that it gives title to the person who works the land. The 1872 law still governs hard-rock mining on the public lands. For oil, gas, and coal, it was amended in 1920 to provide for royalty payments to the federal government.

The price per acre was reasonable in 1872, when land was worth little, and it was the labor of getting the minerals out of the ground that counted. Getting $2.50 an acre for barren land was actually a good bargain for the government. Most people think this level is a little light now and that the federal government should be a greedier landlord. Other systems are available, such as a royalty on gross revenues or net revenues or an auction system with competitive bids. The economics of the matter are not clear. Much of the cost goes into the initial exploration and, when a potential lode is found, into the exploratory mining needed to determine whether the find is commercial. No one knows for sure exactly how a new system would shake down. Richard Gordon, emeritus professor of mineralogy at Penn State, estimates that the federal government's failure to collect royalties costs it only about $90 million per year.[23] Nonetheless, other extractive industries, including timber and oil, have moved in the direction of giving more profits to the government as landlord, and it might be reasonable for mining to go in the same direction.

Note the hedge in the last paragraph though. The system was designed, and still is designed, to encourage lone, low-tech prospectors to explore the public domain looking for valuable mineral deposits. It may be that this is still the best way to explore for minerals, and, if so, the price may not be unreasonable. For actually working the claim, of course, the prospector sells out to a mining company with the capital and skill to conduct actual operations.

The more important issue for mining is the environmental impact. Mining involves two kinds. The first is spoil. Many tons of dirt and rock must be moved to get at the metal-bearing ore. The second is that extracting the value from the ore often involves unpleasant chemicals. Gold mining, for example, usually relies on cyanide. Other metals take sulfuric acid. Unless carefully contained, the chemicals poison nearby, and sometimes not so nearby, soil and water. The extraction process also leaves piles of contaminated ore tailings.

The 1872 law says nothing about cleaning up the mess. The miners had no interest in the land once the ore was gone, so they had no incentive to protect it. The early history of mining was a story of ruthless exploitation, whether the land was public or private. In California, gold fever produced hydraulic mining, in which jets of water washed away whole hillsides to get at the underlying ore. The technique was highly efficient for the producers. By the mid-1880s, a total investment of $100 million in property and equipment had produced $300 million in gold. At its peak, the industry had 20,000 employees. The results were less happy for those downstream, as a river of mud killed fish, polluted water, obliterated river channels, and flooded the countryside. Since "downstream" was the great Central Valley, Sacramento and San Francisco Bay, this was no small matter. (In the Clint Eastwood classic movie *Pale Rider*, you immediately know the bad guys are bad because they are engaged in hydraulic mining. The good guys pan for gold.) In 1884, a federal court stood up for property rights and enjoined the whole industry because of the damage it caused to others.[24]

Most mining damage was not so dramatic. In remote areas it had no effect on anyone else. Whether the mess *should* have been cleaned up is a tricky issue. It is easy to sneer at the miners, as we tend to condemn the clear-cutters of the forest, but this is time blur. The minerals were needed by the industrial revolution, and applying twentieth-century environmental standards would have been impossible. The steam shovel and the bulldozer did not exist in the nineteenth century, and remediation would have required hand shoveling. To spend huge sums refilling holes in the desert or protecting worthless wasteland from chemicals would have struck our forebears as silly indeed. Nonetheless, the residue of the era is half a million acres or more of unreclaimed federal land that offend current environmental sensibilities.[25]

Today mining is like other industries, subject to a panoply of antipollution laws that restrict the costs it imposes on its neighbors or on the environment. Hard rock mining does not leave a big footprint on the land either. Nonetheless, the weight of the past lies heavily on the industry, and it has been steadily pushed out of the public lands. About two-thirds of the federal land is off-limits, and much of the rest is restricted by the Endangered Species Act or other special provisions. Even where mining is legal, the forces of opposition to it are strong.

MONTANA, 1995

"The Beartooth" is a wonderful name for a line of country, evoking ruggedness and even savagery. The place, located northeast of Yellowstone National Park, lives up to the image. The bare mountains jut like fangs, and a roadside sign says: "This is Grizzly Bear country." In a land of 80 miles per hour interstate highways, it takes three hours to travel the 68 miles over the switchbacks of Beartooth Pass from Yellowstone to Red Lodge, Montana. Between October 15 and the end of May, don't try it. The area gets 500 inches of snow per year, and the road is closed. Cooke City, the last town for the next 63 miles on Route 212 out of Yellowstone, shrinks to about 70 people in winter.

Much of the Beartooth is owned by the federal government, as part of the Absaroka, Custer, and Shoshone national forests. It is also mostly in Montana, which is mining country. The official state motto is "Oro y plata"—"gold and silver." As a measure of their importance to the economy of the state, the Montana legislature long ago gave mining companies the power of eminent domain. In the nineteenth century, the Bear Tooth was mined extensively for its gold, silver, and copper—by 1885, 1,450 claims had been staked in the vicinity of Cooke City—and the hills are full of old sites and waste residues. Extraction techniques were crude, and much ore was left untouched because it was not rich enough to be processed economically.

In the past century extraction technology has improved, and some veins of untapped ore are now rich by the standards of the contemporary mining industry. One of these is at Crown Butte, located 3 miles from the Northeast Gate of Yellowstone Park, and it is here that Crown Butte buys up the old claims and prepares to reopen the gold mine.

The proposal to mine at Crown Butte became a vortex sucking in increasing numbers of partisans. Environmental groups opposed it. Business favored it. Local residents were split. The U.S. Forest Service supported the mine, while the Park Service fought it. Many residents of Montana and Wyoming are the new breed of urban professionals who feel quite distant from the Old West of ranching and mining. They opposed the mine, and the polls said that in Montana they had a two to one edge. State officials of Montana and Wyoming were on both sides, and the governors walked carefully indeed.

To add to the stew, the environmentalists gave the fight an international twist. They said that the United States is bound by treaty to protect "World Heritage Sites," that Yellowstone is such a site, and that any menace to it is prohibited, no matter what permits are granted by the appropriate federal and state authorities. An international commission was invited to Crown Butte in the hopes that it would validate that Yellowstone was "in danger," which it did. The expenses of the commission's trip were paid by the Department of the Interior.

The environmentalists' substantive case was thin. Their argument that Yellowstone National Park would be in jeopardy from pollution from the mine was tenuous, considering that two ranges of sizable hills stand between the mine site and the park, the creeks flow away from the park, and no cyanide was to be used for mining. Their argument that contamination might leak out of its holding basins was also thin. This is essentially an engineering question, and the margins of safety planned were substantial. In the end, the argument against the mine was visceral. Mining on public land should not be permitted, period.

In 1996 the government bought off the mine owners. Crown Butte agreed to give up the mine, with its gold having an estimated market value of $650 million, in exchange for other government land worth $65 million. The company also agreed to chip in $22 million for cleaning up prior contamination at the mine site, so its net would be $43 million. The president announced this as a winning deal for all—"win-win" in the current management jargon.

In fact, it is lose-lose. The mining issue is much like the forest issue, except that the opposition is harder to fathom. You can understand why someone values the existence of a forest. It is hard to understand why they value the *non*existence of a mine. The environmental risk was between infinitesimal and nonexistent. The impact of the mine on the country would have been minimal; you go a quarter of a mile off the road up there, and you are deep in the backcountry. It is hard to find the mine site even on a good map. Much of the propaganda is pure time blur, based on the mining practices of a century ago.

The mine would also have made a number of positive contributions. The road over the Beartooth is in bad repair. The mine might have contributed to its improvement, which would have helped tourists going to Yellowstone, environmentalists going into the Beartooth, and residents of Billings and Red Lodge. The $600 million spent on extracting the gold would have gone to a lot of people, including workers. The federal government was the biggest loser. It would have collected taxes on all these transactions. Now they will take place elsewhere, adding to the U.S. balance of trade deficit. The working class has cause to complain that the old bargain that guaranteed them access to the economic base of the commons has been broken again.

The people of the United States have cause to complain that the government is ignoring their interests in response to a special interest group whose real stake is exceedingly murky. The staff at the headquarters of the Crown Butte company in Cooke City will give you a package of information. One of the items is a giant picture of a young woman sitting at a computer. Next to every item in view is a list of the minerals that go into making it: "COMPUTER—petrochemicals, copper, aluminum, steel, gold, lithium, silicon, tungsten, chromium, titanium, silver, cobalt, nickel, gemanium, tin, lead, tantalum, zinc and salt." "COMPUTER SCREEN—silicon, boron, lead, strontium, barium, rare earth elements, phosphorus (Glass is made from soda ash, limestone and feldspar.)" Spin? Sure. Hokey? Yes. But also true. As a personal matter, you probably care little whether gold gets mined at Crown Butte, but you should care greatly that gold and other minerals get mined somewhere so that you can buy your computers cheaply. This means you have an interest in not shutting down Crown Butte for frivolous reasons.

The only one who came out ahead was Crown Butte Resources, which will get paid for its claims, if the bargain holds once the 1996 election is past. Other miners, who lack the leverage of being able to offer a good photo op during an election year, find their rights treated with less respect. The government abrogates claims, then invents complex arguments about why it has not really "taken" them and does not have to pay. One recent newspaper headline sums up a tale that could be told by dozens, and maybe hundreds, of people: "A Man, a Mine, and a 29-Year Battle with Interior."[26]

COOKE CITY, MONTANA, AND DENVER, COLORADO, 1996

In Cooke City, environmentalists celebrating the outcome of the fight over the mine at Crown Butte dance to a bluegrass band. In Denver, headquarters town for the big gold mining companies, the mood is more somber. Executives agree that the fight and the decision increase their companies' incentives to invest overseas. One company has shifted its investment from 100 percent in the United States to 80 percent in Latin America. The largest of them is still investing heavily in Alaskan production ($400 million), but the rest of its budget (and other $400 million) is going to Chile and Russia. Getting an exploration license in the United States can take five years, and a license to start actual production is slower yet. A few weeks ago the president of Uzbekistan came to Denver and made a pitch to the gold miners. He claimed to have $64 billion worth of underground reserves and invited them to come to see, and stay to spend. One U.S. company has already invested $250 million there.[27]

Many westerners are not sorry to see mining go, since only 40,000 people in the West are employed in the hard rock mining industry. They note that the jobs attributable to Colorado's ski industry are double that. This line of argument is superficial, though. The Idaho study found that mining is even better paid than logging, averaging about $43,500 annually, compared with the tourist service industry pay of about $12,700. This makes a big social difference, because it is the distance between a family-supporting wage and a ski bum. It also makes mining more important than the Colorado ski industry. At this rate of exchange, the mining payroll is about $1.7 billion, and the ski industry's only about $1 billion. Besides, why should the West have to choose? There is no conflict between the two. They could reinforce each other by sharing infrastructure and providing year-round support for businesses that would otherwise be seasonal. Its called synergy, and it is crucial to prosperity.

The dancers at Crown Butte are missing another point. People who think the United States can export its industrial base and retain all its services are in for a surprise. When industrial production moves overseas, services will follow. It may take some time but Uzbekistan and Chile will eventually provide engineers, computer programmers, accountants, and lawyers conveniently near the production site. Professionals who thought they could ignore any hemorrhage of industrial jobs will find they have nothing to do with their days *except* listen to bluegrass. Then there will be weeping and wailing and gnashing of teeth, and much searching for scapegoats—everywhere but in the mirror.

Another great resource of the West goes beyond the use of grass, wood, and ore as inputs into various industrial processes. It is the physical nature of the country—its grandeur and charm. The West is a wonderful place to be, and this is worth a lot. From a materialistic point of view, it is an asset that can be sold to urbanites and used by the natives to provide the base of support that lets them live there. The Old West, with its economy based on extraction of natural resources, is being augmented and sometimes supplanted by a new economy based on recreation. This requires a conservation and shaping of resources.

Over time, we have come to accept the idea that most uses of federal lands should pay. We do not think the federal government should give away its grass, timber, or ore. We still tend to think of access to the commons for recreation as a right, though. *Popular Science* surveyed the public about its attitudes toward the public lands. Three-quarters thought that loggers, miners, and oil drillers should pay to use public natural resources, but 85 percent thought that hiking should be free, and only 24 percent thought that boaters and yachters should pay.[28] The attitude carries over into the administration of the great national parks. For $86, you can take two children to Disneyland for a single day. For $20, you can take as many carloads of people as you want into every national park as often as you want for a whole year.

The results are predictable. The national parks tend to be crowded, and the facilities are in poor shape. Lacking any price mechanism to ration and lacking any way for users to express their preference for more and better facilities, the parks come under severe financial pressure. On the whole, recreation users pay less than 10 percent of the cost of servicing them.

One special class of recreationists is especially blessed by the government. This is a group composed of "male[s], relatively young, well-educated, affluent, white, and employed as professionals or executives."[29] These are the users of areas designated as wilderness or similarly locked away from general use, and an increasingly large chunk of the public domain is being reserved for them. This demographic profile is inevitable. The purpose of designating a wilderness is to create an area "where the earth and its community of life are untrammeled by man, where man himself is a visitor who does not remain." Wilderness cannot have roads or structures. Motorized transport is not permitted. The upshot is that no one except the young and fit can go there. Most elderly or even middle-aged people are excluded, and so are the physically impaired, families with children, and anyone else who does not match the profile. The nonrich are also excluded, for reasons that are obvious when you look at the price of equipment in the nearest upscale outdoor store. The land-grab tradition of the Old West lives on, but of all the groups that one might think of to subsidize, the wilderness users seem at the bottom of the list.

Nor surprisingly, various recreational equipment and services companies are strong supporters of the designation of land as wilderness or of rivers as wild and scenic. This is the stock in trade sold by these companies, and the more of it supplied gratis by the government, the more money they make.

It seems clear that recreation policy in the West, like so many other areas, has gone zany. Perhaps it is not necessary to make every place accessible to everyone. When you see people arriving in a park in a trailer big enough to hold a six-room house, you wonder why they bothered to leave home. On the other hand, not many people are into the true wilderness experience. I am not a hiker or camper, but I do go for strolls now and then. Even during high season at Yellowstone, get a mile from the Geyser Basin and you are mostly alone. Go biking in the high, barren hills of Marin County, in the middle of the San Francisco metropolitan area, and readily accessible, and you are also alone. It is fine to make some provision for those who appreciate these forms of recreation, but those who do not also have some claim to consideration in management of the national lands.

Some national land is designated for broader recreational use, but not much. You might think that more land could be devoted to parks than to wilderness, and more money to their maintenance. Congress has created a category of land called "National Recreation Areas," but it contains only 3.7 million acres.

Furthermore, it is not clear why wilderness users can claim the right to displace the loggers or miners who depend on the natural resources of the West for their livelihoods—or why they should displace the needs of those of us who use the resources in the goods we buy. Shutting down the Crown Butte mine seems a high price to pay to enable a limited number of the young and well-off to walk through the entire Beartooth, instead of just 99 percent of it, without seeing another human.

For the most part, the conflict between the older uses and recreation is specious. Yes, totally denuding the forest interferes with recreation, but that day is gone. The existence of logging roads can enhance recreation, even for backpackers, who can motor far deeper into the forest before setting out. Mines have a small footprint and hardly interfere with anything, as long as modern pollution control and cleanup laws are followed. In fact, the mines can support an infrastructure of transportation and commercial activities on which recreation users can free ride. Friends and land speculators living in Red Lodge, Montana, and Cody, Wyoming, would be delighted to have Crown Butte improve the roads to Yellowstone. Tourists and snow mobilers in Cooke City would have benefited greatly from the commercial operations that would have been supported by the mining community. Even grazing is compatible with many recreational uses, as long as you watch where you step.

Chapter 10

Waterless World

Water rights, dams, and other chicanery

In the West, the property that often counts, more than land, grass, wood, or ore, is water. Land is plentiful, water scarce. The needs of the great cities of the California coast and the rise of industry in the Mountain West are putting pressure on the existing structure of water rights. So is the increasing demand that water be devoted to environmental purposes: recreation, wildlife, aesthetics, and wilderness. Much of the conflict is conducted in the language of water law, a form of communication as exotic to most of us as the language of ancient Ur, but its obscurity should not obscure the deadly serious nature of the struggle.

Most water used in the West goes for irrigation and agriculture. Surely, you might think, those 26 million people on the California coast must use lots of water, and in fact they do. But agriculture is incredibly thirsty, and those urbanites, with all their watered lawns, and tossing in all their factories and car washes, and adding in mines and everything else, hardly make a dent. Agriculture uses 80 to 90 percent of the water, depending on exactly how you count.

This heavy agricultural use is good news, especially for the urbanites, because it means there need be no serious crisis in supplying the cities. Relatively minor reallocations can take care of it. One of the leading economic analysts of the issue, B. D. Gardner, estimates that a 10 percent increase in the price of water used for irrigation would result in a decrease of 20 percent in use.[1] This would double the amount now available for other purposes.

This is good news for another reason. There is scope for reallocating water to serve the recreation and wildlife uses that are important to the developing West. This shift is certain to occur, but it can come smoothly and painlessly or with bitterness and trauma. How it goes depends primarily on how well we—meaning society, the government, the environmentalists, western economic interests, all of us—deal with the property rights issues tied up in the region's water.

In all societies, water is a commons. It is not something you own, at least not until you capture it and put it in a pail. It is something you can use.

Usually the right to use a commons is not quite absolute. It is subject to some adjustment in the light of population increases, changing technology, overuse, or some other new event. It is not subject to obliteration, but it is a bit fuzzy around the edges. Sometimes it is in everybody's interest, including the property owner's, not to have rights carved in stone. If people know that a use, once allowed, can never be changed, they will be reluctant to allow it in the first place. A time-honored Lockean function of governments is to make rules about the commons, and water has always been high on the list.

In the United States, the water-logged East developed the doctrine of riparian rights (*riparian* means "related to a riverbank"). The owner of land on a watercourse has the right to use the river for boating, fishing, and transportation. He has the right to receive the natural flow of the water, without significant diminishment or degradation. He has the right to divert and take a reasonable amount of water for use on the riparian property, but he is not allowed to transport water off to use in some distant operation. If uses by different people conflict, courts sort it all out according to a flexible rule of reason. If water runs short, all uses are reduced somewhat.

The West went in a different direction. It made property rights in the use of the water commons absolute. Since mining preceded agriculture, the practice and law of water rights in the West were developed by miners, not farmers. Mining uses lots of water and often takes place far from any watercourse. Besides, all the land was public domain, and if riparian doctrine applied, then no one but the government had any right to use the water. The solution was natural and Lockean. Once you start removing a quantity of water from a stream and putting it to beneficial use, you have a legal property right to keep removing and using that quantity. This use need not be on the land near the stream; it can be anywhere you can move the water. Once you start taking the water, you have a permanent right to the quantity taken that trumps any claims made later in time. No pro-rationing applies. A senior user gets all of his water before a junior user gets a drop. This is the doctrine of prior appropriation.

Water law is state law, not federal, and most of the streams in the West were on federal land. By statute, Congress subjected this water to state rules and the doctrine of prior appropriation—and appropriated it was. In the present day, almost two-thirds of the average annual water yield in the West comes from federal lands, while only about 1 percent of it is consumed there.[2]

In the conditions of the West, prior appropriation made good sense. Security of water supply was the first consideration in making investments of work and money. Clarity was essential. In any situation where a temporary interruption of supply can be fatal and law and courts are not accessible, precision is a great virtue. The system was also somewhat self-regulating. Diverting water meant incredible labor with pick and shovel, so no one would take it for fun or move it farther than necessary.

Naturally, a few complications about the details come up from time to time. A handy guide is David Getches's *Water Law in a Nutshell,* but even a nutshell on water rights is 450 pages big. States retain the right to define the uses that qualify as "beneficial." These have evolved about as you would expect. They vary from state to state, depending on the economic structure, but the list includes mining, agriculture, stock watering, power, domestic, municipal, and industrial. Over the past decades two new ones have been added—recreation and fish/wildlife—reflecting the changing economic base of the West and the growing environmental consciousness. Adding these to the list does not allow them to bump existing rights. It means only that they are recognized as uses for which previously unclaimed water can be appropriated. Adding them also makes them eligible for transfers of existing rights.

In general, no hierarchy exists among beneficial uses. You cannot argue that your domestic use should bump a senior right to stock watering. Some states do classify, and allow a use deemed superior to bump a senior but less important use on payment of compensation. A state can take water rights by eminent domain and pay for them.

Water rights are transferable, but it is tricky. The transfer cannot interfere with the rights of junior holders. In practice, this means that transfers of rights with the land on which they are used are routine. Transfers of rights for the same use are pretty routine, but with limits. Transfers for entirely different uses, and especially transfers out of the watershed, are a jungle. Basic doctrine says you can transfer water, but the issue is now covered by a multiplicity of different state laws and judicial rulings. Generalization is difficult, and so is transfer.

Because of this course of historical development, a lot of water goes into fairly low-value uses, such as growing hay to feed cattle. The road to letting it flow into higher-value uses lies in setting up institutional mechanisms that allow and encourage transfers, and the foundation of this is to recognize the present users' property rights. If water is worth $100 per acre-foot on up to cities, industries, or conservationists and is being used by farmers who value it at $20 or less per acre-foot, there are deals to be made. The trick is to figure out how to let them happen.

So far, all of this seems standard, if not routine. The world is changing, resources are needed for new uses, and the legal and political systems need to figure out how to grease the road to change by securing property rights, inventing new forms of transactions, and in other ways performing as a legitimate government in a Lockean system—not easy, but not impossible. In any event, call this need to let the water flow into new and superior uses western water rights problem number one.

There is, however, a joker in the deck. In a series of decisions interpreting the laws governing water on federal land, the Supreme Court created the doctrine of reserved rights. This says that whenever the federal government reserved land from the public domain for a public purpose, there was an implied reservation of sufficient water rights to carry out that purpose. These rights are effective as of the date of the reservation and can bump any water rights perfected at a later date. In accord with the current legal style of leaving everything up to case-by-case determination by judges, such terms as *public purpose* and *sufficient* are undefined and unpredictable. Given the quantity of water that arises on federal land, this introduces major uncertainties into the whole system. The reserved rights doctrine does not fit at all with the western approach of prior appropriation, because the reserved rights do not hinge on actual beneficial use, are not lost by nonuse, date back to the original withdrawal of the land, and are uncertain in quantity. The general result is a large cloud over many of the water rights of the West. This cloud is darkened by the government's current tendency to interpret every federal law governing western resources in the direction of nonuse. If you thought grass, timber, and ore could cause a rebellion in the West, just wait until the feds start interpreting out of existence valuable water rights dating back a century or more. The implications of an expansive doctrine of reserved rights is western water rights problem number two.

To continue the list of problems, return once again to the roots of the West. By the 1890s, the problem of aridity was known to all. So was the solution, they thought: irrigate. From 1870 on, a multitude of private irrigation efforts beavered away. The Mormons, working under religious discipline, were the best at it. By 1889, 3.6 million acres were irrigated, half of it by the Mormons,[3] out of the 753 million total acres in the Mountain and Pacific West. By 1900, the national total stood at 7.5 million acres under irrigation, most of it in the West. Irrigation took about 20 billion gallons of water per day, half the water used in the nation.

In retrospect, the record of private irrigation efforts looks pretty good. The problem with irrigation is that water is heavy, and great energy is needed to move it. With late nineteenth-century technology, irrigation was mostly limited to good riparian land, which needed only some ditching. In a few cases, a dam can be thrown across a narrow valley and water moved by gravity to a fertile plain, but such opportunities are rare. Moving billions of gallons over mountain ranges to grow hay makes no economic sense, even if it is physically possible. Large-scale irrigation also takes heavy up-front investment, which raises costs still further. The use of capital is not free. All things considered, around 1900 the private irrigation movement was humming along just fine.

To contemporaries, and especially to the land speculators, progress looked painfully slow. The solution seemed clear. The federal government could bring water to the West and achieve the long-dreamed-of Eden. Water for a billion acres! The whole West in bloom! In 1900, both party platforms supported a reclamation act.

LOS ANGELES, CALIFORNIA, 1893

The International Irrigation Congress is meeting. The halls are full of excitement and boosterism. John Wesley Powell rises to speak. He recently completed the government's 1890 irrigation survey, and with his customary realism he estimates that, at most, about 100 million acres of the West can be reclaimed. The survey identified 30 million suitable acres and 200 possible reservoir sites.

Wallace Stegner describes the scene in Los Angeles. Powell listens to the rampant optimism and realizes the delegates have gone mad. He puts aside his prepared speech and tries to tell them so. "'I tell you gentlemen,' he said into their heckling and the rising clamor of their indignation, 'you are piling up a heritage of conflict and litigation over water rights for there is not sufficient water to supply the land.'" The delegates boo him.[4]

Congress had already made its judgment on Powell, out of anger over his handling of the irrigation survey as well as for his pessimism. It cut the budget of his agency, the U.S. Geological Survey, and by 1894 it chivvied him out of government. In 1902, it passed the Reclamation Act. The law created the Bureau of Reclamation in the Department of the Interior. It set up a revolving fund, financed initially from sales of public lands. The bureau would build irrigation projects and sell the water to users, who would pay and replenish the fund.

Congress wanted to ensure that the program did not inure to the benefit of the land barons, especially the railroads, which owned millions of acres. It also wanted to carry out the original purpose of the Homestead Act to create a West of small landholders, so it inserted a limit of 160 acres on land that could be owned by anyone getting water from government projects. The law also required the permit holder to live on the irrigated land.

These requirements did not fit with the changing economics and technical requirements of agriculture. Once again, the story of the West becomes one of evasion and fraud. Everyone, including the government, ignored the acreage limits. Wives, minor children, grandchildren, and cousins can all own land. Excess land can be sold off in legal-size chunks to individual investors, each of whom then leases it back to the original owner to operate. It is best just to forget these acreage limits as unwise restraints on alienation. In all the years from 1902 to 1982, only one acreage limitation case, against the DiGiorgio lands, was pursued to a conclusion,[5] which makes you wonder what political contribution the DiGiorgios forgot to make.

Some accounts might lead you to believe that the whole West is under water and the Bureau of Reclamation is responsible for all of it. Both of these propositions are wrong. In fact, Powell himself was wildly overoptimistic about irrigation. Even now, after almost a hundred years and tens of billions of dollars, the Mountain and Pacific West has about 26 million acres under irrigation, an increase of only 18.5 million acres over the total in 1900.[6] This is 3.5 percent of the land area of the eleven states.

Significant acreage is still watered by diversion of creeks and rivers onto neighboring fields. These are low-cost projects with immediate payoff and clear beneficiaries, and they can be funded privately. Until about 1945, this was the predominant form of irrigation in the Mountain West. The Pacific West began to use other methods earlier, especially in California's great Central Valley.

More irrigation water comes from tens of thousands of wells drilled to tap into the estimated 6.2 billion acre-feet of groundwater that lies below the surface of the West. These too are privately financed. They provide 21 percent of the irrigation water used in the Mountain and Pacific West and 39 percent of California's water. This form of irrigation got a huge boost in 1948, when the centrifugal pump became available for general use. It could pull water up from 300 feet instead of the 25 feet possible with old-style suction pumps. The main impact of the pump occurred on the Great Plains, from the Dakotas south to Texas, where it created the equivalent of an oil boom. Between 1950 and 1975, groundwater use on the Plains went from 2.7 million acre-feet annually to 23.3 million. Allocating the rights to tap these underground aquifers is western water problem number three. Is it strictly prior appropriation, so him as pumps fastest gets most? Is the acquifer a fuzzy commons whose use is to be adjusted by government? Should the water be auctioned off? What *are* the property rights, anyway?

The third source of irrigation water is the Bureau of Reclamation, which builds irrigation facilities and supplies flood control and power as side benefits. The fourth is the Army Corps of Engineers, which builds for flood control and power, and then provides irrigation as a side benefit. The two are not always easy to distinguish. At first, the bureau worked in the West and the Corps in the East, but over time the Corps expanded, and the two competed to grab dam sites. Marc Reisner of the Natural Resources Defense Council wrote *Cadillac Desert,* an entertaining and horrifying set of tales of the great dam-building binge. His term for the bureau and the Corps is "rivals in crime."

After its creation in 1902, the Bureau of Reclamation started slowly. For both the bureau and the Corps, the New Deal was the great event. The government wanted to build public works, and dams were ideal. During the 1930s, creating jobs, for workers and for gasping industrial firms thrown on the beach by the Great Depression, was the name of the game, and dams served the purpose. They were also in accord with the spirit of the times. Huge industrial plants belching smoke, socialist realism art showing noble proletarians at work, Albert Speer's architectural designs for Berlin: these were all part of the 1930s.

The problem with private irrigation efforts was that they were constrained by the market to undertake only projects that made economic sense. There are not many of these, as it turns out, but the government was not so limited. An iron alliance formed consisting of Congress, the Bureau of Reclamation, the Corps of Engineers, local land barons and government officials, and large engineering firms. Pork was spread widely. Because everyone was anxious to build dams, Congress was not interested in asking whether they made economic sense. In fact, it was distinctly interested in being sure that no one asked the question.

TENNESSEE, 1978–1979

The story of the Tellico Dam captures the essence of the dam building binge. The Tennessee Valley Authority proposes a dam that will destroy a beautiful valley and splendid trout and canoeing stream to gain a trivial increase in power generation at a nearby dam. Leaving out any environmental arguments, the dam cannot meet any cost-benefit test. Rational argument against the dam fails, but construction is stopped by the discovery of the endangered snail darter. In *TVA v. Hill* the Supreme Court rules in favor of the fish.

Congress responds by passing a law giving a special cabinet-level committee, nicknamed the God Squad, power to exempt any specific project from the act when the benefits of doing so clearly outweigh any other course of action. Tellico is 95 percent completed, and it is a forgone conclusion that an exemption will be given. The committee, which includes the distinguished economist and Council of Economic Advisers chairman Charles Schultze, says no. Under honest analysis, *all* the benefits from a completed dam do not equal the 5 *percent* of the costs that remain to be paid. Economic rationality says the dam should be left unfinished and the sunk costs written off.

Congress, undeterred, passes a special law exempting Tellico from the act, the dam is completed, and the valley flooded.[7]

Once the dam building machine got rolling, it was unstoppable. By the 1960s, the bureau had 19,000 employees who did nothing but plan and supervise projects and look for new ones.[8] Actual construction was carried out by armies of contractors.

The Bureau of Reclamation became a massive machine to provide expensive water at low cost. Total construction costs for the irrigation portion of bureau projects is almost $20 billion, in 1986 dollars. Eighty-six percent of these costs have been donated to the water users as a subsidy. The subsidy amounts to almost $2,000 for every acre for which irrigation is provided.[9] For newer projects, built on more marginal sites, the economics are even worse. Total costs are $250 to $500 per acre-foot of water delivered. Some water charges are below even the operating and maintenance costs of delivering the water, which are $7 or $8 per acre-foot. Some users pay $3.50.

WASHINGTON, D.C., 1996

My water bill arrives. The District of Columbia charges me $2.868 per 100 cubic feet—half for water and half for sewer. Counting only the water half, this is $625 per acre-foot.

A study of the San Joaquin Valley in California found that farmers pay the government $20 per acre-foot for water. With this, they raise crops with a value of $50 for every acre-foot of water applied, so their net benefit is $30 per acre-foot. A conservative estimate of the federal government's cost to produce the water is $300 per acre-foot, so taxpayers lose $280 in pure waste on every acre-foot of water produced to give farmers $30 of benefit.[10] These calculations are based on only the costs that the bureau assigns to irrigation, which are understated. Projects have multiple purposes, and cost allocation is a dark art. Some costs properly allocable to irrigation are assigned to power production or even to protection of fish and wildlife. Some important costs are not counted at all, because no attention is paid to impacts on environmental values, fish and wildlife, recreation, local communities, or anything except the gods of irrigation, flood control, power, and water supply.

While this is going on, cities just down the road on the coast are willing to pay $100 per acre-foot on up for water.

THE USSR, 1980s, AND CALIFORNIA AND WASHINGTON, D.C., 1995

The Soviet factory makes widgets. They aren't very good and don't sell for much on the open market. When you add up the market prices of all the raw materials and energy used to make the widgets, it turns out that the value of these inputs exceeds the value of the widgets. The factory is a value-subtracting enterprise. If it were torn down and the inputs sold for other uses, Soviet economic performance would improve. Because the prices of the inputs are controlled or subsidized, no one knows this. The production line keeps rolling, making the Russians poorer every day. The Soviet empire is full of such enterprises, from a glove factory in Russia to an orchid greenhouse in Poland that relies on subsidized oil prices.

Ah, those Commies, you think. Luckily, we live in the U.S.A., where capitalism reigns.

Cut to Washington, D.C., in 1995, as the administration proudly announces that after intense negotiations, the Japanese will let us sell them up to 758,000 tons per year of American rice, mainly California short and medium grain, apparently at current market prices. The *Wall Street Journal* lists rough rice, type unspecified, as costing about $200 per ton. In California, rice requires about half an acre-foot of water per ton grown. If the rice is produced with subsidized water that costs the government $300 per acre-foot, then the crop is worth little more than the cost of the water it uses. When you add the cost of necessary inputs of land, labor, and capital, it is clearly a money loser. Like the old joke, we lose on every sale but make it up on volume. Arkansas is the nation's largest producer of rice. California is second.

It is axiomatic that when a valuable commodity, such as water, is being put to a low-valued use and other people are willing to pay a lot for it, there must be ways to get it into the higher use. There are, but it is not easy.

As with most other subsidies, the water subsidy was long ago factored into the sale price of land. When farms are sold, you can be sure the buyer pays full value for the benefits produced by the water. (A forty-year contract to deliver 3 acre-feet of water per year is worth $1,544 per acre in land value.) The person who made out like a bandit was the owner when the subsidy started, not the current owner. And, of course, the initial owner benefited only to the extent of the value of the water, not by what it cost the government to produce it. In the San Joaquin, it is the $30 per acre-foot revenue to the farmer water that got capitalized into the land value, not the $300 it cost the government to build the dam to produce the water.

Given this structure, to switch suddenly to a full-cost system would bankrupt current owners. Even changing to a full-value pricing would make a serious economic dent, and, not surprisingly, current owners resist paying for what, in their view, they already bought from the prior owner. We are irritated because landowners, politicians, and bureaucrats of the post–World War II period were willing to inflict such grievous costs on the taxpayer and the environment for the sake of such paltry benefits to the farmers. Trying to exact present revenge is time blur, though.

No perfect solutions exist, but there are some pretty good partial ones. The starting point is clarity about the nature of the agricultural users' property right. A right to government irrigation water is a partial property right. It is a contract letting the farmer use water for a certain purpose on certain land. Government rules have never defined the right as allowing its sale on the open market or even its transfer to another irrigator. As a result, to say that the farmer's water rights are worth, say, $200 per acre-foot is wrong. The *water* may be worth that to someone else, such as a city. The farmer's *property right* in the water, being partial, is worth only its value as an input in agriculture. In the San Joaquin this is about $30 per acre-foot. This was the price the farmer paid for his partial water right when he bought the land for agricultural use, and there is no moral or economic case for giving him the water free and clear.

Because it is clearly time to reallocate to cities and environmental uses, the government should start buying these water rights at their market value. It can buy from the holders of the rights, or it can buy the underlying lands at a value that reflects the attached rights, then sell it back to the owner or at auction, stripped of water rights. The basic task is to create a pool of tradable water and establish a free market.

Of course, this may not be the way the users see it, so this is another of the conflicts in the West. To a user, he gets the water, so it is his. Those bureaucrats force him to use it for irrigation when he could be making a killing—selling it to some city for $100 on up. So bring on the free market, and give me the water! To convert the current partial water rights into full rights would be a government giveaway on a par with the initial dam building binge. Environmentalists resist this, and they are right.

The other half of the great dam building binge was the Army Corps of Engineers. Its history parallels that of the Bureau of Reclamation and shows the same emphasis on political clout; corrupt cost-benefit analysis; disregard of environmental, ecological, or aesthetic values; and reckless disregard for the people affected by its actions. Reisner, citing chapter and verse, calls it "as opportunistic and ruthless an agency as American government has ever seen."[11]

During the binge, every significant river in the West except the Yellowstone was dammed, many several times, in the name of hydropower and flood control. The results are dubious. Robert Devine, an environmental writer, says that between 1960 and 1987, the U.S. government spent some $40 billion on flood control, while between 1951 and the present, annual flood damage went from $1 billion to $3 billion per year, in constant dollars. The combination of the promise of flood control and subsidized flood insurance triggered a spate of building on floodplains. Devine also cites a General Accounting Office finding that half the flood insurance money is paid out to repeat victims, who make up 2 percent of all policyholders.[12]

Devine points out other problems with the dams. They trap silt, change water flows, and alter water temperatures. These changes devastate aquatic life, as demonstrated by the current controversy over what to do about the salmon in the Pacific Northwest. Dams even change the shape of the earth. The Louisiana coast used to get sediment from the Mississippi. Without it, the coast shrinks and saltwater intrudes. The Corps of Engineers believes that over the next fifty years, the Gulf shoreline will move up to 30 miles inland and a million acres of wetlands will be lost.

The tale of the Tellico Dam is typical of the whole era, but the supply of stories is infinite. You can be impartial, too, reading works by the environmental organizations and the economics profession in equal measure. Devine asked a dam expert to name some "good dams," meaning those with benefits clearly outweighing their costs, including environmental costs. The expert named two, the Hoover and Grand Coulee, then paused. No others came readily to mind.[13]

Still, dams seem to be like the Terminator in the movies: every time you think they are dead, there they are, coming at you. The Central Utah Project was authorized in 1993. In 1990, the General Accounting Office estimated that it will return only thirty cents for every dollar spent on it.[14] It will deliver water to farmers at a cost of $300 per acre-foot. The water will generate about $30 of farm product value per-acre foot, and the farmers will pay $3.[15] The Auburn Dam in California may yet be built. It just shows what you can accomplish if you eliminate markets and property rights and make sure that people getting the payoffs do not have to worry about picky little questions, such as economic costs and benefits or environmental damage.

The question of what, if anything, to do about existing dams is knotty. By controlling flooding and creating riparian land around reservoirs, the dam projects induced large-scale private investment. People built homes and businesses on the floodplains or recreation facilities around the dams. Now they object when they are hurt by government efforts to ease the problems caused by the projects. As Nancy Langston said in connection with the forest, you cannot simply go back up the decision tree and make a different choice.

OROFINO, IDAHO, 1995

Dworshak Dam across the North Fork of the Clearwater River was completed by the Corps of Engineers in 1974. The dam is 717 feet high, 3,287 feet long, and behind it is Dworshak Lake, almost 1 mile wide and 53 miles long. Recreation centered on the lake is now a main industry in Orofino, a town of 3,711 people. The dam's major purpose is flood control. The Clearwater feeds the Snake, which feeds the Columbia, and since the 1930s every part of this system has been dammed and redammed. The Columbia system is a prime salmon river, and the damming has affected the fish. The effect is direct, in that some of the dams keep them from going upstream. It can also be less direct. The dams turn what were once flowing rivers into a series of lakes. As a result, young salmon take too long to make their journey from the spawning streams to the sea. Before the dams, they made the trip in fewer than twenty days. Now it takes up to ninety, and their biological clocks cannot tolerate the delay. One solution is to load the young salmon on barges. Another possibility is to draw down the reservoirs so as to flush the salmon through the system more quickly. In 1995, enough water is released from Dworshak Dam to take the lake level down 20 feet. The action decimates the local recreation industry. The residents are hopping mad.[16]

Clearly there is no legal theory that supports any kind of property right to have the government maintain any given level of water in a reservoir. Nor should there be. Creating property rights in government actions is a sure road to sclerosis and disaster. At the same time, those injured by the action certainly do not believe their interests received fair consideration or that the water release was justified by environmental benefits. The local explanation for the decline of the salmon population is that the courts have interpreted Indian treaties as creating an unlimited right for Indians to take fish at the point where they enter the rivers. This view holds that the water release was a political gesture that did great harm to the people of the nearby towns without doing any real good for the fish. I am rationally ignorant about this matter, so I do not know if the feeling is justified. It is certainly real. Of course, in addition to creating hard feelings toward the federal government, the action sours community relations in the Northwest.

The government is trying to sort out issues of water in the Pacific Northwest. At least it wants to *look* as if it is sorting them out while avoiding blame. Congress created the Northwest Power Planning Council to report on an appropriate governance structure for control over the Columbia River system and efforts to conserve fish and wildlife. The council held a workshop that prepared a report heavy on the need for long-term planning, coordination, consensus, involvement of all stakeholders, dispute resolution, and all the other current buzzwords. No one has control of anything, and no one owns anything. As the workshop report says, "Over the past several decades a constellation of agencies, courts and other entities have been 'in charge' to one degree or another, and authority has shifted among them with the passage and interpretation of various laws and treaties."[17] Nothing in the report would change this. You can predict with total confidence that this issue will continue its downward spiral for the foreseeable future.

Chapter 11

Sorting It Out

Thoughts on the West and other intractable problems

In considering the West, much of the earlier analysis of the endangered species and wetlands programs applies. Western issues present the same hodgepodge of property rights, governmental legitimacy, aesthetic preferences, and militant religion. There is the same difficulty in sorting them out. A reasonable chunk of territory should be set aside as wildlife refuge, where man and woman are visitors who do not remain. It might be a good idea to forbid even visits by people as a way of putting some check on the land hunger of the urban rich. The grizzlies are beginning to enforce this idea without the need for government regulation, though, so maybe it can be left to market forces.

The refuges need not represent any overwhelming quantity of territory. Public domain can remain basically unspoiled while still allowing timbering, mining, and land sales for recreation and home building. These activities simply need not spoil the land in the way that some of the environmentalists seem to think they do. Multiple use is the norm for land all over the country. If you regard the public domain as a commons to be shared by the American people as a whole, creating opportunities for use by other than the most dedicated backpackers is the only ethical course. Most of the absolutist, religious arguments for leaving things untouched come through to me as an effort to lay on a guilt trip as a power move in a game of political manipulation. Few people who call themselves environmentalists are truly dedicated to the absolutist position. Most would be in the wise use camp if they were not rationally ignorant about the details of the argument.

If my slant on things is right and environmentalist rhetoric is more calculation than fundamental belief, the situation has a bright side. Rather obviously, I am not someone the environmentalist community would choose as a spokesperson, but I will hazard an interpretation. Based on conversations with people in that camp, many of them are aware of the moral difficulty of their position on western land and on wetlands and endangered species. They have a problem. They place very high value on the ends served by these programs. They would be ecstatic if these causes were treated as public goods and significant money devoted to funding them. This is not likely to happen, given the grim state of the federal budget. Entitlements are squeezing out expenditures for existing public goods, let alone any new ones. The environmentalists see themselves as caught in a bind. Since funding is not likely, either push the religious, absolutist rationales, whatever the damage to property owners or economic use of resources, or let the environmental values go. Given these choices, they come down on the side of protecting the environmental values. They may feel guilty (a little), but their priorities are clear. Then, of course, they exhibit the human tendency to get mad at the people they are injuring.

This is a bright side? Actually, yes. People in this camp can be persuaded on pragmatic grounds. If they are convinced that better protection of property rights will foster better protection of the environment, then deals can be made. The people at the free-market think tanks are convinced that this proposition is indeed true—that property rights are the royal road to increased environmental protection. The free-market types also think the environmentalists are making a mistake. Taking something that other people regard as their right makes them mad. Eventually it builds up a wave of resistance that turns and swamps you in unpredictable ways. Also, reliance on absolutist rhetoric deprives you of any stopping points. You lose the ability to say no to any members of your own constituency, and you have to demand more and more. This, too, can bite you, in the end.

The Political Economy Research Center in Bozeman, Montana, is a leading purveyor of the free-market view. Senior associate Richard Stroup points out that environmental protection is becoming a highly valued good in the West. This makes sense. We are much richer than our nineteenth-century ancestors. If we want to protect forests or restore mined hillsides, it is economically feasible. We do not have to spend months with a shovel digging by hand. We can call in a bulldozer. Environmental protection is within economic reach in a way that was not true for earlier generations.

Since environmental amenities are within economic reach and since they are valued, they will be supplied in the marketplace. The key is the creation of the transactional capability. Stroup points to two land developments near Bozeman as examples of the way in which the new emphasis on environmentalism is making itself felt in the marketplace. Both rely on land covenants. In one, the residents buy 20 acres and agree to develop only 3 of them; the rest must remain wild for the benefit of the project as a whole. The other is the huge Big Sky project built between Bozeman and Yellowstone National Park, about 90 miles to the south. The developers of Big Sky bought up a large tract, developed part of it themselves, and now sell the rest of it only to people who sign heavy covenants that guarantee the continuing attractiveness of the area. This practice is becoming common in Montana. People who live there value its environmental characteristics greatly and are willing to pay good money to see them maintained.

Putting aside the religious dimensions of the conflict, the West suffers from both too few and too many property rights. Wherever you look, private property rights are partial and incomplete. This is true of grazing rights. It is true for prior-appropriated water and for the rights to subsidized government-generated irrigation water. It is true of cutting wood in the national forests or of claiming mining land. It is also true for recreation in such commons as the national parks. This last one may cry for explanation. How do you have property rights in a national park?

Simple. In my expanded catalog of property rights, you have a right to use the commons. The government could not arbitrarily pick and choose among its citizens. The problem is that the government is failing in its obligations to administer this commons competently because it has not established a mechanism to charge enough. As a result, you and your fellow citizens pay small fees for crowded and deteriorating facilities when you would be perfectly willing to pay higher fees for much better ones. In an effort to be generous in a petty way, the government deprives people of real value. The government has also failed to establish mechanisms for new uses of the land, such as recreation, to bid against old ones, such as grazing and logging.

MONTANA, 1992

Dwellers near state forest land vehemently object to a timber sale. The state offers to sell them a viewshed easement at a price that equals the discounted present value of the future timber harvests that the state will give up if it leaves the trees untouched. The residents are about to accept, then decide that perhaps they can live with a cheaper alternative of a selective harvest that leaves the land looking more natural than would the original plan.[1]

There is even hope for the wealthy white male executives who frequent the wilderness areas. In a study, *Wilderness Designation in Utah*, researchers from Utah State found that 80 percent of this group said they would be willing to pay to have areas designated as wilderness. On the other hand, they might have to bid against other groups, who also expressed a willingness to pay to have the Utah area remain open for multiple use, including motorized recreation.[2] In reality, there is room for both, with each buying up different areas.

The West also suffers because its private economy is tightly bound up with public land and public resources of grazing, water, timber, and minerals. The government administers these resources by political criteria, which makes the situation dangerously quixotic. One of the glories of the market is that it greatly enhances the predictability of people's behavior. This allows others to plan. If you own a sawmill in the middle of privately owned timber country, you know that you can always secure a supply for the mill, at a price. Some owners may hold timber off the market for environmental or speculative reasons, and it is always possible for the price to go so high that you cannot operate, but these are normal business risks. If the land is administered according to political criteria, then your circumstances become fluid, and rational planning is impossible. The people of the West would be better off if the government acted like a greedy property owner or an environmentally conscious steward of the land that maximizes profits within environmental constraints or in any other consistent fashion. Uncertainty is the real killer.

The first result of this uncertainty is to discourage investment, of money or of self, in any activity dependent on federal resources. Go back to the story of the Dworshak Dam. Anyone considering buying a home or setting up a business in the area surrounding the dam must consider the possibility that the government will drop the water level of the reservoir and wipe out the value of the investment. Furthermore, the odds on this event cannot be calculated scientifically. Suppose you want to predict whether Interior will drop the water level. You, being rational, hire a wildlife biologist to tell you whether releasing water will help the fish. She says no, so you build a fishing camp. You then find out that your question was irrelevant; it does not matter whether releasing water will help fish. Lots of people who are not wildlife biologists simply assume that releasing water will help the fish, and they remain rationally ignorant about the truth of the matter. The government officials are concerned with their careers, not with your investment, so their incentive is to release the water even if they know it is pointless. Goodbye camp.

To be evenhanded, the same calculation applies if you are an environmentalist. Political calculations can easily destroy environmental values.

COLUMBIA RIVER, 1967

Marc Reisner, a former staff writer for the Natural Resources Defense Council, tells this story: "In 1967, in order to be ready for Vice President Hubert Humphrey, who was coming out to dedicate the John Day Dam and who wanted to feel the thrum of its turbines, the Corps closed the dam gates before the fish ladders were operational, condemning a migration of *hundreds of thousands* of salmon and steelhead to death. The vice president's schedule couldn't be changed."[3]

Suppose you are back in 1967. You, being rational, dismiss the possibility that the government will wipe out hundreds of thousands of fish for the sake of a photo op. You are wrong. The dam manager does not want to try to convince headquarters that he should make the vice president unhappy. "What do you mean, he came out to dedicate a hydroelectric dam and there was no power because no water was running through the turbines because you were worried about some damn fish? Do you know what he can do to our budget? And to our request for sixteen new supergrade slots for our underpaid dam managers?"

The environmentalists may believe they have no need to deal, since they are now on top. They are wrong.

COLORADO, 1996

Vice President Gore arrives on the South Platte to give a speech on river conservation. Local officials decide to increase the river's flow, and release 96 million extra gallons worth $59,000. As one says, "When you have the river being showcased, you want it to look good."[4]

Despite the difference in outcomes, the two decisions have a family resemblance. Each is political and unpredictable by the people affected. In the Northwest in 1967, fishermen and nature lovers were left to gnash their teeth over pointless destruction of fish. In 1995, Orofino residents who pinned their livelihoods to their investments in recreation facilities feel the same way.

Times may change. The nature of bureaucracies does not.

The consequence of the uncertainty that accompanies administration by politics follows like night follows day. Private actors are encouraged—indeed, forced—to invest in influencing the political decisions. They are often happy to play this game. It can be much cheaper to buy a few politicians than to pay market prices for a resource. But even people who would prefer a market system are forced into the political game. The "special interests" in the West spend large sums of money and effort to obtain the political clout needed to obtain resources "for free." The term *special interests* here includes a wide spectrum: not just the ranchers, timber, mining, and agricultural interests constituting the tried and true pressure groups of western history but the recreation and environmental interests that are striving to build new land baronies. Since no one knows what is spent on these efforts at influence, no one knows whether the total exceeds the value of the resources at stake. It well may. But the political power is about not only the cost of resources but their predictability. A river, for example, can be used by a power company, white-water rafters, fishermen, water-drawing municipalities, wildlife enthusiasts, and irrigators. They all need to know not just what water they can use, but what others can use and when they will use it. One way is by knowing people's rational self-interest or by entering into agreements. If these avenues are closed, often because property rights are ill defined, the backup mode is political control and regulation.

Once a system of political administration of resources gets going, change is difficult. Whichever dogs are on top politically must agree to any reform, and they refuse because they are now getting the resource cheaply. Eventually the political situation changes. Yesterday's top dogs are now ready to deal, but the new ones say no. For example, it is quite clear that the federal grazing lands should be privatized. Maybe they should be sold to the grazing permit holders at reasonable prices or maybe auctioned off to the public at large. Do the ranchers want either of these, even the first? Nah! They want the land on the cheap, and they want all other uses, such as recreation, excluded from competing against them. They do not want a market process that might let the other interests bid for the range. For the nonce, ranchers have the political clout to gain their ends. As the urban and recreational West keeps growing, the ranchers will lose clout, and eventually they will find their opportunity for a rational and advantageous solution has vanished. There will then be cries of "unfair." Actually the cry should be, "Live by the sword, die by the sword."

Perhaps the environmentalists will not repeat the ranchers' mistake. Much of political support for environmentalism comes from urban populations, West and East, who are under the illusion that environmental advocates are saving the West *for* them. They look forward to moving to the West part time and telecommuting, or to using their new four-wheel drive to take the kids on an extended vacation, or to do more skiing. They are in for a shock. The absolutist position is to save the West *from* these well-to-do urban hordes, not *for* them. The rhetoric on this is forthright: the United States has these cancers called cities that must be kept as small as possible. The rest of our territory should be left in a state of pristine nature. Those who want to invest the time and effort to become at home in wilderness will use it. The rest can rot. Instead of having a land used by humans with some wildlife refuges, they want a land used by wildlife with some human refuges.

This is not a winning political hand in the long term. It depends on supporters' not fully grasping the ramifications of the position, on their remaining rationally ignorant. Talking about greedy timber barons is all very well, but Frederick Weyerhaeuser of Chicago, who bought 1.9 million acres of timberland and founded a barony in the Northwest, is dead. He lived long enough to attend the 1905 Forestry Conference and support Gifford Pinchot though. His legacy has turned into Weyerhaeuser Company, which is, according to the gossip of the trade, one of the best long-term, environmentally sensitive managers of timberland and a pioneer in the development of reforestation techniques. If concern for the spotted owl sabotages the company's forestry practices, the result will be long-term damage to the woods. If it sabotages the company's balance sheet, it will do long-term damage to the finances of the upper and middle classes that support the environmental support, since Weyerhaeuser is 60 percent owned by institutions, which means the retirement accounts of the middle class. If the concern shuts down access to the woods for all but dedicated backpackers, it excludes 99 percent of the population. A program that depends on its supporters' remaining rationally ignorant of such realities has a built-in destructive virus. The more it succeeds, the more the ignorance ceases to be rational.

A final virtue of systems that depend on property rights and the market is that they allow gradual adjustments as prices shift. The market can often be brutal, but not as brutal as politics. Geologists tell us that the great tectonic plates underlying the earth are steadily moving past each other. Earthquakes occur where the plates get stuck and cannot slide smoothly. The energy keeps building up until the pressure becomes intolerable, and the sudden release causes an earthquake. So it is when control of resources is political. The plates can no longer slide past each other in smooth adjustment. Eventually there is a release of energy and a political earthquake.

The West needs a lot of sorting out, but all of it should be in the direction of improving property rights of various kinds. Some land should be administered as national commons. In any case, the history of these issues should be respected, and fair claims on the commons by loggers, miners, and inholders should be honored. Some land, especially much of the range land, should be sold off. Some should be tapped for its resources, with other uses allowed to the extent they do not conflict. In many places the federal government needs to act like a profit-maximizing landlord, auctioning off the resources for a market price. Reasonable quantities of land should be set aside for wildlife and the Endangered Species Act scrapped. Water rights should be transformed into a market system, again with due regard for those who relied on the current approach.

None of this is simple. Robert Nelson has parsed through a number of these issues in an interesting collection of essays, *Public Lands and Private Rights*, and a number of other works cast light on the problem.[5] But none of it is impossible, unless the forces—commercial or environmental—that think they profit from rational ignorance conspire to make it so.

How would a reprivatized, market-oriented West work? What would it look like? Who knows? The reason we rely on market processes is that questions like this are too complicated to be answered. If we get the property rules right, then the result will be about as good as we can do, and it will certainly be better than anything produced by wise guardians sitting around crunching numbers, or—the more likely alternative—corrupt guardians sitting around swapping votes and "campaign contributions."

Nonetheless, let us speculate on how it might work. Suppose I am a rancher with grazing rights on some public land. A stream that might provide good fishing runs through the parcel. It is not good at present because my cattle have broken down the creek banks, depriving the fish of sheltering banks and silting up the water. On the far side, the country rises and might make good wildlife habitat. I chase wildlife away though. If it appears, BLM might get ideas about cutting my allotment to make room for it. There is also the horrible possibility that an endangered species might show up. I also exclude human wildlife. My parcel connects to some forest land with trails, and four-wheelers are always trying to cut through my place. I keep them off because they scare the cattle, and there is nothing in it for me to let them use the land. I also worry because I think my permit allows too many cows during this current dry year, but I am afraid to cut back for fear of losing my allotment. I am also afraid to invest in any range improvements because my permit conditions can change before I get back the investment. If this happens, BLM is supposed to pay me for the improvement, but who wants to hassle with the government over depreciation and values? In fact, the way the political winds are blowing, I am likely to get my allotment cut in the future. I better sneak a few more cattle on there and overgraze before I am shut out entirely.

Under the present system, nothing will change. The cattle will munch in excess numbers, the creek will silt, the four-wheelers will go elsewhere, and neither wildlife nor fishermen will find my land attractive. BLM will spend millions of dollars on studies and land use planning, and I will attend meetings of my local advisory council, where I will outjaw and outsit those tree huggers who hate my cows. Or maybe they will outjaw me. Either way, the system will bear a close resemblance to the airline agent deciding who to bump or to the system for allocating land to Hawaiians.

Now suppose a giant government giveaway sells the public grazing lands to us cattle barons for some pittance. ("Cattle baron." Ha! It's a lousy business, with a rate of return on assets of somewhere around 2 percent. The only reason I'm here is because this has been my family place for four generations, and I love it.) This parcel of land is now ALL MINE—an environmentalist nightmare because pillage surely is at hand. The local tree huggers cannot bear to watch. They leave and do not come back for two years. What do they see? I have fenced off my cattle from the creek and now pipe water to troughs (being careful not to spill any because I do not want to create a wetland). I am rebuilding the banks to provide good conditions for fish, and I am working on a deal to sell private fishing licenses. (Those crazy Californians will pay high!) I have cut down the number of cattle because I don't want to ruin MY range. I got an association of four-wheelers to pay for an easement for a trail along the near side of the creek, just on the other side of the cattle fence, and I am installing a gate with a card reader. The association is making similar deals with other landowners across the state. This will provide access for the fishermen too. On the far side of the creek, I am letting the brush build up and encouraging wildlife. Why not? It adds to the glamour, and maybe I can sell hunting rights or add a hiking trail or two and some bird-watching. Did you know that this nation has 25 million regular bird-watchers, that the National Audubon Society has 550,000 members, and that 80,000 people flock to Nebraska each spring to watch the migration of the sandhill cranes?[6] Thar's gold in them thar hills. None of that endangered species habitat, though. How could I build trails for the bird-watchers? If I see one of those (fill in the blank here), that little sucker is a goner.

Of course, that environmental group in California is not happy. They say, "It's not wilderness! We don't want to go there—there's nothing to do but watch the grass grow. We just want to know it exists. You're going to let in four-wheel-drive vehicles; they will leave tracks and a trail! You will know they were there! Yuk! And the land isn't public anymore. That's awful. Californians should not have to pay to dip their expensive fishing rods! They should get streams for free. We know that none of what you are doing was happening before, or could have happened before, or would happen if the government kept the land and kicked you off it, but so what? It's the purity of the thought that counts, not the results."

PART IV

LARCENY, GRAND AND PETTY

Chapter 12

Land Use and Zoning

Games people play; OR, I've got mine and with a little luck I can
have yours, too

To see "nature, red in tooth and claw," you need not go to Isle
Royale to look at wolves and moose. Trot down to your local
zoning board. As two experts concluded, after full body immer-
sion in half a score of bitter land use fights, "something about zoning
brings out the beast in people."[1]

So far this book has covered property rights problems that are remote
from the daily lives of urban and suburban America. Land appropriated
for wetlands or endangered species is mostly rural. To some degree these
programs spill over into metropolitan areas, as in the stories about war-
blers and troglobites from Texas, and the urban effects will spread as the
EPA/Corps of Engineers team continues its imperial ways on wetlands
and the Fish and Wildlife Service keeps multiplying the list of threatened or endangered species. Suburbanites will someday be aroused by
these programs, but that day is not quite here. Conflicts over the public
domain in the West appear similarly remote to urbanites. This is an illusion on their part, because the set of the current tide will provide
some unpleasant surprises for them. They will feel an economic nip as
access to natural resources is cut off, though the chain of causation may
be too remote for the rationally ignorant to recognize. They will feel the
impact directly when they decide to go west and telecommute, only to
find that their own access to the national commons has gone the way of
the loggers and miners. Again, though, this discovery is in the future.

This part turns to the immediate property rights problems of the great metropolitan areas of the United States. Rights are in a state of confusion, and for good reason. The issues are complex in theory and obstinate in practice. Problems of externalities, use of various commons, access to transportation networks, provision of public facilities, and changes in technology are ubiquitous. The whole area is rife with abridgments of property rights, and these do not follow any set pattern. Rules on land use can represent owners' getting together to maximize joint value. They can be one group ripping off another (usually old residents ripping off new). They can be one group against everyone outside. They can be several of these at once. Everybody on every side thinks that their property rights are involved, and all of them are right, at least sometimes. This makes it easy for people of piratical bent to raid their neighbors, and many a respectable suburbanite should be flying the Jolly Roger rather than the Stars and Stripes on Flag Day.

Violations of people's sense of legitimacy are also rife. Between the 1920s and the 1980s the federal courts, particularly the U.S. Supreme Court, regarded zoning and land use as the judicial equivalent of land war in Asia. Its maxim was, "Whatever you do, do not get involved." This shows that judges are not too dumb to have a strong survival instinct, but it also leaves those who feel aggrieved at the mercy of purely local law. In some instances, this has worked well, as state courts have stepped in to fill the gap. In other places, it leaves citizens at the mercy of local kleptocrats.

As is common in human affairs, the lack of outside control on power leads to abuses. In most places most of the time, it might be possible for people to work things out, with give and take and an eye on long-term relationships. In a mobile, urban society this does not work. A few people push the outer bounds of good faith; then others decide that they too can get something for free. The involuntary donees have no way to get anything back, so the original aggression is clearly profitable. In many places the courts, acting in the name of deference to administrative discretion, do not enforce standards of either fair outcomes or honest procedure. Thereafter, it is Isle Royale. The losers are getting madder, of course, and the rumblings of discontent are getting louder.

This chapter seeks to bring some order to this chaotic tale. It starts with a map of the battleground, background on the rise of land use controls, such as zoning, comprehensive planning, and environmental controls. It then looks at some specific problems, such as appropriation by regulation and exactions. It closes by examining some promising institutional innovations that can dampen the conflicts.

The idea of separating land uses to keep like with like and avoid conflicts is so obvious that the practice probably went on back in Ur. You can imagine irate home owners picketing the new Temple of Moloch on the grounds that the screams from human sacrifice diminish their property values and the chariot jams make it hard to get to market. Every city in the United States developed its districts almost from inception, as part of the natural order of things. At the beginning, these were ordained by access to water transportation. Anything that moved goods or raw materials in bulk had to be on the water or, a little later, near the new streams of steel called railroads. Only in the twentieth century, with the highway and the truck, did the options open up. It is no accident that formal zoning became important as the United States turned into a wheeled society. Until then, separation was achieved through the limitations imposed by transportation technology and the doctrines of the common law of nuisance.

Zoning as a municipal legal requirement started in New York City in 1916 and spread during the 1920s, as the United States became suburban. Two-thirds of new urban housing units built between 1870 and 1920 were single-family homes, and by 1929, owner-occupants were 46 percent of all nonfarm households.[2] This meant that suburban land was falling into the hands of people who used it primarily for consumption rather than production. They lived on it but did not farm it, build factories on it, cut timber, or mine ore. For middle-class families, a home was also, and remains, their biggest repository of savings. Both quality of life and savings make home owners extremely sensitive to anything that hurts property values, to externalities. (Once a neighbor who had his house on the market came over and mowed my lawn. It was not meant as a favor or a compliment.)

The suburbs of metropolitan areas became the great bastions of zoning—a new device for residents to shield themselves from urban problems while maintaining access to urban economic opportunities and amenities. Zoning preserved the single-family home on a detached lot against the depredations of apartment houses and commercial development. Even in smaller cities, zoning provided advantages, and it swept the country before World War II.

Builders and land developers got behind the movement. In a time of growth and transition, they were getting burned by uncertainties in the application of the common law of nuisance. A nuisance was not necessarily something noxious in itself. It could be, as one court said, "the right thing in the wrong place." Builders could not be sure that some new structure was legal, which raised the financial risks. A court might decide after completion that the use was a nuisance and require some expensive abatement measures. Zoning promised certainty.

Most zoning took place within the general context of the American optimism about growth and progress. Some towns and suburbs used it to become Brigadoons, villages existing outside time and change. Most embraced growth, including more amenities and rising real estate values. They just wanted to ensure that it was orderly, not destructive of existing values, virtues, and class structures.

Some people argued that zoning regulations took their property without compensation, a position that lost in two Supreme Court cases during the 1920s. Thereafter, local control of land use ceased to be a matter for the federal courts. It remains a major occupation of state courts, which supervise it with varying degrees of rigor. In some states, land use decisions are examined with care. In others, the practice is summed up by experts Richard Babcock and Charles Siemon: "What *can* one say about the California courts other than that one has to be a madman to challenge a government regulation in that bizarre jurisdiction."[3]

The zoning statutes of the 1920s were short and simple. State legislatures delegated general power to municipalities. The cities set up districts for three or four types of use, ranked from "highest" to "lowest": single-family residential, multifamily residential, commercial, industrial. Some only had one residential class. They drew a map showing the boundaries of each district. Within any district, the designated use and all higher ones were permitted. If you wanted a house in the factory zone, you could have it; you just could not complain about the noise. The law added a provision for variances, including consideration of prior nonconforming uses, and that was it.

As time went on, and especially during the great post–World War II housing boom, municipalities found that this simple structure did not give them enough discretionary power. New devices emerged. The "special use," an activity that might or might not be permitted, at the option of the zoning board, came into the law, letting the board look at the specific proposal, and proposer, before deciding. A tony department store can get approval; a discounter cannot. Next came the "floating zone," a list of activities without a spot on the map. Given a specific proposal, the board would decide if activities were acceptable at the suggested spot. Then came the planned unit development, a total unit, including residential, commercial, maybe even industrial, that can be approved as a package, sweeping aside existing zoning.

Views of nonconforming uses reversed. From the idea that all higher uses should be permitted in a district, cities switched to the idea that only the uses specified on the zoning map should be allowed. No more housing in industrial areas, or mixed industrial and commercial zones. Eventually people noticed a problem. The office and commercial zones became ghost towns after 5:00 P.M. because of the lack of residents. At the same time, the residential areas became dull wastelands, devoid of anything interesting. Eventually correct opinion reversed again in some places. The latest rage is to *require* mixed uses, not just permit them.

Succeeding decades brought more new techniques. Private zoning by contract exploded. The developer of a subdivision sets up a regime of control over life in the tract, and anyone who buys must sign on to the program. Contracts of sale for building lots routinely specify such things as how much you must spend on a house and the types of material allowed. They can get downright picky. A friend who bought a lot recently agreed not to leave a snowmobile in her driveway.

This incredible popularity of zoning by contract is a major argument for great caution in interfering with local zoning laws. One slant on zoning by law is to see it as a vehicle for existing neighborhoods to get benefits that new ones achieve by private contract. People give up freedom over their own property in exchange for similar concessions from everyone else. In the legal cases, the phrase used is "the average reciprocity of advantage." In existing areas, some possibility of coercion is necessary because it is not possible to get everyone to agree voluntarily. Transaction costs are too high, and problems of holdouts and sheer contrariness too great. William Fischel, who has the advantage of serving on his local zoning board as well as an education as an economist, observes that people see the right to adopt protective zoning laws as itself a property right and would feel very aggrieved at any authority that tried to take it away.[4] Woe to the politician, judge, or scribbler who comes between home owners and their right to quiet enjoyment and stable and increasing property values.

Over the years, municipal zoning became more complicated. The basic zones were further subdivided. For example, a city may have zones for light, heavy, and medium industrial, with specific industries classified accordingly. Provision was made for cluster housing and garden apartments. Some cities adopted performance zoning, especially for industry. Allowable uses are judged by measures of their external effects, such as noise, vibration, light, and odor. Whatever meets the standard is acceptable. Minimum-lot-size requirements became a standard tool. Architectural review boards (the "Pretty Committee") flourished. In some places, these ensure that every house is alike; in others, they ensure that every house is different. Height limits and setbacks became more sophisticated. Special districts were created, especially for the preservation of historic areas. This idea gets stretched a long way. Designation of a district as historic has turned into a standard device to protect against high-rise buildings, daring architecture, and new technologies. In Arlington, Virginia, a review board in a district of early twentieth-century clapboard houses refused to let a home owner use maintenance-free vinyl shutters to replace wooden ones.[5]

Cities developed ways to deal with nonconforming uses—those that were in existence at the time a rule goes into effect that would not be allowed under the new standard. Most places are reluctant to ban these peremptorily, fearing that courts will classify this a taking of property that triggers a compensation requirement. The standard treatment of a nonconforming use is to allow it to continue but not expand and to prohibit reconstruction if anything happens to the building. Eventually cities got the idea of "amortizing" nonconforming uses. The use can continue for a specified number of years, then must stop. The idea is that the amortization period gives the owner an opportunity to recapture the investment and avoid financial loss.

Throughout these decades of the evolution of land use controls, a few goals were constant. One of these was to ration access to the urban infrastructure. Real estate development always imposes some burdens outside the bounds of the property. It creates externalities, both positive and negative, for surrounding landowners. It puts burdens on the public infrastructure, especially its transportation and utilities networks. If someone puts up a building with offices for a thousand people, someone else will have to make arrangements for moving them in and out. In theory, a city could adopt the land use equivalent of prior appropriation doctrine familiar from western water law. It could let anyone who wants to develop do so, with later comers adapting as they can. If the transportation network is all used up or existing buildings cut off all light to their property, tough.

Cities have chosen not to do this. They impose general rules and limits in terms of densities, setbacks, parking, and so on that reserve some of the commons for landowners who have not built yet. You can look at much municipal land use law as an effort to carry out this principle—a sort of riparian rights doctrine applied to the urban infrastructure. Its great advantage is that it removes the pressure for premature development. In a prior appropriate situation, people must develop or lose the option to do so. Under riparian law, your access remains secure.

Other basic goals of land use control have remained constant: protect property owners, especially single-family houses, try to pass urban problems on to some other city, and give landowners the environment they prefer.

Real estate sections of newspapers may gush about new concepts in design, such as the "new urbanism," which involves narrow streets, small yards, and deemphasis of the automobile. (The developers' code hidden in this text is: "You can pack in more houses, build using mass-production techniques, sell for almost as much as a conventional house and lot, and make out like a bandit.") The public's view of the new urbanism is less gleeful. A recent survey of new home buyers and prospects found them concerned about the same basic things that have driven zoning since the 1920s.[6] By a vote of four to one, they like backyards, cul-de-sacs, and setbacks. Those are safer for the kids, and quieter. Design concepts of smaller lots with houses right up on the street may appeal aesthetically, but they flunk the safety-quiet test and do not provide enough privacy. Buyers reject architectural uniformity. As the head of the survey firm puts it, they dislike the "cookie-cutter suburban look" where the only way to find your house among the look-alikes is "by pressing your automatic garage door opener as you drive by until one opens."

Another municipal goal is the exclusion of land uses that would be heavy users of expensive services but would not pay their share of property taxes. The practice is called fiscal zoning.

CHARLES COUNTY, MARYLAND, 1996

Charles County is a little south of Washington, D.C. About 16 percent of the county's housing stock is town houses, and they hold 12,900 adults. The county commission orders its planners to figure out how to limit construction of town houses. The objection is that the town houses, cheaper and thus more affordable for families with children, do not pay as much in property taxes as do detached homes. The real need is for businesses, which pay more in taxes than they require in services, but the competition among the jurisdictions is stiff.[7]

Another constant of the system is that zoning boards retain freedom to act as they will. Procedures are sloppy; delays are used as strategic weapons; developers are strong-armed into making contributions to the city, not to mention to political campaigns, as the price of admission to the game; neighborhoods are given carte blanche vetoes; and concepts of due process and equal protection are very shaky. Developers know they must deal with the city repeatedly in many contexts, so they tend to bend with the wind rather than fight.

The developers' fantasy that zoning would provide total certainty thudded long ago. A firm knows before building, before making heavy investment in construction, that its project will not be ruled a nuisance. This is worth a lot. Total certainty remains elusive until negotiations are completed, public hearings held, the zoning board's signature put on the dotted line, and all possible judicial appeals exhausted. No one can determine exactly what is allowed solely by looking at the zoning map and reading the regulations. It is a field for political lawyers, not library researchers.

An innovation in zoning was that municipalities began exacting fees from developers in exchange for permission to build. These can be in cash or in kind. A developer can be told to donate land or to build a particular kind of facility that the local government wants. You can trace these back to the nineteenth century, when streets, sewers, and sidewalks were commonly funded by assessments on owners. Exactions on developers started out in the 1920s and burgeoned in the subdivision years after World War II. Municipalities required developers to in-stall their own streets, sewers, water mains, sites for public buildings, parks, and open space buffers. It can even be done by the book; hand-books are published on the costs properly attributable to particular kinds of projects.

Those were the times when most places were still basically pro-growth. They assumed that development—of the right kind, of course, and for our kind of people—would be positive. Over the past twenty years, attitudes have become more skeptical. The impression arose that growth costs more in services than it garners in new property taxes. Maybe a city is better off without it. This idea is probably wrong, but it has become very powerful. It leads to a liberal interpretation of the idea that new developments should pay their own capital costs. Cities are demanding contributions to general infrastructure, such as schools, highways not connected to the specific development, and other general public facilities. These can still be regarded as the equivalent of user charges, though the connection gets remote.

The next-to-final step in the growth of exactions is to sever the link between the costs imposed by the new development and the fees de-manded. In this step, the city simply sells the right to develop, charging as much as the traffic will bear. Sometimes a pretense that the exaction is cost based is maintained. Thus San Francisco justifies extra charges on office buildings on the ground that these bring in new workers, who bid up the price of housing.

The final flowering of exactions is to impose them on existing landowners who want to make changes in their property. This idea reaches its fullest embodiment on the West Coast, and particularly in California. It is also the context in which the constitutionality of exac-tions is getting litigated. Professional developers are used to rolling with the punches, making their deals, and moving on through. Individual home owners can get mad. Several of the important recent Supreme Court cases on property rights, especially *Nollan* and *Dolan*, which are described a few pages on in this chapter, involved government efforts to extort property from individual property owners who chose to fight even though the battle was not a worthwhile economic proposition.

While zoning went through its evolutions, some related concepts were on the march: comprehensive land use planning and the rise of environmentalism. Both interact powerfully with conventional zoning.

Comprehensive land use planning has always been more dream than reality, a spin-off from the faith in central planning of the Progressive era and the New Deal. It is easy to forget now, because the language seems almost quaint, but it was not all that long ago that people *believed*. Wise urban planners would make our cities into New Edens! They would anticipate the trends and steer municipal development in the desired directions! Planning is one of those frogs that looks as if it might turn into a prince, but then just keeps turning into an older frog. The idea of a hundred municipalities in a metropolitan area, each with its own independent, comprehensive long-term plan, makes little sense. Regional planning authorities are set up, of course, but their power is always limited. Each jurisdiction wants to reserve the right to protect its own property owners.

Planning has other problems as well. Inevitably it is done badly. How can it be done well, when it requires total knowledge about sociology, economics, demographics, geography, and everything else, plus perfect foresight? The tale of New York City's efforts to preserve land for manufacturing, used in Chapter 9 as part of my defense of Western land fraud, is par for the course. So is the sequel. The City Planning Commission does not hang its head in shame over its failure or go out of business. Instead, it is considering sweeping revisions in its regulations, though of course it has not actually gotten around to doing anything about it yet. This seems like a singularly bad idea, given the commission's track record. Why not go back to the old four-category classic zoning pattern, and let people sort out the rest for themselves? New York is an amazingly vibrant city—it must be, to survive so much government—but there are limits.

Land use expert Richard Babcock summed it up thirty years ago when he wrote: "Every time I pick up one of the early books on zoning . . . and check a few pages, I have the warm glow that comes with reading a romantic account of some municipal Graustark where a bunch of happy, well-informed people with a social I.Q. of 150 sit around making decisions in complete freedom from outside pressure and without the slightest concern for what takes place anywhere but in their duchy."[8]

The New York experience is not unique. The common result is that municipal planners wind up in a cocoon, cut off from the world. While they play, neighborhoods and developers hustle the local zoning board, where the real tract-by-tract decisions are made, ad hoc and day to day. And while *this* is going on, the really big decisions are getting made somewhere else entirely. Where does the new interstate go, especially the interchanges? Which district gets the water and sewer lines, and which gets left out? Where does Megacorp site its new plant with all those jobs, and what must a town do to get it? What about the federally funded rapid transit line? Where are the right-of-way and the stations?

LOUDON COUNTY, VIRGINIA, 1995

Loudon County, twenty-five miles west of Washington, D.C., has two parts. The eastern one-third is defined by Dulles Airport and the town of Leesburg. It has commercial development, shopping centers, and sub-divisions. The western two-thirds, defined by the town of Middleburg, is bucolic, a land of horses and foxhunting. A main reason for this is that the west has no water lines or sewers. It relies on well water, which is becoming exhausted. The Loudon County Sanitation Authority proposes a study of the feasibility of extending water and sewer service to the western area. The sanitation officials act innocent, saying that they are just studying all the options, nothing can happen without the approval of the County Board of Supervisors, blah, blah, blah, but the supervisors are not lulled by these soothing noises. The chairman of the Planning Commission writes that extending the water lines "will cause a feeding frenzy of land speculation, and will lead to eventual total development." He concludes, "The study must be stopped."[9]

One great impact of planning was not in exurbia but in the central city. Urban renewal, public housing, and giant downtown developments were all children of the planning impulse. They were imposed, often over bitter opposition, at the expense of wiping out viable neighborhoods. They have not been successes. Now the same mind-set that once determined that commercial and residential uses must be totally separated, thus inventing the after-5:00 P.M. ghost town, have gone the other way. Instead of letting people or builders decide, they mandate that new construction be some precise percentage residential, commercial, retail, and so on. Urban governments incapable of synchronizing stoplights or fixing potholes micromanage complex real estate developments.

Planning is done badly for another reason. Most of it is intellectually corrupt. In exurbia, "planning" has become synonymous with slowing or even eliminating growth. The Charles County example given above is typical but more honest than most others. The planners are instructed about the conclusion desired and told to figure out how to implement it. Limiting the types of housing built is one way, but there are other possibilities.

CALVERT COUNTY, MARYLAND, 1995

Calvert County is divided between a northern part populated by commuters to Washington, D.C., who live on large lots and a southern section of smaller lots, less expensive homes, more blue-collar workers, and families with young children. Concerned about the increase in school-age children, the commissioners impose a moratorium on new home construction. A teacher who planned to sell two lots says: "I feel like somebody's just stolen money from our bank account." A court strikes the measure down as illegal. As one possible response, the commissioners ask planning officials for recommendations on raising the school impact fee, which is already at $3,000, to build a single-family detached house, and on the idea of 1 percent county property transfer tax. Since 1989 the county share of school construction has been paid for by the school impact fee, which has collected $18 million from developers.[10]

You might worry about Calvert County, until you pick up the next news clip, which is headlined "Calvert County Stays Thrifty in Prosperity."[11] It describes how Calvert has the highest median income in the state of Maryland, fine schools, more services than other counties, and a low tax rate. The reason? It is the home of a big nuclear power plant, which pays enormous taxes.

Outside the urban core, planning got new invigoration from the environmental movement of the 1960s and 1970s. Statutes providing explicitly for nationwide federal land use controls were defeated in 1974, but other battles for comprehensive planning were won. Controls on development were instituted to protect particular natural assets, such as the California coast, the pine barrens of New Jersey, the Adirondack Mountains of New York State, or the part of upstate New York that provides the water for New York City. These had to be at a statewide rather than a municipal level, thus realizing one of the planners' oldest dreams: release from the straitjacket of the municipality as the sovereign planning authority.

Environmentalism also served to justify less ambitious classifications. Development could be prevented and particular parcels conscripted to the public good by imaginative zoning. Classify something as an environmental buffer zone, for example, and it becomes the equivalent of a public park. True, the owner might theoretically retain the right to exclude people, but what owner would spend money administering a property that is now absolutely valueless? Many a county obtains wildlife refuges and parks this way.

Environmental concerns also teamed up with another preoccupation of county officials: the preservation of farmland near cities. This must be among the silliest of pet causes. Why should farms near cities be preserved? If you want parks, forests, recreation facilities, or anything else, okay, but why farms? So they will be within easy wagon distance in case we forget how to use our trucks and airplanes? In the whole United States, only 92.4 million acres are developed—less than 5 percent of our total surface area of 1.9 billion acres. Cropland takes up 382 million acres. Even in the crowded Middle Atlantic states, only 10 percent of the land is developed.[12] There is no crisis. Nonetheless, planning efforts solemnly worry about this terrible threat, preserving farmland while residential development is forced farther out and commutes lengthen.

Zoning, land use planning, and environmental regulation provide a pretty good set of basic tools for reconciling property rights in an urban area according to Lockean values. There are some problems with them, especially with the tendency to make them overly complicated and underly predictable, but the basics are not bad. It is the application (perhaps one should say the manipulation) of the tools that is raising the level of restiveness. They easily become tools for thievery.

The number of individual situations arising is very large, but a finite set of themes seem to recur. We will look at several of them, not in a comprehensive way, but simply to get a sense of the conflicts.

The first, and in many ways the easiest, is the use of exactions as a pure revenue-raising measure, or as a measure to force a landowner to donate land to the city for some purpose. This is a tricky area, because there is nothing wrong with exactions, properly used, In fact, they are quite a good idea. They are user charges, and the more society as a whole moves toward user charges for the provision of public goods, the better off all of us will be. In connection with the national parks, I suggested that the government treats me and other park users unfairly by not charging us enough. As a result, our preferences do not get factored into Park Service decisions, and facilities are undersupplied in terms of both quality and quantity. Roughly the same analysis applies here. If developers need not convince the government to provide infrastructure, they become free to respond to market forces in deciding on both quality and quantity. This is all to everyone's good. It also makes for cleaner government. When decisions on roads, water, and sewers mean life or death for investments in large-scale building projects, those decisions have a high market value. Market values get reaped in one way or another. If developers pay their own costs of infrastructure, these values are ultimately reaped by the public in the form of tax savings.

A question of fairness arises because in many places existing infrastructure was paid for out of general revenues, not from assessments or exactions. New residents pay for what old residents apparently got for free. The only answer to this one is, Forget it. It is like water subsidies. The values of these facilities were capitalized into the price of existing homes, so the residents paid for them when they moved in. The people who got the breaks were the home owners of 1920 or 1960, and most of them are long gone. If the old infrastructure is still being paid off from taxes levied on new residents as well as old, then the new ones have a legitimate gripe, but not otherwise.

There are, though, many ways to manipulate the system to the advantage of existing residents. Recall the Calvert County school impact fee. The obvious motivation is to mute the objections of childless couples to paying real estate taxes to support the schools. The county says it is levying the impact fee on the developer, but the real incidence is on the seller of the land. So the county is levying a special charge on owners of raw land that is not levied on sellers of existing homes. But prices of existing houses will reflect the value of the schools and will sell for more than houses in neighboring areas with less respected education systems. Thus, the owner of an existing home who sells will also collect an educational premium from the buyer. Unless the county imposes a transfer tax on existing houses, the impact fee looks unfair. Childless couples who do not want to pay taxes for good schools should not get to claim the extra market value generated by the fact that the schools are good.

Exactions easily turn from user charges to extortion. Because land use rules are so amorphous in many places, and especially on the West Coast, landowners cannot be certain of their right to do anything. They must have a permit, and the conditions that govern its issuance are made of smoke. Two recent Supreme Court decisions on property rights came out of the loose exaction practices of California and Oregon.

CALIFORNIA, 1982–1987

The Nollans want to build a larger bungalow on their beach property. The Coastal Commission refuses permission unless they grant an easement for the public to cross the property along the oceanfront line. The commission is putting together a walkway along the shoreline to connect two public beaches. It has already extracted easements from forty-three owners through this technique of granting a building permit only if the owner agrees to the easement.[13]

The problem is that there is no connection between the exaction (the dedication of an easement along the shore) and the permit to build a slightly larger house. The house does not create any problem that will be solved by the walkway. The case went up to the Supreme Court, which said no; the exaction must have a nexus with the purpose of the permit requirement. The requirement of a building permit could not be treated as a free-floating tool to obtain a public right-of-way.

OREGON, 1991–1994

Dolan has a 9,700-square-foot hardware store on a 1.67-acre parcel. She wants to expand the store and pave a small parking lot. Part of the property is within the 100-year floodplain of a creek. As a condition of granting a building permit, the city requires her to dedicate the land lying within the floodplain to serve as a greenway. It also tells her to dedicate enough land for a 15-foot-wide pedestrian-bicycle way alongside the floodplain. The total dedication is 7,000 square feet—about 10 percent of her property. To meet the *Nollan* requirement of a nexus between a condition placed on a permit and the rationale for requiring it, the city finds that the expanded store will increase traffic and that paving the parking lot will increase runoff.

Again the Supreme Court said no.[14] It is not enough to establish the bare fact that the exaction is in some way related to the problems created by the landowner's action. The conditions imposed on the permit must also bear a "rough proportionality" to the burdens imposed on the city by the development. The city cannot say, for example, that because a store will increase traffic slightly the owner must pay for a six-lane freeway into the city.

Exactions are not the only way to steal property. Simple land use rules can do the job. The legal reporters are full of protests against new rules that suddenly require 3, or 40, acres per house, or create an "environmental buffer zone," or impose agricultural zoning, or in some other way transform property belonging to one person into a public facility or a commons.

MARIN COUNTY, CALIFORNIA, 1996

Marin County is a heavily populated, high-income area across the Golden Gate Bridge and north of San Francisco. Andrew Varlow wants to build a 6,292-square-foot single-family house and a 3,264-square-foot horse barn on a 91-acre plot in the less-developed northern part of the county. The plot is already zoned at 60 acres per house, but the county wants more. It wants Varlow to deed 95 percent of it to the Marin Agricultural Land Trust as a permanent conservation easement. At a meeting of the County Supervisors, one supervisor stresses that any house must be "accessory to agricultural use." Varlow is proposing to build a 3,264-square-foot barn, so a 6,292-square-foot house would not be "accessory." The supervisors suggest a 3,903-square-foot house would be "accessory." This just happens to be the size of the largest existing nearby houses. Varlow turns down the deal and, according to press accounts, leaves, talking about lawsuits and comparing the most active supervisor "to an emperor and to former Ugandan dictator Idi Amin."[15]

The Varlow affair illuminates the absurd concern about farms so often expressed by county officials and their planners. They are hypocrites rather than idiots. Farms do not require new schools, roads, sewers, or other infrastructure, do not complete with existing residents for existing facilities, and make nice open space for existing developments. A frank admission of these motives might trigger legal problems with the farmers, who would regard this as a confiscation of their land. Saving "vital agricultural resources" makes a good sound bite.

The Varlow case also illustrates another common characteristic of these situations. Reading the minutes and news accounts of the supervisors' meetings on the matter is like entering a novel by Franz Kafka. The objections are vaporous. Opponents talk about preserving agricultural use and rural character, but they are talking about the middle of a large metropolitan area. Their dreams are not possible. One rancher-neighbor punctured the nonsense surrounding the affair: "How many cows can he graze there, twenty? Sheep would be worse. He's not agriculturally feasible."

The planners fret about size of the house, the effect on views, future development in the area, the possible impact on local real estate prices, and "the project's inconsistency with the goals" of the planning group (whatever these may be; the meeting minutes do not say). No standards are announced. Varlow and his people have spent over two years working on the project without any firm guidance that "you can do this but not that." This is not "planning." It is government by whimsy, which is the cause of much of the unhappiness fueling the property rights movement. It is not within the bounds of legitimacy, of the unwritten constitution. It is like the story in Chapter 2, where a member of an advisory group can vote to disapprove a design because of what she saw in her former life as a seagull.

Around Washington, D.C., a special technique is available, called history. Much of the Civil War was fought in the territory between Washington and Richmond. Add the Revolutionary War and the many Virginians listed among the nation's founders, and it becomes hard to throw a stone without hitting something awash in historical significance. Whenever development is proposed, history buffs appear who have theretofore kept their intense interest a complete secret. Historic preservation of buildings is discussed in the next chapter, but appeals to history are also surprisingly successful as a means of keeping property totally undeveloped.

STAFFORD COUNTY, VIRGINIA, 1996

George Washington lived at Ferry Farm from the ages of six to twenty. The house burned down two hundred years ago, and only the foundation remains. Nothing has ever been done with it as a historic site, and much of the farm's original 600 acres are covered by houses, stores, and fast food restaurants. In 1990, the owners of the remaining 70 acres got the county to rezone 25 acres as commercial. As the price, the county exacted a donation of the rest of the tract, including the site of the residence. In 1996, the owners made a deal for Wal-Mart, the big discount retailer, to build a store on the 25 commercial acres. The local residents went ballistic over the loss of this suddenly important site, and the county's Architectural Review Board voted five to zero to turn down the development plan. As of June 1996, the matter rests in the hands of the county Board of Supervisors, some of whom negotiated the 1990 deal.[16]

"Historical preservation" of this type is highway robbery. This started in 1990, when the owner was forced to give up more than half the land in exchange for zoning that should have been granted as of right. Now the Architectural Review Board is trying to rob it again, for the sake of a site that no one for two hundred years has thought worth more than a commemorative plaque.

Another imaginative use of history is to combine it with a concept called the "viewshed." Thus, it is asserted that nothing should be allowed within the viewshed of Monticello, the famous home of Thomas Jefferson. Since Monticello sits on top of a small mountain, this is a large claim. It is also a pointless one. The view now bears no resemblance to that seen by Jefferson. There is no prospect of restoring the early nineteenth-century view. We do not even know what it was. Besides, why bother? Seeing what Jefferson designed and lived in is fascinating. Extending this to say that we should see only what Jefferson saw is pointless. Jefferson also traveled from Monticello to Washington by stagecoach over rough roads. We drive it in two hours by car. When he looked out, he saw the eighteenth and nineteenth centuries. We see the twentieth. Why pretend otherwise? If you can convince the public and the legislature to appropriate the money needed to buy scenic easements from all the owners of the land in sight of Monticello, I will revise my opinion of the value to be placed on this particular benefit. Until you do, inventing a concept of a sacred viewshed is an effort to print your own license to steal.

Thefts also take the form of downzoning undeveloped parcels to allow significantly lower levels of use than allowed on existing parcels.

When a suburb full of houses on 1-acre lots adopts 3-acre zoning, it is difficult to see it as anything except an appropriation of value. This conclusion is supported by the market values involved. William Fischel notes that his area of Hanover, New Hampshire, upped the zoning from 1 acre to 3. The 3-acre lots from newly divided land do not sell for any premium over the 1-acre lots that were grandfathered in. The same principle applies when a town of apartment buildings discourages any more by downzoning not-yet-developed property.

Many of the environmental zoning matters are equal protection situations. We would not be concerned if the community were imposing a set of consistent standards on all of its members. These would be like the zoning-by-contract situations, and you would assume that people know best what they want. But nowhere in the annals of land use control do you find a case in which an area is dedicated to open space or environmental protection and all existing structures on it are torn down. These decisions involve a judgment by the supporters of the restriction that someone must sacrifice, and your friends and neighbors have selected you. Too bad, but why are you so grumpy about it? You must be against the environment! Where is your sense of community?

A recurring feature of treacly discussions about "community versus property" is that the speakers assume that obligations run in only one direction: property owners have obligations to the community. In particular, the owners should let their property be used by the community for free, and not whine about it. This duty runs to anyone wanting to use the property for any purpose that lends itself to a feel-good sound bite. I keep waiting to read something in which a spokesperson for environmentalism, or historical preservation, or open space, or any other cause characterizes the obligations as reciprocal. He would say that it is fair to ask landowners to respect and accommodate his group's cause, and his group should figure out how to promote its ends while respecting both the property that hard-working people have built up and the general benefits of an economic system based on private property and a free market. He would also comment on the usefulness for his cause of the concept that property should be bought, not taken. If you must pay, then it forces thought about what is really valuable and what is not. If the property is free, the outcome is obvious: take everything you can get your hands on.

There is indeed a breakdown of community, but its nature is not what these advocates would have you believe. The eagerness of so many people to inflict substantial financial losses on others for the sake of often-trivial personal gratification or poorly thought-out environmental symbolism, and the air of sanctimony with which they do it, demonstrates a shocking breakdown of community feeling.

Substantively, many of the problems are not easy to analyze. When is the community imposing standards on itself to limit the external effects of the use of property, and then applying these to a particular landowner, and when is it taking property? Robert Ellickson, a law professor, and William Fischel, an economist, take the view that the benchmark should be the land use that is normal within the community. Fischel uses the diagram shown;[17] in this schema, neighbors have no right to keep a use from moving from D to A, or even to B, without paying the owner compensation. (Fischel would allow the community to make reasonable exactions for a move from A to B, an idea that seems questionable to me.) The community could prevent a move to C. He also thinks a community should generally be able to insist that a C use predating current standards should be raised to point B without compensation.

Subnormal	Normal	Supernormal
(maximum intensity— *least* desired by neighbors)		(minimum intensity— *most* desired by neighbors)

C	B	A	D

The key is how to define normal use, and this cannot be done in the abstract. It depends on the specifics of time and place, and on history.

SOUTH CAROLINA, 1986–1992

Lucas buys two beachfront lots in 1986 for $1 million. A number of similar lots already have houses on them. A 1988 beach protection law prohibits any new building along the beach. The key findings underlying the law are that the beach and dune system is very important to the people of the state, and that past "development unwisely has been sited too close to the beach/dune system," which jeopardizes the stability of the system, accelerates erosion, and endangers adjacent property. The introduction to the law says it is intended to discourage new construction and encourage people who have built close to the beach to retreat from it. Lucas is forbidden to build, and the value of his lots drops to zero.

Lucas v. South Carolina Coastal Council, decided in 1992, is one of the crucial Supreme Court property rights decisions of the past decade.[18] The legal rationale for finding in favor of Lucas is covered in Chapter 14, which takes up legal matters in general, but the facts lend themselves nicely to the Ellickson-Fischel analysis. The state was forbidding a use that was absolutely normal for the neighborhood. Whatever its reasons, it could not change the rules and single out the owners who had not yet built and force them to go to point D on the diagram without compensation.

South Carolina was blunt about what it was doing. In some places, the pilferage is more subtle. Take the story told back in Chapter 2 about the group of families with a home lot on Broad Creek, which flows into a river that flows into Chesapeake Bay. Yes, the Chesapeake is under environmental pressure, and action is needed. At first thought, it seems appropriate to check new construction because of the need to prevent pollution. At second thought, things get more complicated. The most expensive requirements have no connection with any need to protect the Chesapeake. Why require a full biological survey, for example? This looks like an effort to find an excuse to forbid any development, or a prelude to taking the property for endangered species habitat. At the least, it is a way to make development expensive and to discourage it. It is in the theft category.

The Broad Creek story is useful because it segues nicely into another major theme running through these land use cases. In many situations, existing owners do not really care about the specific piece of property when they freeze development. What they are really doing is appropriating a commons for their own personal use. To illustrate this, start with a situation that has become exceedingly common.

WASHINGTON, D.C., 1996

The street shall go unnamed because I live on it. It runs for half a mile between two arterials and could provide a convenient shortcut for some drivers. It is also close to a major university and two major bus routes, and would provide convenient parking. Under D.C. law, it can be used as neither a shortcut nor a parking lot. Parking is limited to two hours except for those with the proper residence stickers, and one block at each end of the street is one-way, in opposite directions, to prevent through traffic. We residents, like the residents of many other streets all over the District, have appropriated our street for our personal use. Of course, we complained bitterly last winter when the District government made it low priority for plowing.

With this introduction, go back to Broad Creek. After you strip out the requirements designed to appropriate the lot as a wildlife refuge, the structure of the deal becomes clearer. The capacity of the Chesapeake to absorb contamination is a commons, just as the capacity of a pasture to support sheep is a commons, or the use of my street. At Broad Creek, the old residents are discouraging any new development to that they do not have to cut back on their own discharge of contaminants. They are appropriating a commons.

This, and many another commons, including streets and general congestion, sound echoes of the West and its doctrine of prior appropriation of water. The residents are saying that whoever got there first has the right to use the carrying capacity of the bay, to the exclusion of later comers. My neighborhood is arguing that we have the right to appropriate the street, to the exclusion of others.

As with respect to water, you can make an argument either way on this point, as you can argue for either system of water rights. You can say they ought to be riparian rights. It does not matter who was first; everyone involved has equal rights as long as they act reasonably, and reductions must be pro rata, with everyone chipping in. On the other hand, you can take a prior appropriation view. People need to know that their use of the commons is secure if they are to make investments necessary for development and progress. There is also, as William Fischel points out, a powerful human sense that first in time is first in right, and that it is not fair for a later comer to dispossess you. On the other hand, there is a problem of fair notice. If prior appropriation is the rule, then someone should have told the people who now want to develop their property. The owner of a vacant lot might have built on it if he had known that his rights might be lost. Of course, a doctrine of prior appropriation encourages uneconomic races to develop and appropriate the commons.

You can also look at much regulation of sea coasts, lakes, and rivers as involving commons problems of a different sort. Water is a commons, with a couple of minor exceptions. A lake completely surrounded by private land may be private, and some places recognize ownership of a lake bottom and the waters above it. In general, the public is allowed to fish and boat. The ocean is a commons and so are ocean beaches, up to the high-tide mark. A good chunk of the value of riparian land is in its proximity to these aquatic commons. The owners of this property have a strong collective interest in sealing off access, because then they get all the value for themselves.

NEW YORK, 1996

The beach at the Long Island town of Neponsit is open to the public, so the city closes the streets, more or less. From May to September, no parking is allowed anywhere within a half-mile of the ocean.[19]

One purpose of an enterprise like the California Coastal Commission is to prevent appropriation of the ocean commons by the abutting owners. Once such a commission is created, it is likely to become an instrument of another purpose, incorporating as much private property as possible into the commons.

Of course, some problems are just hard.

SAN JUAN COUNTY, WASHINGTON

This is a county of 172 islands between Vancouver Island and Washington State. It has just banned jet skis, the personal watercraft that sell for $4,000 or more. Sales are increasing fast, and more than a million of the things are in operation. San Juan's theory is that its economy is dependent on its reputation as a "tranquil oasis." Of the 12,000 people in the county, 4,800 are self-employed, working out of their homes. The noise of the jet skis is described as an "incessant, whining pattern," especially irritating when skiers travel in packs. There may also be a bit of snobbery involved. One comment was that the skiers "are nautical illiterates. . . . All you need to ride one is a bank card." The manufacturers vow to fight: "Times change, and they will just have to get used to it." They sue the county on the ground that it is violating the skiers' rights to engage in interstate travel.[20]

Who is impinging on whom here? Are the residents appropriating the ocean? Are the skiers creating a nuisance? Is the invention of the jet ski like the invention of the airplane or the railroad—a technological change that forces a basic readjustment of some property rights? Is the jet ski really louder than a motorboat, or is the problem due to the fact that their price is low enough so that the number of riders is getting large? Who should win this case? Darned if I know.

This covers the first three themes running through these land use situations: theft by exaction, theft by rule, and appropriation of the commons. A fourth theme is bound up in the process of growth and change in a community, and the problems get very difficult. They involve externalities, various commons, and the transportation network. I am all for property rights, if only I could figure out what these are.

One common situation is gentrification. The new people come in and find that activities of the long-time residents are déclassé.

MONTEREY COUNTY, CALIFORNIA, 1996

The Coxes have owned an 11-acre goat breeding farm for over twenty years. In 1987 they get a dairy license and start selling goats' milk and cheese. In 1992, acting at the instigation of neighbors wanting to protect their viewshed, the county amends the zoning law: minimum size for a dairy is now 40 acres. Goat breeding is still legal but milking is not.[21]

This situation is from the newsletter of the Defenders of Property Rights, an advocacy group helping the goat farmer. It has another case for a farmer in Virginia involving hogs.

The viewshed concept is becoming increasingly common, and it is a truly bad idea. Usually it is used defensively. Existing property owners fight development on the ground that it will interfere with their view. The idea seems to be that everyone has a right to be monarch of all he has ever surveyed, preventing every use that he finds personally offensive. One estate owner recently sued another for building a house within his viewshed. There was nothing particularly wrong with the architecture; the plaintiff just preferred the open countryside. In addition to being contrary to several centuries of settled law, the idea seems inherently silly because it has no limit. "You don't like my goat farm? Well, my goats don't like that hackneyed colonial design you call a house either, and it's causing their milk to sour. I'll sue!" Viewshed protection is hard to take, unless even a goat would agree that the activity is a true eyesore.

When the externalities of an existing use are more serious, these situations are tough, and they have bedeviled legal doctrine for a century. Some courts use the concept of "coming to the nuisance," which says you cannot complain if something exists when you move in. This rule does not work, because it means that the perpetrator of the nuisance gets to appropriate the property of the prior owner. Suppose you own a farm, and the city puts an airport nearby. The noise does not bother your wheat, so you have no immediate loss of value. Eventually the city expands, and your wheat field would make a good housing development, except for the airport noise. If the developer who wants to buy it cannot object to the noise, then your property has just been conscripted into an airport buffer zone, with no payment to you.

This is not a good result. If the city wanted to secure its right to pollute your property with noise, it should have bought an easement. There is no reason to say that it can take your property. Besides, the coming to the nuisance doctrine is not even in the interest of the airport. If it applies, the savvy landowner will object to the airport from the outset so as to avoid losing rights. Yet it may be that the land will never be valuable for houses, and the fight is pointless.

The farming cases are tougher, because at one time the smells from the hog farm wafting over the neighborhood were part of a system of reciprocity. The neighbors were farmers, too, and they stunk up the hog farmer's land. Now the neighbors have been bought out, and the reciprocity is gone. The farm is surrounded by new hoity-toity people who cannot stand the sight of goats. (Smell was not an issue in the goat case; it was a dairy, and kept clean.)

The right result here is for the new neighbors to buy out the farmer, who can then take the goats or hogs to some more welcoming place. The problem is a lack of the mechanisms necessary to make the deal. The neighbors face free-rider and transaction cost problems, so they take the easy route of conscripting the powers of the state into labeling the farm a nuisance. If the powers of the state are to be used, they would be better used to force the benefiting landowners to pool their resources, buy out the hog farmer (including his moving costs), and sell off the land for houses.

Usually problems of growth present the reverse of the goat farm case. Instead of new owners' aggressing against old, the existing residents get a veto over anything that might affect them. The result is gridlock and stalemate. Residents complain about poor services and rising taxes even as they nix new projects that could share the cost. Property owners who could turn a buck selling for development are gnashing their teeth, objecting to this abridgment of *their* property rights. Existing schools, businesses, and other institutions are frustrated by their inability to adapt to new circumstances by modifying their plant. Hark back to the Fordham radio tower in Chapter 2. You can also look at the experience of Georgetown University with my neighborhood in Washington, D.C., where any university effort to do anything with an impact on surrounding territory sounds an alarm. And residents of my area are pikers at the game compared with the professionals over in Cleveland Park, an area of 1900-era Victorian million-dollar houses owned by high government officials, lawyers, and journalists, located a five-minute walk from a subway stop and a five-minute drive from downtown Washington. Cleveland Parkers stop *everything* in or anywhere near their turf. They once pleaded for the historic significance of a rundown strip mall on the grounds that it was one of the very first strip malls in the United States, and thus deserved preservation. They won, too, and I must admit that the old place has been restored most attractively.

The gridlock has effects on the shape of metropolitan areas. If facilities ranging from baseball stadiums to factories to subdivisions cannot be built near existing clusters of citizens, only one solution exists: the builder goes farther out, to where fewer citizens are found. These may be few enough in number to be overrun, or bribes in one form or another become feasible. The result is a continuing pressure for urban sprawl and leapfrog development, which then intensifies the automobile dependency of the metropolitan area. This generates more sprawl, since cars are voracious users of space. Anyone who cares about this issue should want to explore ways of removing the pressure and giving more options to people who would prefer not to live about 40 miles out from the city. There may be no crisis of loss of farms, but the amount of land classified as developed jumped 19 percent between 1987 (77.3 million acres) and 1992 (91.9 million acres). Something is going on.

The effect of the local resident veto on nonresidents is also substantial. A young couple with a new baby living in an urban apartment might like to move to Nearby, a close-in suburb. A landowner there might want to sell to a developer, who is eager to put up a bunch of affordable town houses. So far, so good. It look as if everyone will be happy. Then existing residents object. Town houses erode the tax base. Town houses do not fit with the architecture. Whatever. The young couple is left without an effective champion. The land seller would like to make the deal, but his power is drastically limited. He has no right to build, so he is at the mercy of the local authorities, who have distributed vetoes to all his neighbors. The developer would like to build in Nearby but does not really care much. For him, land is just a raw material, like lumber or labor. If he cannot buy it one place, he buys it in another. If the basic demand exists, he can build somewhere, even if he must go out 40 miles to Wayaway. As long as no one else can build in Nearby, he is indifferent. The young family will have to go to Wayaway to find anything in its price range, and he will make the sale in the end. The reason, although the family will not know it as it rises at 5:00 A.M. every day to cope with its 40-mile commute, is the dilution of the landowner's right to build. Urban sprawl, like so many other of our society's current problems, turns out to be a product of government policies that undermine property rights.

Not that you would know this from reading your local newspaper. It is bizarre to browse through my pile of clippings on land use. Complaints about sprawl and suburban development alternate with stories about the need to limit town houses in favor of single-family detached houses, the more expensive the better and the larger the lot size the better, to keep up the tax base. An occasional story on the need to protect agricultural land and rural zoning, such as one house per 25 acres, is tossed in, before the next story on the evils of sprawl, which is assumed to be totally the fault of an evil group called "the developers," and has nothing to do with any government policies, or with any erosion of the freedom of action of property owners. The usual prescription is for more power to the local officials, who made this mess in the first place.

Commercial developments and clean industry contribute to the tax base, so cities vie for them, but they still have problems. The benefits accrue to the city as a whole and, insofar as job creation is concerned, to the region as a whole. Externalities are concentrated on a small proportion of the residents. These object, loudly. Big tax-producing projects may override the objections, but lesser ones have trouble, and so do basic public facilities. A railway commuter line station could not be put in a town because of objections to the building of a parking lot. A town with a lack of restaurants objected to a proposed national chain because people thought its sign was ugly. A 200-foot police/fire communications tower was nixed in another municipality. Elected officials are frustrated because they see the need for tax-paying commercial development and new jobs, but they have a broader focus than the neighborhoods.[22]

In a different time with smaller communities, development issues could be resolved by informal relationships. Someone could be induced to act for the good of the town as a whole. Implicit in this is an awareness on everyone's part that he was now owed, and people would reciprocate at some point. In the metropolitan areas, the informal mechanisms have been swamped by growth and mobility. If you accept the 200-foot communications tower because it is good for the community as a whole, the value of your property might do down and you have no formal or informal way of getting a payback. So why accept it?

As in the West, the erosion of property rights in metropolitan America is producing not progress and happiness but quite the reverse. The planners and local officials say that they need yet more discretion to override property rights, and then all will be well. The reaction of these people to the rather mild recent Supreme Court decisions upholding owners' rights verged on the hysterical. The basic process of land use regulation has gone deeply awry. We are a long way from the original, sensible concept of separating conflicting uses and putting the boundaries on a map. Urban officials, and a growing corps of supporters of national land use planning, are dedicated to the view that a bevy of wise guardians can fine-tune an urban area, a region, or a nation, arriving at some optimum. The fact that this idea of comprehensive planning has failed utterly in every other context in which it once held sway—economic planning, transportation, telecommunications, finance, utilities, Russia, name it—has not sunk in. They believe! Others may falter, but the old faith still lives in city hall.

The overall situation is much like that with federal lands in the West. The property rights are either too much or too little. The political system has created so many criss-crossing rights that anyone can say no to a suggested use of property, and has an incentive to say no, while no one can say yes. No mechanisms exist to create an incentive for people to say yes. Home owners may have veto power over a proposal for nearby development, but they do not have a clearly defined property right that a developer could purchase, and they have strong incentives to exercise their vote. The costs in terms of urban sprawl and inefficiency are borne by the residents of the area as a whole. The benefits of the veto go to the nearby property owners. Of course they say no.

Several things are necessary to restore the balance. The first is to re-assert the boundaries and certainties of property rights. Cities need to get their basic rules in place, and then let people act, without more nit-picking detailed review. A recent news article reported on the success of city planning in Portland, Oregon. What does Portland do? Well, for one thing, it follows its own zoning law. If the code says you can build apartments somewhere, that is what you are allowed to do, without fur-ther ado. The story said planners the world over are coming to marvel at such an innovation.[23]

As a part of reform, people need to understand that they do not con-trol their neighbors' property, except to the extent defined by clear codes that are enforced against all, such as universal setback rules. You do not have a right to impose any conditions on new construction that are not imposed on you, nor do you have the right to appropriate the commons of roads, parks, and other facilities against continuing devel-opment. When you paid for your land, you did not buy an easement on everybody else's property. If that is what you wanted, you should have bought it, as did my friends in Bozeman who purchased an easement over the parcel next door. One of the big advantages of the private zon-ing created by subdivision developers is that land grabs are barred. If the basic map shows that an area is for building more houses, not for an empty field, the decision stands. People cannot move in, then bar the door behind them by appropriating the empty land in the name of "pre-serving open space" or "saving farmland."

The next step is to recognize that major public facilities do indeed impose special costs on some property owners while scattering benefits around the region as a whole. The answer is simple: buy off those who are hurt. Suppose residents of the area near a proposed baseball stadium are concerned about the increase in traffic. The stadium is in the inter-ests of the town and region as a whole, but these residents put the heavy arm on their councilwoman, who vetoes it. Stalemate. The stadium goes somewhere else. It would be better to say, "We recognize that you residents have some right—call it a property right—to your access to the commons of the road network, and that this stadium will put an extraordinary burden on it. After the stadium is built, including, of course, some road improvements, we will pay you $X for every annual hour that the facility adds to the time you spend driving." If the estimated bill would be too high, the stadium does not get built. If the bill is acceptable, it does. As a bonus, the town has an incentive to try to minimize the inconvenience to the residents.

Is developing such mechanisms easy? Of course not. Who is within the compensation area, and who is not? How much should the payment be? How do you gauge the level? Must the city enter such arrangements every time it puts up a stop sign? If not, when does it kick in and when not? And so on. Good questions, all. The answers will always be rough. But as the old saw goes, it is better to be roughly right than precisely wrong, or it is better to be going slowly in the right direction than fast in the wrong one. At the moment, total gridlock is the wrong way. Besides, this situation is not really so novel. Our suburban residents are actually in the same position as A. Webster Richards, who lived next to the railroad tunnel back in Chapter 3. The Richardses are in the suburbs, and they are not only thinking about monopoles. They are next to the site of a proposed baseball stadium. The issue is the same as the one presented in 1914 by the tunnel. When does change impose special burdens on a landowner for which she should be compensated?

Writing in the 1960s, Richard Babcock bemoaned the lack of intermediate mechanisms between eminent domain, which requires full compensation, and regulation, which requires no compensation. He expressed the need for mechanisms of partial compensation that reflect the partial financial damage imposed by various forms of regulation and restriction.[24] His basic concern is absolutely correct. Intermediate mechanisms are badly needed. But he was overly pessimistic about the possibilities of developing such mechanisms. A number of interesting ideas are floating around, and the only limit is our imagination.

One of the problems of the current system, which has legitimized the appropriation of property for any use that can be made to sound noble, is that it blinds people. They do not even think about alternative ways to achieve their desires.

WASHINGTON, D.C., 1996

Twenty-two tenants of an apartment building share a lovingly tended communal garden that has existed on an adjoining lot for over fifty years. There is a possibility that the owner of the lot will sell it for building. Instead of negotiating to buy it, the tenants petition to have the garden declared a historic landmark. Suddenly facing the possibility of total loss, the owner bulldozes the garden and surrounds the lot with a chain-link fence. Regardless whether the lot is sold, the garden is now an ugly mudhole. In the newspaper story about this event, the tenants express rage, sadness, and loss—but no one ever says, "We should have bought it."[25]

The environmentalists have pioneered the creative use of easements. For the sake of his own conscience or in exchange for hard cash, or as a tax dodge, a landowner dedicates some of the sticks in his bundle of rights to the cause of the environment. The process is made formal and legal by recording the restriction as part of the chain of title, which makes it binding on future owners and enforceable against them by others who might be interested. The devices can include restrictions on density or on type of development. A scenic easement can be granted, ensuring that the view across the property remains unimpaired. Any of a number of environmental groups will give you guidance on doing this, if you are so inclined. Call the Nature Conservancy in Washington, D.C. or the Lincoln Institute of Land Policy in Cambridge, Massachusetts.

Environmental easements may build up some problems for the future, since the land becomes unavailable no matter how much circumstances change. From the standpoint of municipal authorities, it also goes off the tax rolls. This could be a big issue some day, just as the land held by the church became an issue in the Middle Ages. But that is tomorrow's problem, and the easement device is useful today.

Another promising device is auctions. Herbert Inhaber, an expert on safety and waste disposal issues in the nuclear power industry, suggests that undesirable facilities can be sited by using a reverse auction.[26] The federal government or the state pays a town to take the facility, with the winner being the place demanding the lowest sum of money. For example, if a waste dump needs to be put somewhere in a state, Town A might take it if the state gave it $100,000, Town B might ask $250,000, and Town C $1 million. Town A would get it. This process makes everyone happy. Town A has said that it would like to have the $100,000 and the dump, and the others are happier as they are, without the money. The alternative to the auction is some elaborate planning process where the "right" location is supposedly found. Usually this takes forever, makes everyone unhappy, and makes a final decision in random fashion. There is no way to decide where a dump "should" go, any more than there is a "fair" way to decide who gets bounced from the oversold airplane.

Completely private action is also a fast-developing alternative. Too much discussion of property assumes that the government must intervene or all property will be trashed. A conference announced on the Internet is labeled "Property Rights vs. the Common Good." Nothing could be further from the truth. People place a high value on environmental amenities and are willing to pay for them. They will not pay much for the amenities wanted by the far-out fringe of the environmental movement, which consists of land that is removed from all interaction with humans, but they will pay handsomely for human-oriented environmentalism. As one of the Calvert County commissioners commented, "People are willing to pay a good price for this rural environment." He did not add, though he could have, that they will pay a good price to live in it; they will not pay just for the knowledge that somewhere it exists.

People are also willing to pay a good price for recreation. Fifty companies make over a thousand different kinds of hiking boots, and sales grew from $500 million in 1993 to $795 million in 1995.[27] Even if a good chunk of this increase is merely the latest fashion statement, the fact that hiking boots are "the thing" is itself important. Four-wheel-drive sports utilities are the hot-selling cars. Jet skis have already been covered. Visitor hours to federal recreation areas went from 6.4 billion in 1980 to 8.0 billion in 1992.[28] Between 1980 and 1994, sales of all sporting goods rose from $16.7 billion to $46.2 billion. Of this, recreational transport—boats, bicycles, snowmobiles, recreational vehicles—accounted for $5.3 billion in 1980 and $15.7 billion in 1994.[29] In *Cadillac Desert*, Marc Reisner comments that in the 1930s about 5,000 people then alive in the United States had ever floated on a whitewater river. By the early 1990s about 35 million had done it.[30] He sees in this a revolution in the West. He is right, but you cannot limit the vision to the West and the management of the public domain. It is a revolution in the nature of land use nationwide and in the incentives at work under a free-market system based on property rights.

The combination of increasing affluence and improved information technology opens up new vistas of user-charge recreation facilities. In Japan, Toyota spent $3.5 million building a rugged road for four-wheel-drive vehicles and charges drivers twenty-six dollars per hour to use it.[31] My rancher in Chapter 11, the one who installed the card reader for fishing rights, can become a nationwide chain. He moves east, buying up easements over private property for trails that serve for horseback and bicycle riding from spring through fall, snowmobiling in the winter, and, on a separate track, year round four-wheeling. Access is through gates controlled by the reader or by licenses checked randomly, just as fishing licenses are checked. Then he breeds horses in the West, ships them to the East in the summer and the Southwest in winter, expands into riding lessons, adds a franchise operation of roadside bicycle–sport utility repair shops, and the next thing you know he is bought out by a running shoe giant, which integrates with jogging tracks and forms a joint venture with the National Rifle Association to create shooting ranges at remote locations.

This is not as fanciful as it sounds. All kinds of new markets are in creation in areas once consigned to the purgatory of command-and-control regulation. Transportation is deregulated. Telecommunications is on the same track. The creation of transferable pollution credits is reducing pollution in an efficient manner. Competition has hit the market for electricity. Customers, once prisoners of the deadly hybrid of the sloth inherent in a regulated monopoly crossbred with the social engineering impulses of regulatory commissions, are free to seek the best price. There is no reason to exclude the business of providing environmental amenities from this revolution.

Approximately a hundred jurisdictions have adopted a device called transferable development rights (TDRs). In this system, areas where the development is encouraged are called receiving areas. Those where development is banned are called sending areas. Owners of land in each are accorded development rights to build on their property. Owners in sending areas cannot actually use their rights; they must sell them to owners in receiving areas. Owners in receiving areas do not get enough rights of their own to build out to the limits allowed by the zoning. They must buy more. Often the first step in setting up a TDR system is to downzone the receiving area so as to force owners there to become customers of TDRs.

You can look at TDRs in two different ways: as a blatant appropriation of property from both sets of owners or as a reasonable approach to solving problems of externalities and commons. In particular, they represent a solution to the "givings" problem. The theory is that by limiting development in some areas, the city is enhancing the value of the remaining land. TDRs are a way to integrate these transactions and split the total value among all the landowners. On balance, and if implemented by governments concerned with perfecting property rights rather than appropriating them for favored constituents, TDRs are an intriguing innovation. As if to prove the old saw that there is nothing new under the sun, they evoke memories of nineteenth century land grants to railroads. Like the land grants, they are a device for integrating the costs and benefits of spillovers and infrastructure with ownership. They are the kind of institutional innovation that is necessary to revive property rights in the nation's great urban areas, and break through the deadlocks that are strangling them.

Chapter 13

The Quick Tour

Lots of issues in a few fun-packed pages: historic preservation, coastal zones, forfeitures, rails-to-trails, and a few other things

T he increasing propensity of government to run roughshod over rights to property goes beyond the areas covered so far. There are many more, but the issues get repetitive. However, the sheer number and variety of assaults on property is a significant part of the story, so I hate to skip them entirely. This chapter compromises by fast-forwarding through some other topics worthy of chapters of their own.

HISTORIC PRESERVATION

The urge to preserve places important to the nation's history is a strong one. By 1978, fifty states and over five hundred municipalities had passed some kind of historic preservation law. The federal government also has a large-scale effort. In 1949 Congress chartered the National Trust for Historic Preservation, an organization with a budget of $33 million and $68 million in assets. Congress gives it $7 million a year and allocates another $33 million to state historic preservation offices.[1]

Local programs vary widely. Some are like the Maryland program described in one of the stories in Chapter 2: your property can be appropriated for the preservationist cause. Others are voluntary or even good news for the landowner because designation results in tax breaks.

Preservation programs can include designation of certain districts as historic, forbidding change in any outward appearance without the approval of a review board. These are often strongly supported by the landowners and are defensible as instances of people getting together to preserve property values. The device is tending to get overused, with any neighborhood that is old recasting itself as historic. The harm here is probably not to the landowners. Some evidence indicates that designating a district as historic does not damage values,[2] and local residents tend to support it. The harm is to nonresidents and to the metropolitan area as a whole. By declaring itself a "historic district," residents of an old neighborhood can stave off competition from people who cannot afford the high price of an existing home but would accept less space in exchange for an in-town location. It is a good bet that Arlington neighborhoods became interested in the program as the Metro transit system pushed into northern Virginia and created pressure for more intensive use of land.

Designating individual buildings without the consent of the owner crosses the line into appropriation. Someone whose property is frozen by the program is robbed for the benefit of friends and neighbors, especially for people like me who enjoy history. Preserving things important to the nation's historical heritage is a quintessential public good. The incongruity of providing this preservation by stealth and regulatory taking rather than by honest purchase is an ironic commentary on where that noble history is trending.

The problems are worsened by the ease with which historic preservation programs are manipulated. Any old rattrap can be called historic if some neighbor's interest lies in freezing its use, and the standards are too vague to contradict. Especially outraged are churches caught in the preservation trap, which believe that being forced to put their money into supporting a building rather than their religious purposes is a violation of their freedom of religion.[3]

New York City is the paradigm, though it is not unique. In 1978 the Supreme Court upheld the constitutionality of an uncompensated historic designation of Grand Central Station in New York City in the *Penn Central* case.[4] Thereafter the city binged on preservation. By 1996, it had put 20,135 buildings on the list. (Chicago, the home of modern architecture, designated only 4,216.)[5] The examples reach the ludicrous. Efforts to improve New York's SoHo area with trees were stymied, for example. There were no trees when it was a manufacturing district in the nineteenth century, so it cannot have trees now. Or take the following tale.

NEW YORK CITY, 1993

The owners of a cooperative building need to replace windows dating from the 1930s. Upon learning that wooden replacements would cost $60,000, they spend $16,000 to install metal-framed windows. The New York Landmarks Commission objects, insisting that the job be done over with wooden replacements. The irony is that the building was erected in the 1890s, and the 1930s windows replaced original windows of an unknown aspect. So the commission is insisting on a costly return to a corruption of the original style, not on a true restoration. One tenant describes her session with the commission: "Not more than 60 seconds of debate—or even conversation—ensued among them in making a judgment." The commission acknowledges that cost to owners is not a concern.[6]

As Terry Anderson of the Political Economy Research Center, a leading writer on the economics of property rights, put it in a different context, "No sacrifice is too great for someone else to make as long as it is free to you."[7] Even the architectural critic of the *New York Times*, a strong supporter of *Penn Central*, began to have second thoughts about preservation, suggesting that perhaps a city needs to evolve over time.[8]

The National Trust has also wandered considerably from its cause. Its most recent conference, "Preserving Community: City, Suburb, and Countryside," included sessions on preserving everything—not just historic sites in a conventional sense but skyscrapers, barns, landscapes, roads, old downtowns, urban fringes. Name it, and it is worth preserving. It has also decided that the low-price superstores such as Wal-Mart, Price Club, Home Depot, and their ilk are responsible for urban sprawl, and has joined the crusade against them. It sells a guide, *How Superstore Sprawl Can Harm Communities (and What Citizens Can Do About It.)*[9] The conservative Capital Research Center says, "The anti-Wal-Mart crusade is less about preserving history than it is part of a general campaign against suburban development. In this campaign, "historic preservation functions more as an argument than an objective.""

The issue for the future is a strange, ill-defined effort, the American Heritage Corridors program, to set up corridors, mostly along rivers, to preserve the landscape from any meaningful change. Six minor individual Heritage Corridors already have been named by Congress. A number of others are under consideration, including the Mississippi River Corridor Study, which would cover 2,400 miles in ten states. At least ten more specific corridors were proposed in the 104th Congress, along with general legislation. The proposal is full of ringing language about comprehensive planning, government-private partnerships, and other concepts that have proved disastrous in practice, but it is difficult to determine the purpose of the whole enterprise.

RAILS-TO-TRAILS

Rails-to-trails (RTT) is an ingenious idea. The rise of the highway and airplane caused a steady decline in miles of railroad track in use. At the peak, around 1930, railroads operated 230,000 miles of mainline. By 1993, this was down to about 131,000 miles. Rails-to-trails is based on the idea that these old rights-of-way would make excellent trails for walking, biking, cross-country skiing, and other healthy recreations. As a blurb for the annual Rails-to-Trails Conference puts it, "A vast network of trails across the nation connecting our city centers to the countryside and countless communities to each other . . . linking neighborhoods to workplaces and congested areas to open spaces . . . serving both transportation needs and the demand for close-to-home recreation."

In 1983 Congress enacted the Rails to Trails Act, which rests on the premise that the nation might someday need these railroad rights-of-way again. Therefore, it would be foolish to let them disappear. A railroad is not allowed to abandon trackage without the approval of the Surface Transportation Board of the Department of Transportation. The law provides that when abandonment is contemplated, the railroad must give private groups or states an opportunity to take over the right-of-way and turn it into a trail. In theory, it is not abandoned but banked against the day when the trains must roll once again. To sweeten the pot, starting in 1991, Congress decreed that states can use money from the Highway Trust Fund to create these trails.

The program has caught on. Over 800 trails containing 8,000 miles are open, with another 800 or so in development; $200 million of Highway money has been allocated. The national association boosting the program, the Rails-to-Trails Conservancy, claims it is also a money-maker for localities. It says existing trails generate $1.5 billion annually in spending on lodging, food, bike services, and other tourism.[10]

Rails-to-Trails is a fine program, for me. My house lies about one-quarter of a mile from the Capital Crescent Trail, and from there I can get on the Washington & Old Dominion, which is another rail turned trail or on numerous other hiking and biking paths. Most people seem to agree with me. A survey of Marylanders found that 86 percent support the program.[11]

Many people who are a little closer to the action—the trail runs through their backyard—hate it. Having an occasional freight roll by was no problem compared to the intrusion of a parade of bikers, walkers, and packs of snowmobiles. Landowners have put up barricades, yelled at passers-by, and dumped manure on trails.[12] Some owners cite examples of drunken parties and express concern about trails as natural routes for criminals, but it is impossible to pin down the legitimacy of this concern. Certainly, in a time in which people pay heavily to live in gated communities with security guards it is not fair to dismiss it out of hand.

Because many people dislike a rail-to-trail in their backyard, the program lessens the value of their homes. The quarter-mile difference between my homesite and theirs is crucial. The proximity raises the value of my house, since I have the advantages without having strangers traipsing through my backyard. The National Association of Reversionary Property Owners (NARPO), which is fighting the program, cites numbers showing serious losses by its constituents, ranging as high as half the value of their homes in some cases.[13]

Other economic interests are also at stake. Railroad rights-of-way are used for cables and pipelines. Whoever owns the land has the right to collect the tolls for these, and they can be substantial. The railroads also make a good thing out of rails-to-trails. The railroad's consent must be obtained for the conversion of the right-of-way into a trail. Consent does not come cheap, so part of the cost of the program is that the railroads get cash payments. The railroads profit in another way.

Wooden rail ties are treated with preservative, which over the years soaks into the soil. Railroads also spill chemicals out of tank cars and spray heavily with herbicides. Just about every mile of old right-of-way is contaminated with these chemicals, which makes them Superfund sites under the antipollution laws. To be responsible for a Superfund site is bad luck indeed. You are legally liable for cleaning up any contaminants found there, and the standard of "clean" imposed by EPA can be stringent indeed. If the rails-to-trails program lets railroads avoid this liability, it is like money in the bank for them.

Some of the unhappy landowners are not limited to cursing their fate. NARPO estimates that 85 percent of all railroad trackage was built on easements, not on land owned by the railroads. This means railroads did not buy the land. They got only the right to use it as a railroad right-of-way. The standard clause in the deed is that if the land ceases to be used as a railroad, it reverts to the owner of the parcel containing the easement.

The owners contend that the Rails-to-Trails Act takes their property by overriding the clause in the deed that says the land returns to them when rail use ceases. The government and the proponents of the program counter that railroad use has not really stopped; it is just suspended. The right-of-way is railbanked, against the possibility of future need. No one really believes this, and it is amusing to imagine the reaction of the hikers and bikers if the government tried to take the trails back for railroad use. The banking idea was a convenient fiction to justify keeping the rights-of-way.

A number of cases challenging this program are pending in the courts. So far, the results are inconclusive. The Supreme Court has ruled that the program is indeed legal, but it has not ruled on whether it is a taking that requires compensation. As that issue bounces around in the courts, the reversionary owners are becoming increasingly active politically. If NARPO is right about the magnitude of the potential losses imposed by the program, this opposition is sure to increase as the number of trails increases. One hundred thousand miles of unused right-of-way affects a lot of landowners.

Rails-to-trails is a good example of the point made earlier about the loss of community, as embodied in the callous willingness to inflict hefty losses on others for one's own minor gratification. The issue of trails is not cluttered up with concerns about endangered species, or wetlands, or old-growth forests, or anything else. It is not even cluttered with issues of the economic need to provide a transportation net. It is purely about the pleasure people get from this source of recreation. Personally, I like this program. Washington and its suburbs have a wonderful network of greenways, parks, and trails, and they add substantially to the quality of life. Nonetheless, it is hard to fathom why I should be allowed to impose losses on others because I like to walk and bike. For a start, it is hard to fathom why the railroads should collect the value of easements that they are abandoning. Why doesn't this money go to the landowners? It also seems worth investing considerable energy to create mechanisms (card readers, trail use stamps, whatever) for charging us trail users and compensating the property owners. I would be willing to use the government's power of eminent domain to force the property owners to sell the right-of-way for public use. Otherwise holdout problems and transaction costs will make it impossible. But I am queasy about going even this far, and outright stealing is way beyond the bounds.

Besides, we trail users should get the landowners on the side of the trails. Maybe they should be compensated according to usage. They could compete, putting up rest rooms, picnic areas, and other amenities. Maybe they could be allowed to improve the trail, adding hills, twists, and other things to make it more fun. As with endangered species, it is far better in the long run for the visitor to be welcome. The motive for this extends beyond elementary justice to long-term self-interest. If trail advocates do not deal fairly with the landowners, in a few years trail users will find themselves biking or jogging along paths that stretch for miles between walls of 10-foot-high privacy fences. This is not the trail experience that people have in mind.

BILLBOARDS

Billboards have always presented particular difficulties for takings analysis. They are purely visual, so they are not within the general definition of pollution, which requires an offense to some other sense or to health or safety. They are not quite an eyesore that would justify abatement as a nuisance. At the same time, the sole function of a billboard is to be an externality—to affect people who are not on the property itself. This leads naturally to a gut feeling that the community ought to be able to control and limit this impact. The feeling is strengthened by the fact that the whole value of a billboard derives from its location next to a public transportation commons, a highway or street. The owners of the highway—us, the public—ought to be charging the billboard advertiser for providing it with access to an audience. We are like a TV station, only we are giving our audience away to the advertisers instead of collecting from them. Furthermore, it seems as if the landowner who is collecting the rental fee from the billboard company is actually charging for access to an audience created by the commons.

In the early twentieth century, various antibillboard laws were ruled unconstitutional by the courts. In response, governments devised rationales that they were protecting public health and safety. After all, thieves can lurk behind billboards, and immoral activities can take place in their shelter. Later the idea came into vogue that billboards distract automobile drivers and should be controlled as a matter of highway safety. More recently, the tendency is to regulate them on frankly aesthetic grounds but to treat those in existence at the time a ban goes into effect as nonconforming uses and allow their amortization over time.

Billboard companies are not without resources. A lot of laws have been passed dealing with these issues, and a lot of lawsuits have been brought. The results are all over the place.

ARTISTS' RIGHTS

This program is not important compared with many of the others, but it is too amusing to pass up.

Thinking about covering that weird mural that someone painted on the side of your building or maybe in the hallway? Think again, and read the Visual Artists Rights Act (VARA) of 1990. For visual art of "recognized stature" created after 1991, the artist is entitled to prevent destruction. If removing the work from a building would result in the work's destruction, then it cannot be removed. It is protected for the lifetime of the artist. If this prevents remodeling or razing the structure, tough.

NEW YORK, 1991–1995

A partnership leases a commercial building. It engages three artists to install sculpture in the lobby. They create a giant walk-in work that fills the entire lobby, inextricably linked to the structure. In 1994 the lease expires, and the owner, who takes over the building, expresses an intention to remove the sculpture. The artists get an injunction against any renovation that changes the sculpture. On appeal, the owners win on the ground that the work was done "for hire," which is a concept embodied in the copyright law. Works for hire are not covered by VARA.[14]

VARA is typical of nice ideas run riot. The basic purpose of the law is to protect artists' "moral rights." These, long recognized in Europe, are rights beyond those covered by the copyright or the physical ownership of the work. They include attribution, which means a right to be recognized as the author, and integrity, which means a right to prevent mutilation or deformation of the work. In some places, the right of integrity includes the right to prevent destruction. (If you oppose colorizing old movies, do not get your hopes up. The law does not apply to motion pictures.)

The basic idea of VARA is to make these moral rights of attribution and integrity enforceable. Then the law was pushed further. It says the artist has a right to prevent the destruction of a "work of recognized stature." Anyone who plans destruction must notify the artist and give him or her a chance to remove the work. So far, this is okay. It seems to be a reasonable effort at balancing people's interests and rights and in recognizing a new property right for artists. The standard is too vague, but notification is not too much of a burden. This is an evolution of property rights that seems reasonable. It seems fundamentally fair that someone who plans to destroy the work some struggling artist painted with her own blood and sweat be required at least to notify the artist and give him or her a chance to save the work. It is, after all, what any decent person would do without a law.

Then the law goes that yard too far; it deals with works that cannot be removed. It says that if the work cannot be removed, the building cannot be touched. This makes the building into an endangered species habitat for artists. The result will be the same too. The owner who gives refuge to art, like the owner who makes property attractive to animals, runs the risk of ruin. So owners will not allow art anymore if they have any sense. Driving around New York City or Washington, D.C., you see large murals painted on rundown buildings. In Washington, the number has grown from about a dozen in 1991 to, in 1996, "hundreds, depicting everything from black history to neighborhood pride and advertising nightclubs and theaters."[15] Many are interesting. Some are good. As owners of buildings learn about this law, the number will drop because the owners will refuse to take the chance. An artist who mingles her work into the structure of a building knows that the building may be changed. When she gets the commission, she can bargain over what will happen if this occurs. Why pass a law that ensures that the commission will never be given in the first place?

VARA has other morsels for the legal profession. The act has an exception: if the artist signed a waiver when the work was created, VARA does not protect the work. But the law does not seem to require that a building owner consent to the installation of the art. It is hard to get a waiver if you do not know what is going on. If you rent an apartment to a wannabe Picasso who paints a mural on the wall, and he has an art critic buddy who swears it has "recognized stature," does he now control your building?

What about New York's campaign against subway graffiti? Do you think I can find an art critic in New York who will swear that graffiti has "recognized stature"? Time me—10 minutes with the Yellow Pages will do it. Must the city pay off the writer every time it cleans a subway car? If you do not believe this could happen, read *Subway Art*, published in 1984: "Few 'pieces' survive long . . . it is rare for more than one or two undamaged graffiti masterpieces to be running in the entire transit system at any one time."[16] A recent news article noted that "much of the stigma has been removed from graffiti art in Europe. For a handful . . . the medium has developed from an underground, criminal activity to a lucrative and respectable career."[17] Surely, you might think, Congress could not have meant to allow graffiti writers, who can be jailed for vandalism, to appropriate whole buildings. Given the history of endangered species and wetlands, how much do you want to bet on this proposition? Will you bet a multimillion dollar building? Maybe there must be a trial, complete with learned experts, over whether this particular piece of graffiti has recognized stature. I can hear it now: "Well, Doctor, are you claiming that Wrekonize's writings on the IRT are of the same stature as Skeme's classic on the BMT? Come now!" (The names are real, from *Subway Art*.)

AMERICAN INDIANS

The United States government recognizes 319 Indian tribes, ranging in size from 3 members to 308,000. Another 120 are in the process of petitioning for federal recognition. About 1.9 million people identify themselves as Indians on census forms, and 700,000 of these are enrolled in a recognized tribe. (Most tribes require 25 percent Indian ancestry for enrollment.) Another 10 to 15 million people have a discernible degree of Indian ancestry but do not identify themselves as Indians.

Four hundred thirty-seven thousand Indians live on three hundred plus reservations containing 55 million acres. About 20 percent of the land is owned by individual Indians. Title to the rest is held by the Department of the Interior in trust for the tribe. At the same time, about 11 million acres within reservation boundaries are owned by non-Indians, and 370,000 people—46 percent of the population living within the boundaries of reservations—are non-Indian.

The long pain of the relations between the waves of immigrants to the United States and the Indians has left a welter of problems involving property rights. During the nineteenth century, some land was acquired by non-Indians in violation of the Nonintercourse Act of 1790. Indians are now claiming this land back from the successors of these purchasers. Not surprisingly, people who emigrated from Europe in 1910 and bought land in perfectly legal style do not believe they should be pauperized because some frontiersman in 1850 did not understand, or care about, the Nonintercourse Act, and they fight back.

The non-Indian holders of land within the boundaries of reservations contend that they are treated like second-class citizens. Indian tribes are sovereign nations, sort of. Reservations are ruled by tribal councils. Non-Indians cannot vote in the tribal elections and have no voice in the government. The uncertainties of governance drastically cut the value of their property. Who will buy in a place where they have no control over tax rates or their government?

The Indians themselves find the system less than perfect. The Bureau of Indian Affairs (BIA) cannot seem to account for over $2 billion in Indian trust funds. BIA must approve many tribal contracts and

leases, and severe restraints are imposed on alienation of many tribal resources. These inhibit development and make it difficult for tribes to
enter into contracts. Many Indian lands are rich in undeveloped resources while individual Indians are extremely poor.

Inefficient inheritance rules imposed on many individual allotments
have fragmented ownership. The transaction costs of getting the multiple owners to agree are often so high that there is no point in even trying to use the land. Also, much Indian land is held in common, in the
form of a trust for the tribe. Studies comparing trust land with nontrust
land of equal quality find that trust status reduces productivity by about
50 percent.[18]

This by no means completes the roster of property issues. Nineteenth-
century treaties between Indian nations and the U.S. government often
gave Indians extensive hunting and fishing rights over public domain
lands, including lands that were later sold or homesteaded. These rights
are now the subject of intense controversy. (See, for example, the Mille
Lacs claim in Minnesota described in the Introduction.) If the Indians
have the property right to the large harvest of fish and game that they
claim, then the recreation-based economies of large parts of the Midwest and Northwest face serious disruption. The Indians, of course, believe that they are only trying to enforce still-valid property rights that
have been ignored for decades.

As always in the West, water rights too are in turmoil. Unsettled Indian claims in the West could exceed 45 million acre-feet per year and
be worth $20–$50 billion. Since western water is a zero-sum game—
what one person gains, someone else must lose—the other claimants
are not happy about this prospect.

These multiple conflicts are causing serious frictions between Indians and everyone else. Most of them are unnecessary. They are products of uncertainty. Rights to property have been left unresolved,
sometimes for over a century. In many cases there is a conflict between
the likely result under a strict interpretation of the law and the realities
of social practice over the years. For example, the Nonintercourse Act
of 1790 does indeed say that a transfer of title to land made by an Indian tribe has no validity unless it was done under a formal treaty.
Nonetheless, courts are reluctant to come to this conclusion, and litigation gets back-burnered while people try to work out a political set-

tlement. But the uncertainty plays hob with property values and people's ability to plan.

The same problems beset the controversies over hunting, fishing, and water rights. Whether the water behind the dams gets taken down a few feet is a matter of economic life and death to many people in the Northwest. Having the matter left up in the air indefinitely arouses serious bitterness, which tends to take the form of antagonism to the Indians. The hostility should be directed toward the government, or perhaps the lawyers, for their inability to reach fair closure on the issues and let everyone know where they stand.

FORFEITURES

Pick up the Business Section of the Sunday *New York Times,* and turn to about page 10. You will find a list of assets seized recently by the federal government: cars, homes, boats, you name it. These are the fruits of one of America's fastest growing industries: forfeitures of property to the government.

The theory behind forfeitures started out with the proposition that property used to commit crimes should be forfeited. Then it moved on to the idea that the fruits of crimes should be forfeited. Between them, these account for just about any property owned by someone who commits or is accused of a crime, so the field has grown apace. The U.S. government now collects a steady half-billion dollars a year in forfeited assets, and states collect an unknown amount under their own laws.

The list of favorite targets includes drug dealers, of course. It extends to financial criminals. It has been proposed for use with environmental offenses. In early 1996 the Senate voted to apply severe forfeiture provisions to doctors who commit any of a series of vaguely defined crimes. Clearly this idea has now reached the point where forfeiture will be attached to every new regulatory bill as a matter of routine.

In 1995 the Supreme Court upheld forfeiture of a car belonging to a woman completely innocent of any crime whatsoever. Her husband used it to have sex with a prostitute. The state of Michigan, like many others, seizes forfeiture of property used in connection with vice offenses. This creates many opportunities for mischievous merriment. Mad at your neighbor? Throw a few marijuana seeds over the fence, wait until they sprout, then turn him in. That'll teach him to throw a loud party without inviting you. Want to get even with the airline for sticking you in that middle seat? Stick a little coke in the seat back pocket, call the narcs. (Actually, you do not hear of many airplanes, cruise ships, or hotels getting seized. Maybe some innocent property owners have more political clout than others.)

Forfeiture practice is becoming the cesspool of law enforcement and the favored instrument of local tyrants. In one town, an eighty-year-old African-American woman owned a rundown motel coveted by the local authorities. They had the police stake it out, waited until a prostitute came with a customer, and confiscated the property. In a cause célèbre in California, police burst into a ranch house and killed the owner when he resisted. They claimed an informant had told them of drugs on the premises, but no drugs were found. Surrounding circumstances create deep suspicions that the real goal was to seize the ranch, which was adjacent to a park. In Florida in 1992, the sheriff's deputies stopped thousands of motorists traveling on Interstate 95 on the grounds that they fit a "drug-courier profile." Seventy percent of those stopped were black or Hispanic. The deputies confiscated on the spot any cash carried in excess of $100 on the assumption that it must be the fruit of an illegal enterprise.[19]

Procedural protections are minimal. The Supreme Court finally decided that an owner must be given notice before his property is seized. You are not entitled to the benefit of the criminal law's requirement that guilt be proved beyond a reasonable doubt. Property can be seized on a civil "more probable than not" standard. In the real world, the way it usually works is that the property is seized upon the allegation that it is in some way connected to a crime. You must sue the government to get it back. Obviously, for anything except the most expensive property, there is no point in fighting; the legal fees will cost you more than the property is worth. In practical effect, the allegation is all that is required to complete the seizure.

Much forfeited property is kept by law enforcement agencies. If your new car is seized because you are accused of using it for solicitation, it can—assuming its up to their standards—be assigned to detectives for official use. The rationale is that undercover cops cannot drive low-rent Chevies; they need top-of-the-line wheels. Of course, you might want to check the department's policies on whether cops get to drive their official vehicles home at night and whether "official duties" include visiting the mall on Saturday.

COASTAL ZONES

People like water. The density of population in U.S. inland counties is fewer than 50 people per square mile; for coastal counties, it is 275. About 65 percent of the U.S. population lives within 50 miles of an ocean or great lake. The Coastal Zone Management Act is a federal law that encourages states to engage in comprehensive planning for coastal areas. State participation is voluntary, and the major import of the whole thing is to get states to engage in statewide zoning for coastal areas rather than leaving land use up to each municipality. The program also requires a participating state to install a program to control pollution from nonpoint sources. (In environmentalese, things like factories are "point sources." "Nonpoint sources" are things like farms, parking lots, and roads, where any release of pollutants is diffuse, and cannot be controlled by installing a control device at a single point.) The carrot is federal grants to states that participate. Also, if a state participates in the program, then no federal permit can be granted unless the permittee has the sign-off from the state agency.

Twenty-four states have enacted coastal protection laws, some in partnership with the federal act and some separate.[20] In terms of their effect on property rights, the basic doctrines and problems are the same as those affecting land use issues in general. There are a lot of problems, though, since states have come to regard the existence of a coastal zone as a regulatory carte blanche. From an analytical point of view, the question is whether state rules are reasonable controls on externalities, or reasonable efforts to allocate a commons, or straight-up appropriations for the sake of existing owners.

For example, the federal government controls drilling for oil and gas on the continental shelf beyond 3 miles from the shore. It owns the shelf, so to speak, on behalf of all citizens of the United States. Under the Coastal Zone Act, federal activity must be "consistent with" the state's program of coastal zone management. North Carolina has indicated that it will veto development of a promising field 140 miles off the coast out of fear of coastline contamination. There is a flaw in the logic though. The field will produce natural gas, so coastal contamination is impossible. Nonetheless, the state power is absolute. If it wants to pre-empt productive use of the property, thus taking it from all of us, it can. The oil companies are like the real estate developers. They do not re-ally care one way or the other. They will take their rigs and go where they are appreciated.

Public access to the beach is an interesting issue. By ancient law, pri-vate people can own the beach only to the mean high-tide line. Sea-ward of that, the beach and the water is a common—which raises the question, How do people get to the common if all the property on the landward side is privately owned? No owner has any incentive to allow access. As a group, the owners would rather they were the only ones who could get there. Nope. The law has thought of this. It is called dif-ferent things, such as *prescriptive easement, implied dedication, implied reservation,* or *custom* (the terms vary from one place to another). Some-how the public has the right to get to the beach.

Of course, while some parts of government are protecting beaches by prohibiting development, others parts are happily subsidizing develop-ment. Coastal areas have benefited from subsidized flood insurance, which ensures that property owners need not run the inevitable risks of being washed away by storms or tides. Infrastructure such as highways and bridges gets rebuilt regularly with government money. Millions of dollars in taxpayer money are spent in the usually futile efforts to stop erosion of beaches. Shoreline dwellers come to regard the right to these expenditures as a kind of property right. So anyone with a taste for irony can watch as David Lucas is arbitrarily deprived of the right to use his property, while other owners are subsidized to build in vulnerable spots or have big bucks spent to keep their beaches from washing away.

AND THERE IS STILL MORE

We can go on to look at restrictions on floodplains, or at the Depart-ment of the Interior's newest gambit, which is ecosystem protection. We can discuss the Heritage Corridor program in more detail, and the issues in the Adirondacks and the Northern Forest. Cities such as New York are trying to control activities in vast upstate regions to protect the purity of their water supply. The city dwellers see themselves as having a right to uncontaminated water; the upstaters think the New Yorkers are trying to avoid paying for treatment plants and do not mind inflicting huge losses on other people in pursuit of this selfish goal.

We could take up farmland preservation. It has been touched on a couple of times, but textbooks on property law give it a whole section of its own. The expansion of national parks and monuments raises continuing controversy. When property is taken for additions to these facilities, it is paid for under eminent domain, but there can sometimes be years between the date additions are planned and the time they are actually taken and paid for. The result is called *condemnation blight*, a familiar concept in takings law. It means no one wants to buy or invest in property that is going to get taken, so it sits there and rots. The owner can be immobilized for years, unable to start over somewhere else and unable to continue in that spot.

We could take up some of the programs that deal with pollution. Superfund, which is directed at even minor releases of chemicals, covers hundreds of thousands and maybe millions of old industrial and commercial sites and involves a massive shift in property rights. The Leaking Underground Storage Tank program covers petroleum tanks. It too affects over a million sites and makes drastic changes in historic property rights.

Oceans present property rights problems. The ocean is a commons, or perhaps is better described as a multitude of different commons. Fisheries are susceptible to overexploitation, since every fisherman and every fishing nation knows it had better catch all those fish before some greedy person gets there. Controls are exercised by a mosaic of treaties and rules, some of them sound, some silly. For example, nations impose limitations on the numbers of days that fishing boats can work, which triggers a fishing equipment arms race. If a boat can work for only a limited time, it better be equipped with the most up-to-date efficient equipment so that it can cut a real swathe through the fish population during that time.

The book has not covered an area rich in potential for future conflict. The United States has entered into a number of international conventions that affect the use of property, such as the World Heritage Treaty, the Convention on Biosphere Reserves, the Convention of Desertification, and the Framework Convention on Climate Change. These could impose obligations on citizens that override their rights under state and even federal law.

My mail this morning had a blurb for a conference, "The Native American Graves Protection and Repatriation Act: Its Legal Effects on Private Industry." This is the latest in a series of laws dealing with archeological artifacts, fossils, and cemeteries. If you find any of these on your property or in the course of your building project, you lose control in an expensive way. As always, the cause seems worthy. Who can quarrel with the idea that the dead deserve respect and should not be used as the foundation for a suburban patio? But it turns out there are thousands and thousands of unmapped cemeteries. A sleuth has turned up over a hundred in a single county in Virginia.[21] The standard government reflex—make disturbing a cemetery a crime—does not solve the landowners' problem.

Rent control has not been discussed, except in a couple of brief anecdotes. It is, like many other abuses of the right to property, an unsavory tale of how the rich use assaults on property to steal from the working class and the poor. Nothing said here could improve on William Tucker's devastating 1991 book, *Zoning, Rent Control and Affordable Housing.*

If pressed, the list could be expanded, but the primary point is made: the assault on property rights has breadth as well as depth. Serious intrusions exist not only in the areas detailed in this work but in many others as well. The sheer number is impressive.

Although the contexts change, the same themes recur. Over and over you start with a problem. It may or may not present a cause for legitimate concern. It certainly lends itself to sound bites. Historic buildings get destroyed. Coasts are crowded. Old railroads make good trails. Farmland is disappearing. Species are endangered. Wetlands are valuable. Then the government, instead of dealing with it in any sophisticated way, picks up the sledgehammer of regulation. Before you know it, a set of inflexible rules is in place that fits ill with any specific situation. The usual effect of these is to remove some of the sticks in the bundle of rights that makes up property. Sometimes these sticks are given to other owners. Often they are destroyed. Wetlands regulation does not transfer ownership of rights. It destroys them. No one can exercise dominion over the property anymore. Sometimes the regulation takes almost all the sticks, leaving the owner with only a few twigs.

Humankind's capacity to get these issues wrong throughout history is enormous. In particular, the tendency of governments to choke off economic improvement is a constant factor in human affairs. As the philosopher George Santayana said, "Those who cannot remember the past are condemned to repeat it." An addendum to this, attributed to a famous historian, is, "Unfortunately, those of us who do remember the past are condemned to repeat it with them."[22]

Chapter 14

Legal Issues

Protection of property by the legal system, OR, Can't anybody here play this game? Plus some comments on finality, the Tucker Act shuffle, and other trickeries of the trade

FLORIDA, THE 1940S

A story is told about Leo Durocher, the abrasive National League manager of forty years ago. During spring training, he watched as a rookie playing third base booted several grounders. Durocher grabbed his glove and ran out on the field. "Move over," he said. "I'll show you how a pro plays third." The first grounder came down the line, and Durocher booted it. He threw down his glove, glared at the rookie, and said: "Hell, you've got this position so screwed up that no one can play it!"

That is the story of the law of takings under the Fifth Amendment to the Constitution: the position is so screwed up that no one can play it.

During and after the New Deal of the 1930s, when the federal courts withdrew from the business of protecting rights to property, an exception remained. The compensation clause of the Fifth Amendment to the Constitution says specifically, "Nor shall private property be taken for public use, without just compensation." This protection also applies to actions by state governments, since it is incorporated into the meaning of due process of law guaranteed by the Fourteenth Amendment. Even without this incorporation, people would be protected against confiscation by their state governments. The principle that governments must pay for what they take was well established in the states by the early nineteenth century. Twenty-six state constitutions go further than the U.S. Constitution: they require states to pay for property they damage as well.[1]

For purposes of federal law on takings, state law defines property. However, a state cannot arbitrarily define something as "not property" and therefore not subject to the Fifth Amendment. A federal court will look at the rights created by the state and decide whether they rise to the standard of being property for purposes of the compensation clause.[2] The reason behind this doctrine is obvious. Without it, a state law could say, "Land [or automobiles or copyrights] is not property, and therefore we can ignore the requirement that we pay them when we take it."

The scope of the term *property* is broad. It includes real estate, such as land and houses; personal property, such as cars, boats, and appliances; intellectual property, such as patents, trademarks, and trade secrets; usufructs, such as rights to use land for grazing or firewood; water rights; and almost anything else you can think of. Liens and contracts count as property. Leaseholds are property. The bounds of a particular property right may be narrow, as in the distinction made earlier between your right to social security (not property) and your right to a specific social security check (property). However narrow the bounds, whatever is within them counts as property.

Also, remember the bundle of sticks theory. The term *property*, says the Supreme Court, means the "entire 'group of rights inhering in the citizen's [ownership.]' . . . It is not used in the 'vulgar and untechnical sense of the physical thing with respect to which the citizen exercises rights recognized by law. [Instead, it] denotes the group of rights inhering in the citizen's relation to the physical thing, as the right to possess, use, and dispose of it.' "[3]

Besides guaranteeing due process, the Fourteenth Amendment contains the equal protection clause, which says that a state cannot "deny to any person within its jurisdiction the equal protection of the laws." This does not mean that a state cannot treat people differently. Many laws do indeed make distinctions. One activity is taxed and another is not, or one is regulated and another left untrammeled. The courts read the equal protection clause as meaning a state must have a rational basis for treating its citizens in different ways. The fundamental purpose of the clause when added in 1868 was to prevent racial discrimination, and it stands as the bulwark to prevent all kinds of state discrimination against minorities. Differences in race, gender, religion, or national origin are not valid grounds for making distinctions.

For practical purposes, equal protection does not shield property from governmental action. For a time during the nineteenth century, it was used as an argument against regulation of property and business, but during the New Deal retreat of the 1930s, the Supreme Court developed the idea of "preferred freedoms." In this construct, which still rules constitutional adjudication, a presumption of constitutionality attaches to all state laws. The force of this presumption varies with the situation, though. Laws regulating property are upheld if the court can find any "rational basis" that would justify the state's action. Laws directed at minorities receive much more stringent review, called "strict scrutiny," under which the courts look intently at the underlying facts and at the state interest served by the legislation. Laws affecting particular religions are also viewed skeptically, as are laws that inhibit the operation of the political process in some way.

Much constitutional adjudication is about the standard of review. Many laws go down when subjected to strict scrutiny. Almost any law can survive when given the full benefit of the presumption of constitutionality under a "rational basis" test. Only a truly dumb legislator is unable to invent some connection between a legitimate state purpose and a desired law, no matter how cockamamie. Equal protection in theory may protect a property owner against irrational discrimination, but it is hard to find situations in which the protection amounts to much. As long as the government can articulate some reason for treating one group of property owners, or even one owner, differently from others, the decisions will stand. This leaves the compensation clause as property owners' only realistic constitutional refuge. When the compensation clause is invoked, the level of scrutiny is "intermediate"; it is not "strict," but not totally deferential either.[4]

Throughout the nineteenth century, courts found takings only when the owner was deprived of physical possession or formal title to property.[5] In 1922 came the case of *Pennsylvania Coal Company v. Mahon*, the seed of modern takings law, a Supreme Court opinion written by the revered Justice Oliver Wendell Holmes.[6] The decision departed from the assumption that only a physical occupation counts. It said that a regulation limiting the use of a tract could amount to a taking. The decision acknowledged that not all regulation meets this standard. After all, "government could hardly go on if to some extent values incident to property could not be diminished without paying for every such change in the general law." On the other hand, if government is allowed free license to use regulation rather than purchase to acquire property, then "the natural tendency of human nature is to extend the qualification more and more until at last private property disappears." Because this extension "cannot be accomplished in this way under the Constitution of the United States, if regulation goes too far it will be recognized as a taking." Justice Holmes, who liked to keep his opinions terse, did not furnish any further definition of "too far."

As a seed, *Pennsylvania Coal* was long dormant, because nothing happened in the field of taking by regulation for almost sixty years. During the 1920s the Supreme Court upheld states' rights to engage in zoning and land use planning, and it looked as though takings law as a limit on regulatory action had gone the way of the dodo, like other protections of property. The Supreme Court did a business in takings law, but it all concerned gray areas that arose in connection with physical intrusions or seizures of title, not with taking by regulation.

The seed got a little water in 1972. *Lynch v. Household Finance Corp.* was a complex case involving debt collection.[7] HFC got the local sheriff to seize Lynch's savings account without giving her any advance notice. She sued under federal civil rights statutes, arguing that seizure without notice deprived her of her rights as a U.S. citizen. The trial court dismissed the suit on the grounds that the law protected only "personal" rights, not "property" rights. The Supreme Court, presented with an opportunity to drive home the idea that property rights are inferior, went the other way, ringingly: "The dichotomy between personal liberties and property rights is a false one. Property does not have rights. People have rights. The right to enjoy property without unlawful deprivation, no less than the right to speak or the right to travel, is in truth a 'personal' right, whether the 'property' in question be a welfare check, a home, or a savings account. In fact, a fundamental interdependence exists between the personal right to liberty and the personal right in property. Neither could have meaning without the other. That rights in property are basic civil rights has long been recognized."

In 1978 the seed sprouted a little. New York City classified Grand Central Station as a historic landmark, which meant that the owner was forbidden to tear down the station or even to build something in the air overhead. The U.S. Supreme Court, in the *Penn Central* case, said this was not a taking.[8] In the course of rejecting the claim, though, it reaffirmed the dormant *Pennsylvania Coal* doctrine that regulation could indeed be a taking if it went too far. Since many had thought the doctrine dead, this was cheering news for the property owners, even if not for Penn Central itself.

Before going on to developments after *Penn Central*, one point must be reemphasized. A court determining whether a taking has occurred is *not* reviewing the legality of the government's action, it is accepting that the action is legal and effective. In *Pennsylvania Coal*, the determination that the regulation "went too far" did *not* mean that the regulation would not be applied. It meant only that the state must pay for the value of the property taken by it. Similarly, if the property owner had won in *Penn Central*, New York's historical preservation ordinance would have remained in effect. The owner would still have been forbidden to tear down or build on top of Grand Central Station. The difference is that the city would have paid for the loss of value.

This point is easy to forget but crucial. When an owner sues for compensation for a taking, the government action or regulation affecting the property stands as valid. The court does not look at the merits of the regulation but only at who bears the cost: the government or the owner. The compensation clause "is designed not to limit the governmental interference with property rights *per se,* but rather to secure compensation in the event of otherwise proper interference amounting to a taking."[9]

Following *Penn Central*, more cases arose alleging takings. In 1987, the landowners finally won a couple. Since then the federal courts have decided two or three dozen more. Most have gone in favor of the government, but the owners win enough to keep people's hopes alive.

Starting with its opinion in *Penn Central*, the Supreme Court has developed a standard choreography for takings cases. One factor that might seem relevant is dismissed. The compensation clause refers to taking private property "for public use," so some have argued this means their property cannot be taken if the use to which it is put is essentially private rather than public. No dice. If a legislature is willing to order the use of eminent domain, the purpose is public and that is the end of it. The same principle covers takings by regulation.

Three other factors are relevant to deciding whether a taking has occurred: Factor One, the character of the government action; Factor Two, the economic impact on the landowner; and Factor Three, the degree of interference with investment-backed expectations, or maybe reasonable expectations; the correct formula is unclear. (If you find the distinction between Factors 2 and 3 unclear, welcome to the club. It will not be your last point of confusion.)

Factor One—the character of the government action—includes many situations so clear they never get to court. When the government takes title to your property, it is a taking. No question. If it builds a courthouse in the middle of your land without bothering to take title, this too is a taking. Any legal seizure or physical occupation qualifies, whether temporary or permanent. The intrusion need not be serious. If the state authorizes a cable TV company to invade your apartment house to install the equipment needed to provide cable service to tenants, that is a taking. The "just compensation" required for such a trivial invasion may not amount to much, and in the cable TV case it equaled one dollar, but it is still a taking.[10] If the inquiry into the character of the government action finds a physical intrusion, then there is no need to examine the other two factors. The physical intrusion settles the matter.

As in any other legal area, there are big gray areas, even for something as clear as physical occupation. What if the physical intrusion is temporary or intermittent? What if government airplanes fly over your property at a height of 100 feet? At 10,000 feet? In between, at 1,000 feet? What about flood waters? Or smells? In general, noise, smells, flood waters, and so on count as physical intrusions if they are bad enough to prevent use of the property, but there is always gray.

When the government regulates but does not physically take over, then the judicial probe into whether the regulation goes "too far" and can qualify as a taking becomes fuzzier. (We are still on Factor One of the test—character of the government action.)

If the state bans a pernicious activity, such as gambling or making liquor, the loss of value inflicted on owners of slot machines or distilling equipment is not a taking. Similarly, if the state bans or controls something regarded as a nuisance under conventional property law, it is not a taking. However, the 1992 *Lucas* case imposes an important limit on this use of nuisance: the activity must be a nuisance under the state's historic principles governing property ownership. The state cannot simply decree that a particular use hereafter is noxious, so no compensation is due: "Any limitation so severe [that it prohibits all economically beneficial use of land] cannot be newly legislated or decreed (without compensation), but must inhere in the title itself, in the restrictions that background principles of the State's law of property and nuisance already place upon ownership."[11] If you start up a fireworks factory or a pig farm in the middle of a residential area, the state could call it a nuisance. It could not decree that a house built in the future on a lot that is now vacant shall be classified as a nuisance and that the lot must remain open space.

If the restricted activity is not a nuisance (or a noxious use, as it is sometimes phrased), then other questions about the character of the government's action come into play. A major question is, Does this law force one individual to bear burdens that should be borne by all? Here is another: How legitimate is the government's interest? The more important the purpose is to the public, the less likely a court will call the action a taking. In some cases, the Supreme Court has referred explicitly to the bundle of sticks view of property rights and said that depriving the owner of a big stick is a taking. Thus removing his right to exclude others from his property can be a taking, even if he can still use it himself. On the other hand, maybe not. In cases concerning conditions on zoning variances and land use requirements, there must be a connection between the condition and the purpose of the law. There must also be a "rough proportionality" between the condition and the cost of the exaction.[12] Some state courts add a "natural use" doctrine: no taking occurs if property is being limited to the uses for which it is suited in its natural state. Decoded, this means that regulation of wetlands is not a taking. The U.S. Supreme Court has never addressed this one.

To recap the effect of Factor One, if the character of the government action is a physical intrusion, then a taking *has* occurred, regardless of the other two factors. If the government is suppressing a nuisance or noxious use, than a taking *has not* occurred, regardless of the other two factors. If neither the permanent physical intrusion test nor the nuisance–noxious use test is met, then the character of the government action does not determine the outcome. It is thrown into the pot to be considered in connection with the remaining two factors.

Factor Two is economic. What is the impact on the owner? Has the government deprived the owner of all economically viable use of the land? Does the property have any remaining value, or is it reduced to zero? If the economic value is gone, does the property have any remaining value to the owner, such as her enjoyment of possession? The basic rule seems to be that even if the activity suppressed is not a nuisance, no taking occurs unless the owner is deprived of all economically viable use of the property. The exact point at which economic viability is gone is unclear, though, and in *Lucas* the court holds out hope, but no certainty, that a partial loss is compensable in some cases.

Factor Three is whether the government is frustrating "investment-backed expectations." If you actually invested money in reliance on the assumption that you could do something, then a sudden change of heart on the part of the government tilts the scale toward a finding that a taking occurred. Thus, if you buy a parcel and the government suddenly downzones it, this might be a taking. The interaction of this test with the others is unclear. So is its scope, since local governments downzone all the time, and it is always held not to be a taking unless construction on a project has actually started. Simply buying the land and spending a zillion dollars on plans is not enough to give you any rights. The most likely rationale behind the Factor Three test is to prevent the following situation: A speculator buys a wetland cheap because it is a wetland and cannot be filled. He then argues that the designation as a wetland takes the property, and wins. Now the value of the property jumps up to its former value, and he has made a bundle. Applying the investment-backed expectations test gets him thrown out of court. This is a bad result, because the previous owner of the wetland *should* be able to sell off the land plus the possibility of winning a takings lawsuit, but courts are biased against traffic in lawsuits.

As many, many commentators have noticed, this body of law is thoroughgoing mush. No clear line of analysis emerges, results are unpredictable, cases are inconsistent, and many of the tests make no sense. Are *Nollan* and *Dolan*, described in Chapter 12, on land use, physical intrusion cases or regulation cases? Can anyone pretend the decision in *Lucas* is consistent with the decision in *Penn Central*? How can the courts say the legitimacy of the state's interest is relevant to deciding whether a taking has occurred? If the government condemns land for a courthouse, its interest is totally legitimate, but this does not eliminate the obligation to pay. As Loren Smith, chief judge of the Court of Federal Claims, observed, "The protection of the Fifth Amendment is most needed to protect the minority against the exercise of governmental power when the need of government to regulate is greatest, and the desire of the popular majority is strongest."[13]

More questions: Some cases indicate that a temporary regulatory taking creates a right to compensation. How can this be? If the effect is temporary, by definition it does not deprive the owner of all economic value. But a deprivation of all, or maybe nearly all, value is necessary before the court will find that a taking has occurred. By the way, what is the economic test: "economically viable use" or "all economic value"? Both phrases are used, as if they are interchangeable, but they do not look interchangeable to me, and what does either of them mean? Do you get paid if you have a big mortgage that requires a big cash flow to service, but not if you own the property free and clear?

Under the economic value test, can the government regulate to reduce the value of the property down to a nominal level, then take the remaining estate and pay only this nominal price? For example, suppose you own an acre of prime commercial property, worth $100,000, that the city wants as a park. Can it zone it low rise only, reducing the value to $10,000, then the next day take it by eminent domain, paying you only $10,000. If not, why not?

FLORIDA, 1958–1995

In 1958, eight retirees buy 80 acres of unimproved land zoned for residential construction next to Everglades National Park. In 1981, Dade County downzones the property to allow one house on every 40 acres. In 1995, a federal-state partnership agrees to acquire 110,000 acres, including this tract, to add to the park. The government offers $500 per acre compensation, representing its value with 40-acre zoning. On land immediately outside the takings zone, building lots are small, and land goes for several thousand dollars per acre.[14]

Should economic impact be measured against the entire parcel or only the portion affected by government action? If you own 100 acres and regulation makes 10 acres completely useless, have you lost 10 percent of 100 acres or 100 percent of 10 acres? The loss is exactly the same, but under the "entire value" test, calling it the former means you get nothing, and calling it the latter means you get paid for the 10 acres.

Lucas has a footnote saying that it is not clear how the Supreme Court will look at this issue. This is not much help to litigants. It just shows the absurdity of the test.

What are "investment-backed expectations"? If your family has owned a building lot for a hundred years and the state downzones it into a park, have you have lost nothing because you had no investment-backed expectations? What if the owner of the identical lot next to you sold it last year, and the state downzones it? Does the new owner of that lot get paid while you do not? What is the impact of the fact that the justices have shifted toward the phrase "reasonable expectations" instead of "investment-backed expectations"?

Because of all these uncertainties—absurdities—an argument in a takings case is not an orderly analysis conducted within a logical structure. It is a battle between competing aphorisms. The parties toss quotations at each other, like lobbing mortar shells at an unseen target in the hope that something will hit. One side fires off, "Regulation is justified because the legislature is 'adjusting the benefits and burdens of economic life' to secure to everyone 'an average reciprocity of advantage.'" (Pow!) This brings counterfire: "The purpose of the takings clause is 'to bar government from forcing some people alone to bear public burdens which, in fairness and justice, should be borne by the public as a whole.'" (Bang!) Here comes a bomb in the form of Holmes: "Government could hardly go on . . . ," only the good justice is promptly loaded into the cannon as return fire: "If regulation goes too far it . . . [is] a taking." (Bam! Bam!) "Substantially advance[s] legitimate state interests" is met with "no economically viable use," and "reasonable investment backed expectations" countered by "police power."

Professor Richard Epstein of the University of Chicago called it right in his seminal and influential 1985 book, *Takings*. He said most of these restrictions, and many others to boot, should be classified as takings. The real question is whether the owner is receiving just compensation. In many cases, compensation is provided, often in the form of reciprocal restrictions on other owners. The compensation is just, and no payment is necessary.

Even without a complete shift to the Epstein approach, considerable progress is possible. *Nollan* and *Dolan* are good decisions, but their impact is largely in the limited field of exactions. It is hard to translate them into more general rules on property rights. *Lucas* is the most important case, and provides the best foundation for developing the law in the future. It says that property law developed slowly and that present titles are held subject to all sorts of understandings and limits—the types of things that this book presents in its first few chapters. These limits are inherent in the title, and no one can claim unfair surprise when they are adjusted at the margin as new circumstances arise. On the other hand, the wholesale revampings of the past twenty years are a different matter. These represent a marked departure from the Lockean structure and its effort to perfect property rights. They are an effort to provide all sorts of public goods: wetlands protection, historic preservation, scenic easements, endangered species habitats, and similar benefits. These limits were not inherent in the title and cannot be engrafted on the preexisting law of property. They are major shifts, not adjustments at the edges, and fairness requires that they be bought, not seized. They are departures from, in the words of Justice Scalia in *Lucas*, "the historic compact recorded in the Takings Clause that has become a part of our constitutional culture."

If the Supreme Court meant what it said in *Lucas*, the case could serve as the foundation for a reasonable law and practice of takings. Such optimism is reinforced by a comment by Chief Justice Rehnquist in *Dolan*: "We see no reason why the Takings Clause . . . , as much a part of the Bill of Rights as the First Amendment or the Fourth Amendment, should be relegated to the status of a poor relation." To those who want to bring back the Constitution-in-exile, this can be read as meaning that the Court is seriously considering reversing the 1930s decision that protection of the right to property should be the part of constitutional protection that gets no respect.

That is the good news. The bad is that the Supreme Court in *Lucas* and *Dolan* was deeply split. In *Dolan*, three dissenting justices repudiated the whole idea that state regulations that go "too far" violate the Fourteenth Amendment. They said, in essence, that the amendment did not incorporate the compensation clause after all, contrary to the jurisprudence of the last century. It is clear that these justices want no part of the promise of *Lucas*.

A broader cause for pessimism is that most of the Court's decisions are not based on any sense of the role of property in society. The result is amorphous interest balancing under vague criteria, many of which make little sense, are inconsistent, or both. Interest balancing of this stripe makes lawyers rich because everything is relevant and nothing determinative, so the litigation is endless. South Carolina eventually paid David Lucas $1.5 million for his two lots, and he paid out $525,000 in legal fees and $75,000 in court costs.[15]

This balancing also stacks the deck against the property owner. The contest is described as between the public's interest in wetlands, or what have you, and this particular owner's vulgar desire to make money. A proper description would emphasize the stake we all have in preserving a mechanism that balances the many complex functions served by property and makes the trade-offs that benefit everyone.

Another problem runs through the cases: the theory of government underlying them is about sixty years out of date. The assumptions are those of the Progressive Era of 1900 to 1920, the New Deal of the 1930s, the Great Society, and the assumptions that still dominate comprehensive urban planning. In this view, Congress or state legislatures enact vague laws to promote the public interest. They delegate implementation of these to administrative agencies. The agency staff acts as wise guardians, disinterested experts bringing to bear the best in technical knowledge to achieve some social optimum, often through long-term planning. Courts are heavy on presumptions of regularity and constitutionality, on deference to agency expertise, and on the gospel that all government officials are operating in disinterested good faith. It is sort of a smiley-face view of government.

When analyzing the motives of ordinary citizens, we assume that their behavior is motivated largely by self-interest. They seek their own advantage and that of the groups with which they are closely associated, such as family, employers, professional groups, and so on. Yes, people are motivated by the idea of craftsmanship, the desire to do a good job, and altruism. These are all givens, and they can be important components of self-interest. But for day-in, day-out prediction of human behavior, it is hard to beat knowing where lies their personal advantage, judged in the coin of money, power, and security.

When analyzing the actions of government workers, there is no reason to suspend this assumption about the importance of self-interest. Bureaucrats are moved by the concerns that move everyone else, such as pay, promotion, benefits, security, power, and convenience. They want to do a good job and protect wetlands or collect taxes or whatever, but if it comes to a conflict between these goals and personal concerns, the latter win. If it comes to conflict between personal concerns and some goal that is not even on their agency's radar, such as somebody else's property rights, there is no conflict at all. Self-interest exercises a potent magnetic field, and to a large degree we are all iron filings.

This focus on personal advantage is harnessed by organizations, which all foster a kind of groupthink. They develop mechanisms of internal rewards that force their members to assume the virtue and competence of the organization, shut down internal self-criticism, and foster pursuit of the organization's growth and power. These mechanisms harness the individual's pursuit of self-interest to pursuit of the organization's goals. Government organizations are as ruthless as private ones at this. In fact, they are probably a bit more ruthless. Private organizations can get killed in the marketplace. If something is going wrong, there is survival value in getting the information first. Good ones learn, though sometimes reluctantly, that self-criticism is useful for survival. Government agencies are different. They get damaged by politics but not by the market. Confessions of error are likely to be seized on by political opponents, so they place great value on keeping a solid front and giving no ammunition to ill wishers. If this deprives them of information essential to good internal management, well, good management isn't everything. In fact, in the world of government agencies, it isn't much of anything. Staff soon learns that criticizing the organization is not the road to personal success.

This does not mean government people are worse than private actors. They are not, but neither are they any better. The precise reason we want private organizations submitted to the market is to put a leash on this personal and institutional will to power. What have we got to serve this purpose for the government?

During the Progressive and New Deal eras, this elementary wisdom got forgotten. Even now, to assert the truism that government officials and agencies look out for themselves and that we ought to think carefully about the implications of this—propositions regarded as elementary by the founding generation—is characterized as "part of the radical right" or "against government." It is neither of these things. It is part of the ancient wisdom of our people. In the end, it can be boiled down to Lord Acton's axiom: "Power tends to corrupt and absolute power corrupts absolutely." Or to quote the Federalist Papers: "If angels were to govern men, . . . [no] controls on government would be necessary. In framing a government which is to be administered by men over men, . . . a dependence on the people is, no doubt, the primary control . . . but experience has taught mankind the necessary of auxiliary precautions."[16]

During the past half-century, most disciplines concerned with government have reoriented themselves away from the New Deal's smiley face view of government. The law has not kept pace, and the world of government depicted in Supreme Court opinions is far from the messy world of rational ignorance, single-value agencies, personal advantage, capture by special interest groups, political action committees, pure ego, and policy entrepreneurs with a sharp eye for the main chance. In the fictional legal world, no official ever games the system, taking advantage of the legal fictions to bamboozle the citizenry. In the real world, the public increasingly thinks, and with good reasons, that many officials do little else.

The Progressive–New Deal faith had another branch that fostered the legal profession's deference to government officials. It emphasized the primacy of government as the main decision maker in society. Officials need as much flexibility as possible. They are not required to lay down clear standards for private actors, who are regarded as a selfish breed, not governed by the unselfish motives of the wise guardians.

The current renewed faith in private decisions and skepticism about government has changed these attitudes and left the legal profession's view of administrative agencies now 180 degrees out of kilter with contemporary political thought. Government is not and cannot be the moving force in society, and tailoring the legal system to the assumption that it should be is an error of stupendous consequence.

Many officials are motivated by a strong sense of duty and craftsmanship, but these traits do not always produce either justice or efficiency. If the sense of duty is to achievement of total fairness, it can create paralysis, as in the airline seat example back in Chapter 3. If the duty is to a single value, such as protection of wetlands or endangered species, the stronger the sense of duty the more it turns into a fanaticism that ignores any competing considerations, such as property rights. You can make all the assumptions you want about an official's expertise on wetlands, endangered species, or grazing lands. None of them support the suggestion that he can be relied upon to protect the property rights of private citizens if they in any way impede the agency's mission, or even its convenience.

Government has an important role in defining and protecting property rights, but it is not the prime mover in society. Quite the reverse. If you put government in the role of prime mover, it tries to remake everything it touches, in the image of big government: slow, bureaucratic, and often corrupt. Government must be kept small so it can be watched, and the rules government makes should be sharp and clear so private actors know what they are and can make their decisions.

SOUTH CAROLINA, 1993

In 1991, the *Lucas* case is finally over. After the state spent six years defending its position that prohibiting construction on Lucas's lot was essential to the protection of the beaches of South Carolina, the Supreme Court has ruled. The state's view may be right, but if so, it must pay the costs of leaving the lots empty. Lucas gives South Carolina a deed to his property, and it gives him a check. The state can now keep the lots bare.

In 1993 South Carolina puts the lots up for sale. It refuses an offer of $315,000 on one lot from a neighbor who wants to buy it and keep it vacant. It then sells the lot for $392,500, and as part of the deal the buyer gets a permit to build. For six years, the state has fought to keep the land empty, insisting this is crucial to the public welfare, no matter what the cost to Lucas. In the end, with its own money at stake, the state does not think nondevelopment worth even $72,500.[17]

This farcical ending to the *Lucas* case makes the government people look like fools. Some other government choices are making them look like knaves. The earlier discussion of political legitimacy noted that citizens think they have a right to expect the government to implement methods for quick, economical resolution of disputes between itself and its citizens. In the area of property rights, the exact reverse is happening: the government's minions dig in and use every possible procedural technicality to delay proceedings and to make getting paid for a taking, or even getting a decision whether a taking did or did not occur, as slow, expensive, and improbable as possible.

Several devices serve this end. The sturdiest is to manipulate the concept "final agency action" or its sibling, "ripeness." A court will not review an agency action until that action represents a final decision on the matter at issue. The matter must also be "ripe" for review, which means basically that no loose ends are dangling that might make the court's decision pointless. In theory, these are sound doctrines that avoid piecemeal intervention and let an agency do its job without random intervention. In practice, they are less benign.

Suppose you own 100 acres in a wetland. You know the Corps of Engineers will not let you fill it in and build because it denied permits to ten other owners in identical circumstances. Nonetheless, you must request a permit. You must furnish all the information required by the agency, which can be expensive to obtain. If the Corps asks for more information and you fail to supply it, then the permit will be denied for "failure to supply information." A reviewing court does not sympathize with an owner who is being uncooperative, especially when the agency says, "How do we know what we would have done if he had given us the information?"

Suppose that the permit is denied on the merits. The agency says, "We have all the information we need, and the answer is no." Even this is not necessarily final. The agency can say, "We only denied a permit to fill in 100 acres of wetlands; we might grant one for 90 acres. We know we turned down ten identical applications from neighbors without granting any, but, gee, you never know." The owner says, "Well, does that mean you *would* grant it?" The agency answers: "How do we know until we see the application? Put it together and send it in." So a permit for 90 acres is submitted, reviewed at length, subjected to a flood of new information requests—and eventually denied. This game can go on a long time.

The Court of Federal Claims says you need not go through this process if it is not a reasonable variance procedure or is so burdensome that it effectively deprives the property of all value. These are highly subjective tests though. You can go through years of litigation, only to have an appellate court throw out the whole case on the grounds that the agency decision was not final and a trial court should not have heard your case.

The name of this game is transaction costs. By making the permitting process long and expensive, the government ensures that only the most serious cases will ever go to court. This effort is aided by the difficulty of winning once you do sue. It is no accident that few wetlands cases have been litigated to success by the owners, and these involve land worth millions of dollars owned by people with enough money to finance the effort. The need to prove a denial of "all economic value" is hard to meet, and most cases are lost on this point. Other owners take note and do not try. Even if all value of your property is gone, the loss must be large. If it is not, any payment from the government will not even cover the lawyers' and experts' bills. It is easy to go broke defending your constitutional rights.

If a state is involved, the finality and ripeness hurdles are even higher. An owner must go through all the state agency processes and lose, then go through all appeals to state court and lose, and then sue the state for taking the property and lose again. Then he can go to federal court arguing that his federal rights to just compensation have been violated. An angry land use lawyer summed it up: "The effect . . . is to 'close the federal court house door' on almost all land use taking cases." He went on to explain why the doctrine closes the state's courthouse doors as well, which pretty much leaves owners with no relief at all, doesn't it?[18] Substantive legal doctrines mean little if you cannot get to court in the first place.

To grasp the full power of these doctrines, imagine your city enacts an ordinance saying, "To protect the view from the west side of 50th Street, all houses on the east side are declared nuisances and must be torn down, at the expense of their present owners. However, in case of hardship, the city may grant a variance allowing a house to remain standing for a period of years to be determined by the city." You own a house on the east side. You cannot challenge this law on its face, so you apply for a variance complying with the city's regulations requiring you to provide extensive personal financial information to establish that tearing down your house would be a hardship. Say you apply for a fifty-year variance. The city turns you down. You go to court. The city says, "This is not ripe. The owner should have applied for a thirty-year variance; we might have granted that." The court disagrees and allows the suit. You win. But the city appeals, and the appellate court says that it was not ripe and should not have been tried, so it dismisses the case. You now apply for a thirty-year period, supplying lots of new data. The city says, "Nope, not thirty, either. Maybe twenty?" At this point a court will say enough is enough, and you can finally get to court with your

substantive claim, which is, "They can't do this to me under *Lucas!*"
You should win if you still have the money to pursue the claim after all
these legal expenses. Now change the law a little, and suppose the city
passes a zoning law allowing high-rise apartments on the west side and,
to protect the view, no new development on the east side, and no major additions to any existing houses, but you can let your present house
stand. Now they darn well *can* do it to you.

Other games are played with finality. The government can amend
the regulation, or even the statute, and then contend that the plaintiff
must now start over. "After all, that was under the *old* law that we made
his beachfront lot into a public park. Now, we changed some commas,
and the result might be different. He needs to apply for a *permit*. Of
course, the law is different now, so we need lots of new information."

OREGON, 1996

**Following their Supreme Court win, the Dolans reapply to the city of
Tigard for permission to expand their hardware store. The city says they
can if they make the improvements and modifications originally required, with some slight modifications. The matter has started its way
back up through the appeals process.[19]**

One municipal attorney explicitly advised his fellows, "If all else fails,
merely amend the regulation and start all over again."[20] This attorney
was from California, which is not surprising because California developed the games of finality and ripeness into an art form. For over a
decade it managed to read the takings clause out of the Constitution.
(The tale is well told in economist William Fischel's *Regulatory Takings*.)
Californians pay the price for the state's antidevelopment bias. In 1960,
the median value for California houses was 27 percent higher than the
median value of houses in the United States as a whole. By 1990, the
California value was 147 percent higher.[21]

Federal lawyers have special tools to deter any pursuit of takings
claims. If you are denied a federal permit to build in a wetlands or your
property is turned into an endangered species habitat, your logical
course of action is clear: go to a federal court and file a complaint claiming that the government decision was wrong. Maybe the agency misap-
plied the rules, or the rules themselves are not legal under the statute.

You also want a backup position: if your first claim is wrong, and if the agency action is in fact legal and correct, then the government took your property and should pay you for it.

You can make both these arguments but not in the same court. The district court is the place to argue that the government decision was wrong, but it cannot hear your contention that the action, if it was legal, took your property. The Tucker Act says that monetary claims against the United States for over $10,000 must be brought in the U.S. Court of Federal Claims. This is a court of eighteen judges with nationwide jurisdiction, and it holds trials all over the country. You cannot ask the Court of Claims to review the legality of the agency action, though. It looks only at monetary claims.

This is inconvenient but not too serious. You decide to file two lawsuits: you ask the district court to review the agency action and you file in the Court of Federal Claims. You plan to let the second suit sit and then pursue it if you lose the first case. Now you get to learn something called the Tucker Act Shuffle. The government asks the judge in the Court of Federal Claims to dismiss your case on the ground that you have another case based on the same facts pending in district court. If you lose your case in district court and then refile in the Court of Federal Claims, the government argues that the statute of limitations has expired. If you try to outfox them by filing only in the Court of Federal Claims, then the government argues that you are *really* challenging the rule, not seeking compensation, and that the Court of Federal Claims should not hear the argument. Wherever you go, the government will argue that you should have gone to some other court. When you go to another one, it will argue that you are too late or too early.

NEVADA, 1996

Wayne Hage brings a complicated takings case. Part of it involves rights to the water from a spring on Forest Service land. Hage says the government diverted water to which he had a prior right and kept him from using it. The government argues that the diversion did not take Hage's water rights. Such rights apply only to water that is put to beneficial use. Hage did not use this water; the government did. Therefore, he failed to put it to beneficial use and had no right. The judge describes the government argument as akin to the old joke about the person who kills his parents and then asks for sympathy because he is an orphan.[22]

Even if using such arguments is technically within the law and the canons of professional ethics, an odor of bad faith hangs over them. The government lawyers seem to believe they are defending the environment against mere property, so they are entitled to use whatever tricks work. There are also strong peer pressures in the legal profession to show how hard-nosed you are.

A final procedural hurdle exists. Federal law says that anyone bringing a claim for a regulatory taking must still own the property that is the subject of the claim. This prevents anyone who is not rich from protecting his rights. Even if your claim is ironclad, you must have the money to finance the litigation or it is not going to be worth anything. The ordinary course of action for an owner who has a good takings claim and no cash would be to sell the property, including the claim, to someone with money. By making this impossible, the government ensures that many valid claims will never be brought. Like most other restraints on alienation, it damages the owner of the restrained property and society at large.

The requirement that the property not change hands is a relic of long-ago legal doctrines. The other diseases, finality and ripeness, are much more difficult to treat. These concepts, used properly, are reasonable. They are extremely important to the efficient operations of both agencies and courts. Without these doctrines, landowners would certainly try to game the system, applying for permission to do something awful and then suing when it is denied. Courts, especially federal courts, do not want to become super zoning review boards for every hamlet in America, or official second guessers of every agency in the U.S. government.

On the other hand, the doctrines are not used properly. They have become prime instruments by which government agencies manipulate the system. The basic problem in an area such as wetlands or land use law is that an owner can do nothing as a right. The structure of the law is that everything is declared illegal, and then exceptions are made ad hoc. Every action needs a permit, and permits are granted only after negotiation under unpredictable standards. The doctrines of finality and ripeness are important bulwarks of this system. They say, in essence, that reading the law is not enough because the government can change the law ad hoc, so you must ask for the change before the decision is final. If the standards were certain, including the standards under which exceptions would be granted, then people would know their rights and could act within them. The problems caused by manipulation of the procedural gimmicks would then disappear. The constitutional question would move to where it should be: into whether the *standard* works a taking, not whether a single ad hoc decision does so.

Current efforts to improve protection of property rights devote themselves to writing some magic bullet of a statute that will cover all the situations described in this book in a few sentences. It probably cannot be done. In particular, most proposals define a taking in terms of some percentage of the value of property lost because of government regulation. They provide, for example, that a regulatory taking does not occur unless the value of the property is reduced by, say, 30 percent. The impulse behind this seeks to avoid litigation over trifles, especially when the government is adjusting the use of a commons or is limiting externalities. Defining the exact point of fairness is difficult, and a law must allow for rough justice. But the percentage approach cannot work. The problem of defining the baseline for calculating the allowable percentage is impossible. Suppose that a statute says a reduction of value of over 30 percent is a taking and must be paid for. You own 100 acres, worth $100,000. The government takes 20 of them for a road, zones 20 more as an open-space buffer zone beside the road, and says you cannot build on the remaining 60 for three years. Under the 30 percent rule, how much does the government pay you? Reasonable lawyers could give you an answer of anywhere from zero to $60,000, and there is no conclusive argument for picking any one number over another.

Even without a percentage clause, drafting a test to distinguish between laudable collective action for mutual benefit and brazen theft of other people's property is not easy, even if efforts are limited to one area, such as land use. Trying to write a general law is even more difficult. Many different programs and fact patterns must be considered, and calculating the ramifications eats you alive. So far, efforts at the federal level have been picked apart. It is easy for the opposition to come up with a long list of uncertainties and horrible possibilities.

Most of these arguments used against proposals for increased protection of property rights rely on distortions of standard doctrines of property and nuisance law. The federal government, in particular, is devoid of any sense of professional responsibility or craftsmanship. If the documents submitted to congressional committees by the Departments of

Justice and Interior were submitted as papers in any respectable law school, they would get a D. Nonetheless, some real problems exist, and they are not easily solved.

Despite the difficulty, many states are trying to do something. Between 1991 and early 1996, every state except Connecticut considered legislation to protect property rights. Eighteen states actually enacted something. Most of these efforts are cautious. Four require the attorney general to review regulations and inform the issuing agency of takings implications. Ten require the state agencies to assess the impact of regulations on private property. Six expand existing rights to compensation, but carefully.[23] None takes a shotgun approach.

Many problems are due to defects in the underlying programs, such as wetlands and endangered species. Takings problems involving wetlands would disappear if the Clean Water Act were returned to its original purpose of guarding against contaminants, and if navigation were protected by a specific statute directed at this purpose. Preserving wetlands is not related to either of these purposes. If it is important to protect them, it would be easy enough, and not very expensive, to buy easements and create new wetlands as necessary. Similar considerations apply to endangered species habitat. In both areas, Congress is trying to write a law on takings to remedy the problems that it created by failing to make its delegations of authority clear, twisting statutes to serve new purposes, and failing to control agencies that turn delegations of power into licenses to steal. This is theater of the absurd.

Another problem adds to the difficulty of drafting any law creating across-the-board protection of property rights. Judge Loren Smith, the chief judge of the Court of Federal Claims, has presided over several of the major cases and is extremely highly regarded by the professionals in the field. He notes that takings law has become the only avenue by which citizens can seek redress from government intrusion: "The protections of federalism and the doctrine of enumerated powers, the Ninth and Tenth Amendments, the Contract Clause and the non-delegation doctrine, and the Due Process and Equal Protection Clauses—all have been abandoned by the courts as real or viable limitations on government actions affecting economic relationships. Only the . . . Taking Clause retains any life."[24] As a result, problems that should be analyzed as equal protection cases or as possible violations of due process rights are shoved into the pigeonhole of takings. The fit is awkward.

This point is worth pausing over. A direct assault in the form of a statute elaborating the meaning of the compensation clause is not the only way to deal with issues of takings and property rights. For many problems, it is not the best way. For example, a system that makes federal courts into super zoning boards deciding tiny issues of local land use on a case-by-case basis would be everyone's nightmare. The need is for doctrines of administrative fairness and due process that require local authorities to anchor their decisions to specific parts of the Lockean basis of our property system. They should be talking about externalities, and the transportation network, and exploring the extent and limits of the various commons. Local authorities should also make their standards clear and universal. Zoning rules should mean what they say. Landowners and builders should know what they can and cannot do by reading the law. What is needed is a restoration of government of law rather than government by whimsy.

Many of the questions that come up are, at their core, problems of equal protection. Look at *Lucas*. Who knows whether protection of South Carolina's beaches requires the state to prohibit further construction along the shore? Maybe this measure represents an effort to protect the property values of all existing beachfront owners, including the state as the trustee of the public beaches. If so, the problem is one of equal protection. Burdens are being put on Lucas that are not put on owners who have already built. If the law is for the benefit of all owners of beachfront property, it is not the taxpayers who should pay but the owners. What is missing is a mechanism for pooling the interests of all beachfront owners and paying off the owners whose property is made unusable. Reviving the principle of equal protection would shake governments—perhaps even the Department of Justice—out of their current intellectual sloth. As long as official theft is available as a remedy, why look for anything more creative? More rigorous scrutiny would force the invention of new types of transactions that keep benefits and burdens together.

The picture that emerges from this chapter is somber. It shows not just an area of the law in a state of intellectual anarchy but a whole legal system in disarray. The institution of property, one of the bedrocks of human liberty and autonomy, is a great engine of the wealth with which this nation has been blessed. The reasoning that places private property in opposition to community values is precisely wrong. Property is one of the major tools by which the community achieves its values. Given all this, defining property rights and protecting people's personal right to property should be a major, and highly honorable, preoccupation of the legal system. Instead, a large part of the legal profession, especially government lawyers, have abdicated this duty in favor of a mushy reliance on uncontrolled government whim, faith in discredited doctrines of central planning, and sentimentality. It is not a pretty landscape.

PART V

SHAPES IN THE MIST

Chapter 15

Matters of the Mind

Information as property—the wealth of the future and the future of wealth

Songs are heard all the time, over radio and television, at concerts, in clubs, and under copyright law, a composer is entitled to a fee for each public performance. Violating the composer's right can be criminal, carrying penalties of up to a $25,000 fine and a year in jail. In theory, an artist who wants to perform a work should call the composer and negotiate a fee. The composer might ask how many people, how many other songs, and so on, and they could bargain for a while. If the price were too high, the artist would call another composer and begin negotiations anew.

This system would be like the pursuit of fairness in bumping airline passengers: the transaction costs would eat everyone alive. So we invented a system. Composers join an organization such as the American Society of Composers, Authors and Publishers (ASCAP), which then sells blanket rights allowing performance sites to use music by any of its members. The proceeds are split among the members according to a monitoring system designed to assess how often the music of each member is performed. ASCAP is big—68,000 members and 4 million songs, including "God Bless America." It collects about $320 million each year and distributes $254 million of it to the members. A few similar organizations exist, each with its own stable of composers, but ASCAP is the largest.

ASCAP has always collected fees from radio and TV stations, clubs, concerts, and other major users. Over the past decade or so, it has gone on the offensive against smaller users, including rodeos, businesses that rely on the radio for background music, and even funeral homes.

THE UNITED STATES, 1996

ASCAP notifies eight thousand summer camps that they must pay for any songs they use, as when campers sing around the fire. It negotiates a special fee with members of one camping association but hangs tough with others, including the Diablo Day Camp of Lafayette, California, which is a Girl Scout operation. ASCAP wants $591 in royalties for the summer. Other composers' groups might want fees for their songs too, and Diablo decides it cannot afford it. Counselors go through the song books crossing out forbidden music, such as "Puff the Magic Dragon" and "This Land Is Your Land."

The story becomes a public relations disaster. The *Wall Street Journal* puts the incident on its front page, other papers pick it up, and ASCAP drowns in protests. It defends itself, pointing out that the camps do not get their craft supplies for free, so why shouldn't they pay for music, and that songwriters must make a living too. No go, and soon after the head of the organization is described as "in seclusion." Within a week ASCAP retreats, claiming it meant only to collect royalties from big, profitable summer camps, "the sort that brings in bands for square dances, have music by the pool," and that sort of thing. It puts an ad in the Sunday *New York Times* to say it loves the Girl Scouts, and the Boy Scouts, too. It does not give in on principle, though, or say it lacks the right to collect from the Girl Scouts; it says only that it is not going to try. Its ad does not give ground on non-Scout camps.[1]

This tale is useful because it captures so much of the ambiguity inherent in intellectual property. Songwriters do have to make a living. If there were no way for them to get paid, then many fewer songs would be written. Some would still be composed out of ego, and every culture manages to produce art, copyright or no, but social incentives alone are not as reliable as social incentives plus cash, and the output would shrink. Besides, composers would lack the time and energy to write, since they would have to do something else to make a living. You cannot sing "Puff the Magic Dragon" if no one ever wrote it, so all of us, including the Girl Scouts, would be the poorer. The situation is like the national park example, where park users get shortchanged because they are undercharged and cannot express their preferences in the marketplace. It might seem strange to say, "We would like to let you sing 'Puff' for free, but that would cheat you because then fewer such songs would get written. We cannot bear to deprive you, so off to the slammer you go," but there is a lot of truth in it.

On the other hand, the songwriters draw heavily on the efforts of other people, such as those who invented the musical notation they use to put their ideas into marketable form, a rich tradition of folk music written without benefit of copyright, and old works no longer covered. The composers are tapping into a sort of intellectual and cultural commons without which their efforts would be bootless. In connection with the ASCAP affair, a reporter contacted folk singer Pete Seeger. Seeger says that "music really comes from and belongs to everyone." His father was a musicologist who, after studying Beethoven, judged that even Beethoven's music was about 90 percent musical tradition and 10 percent his own. Be that as it may, Seeger himself holds over 200 copyrights and makes enough to pay his annual income taxes off the royalties from just one of them, "Where Have All the Flowers Gone?"

A more formal basic economics argument is sometimes brought to bear against payments for intellectual property. The marginal—extra—cost of an additional rendition of a song is said to be zero. The time and effort that went into producing the song have already been spent. For the Girl Scouts to sing it does not add any cost. A maxim of economic theory is that prices should be set at marginal cost. Since marginal cost is zero, the price should be zero.

This argument is wrong. The economics books that talk about marginal cost pricing always have a little aside that says something like this: "Marginal cost, properly defined, includes interest on the capital invested in the business, amortization of that investment (depreciation), and an appropriate allowance for the risk that no return at all will be received." In other words, the marginal cost of producing the song is not zero after all. It includes all the costs of producing the work originally, spread over time. The argument stated in the preceding paragraph confuses marginal costs with variable costs, which are indeed the direct costs attributable to producing one more unit. For a song performance, variable costs are zero, but no book says businesses should charge variable cost. Any that tried it would be out of business fast, since they would never get their original investment back.

Intellectual property is like other businesses that require heavy up-front investment. If you have an airline, once you decide to fly one passenger from New York to San Francisco on a 747, the variable costs of flying an additional 250 people are close to nil. No one suggests economic theory says only the first passenger should pay and the rest should ride free. Sellers make predictions about what they should charge each person to keep the system operating over time, aiming for some mix of prices that makes the balance sheet come out right in the end.

A more cogent form of this argument is that songs, books, and other forms of intellectual property are not exhausted by use. If you farm an acre of ground, I cannot use the same property. One function of property rights is to force us to bid against each other for the right to engage in this action, and the auction serves to channel the resource to the person who can get the most productive use out of it. For intellectual property, this is not true. Girl Scouts all over the world can be singing "Puff the Magic Dragon," all at the same time. No rationing is necessary, and no one else is helped if the girls at Camp Diablo are forbidden to sing it. Again, though, the same argument can be made about the airliner. If it is going across the country with only one passenger, why not put up a sign saying, "Free trips to San Francisco"? The reasons are simple. One is the Argument from Justice. Why should the creator of the song or the airline give away what it produced? It is only fair that those who get utility from it show their appreciation, tangibly. Another reason is that if you take the free-ride view you cannot make the system work, and you will have neither songs nor airlines.

That fact that intellectual property is not exhausted by use has another crucial impact, though: we need not devise rules for property rights in the use of the intellectual commons. If only so many sheep can eat the grass on the village green, the rights to the grass must be allocated somehow. If only so much water flows in a western stream, people must have property rights that determine who gets to use it. But we can all graze our mental sheep on the intellectual commons at the same time without displacing anyone.

The ASCAP story is also about monopoly. Our society relies on competition to keep prices down. In the Camp Diablo situation, the real problem is that ASCAP wants a fee of $591 from a small camp. The normal rules of antitrust would keep composers from banding together to fix prices. These have been suspended because of the impossible transaction costs involved in forcing everyone to negotiate song by song. ASCAP is responding like a nineteenth-century railroad with a hammerlock on a rancher's ability to ship cattle to market: it wants to snatch as much as it can of the value of the entire camp. When trucks are available, rail rates fall. If the Girl Scouts could force composers to compete, the cost of song rights for the season might be about $20, which would better accord with our sense of where it ought to be, and the *Wall Street Journal* would not have had a story.

Intellectual property, including that used for entertainment—songs, books, movies, plays—does deserve to be treated as property. All the arguments recounted back at the beginning of this book apply. Here, as with land or tangible things, rights to property are the great engines of Justice, Economic Efficiency, Political Freedom, and Personal Autonomy. The right is recognized in the Constitution. Section 8 of Article I gives Congress power "to promote the progress of science and useful arts, by securing for limited times to authors and inventors the exclusive right to their respective writings and discoveries."

At the same time, the problems are sticky. Copyright law has some compromises designed to deal with these complications, and it does a serviceable job. You can copyright a specific text, such as *Romeo and Juliet* or "Puff the Magic Dragon." This gives you the exclusive right to control its use. You cannot copyright an idea; you cannot file on "any play about star-crossed lovers from feuding families" or "all songs about dragons." The phrase in the statute that supplies the basis of these decisions says that copyright cannot protect any "idea, procedure, process, system, method of operation, concept, principle, or discovery." This recognizes, roughly, the ambiguity of the split between the individual contribution and the cultural commons.

The dual nature of intellectual product is recognized further by making the author's exclusive right limited in time. Copyright lasts for the author's life plus fifty years. After that, the work goes into the public domain, which means it becomes part of the great cultural commons whence it in part arose. Someday "Where Have All the Flowers Gone?" will indeed belong to everyone.

Copyright is limited further by a series of doctrines revolving around the idea of fair use. You can look at these in a variety of ways. They could be based on the role of the cultural commons and a belief that the copyright holder should not be completely chintzy about giving something back. They could be realistic recognitions of transaction cost problems, representing a decision that it is better just to let some infringements go. The doctrines could represent a view that some uses may take the copyright holder's property without really damaging him, like the cable TV installation, where the damages for the taking were one dollar. They could represent political favoritism for especially deserving groups, such as professors copying materials for classes, or Girl Scout camps, or home videotapers; we will set up a system that provides payment for creators but lets some people free-ride. The question, of course, is: Who? Political favoritism begins to look perilously like taking, rather than a legitimate effort to define property rights and reduce transaction costs.

Take your pick of rationales, but checking "all of the above" is pretty safe. The result is a complex body of law involving judgments on parodies, copying articles from academic journals, using radio to provide background music in a store, lending libraries, compulsory licenses and legally set fees, and other complexities. Over the past twenty years, the issue of home copying of audio and visual works—tapes and movies— has moved to the fore. Congress, in its 1976 revisions of the Copyright Act, managed to duck the issue. The Audio Home Recording Act of 1992 levied a tax on blank tapes and equipment, which is deposited into a fund to pay creators. In England, authors are compensated when their books are borrowed from libraries.[2]

Aside from the protections of the law, copyrighted works once had some physical defenses. It was expensive to copy them. Anyone wanting to copy a book and undersell the publisher had to set up an industrial-scale print shop and could be easily found by the long arm of the law. This did not always help the creator because whole nations could turn to piracy. The United States in the nineteenth century did not subscribe to international copyright conventions. While westerners were pilfering tracts of arid land, for which they have been abused ever since, the literary classes of the East stole the works of English authors en masse, reprinting them without permission or payment.

The photocopier, the scanner, the VCR, the computer, and now the Internet have created a new world of piratical opportunity. Copying is cheap, and distribution can be practically instantaneous. Piracy can also be international and difficult to trace, which puts it beyond the reach of the law. There is still one saving grace. If you're willing to contravene the law, you can scan the latest Tom Clancy novel into your computer, set up a Web page, and let anyone download it who wants to. But why would you do this, unless you have a personal grievance against Clancy? It might also be cheaper and easier for the downloader to buy the book rather than pay the access charges to the Web, the cost of the paper, and download time. Also, for you to make piracy pay as a commercial venture, customers have to be able to find you. As in any business, you must advertise and get yourself known, which means that Tom Clancy's process servers can find you, too. Without government acquiescence, commercial-scale piracy is a difficult way to make a living.

CHINA, 1996

"A detailed study . . . of Chinese factories that are pirating billions of dollars worth of American software, music and videos shows that almost all the operations are partly owned by foreign companies, some of them working from nations that are close allies and trading partners of the United States," says a news account. The U.S. government releases a list of thirty-one pirate factories, including locations, plus telephone and fax numbers. A senior official says, "We didn't want to hear the excuse that they couldn't find the offenders. By handing them the list we are doing everything but picking their officials up and taking them to the factory door."[3]

The international dimensions of protecting intellectual property is a serious matter for the U.S. government. Charles Dickens, wherever he may be, must be vastly amused, since he was one of the chief victims of American piracy 150 years ago. Now, the United States has got religion. As a major producer and exporter of movies and videos, we have discovered the immorality of theft, and the effort to suppress it is a major component of our international relations. If we are not going to allow mining or timbering, or a lot of industry, we have to sell something to the world to pay for our imports of these things, and entertainment seems to be it. Besides, the entertainment industry is a political giant, largely because quirks in the campaign finance laws give it tremendous fund-raising clout. A normal person, no matter how rich, can donate only $1,000 to a campaign. A star can appear at a fund raiser and rake in hundreds of thousands of dollars without violating the law. Politicians listen carefully to the industry's ideas on government policy. People used to worry that war and peace might hinge on the interests of the arms merchants or the oil industry. Now it may hinge on the interests of Hollywood. Maybe Arnold Schwarzenegger's next role will be to play a two-fisted secretary of state defending the vital U.S. interest in controlling reruns of *The Brady Bunch*.

The producers of intellectual property fret about private copying and the constant circulation of videos, tapes, and software among friends, but this is not as serious. They also worry about the ideological violator—the hacker who pirates intellectual property out of conviction that "information wants to be free" or some other quasi-religious slogan. It is always hardest to defend against people who are not responding to economic incentives, just as it is hard to protect against people with an ideological commitment to physical terrorism.

The problems will remain until some technical solution is found—an equivalent of barbed wire that prevents copying. The three D's still dominate. Property must be definable, defensible, and divestible. Intellectual property is definable, albeit with difficulty sometimes, and it is divestible in law. It is not fully defensible, any more than rangeland is fully defensible even with barbed wire. The most valuable material, such as software, might be booby-trapped, but any text that can be downloaded and printed can be scanned and uploaded again.

The current hot topic is the liability of third parties for copyright violations. If you run a bulletin board and your subscribers post copyrighted material that others download, are you responsible? The bill proposed by the administration in 1995 said yes, and aroused a storm of protest. The answer will almost certainly be no when the issue gets finally resolved. Transaction costs again. To put this burden on the third parties, on operators of the Internet, would raise the costs too much. It would be like making the Post Office responsible for every misleading advertisement sent through the mail. The burden of checking would eliminate the mails completely.

Copyright, fair use, international conventions, and the other travails of the entertainment industry only scratch the surface of intellectual property. These issues are a subset of the fruits of the information revolution of which we are reminded a dozen times a day.

The information revolution means that technological capability to generate ideas and to gather, record, process, store, and transmit information has grown enormously. All of these processes keep getting cheaper, which makes it possible to use them in a rising number and variety of contexts. These two sentences pretty much exhaust discussion of the general idea of the information revolution, though. Digging deeper requires analysis of the specific contexts and uses of the information. Once you get beyond the area of entertainment, information is always *about* something. To consider it seriously you must bring the *about* into focus because information as an abstract concept is too mushy to analyze. The emptiness of information that floats free of any *about* is illustrated by much of TV (fifty channels and nothing on), by Web discussions that are all opinion and no fact, or by five hundred e-mail messages per day. Hell is being trapped in the Net with a disabled log-off.

A fundamental error in musing on the information revolution is to see it as a successor to the agricultural or industrial revolutions. Useful information is usually *about* agriculture or industry, including service industries. During the nineteenth century, one of the most profound areas of industrialization was the agricultural sector. In half a century, we moved from a society of hand labor and horse-drawn transport to numerous kinds of agricultural machinery and the railroad. The farm became a food factory. One of the most important effects of the information revolution is to revolutionize agriculture still further.

ILLINOIS, 1996

Farmers are using global positioning satellites to micromanage their fields down to the square yard. Data on soil conditions are fed in and mapped on a computer, and signals from the GPS to the tractor tell the farmer as he works how much seed or fertilizer to spread exactly where he now is. Units sell for $6,500. One farmer estimates he can save $10 per acre per year on fertilizer alone, or $16,000 a year on his 1,600-acre spread.[4]

Comparable examples in industry abound. The oil industry is using satellites for real-time seismic exploration of the ocean bottom.[5] The Japanese revolution in quality control in the automobile industry was a revolution in the production and use of information in an industrial setting.[6] A revolution in blue jeans is in the offing. For decades, women have complained about the difficulty of getting properly fitting blue jeans. The problem affects stores, too, because carrying a large inventory is expensive. In a new service, the customer goes to a retail store, where measurements are taken. These are wired to a central facility, and the jeans are cut to measure and shipped. Happy customers, and no inventory cost. At the moment, this is a premium service, but as the inventory costs disappear, jeans will become cheaper, especially as the information revolution in manufacturing eliminates the need for long production runs of a single size. The key to the service ultimately is the ability to make one pair at a time for the same unit cost incurred in mass production. The same revolution is hitting the shoe business. Feet are scanned electronically and the data transmitted to a factory in Italy. The price is about $140 per pair, as opposed to $500 for normal hand-made shoes.[7]

The information revolution was responsible for ASCAP's abortive effort to assert its rights against camps. In the good old days, there was no way this effort could have made economic sense. Now, ASCAP can buy a mailing list with the names of eight thousand camps, on disk of course, draft a form letter, punch Mail Merge, and out it goes. ASCAP can also set up a database to monitor the results, feeding in continually updated information on individual camps. This would not have been possible with quill pens or even ballpoints. Changes do not always represent progress because technology also opens up new frontiers of foolishness, but you cannot expect to find silver linings without clouds.

Information can be about other types of property and can affect agriculture, industry, and consumption goods through this medium. A point made several times in this book is that the property rights that can exist are limited by a society's informational capacity. An illiterate medieval world can recognize rights that are memorable years later by the boys who got beaten on the day they were transferred. "It's Odin's" is about the extent of it. When literacy becomes common, more complexity becomes possible. "Odin owns it, but Thor can cut mature timber, and Freya is leasing it for ten years." (This short-changes our medieval ancestors a little. At the local level, patterns of rights were reasonably complicated. The recording mechanism was the collective memory of the village, which made them inflexible.) As information technologies keep improving the level of possible subtlety and flexibility grows. Eventually, you have Trails, Inc., which sells licenses to use its nationwide network, paid for in advance over the Internet, recorded on cards, and automatically debited at the point of use by automated readers. Or Software, Inc., which sells one copy for $100 or one copy with the right to make 10 more for $500, enforced by an automatic destruct feature.

All of these developments depend on devices that generate, collect, and process information. The people who invented and developed the devices—the card readers for Trails, Inc., the mailing list of camps, the technique of blues jeans or shoe measurement—have created intellectual property. The hardware is trivial. It is the information component that counts. They have made the use of other property more efficient, and they get paid for doing so by the owners of the other property. Intellectual property must be protected to give people an incentive to create these devices. The inventor of the card reader must be able to patent it; the creator of the mailing list must be able to protect it from theft. The originator of the blue jean measurement system is out of luck, though. Someone who sees how it is done can easily copy it. There is no enforceable way to create an exclusive right to measure people's bodies. The shoe people will probably fare better because of the need to use a machine that can be protected by patent. But it might be possible to invent a machine that makes blue jean measurements perfectly every time, unlike error-prone customers, and thus develop defensible property.

We have now segued into the second great domain of intellectual property, patent law, which protects devices embodying ideas and information. The interaction between information and other kinds of property enhances the value of both. Take a simple idea that had monumental impact on human history: the horse collar. The Greeks and Romans harnessed a horse by putting one strap around its belly, another around its neck, and joining them on top of its shoulders. The connection to the load, to the wagon or chariot, ran to this juncture of the straps. Under load, the neck strap pulls tight and chokes the horse, which cuts its ability to pull by about 80 percent. One of history's curiosities is why nobody noticed this. Probably it was because they used oxen for pulling heavy loads, and did not realize the extent of the advantage in speed of using horses, but who really knows.[8]

About 250 B.C. the Chinese invented the horse collar. Europeans were a little slower; it took them another 1,000 years. This devise uses a broad collar rather than a strap. It still goes around the neck, but two connections to the load are used, placed lower down and to the sides. The strain is taken on the front of the horse's shoulders, not on the windpipe, and the animal's pulling capacity is increased by a factor of five.

The idea of the horse collar is a piece of intellectual property, and an extraordinarily valuable one. It also illustrates many of the problems inherent in such property. Ordinary physical property can be protected by physical means. You protect your land and cattle with fences and guard dogs. You protect your car or your jewelry by keeping it close to you and by locking it up. In addition, it is obvious when someone has taken it and easy for the law to recognize that you have been deprived of it.

The horse collar is not physically defensible. Anyone who sees it can grasp the principle and apply it. Now the inventor's ability to control it is gone. Furthermore, it is not obvious to people that you are deprived if someone else copies your idea. After all, you still have your horse collar. It took a long time—until the Lockean era, in fact—for people to begin to understand that there was indeed something amiss when ideas were copied.

If intellectual property cannot be protected physically and is not protected legally, then the incentives for people to dream up and perfect horse collars and other useful gadgets are inadequate. The impact of the horse collar on overall productivity is immense, but only a tiny part of this can be captured by an individual farmer-inventor, so few people spend serious time on invention, and everyone is the poorer, as thousands of years go by while the full potential of the horse goes untapped.

The logical solution is the patent system. Society makes the horse collar into property protected by the law and says that anyone using it must pay a toll to the inventor. This changes the incentives, and soon creative people are beavering away, inventions are rolling out, and productivity is taking off like a rocket. On the time scale of history, it is a mere blink from the horse collar to micromanaging fields with a GPS.

The two big problems are what qualifies as a patentable invention and how much the inventor gets. The first of these leads into the exotica of patent law. Many of the important concepts are familiar, particularly the problem of distinguishing the fruits of individual effort from the great sea of the intellectual and cultural commons. The basic answers are pretty commonsensical. The invention must be novel and nonobvious, and it cannot be contained within prior art. You can patent a device but not an idea. You cannot say, "Wouldn't it be neat to have some way to let horses pull without choking themselves, and I hereby patent it." You must say, "Here is my design for a horse collar that works, and I patent it." You cannot patent laws of nature; Albert Einstein could not patent $E = mc^2$, to the regret of his heirs.

Millions of dollars turn on these questions of originality, and fighting over them is a large and lucrative industry. It is also an increasingly troubled one. As technology proliferates and becomes more specialized, it becomes harder for the Patent Office to keep up with what is going on. The suits for infringement, challenges to patents, and defense of patents also become more complicated, but they all turn on the basic questions of what is novel enough to be protected as individual effort.

The second question—how much the inventor gets—takes us into the realm of economics and antitrust law. The horse collar still provides useful fodder for illustration. To haul a wagon load of produce requires a wagon, a horse, and a collar; call it a cartage system. Say the load is worth $100 at point A and $200 at point B. If each of the three elements of the system is owned by a different person, how do they divide the profit from moving the goods? The answer of our economic system is to let them bargain and compete. There are lots of owners of horses, wagons, and collars, and they make contracts with each other. The share going to each will depend on their costs and the scarcity of each factor. In addition, much of the value should go to a fourth party: the customers. The owners of the factors will put together lots of competing cartage systems, which will drive down the price of the hauling. In the end, most of the value added by carting produce from A to B will go to consumers.

Giving a patent to the inventor of the horse collar changes this system. Without the collar, a horse and wagon can haul only one-fifth the amount of goods and make only $20 in profit. Adding the collar adds $80 to the return from the trip. If we give the inventor of the horse collar a monopoly, we remove the price of the collar from the discipline of competition. Its owner will demand that owners of horses and wagons give him almost all of this added value or he will not deal. They will agree, because they are better off to take $21 of the profit and give him $79 than to make the trip without the collar and make only $20. Furthermore, the owner of the patent on the collar can control the whole cartage industry, making sure that cartage systems do not compete with each other. Thus prices will not fall, and consumers will not get the benefit of the increase in efficiency.

This is a highly unstable system, since everyone is going to be unhappy with the inventor. In particular, the owners of horses and wagons will protest that their assets have some value without the collar, but the collar without a horse is worth zero—so how does it turn out that the inventor gets most of the money? Appeals to the greater good of the system over periods of decades are not likely to be effective.

The solutions are not pure, since they reflect considerations not easily reconciled. We want to foster invention but not reward it too much at the expense of other factors. We recognize the inventor's natural Lockean right to the fruit of his labor, but does this mean that he has the right to 80 percent of the increase in efficiency? Without the horse and wagon, his collar is worth zero. Raising "theory of value" at a session of economists guarantees hours of inconclusive debate. We also need something that is socially acceptable over the long term, that people regard as a legitimate division of the fruits of cartage systems.

The first and most obvious approach is to limit patents in time. In the United States, the term is twenty years from the date the application for the patent is filed, or seventeen years from the date of grant if this is later. (The term changed in 1995. For pre-1995 patents, the term is seventeen years from the date the patent was granted.)[9] After this the invention becomes part of the commons.

The limit on what is patentable is also a limit on monopoly. You patent a specific horse collar, not all devices that allow horses to pull more easily. Someone looking at what you have done can invent another device to accomplish the same thing. If this happens, we have competition, which is our normal way of checking rapacity, and our system is working again.

We also have developed antitrust doctrines to keep patent holders from extending the market power given them by the patent into other areas. Antitrust law is sort of like takings: the position is so screwed up that no one can play it. The problems extend to the treatment of intellectual property when these come into contact with antitrust law. In the long run, the best answer to the problems of monopoly granted by intellectual property is more intellectual property, not the formalism of antitrust law. Monopoly does not come up much in copyright because for entertainment there is always competition, except in such special cases as the ASCAP consortium. The power of the author of a play to extract monopoly profits is limited by the existence of many other plays. You have a wide selection of books, or movies. The same thing usually holds in patent situations. There are few products, if any, that are absolutely without substitutes, and it is far from clear that the monopoly use of patents is a practical, as opposed to a theoretical, hobgoblin. The more the forces of inventiveness are unleashed, the less of a problem it will be.

When copyright would create a serious possibility of monopoly, the courts tend to disallow it. You cannot copyright a method of accounting, an issue settled in 1879 in one of the big cases of copyright history.[10] In *Lotus v. Borland,* a federal court of appeals said Lotus could not copyright the menu command hierarchy of its Lotus 1-2-3 program and thus could not keep Borland from adding a feature to its Quattro spreadsheet allowing Lotus users to use their existing knowledge and macros. The case was argued in terms of the technicalities of copyright law. Is the command hierarchy a "method of operation," and thus uncopyrightable under the terms of the statute? Two of the appellate judges said yes. A third judge, Michael Boudin, agreed, but on a broader basis. With a copyright, Lotus could maintain a grip on its installed user base by making it inconvenient for users to switch to Borland's product. But the investment in learning the commands and drafting macros was made by the users, not by Lotus. Boudin asked why the company should get to appropriate the value of its customers' work."[11] If you think of the case as a problem in defining property rights, this line of analysis is the most fruitful. The standard approach recognizes only Lotus and Borland as possible owners of the customer's knowledge base, but clearly the customer has a claim as well. Judge Boudin's question leads you to the answer that the investment in learning to manipulate the menu belongs to the customer, which means it should be portable from one system to another. This is the right answer.

Lotus v. Borland was a big case, with everyone in the computer industry jumping in, mostly against copyrightability. The Supreme Court took it for review, then split four to four on the outcome, which means the lower court opinion stands, and the law remains in disarray.

The law and policy governing intellectual property are in better basic shape than the systems governing other types of property. Intellectual property has not been subject to the raids mounted in other places in recent years, and the system is asking the right questions. The answers are not always easy, but trying to do the right thing is half the battle. A debate is going on now between those who argue that the intellectual revolution requires a wholesale rethinking and revamping of the law and those who think that the structure is sound and can be built on. The latter view seems correct. The fundamental questions are constant, whether you look at the contribution of the horse collar to the value of a cartage system or the impact of the graphical user interface on computer systems, and the calls for "fundamental rethinking" have an ominous ring. They probably mean that someone has figured out something tricky that will not be to the advantage of the rest of us. I echo science writer James Gleick when he notes that the motto "information wants to be free" means only that someone wants information to be free to him.[12]

The usual start in figuring out who is up to something is to look at who would profit from the change. If you begin receiving propaganda about the horrors of allowing patents on horse collars, the chances are the mailings are paid for by the horse and wagon lobbies. These mailings will not suggest, you might note, that horses and wagons ought to be free—only horse collars.

If you see arguments that, for example, computer software should not be protected, it would be logical to look at what big software companies are doing. You would expect them to favor leaving software unprotected by either patent or copyright. They can pay people to write software. The lack of competition from independents will increase their grip, and any software that does get written by an independent can be appropriated. The existing company has the marketing network to sell it, something that is hard for the independent to develop, especially if she is a one-product operator. As a bonus, if software cannot be protected, then it becomes harder for employees at big companies to jump the reservation and make a living as independents. You will not see suggestions that "information in the form of customer lists want to be free" or "savings from economies of scale want to be shared with our competitors."

VIRGINIA AND NEW YORK CITY, 1996

A broker with a small Richmond firm sues SmithBarney, a giant New York investment firm. He says he developed a package of specialized securities for financing certain types of corporate deals and tried to sell it to SmithBarney, which signed a nondisclosure agreement as part of the negotiations. The parties never made a deal, but a similar package—consisting of a debenture, two call warrants, and a contingent note—showed up as part of the financing in a giant merger orchestrated by SmithBarney.[13] Smith-Barney says it developed the package used in the merger independently.

It is a novel case. Wall Street firms generally regard any idea as fair game for use by all, and the idea of claiming exclusivity for any type of instrument seems strange to them. This position is not based on charity. They have access to the major corporations, and the Richmond firm does not. If ideas are free to all and access is not, then he who has the access gets the money. The *Wall Street Journal* points out that the SmithBarney partner on the deal makes about $5 million per year; the Richmond broker makes $50,000. Once again, property rights are the protector of the little guy rather than the megacorp.

Our improving capacity to turn information into property promises other interesting changes. For example, the industry that information is "about" can be the information industry itself. In classic television broadcasting, the product is an audience, which is sold to a sponsor. The entertainment is only the bait used to hook the fish. This leads to the lowest common denominator programming that has cursed television forever. There is a little variation for demographic characteristics, but basically a body is a body, and the more the better. Viewers are not in the role of purchasers who pay for a product called entertainment. They cannot offer to pay more for a premium product, thus giving the creators of programs an option of collecting more per viewer from a smaller audience. The growth of pay-per-view, which depends on two-way information transfer and encryption devices, will change this profoundly. Selling entertainment product to consumers is a different business from selling audiences to sponsors.

Pay-per-view, with all its promise, depends on sophisticated two-way information transfers and on encryption. So does the use of the Internet as an effective device for the distribution of information. Some experts argue that the ease of piracy on the Internet will render intellectual property indefensible both physically and legally. As a result, creators will not be able to make a living from producing it. They will be forced to produce as hirelings paid by a sponsor with an interest in getting the message out. It is important that inventors be encouraged to falsify the prediction of these experts and that a combination of encryption and improved civil justice maintain the defensibility of intellectual property. As with television advertising, the motives of a sponsor are not the same as the needs of the viewer, and it is foolish to assume they are. You can see the problem on some Internet search engines. These purport to give you the Web sites most relevant to your search request but in fact steer you to the sites that have paid them. They are not selling information to you; they are selling you to the sponsor. You, as a Web searcher with limited time and a low tolerance for nonsense, are far better off with a system in which *you* pay a search engine to exercise independent expertise in finding relevant sites.

The next step in the downward spiral of sponsorship would be for the search engine to tell you it is exercising its independent judgment, then sell you to a sponsor in secret.

BOSTON, 1996

An investment banker with Lazard Freres & Co. is convicted of depriving his clients of their "right to honest services." He was hired by municipalities to advise them on the best financing for projects. He steered deals to Merrill Lynch & Company, without telling the clients that any fees they paid to Merrill were split with Lazard. The firms pay the government $24 million in civil penalties.[14]

There is a lot of this virus going around. The lawyer on your personal injury case says: "You need a tax lawyer, eh? Well I can direct you to the best one in town, and it just so happens she is right here in this very law firm! Funny coincidence, what?"

The moral is, Be the buyer, not the product. Pay someone for her intellectual property in her own disinterested advice. But you cannot achieve this happy state unless three-D property rights exist. There must be an owner of a defined right who can defend it from piracy and sell it to you.

This discussion could go on for a long time. For those with a taste for difficult puzzles, the legal specialty called IP—intellectual property—is a lode of pure ore. Assuming that computer software should indeed be protected, the details give people fits: Patent or copyright? What parts of the software? To what extent? My newsclip file is a mine of comparable questions. In California, doctors took some spleen cells from a patient, started a new line of genetically engineered cells, and patented it.[15] How to treat the products of biotechnology is an industry all its own. One headline reads, "Move to Patent Cancer Gene Touches Off Storm of Protest."[16] If that seems too exotic, what about traffic circles? Engineers with computers are inventing new types of intersections, including the Florida-T, the Continuous Flow, and the Mini-Roundabout. Patents have been requested on some of them.[17] Another puzzle gives people fits and will continue to do so: the long-term clash between the idea people and money people over their respective shares in intellectual property. Is the owner the person who thought up the invention? The company that paid her to look out the window and think? The review team that refined it to commercial viability? What happens when some of the people involved hit the road? Who owns the information in their heads?

If you want to go further afield, ponder the impact of the information revolution on land use patterns in the West. People who want to live close to nature and telecommute will not be happy to learn that most potential home sites are locked up as wilderness, unavailable even for environmentally sensitive development. (Incidentally, this will raise the prices of available sites even higher, which will ensure that the urban rich not only appropriate the wilderness areas for their own use but are the only ones who can afford to live near them.)

Think of the impact on urban land use patterns of the revolution in tailored blue jeans and shoes. You might not need the retail store at all, or you might have one small store selling a huge variety of bespoke clothing. The manufacturing facility might provide directions on measuring over the Internet, the customer or the store send the measurements in, and that's it. Think of the impact on stores and malls, and thus on traffic, commutes, and land use. It is already axiomatic that changes in work patterns, largely based on the information revolution, are affecting these. Imagine the change if the huge variety of goods now available cheaply only at massive malls becomes available at home or at the equivalent of your village store. The new urbanists may yet be right.

As long as the basic structure of our system of dealing with intellectual property evades demolition by the forces of darkness that are operating in other areas, the future looks bright. The information revolution will make it possible to protect intellectual property effectively in ways that have been impossible in the past. New devices for metering will allow creators to sell directly to mass audiences, charging a few pennies to each customer and free of the need to work through media conglomerates. The result should be a broad burst of creativity and progress. As with other types of property, the purported conflict between property rights and community values is a false flag, and those who trumpet it should, like suburban landowners, be flying the Jolly Roger. Property rights are the most effective device we have for supporting and expanding the values of our community.

In the area of information and intellectual property, as in so many others, property rights are the key to justice, economic efficiency, political freedom, and personal autonomy. Cyber guru Esther Dyson captured the essence of all these arguments when she talked about a trip to Eastern Europe: "Having seen a non-market economy, I suddenly understood much better what I liked about a market economy. . . . Number one, that it works. Not always, and not everybody in it is moral, but the system is, I think, a moral one . . . in the sense that people who produce things and work get rewarded, statistically. You don't get rewarded precisely for your effort, but in Russia you got rewarded for being alive, but not very well rewarded. A worker's paradise is a consumer's hell. People were beaten down. Everybody drank too much. Everything was hostile and dysfunctional. It was a good education about why the U.S. was a better place."[18]

Chapter 16

Confused Alarms

And we are here as on a darkling plain
Swept with confused alarms of struggle and flight,
Where ignorant armies clash by night.

—Matthew Arnold, "Dover Beach"

Prisoner's Dilemma, the uses of greed, and other responses to current woes

There are many ways to interpret these events. One slant emphasizes environmental protection. In this view, people are learning that our physical world cannot be ruthlessly exploited. The iron laws of greed and self-interest dictate that property owners, left unleashed, will impose external costs on everyone else and on the commons of our collective physical environment. Look what happened to the nation's rivers, appropriated for purposes of waste disposal. These same incentives dictate that individual commons, such as oceans and forests, will be overexploited and ruined unless rules of conservation are imposed. We are seeing a new ethic that recognizes humankind's interdependence with the world and emphasizes the need to do as little harm to it as possible. "Tread lightly" on a massive scale.

In this perspective, the tribulations of many of the landowners might be unfortunate, but change is always difficult, and they must adapt. The cowboy ethic, as it is often branded, is unsustainable. The alternative to the present policy is to let owners persist in an outmoded ethic of exploitation. The taking of property by regulation is not a real issue, because ruthless exploitation is immoral anyway and landowners should not engage in it.

This perspective cannot be dismissed, largely because it has some truth in it. Property owners do not always have a good sense of boundaries—of where their property rights end and those of other people

329

begin. Respect for the environment, like true respect for property rights, dictates that owners be held within proper limits.

These situations where property owners are being pushed back with their proper boundaries represent only a fragment of the whole picture, though. Looming larger and more important, and much more bitterly felt by the property owners, are the conscriptions of property for purposes only marginally related to environmental protection and hardly an effort to stop rapacious landowners. Seizing land for wetlands, wildlife refuges, or rails-to-trails, eliminating trivial impacts of mining, making the world safe for 3-acre lots, and fighting superstores are far removed from any effort to keep landowners within proper bounds. The number of these situations is large and has grown fast. We must seek some explanation beyond environmental protection.

One broader theory is oriented toward the changing nature of property. It holds that the decline in the importance of land makes upheaval inevitable. As other forms of property become more important for the production of wealth, society's attention shifts to those. This explains the current concern with intellectual property, and with repositories of wealth such as retirement accounts and pension funds. Real estate is becoming more of a consumption good, like clothes or entertainment, and the events recounted in this book simply document this shift. The holders of new forms of wealth value land and natural resources for purposes of recreation and aesthetics and are making their weight felt against the old groups that rely on land for the production of wealth. So be it.

This theory, too, has a lot of merit, but it does not explain why the shift is assuming the form of expropriation rather than simple purchase. If rising and wealthy classes value wetlands or endangered species habitat, why do they not just buy it? Why is the shift taking the form of confiscation?

Another view is that America's suburban upper middle class is appropriating from everyone else, and this class is increasingly dominant politically. The events recounted in this book fit neatly with the argument that this group is using its position aggressively. It is cutting off the outnumbered rural westerners from their historic access to natural resources so that these can be devoted to the amusements, or ideological preferences, of the suburbanites. It is appropriating endangered species habitat and wetlands, which are not usually found in suburban areas. It is shifting the cost of providing greenways and open space onto farmers, with the occasional sacrifice of some suburbanites. Historical preservation maintains the cities as museums for weekend pleasure, at considerable cost to the cities themselves. The power of zoning is exploited to push the problems of the cities back into the cities and the problems of growth out into the boondocks, sparing the suburban doughnut in between. Again, there is some truth here.

Another possibility is broader. Maybe the assault is less on property than on the terrifying rate of change of the twentieth century. In this view, many areas of change are too elusive to pin down. How do you check the growth of invention, or the shift in patterns of production that goes with the growth of the world market for goods? It is hard. Property in the form of real estate sits in one place, so it is a good target. You can draw a bead on it and see a result. Changes in land use also affect groups of specific neighbors in a concrete way, galvanizing them to action. The property owners are a rod for powerful social lightning.

All of these theories focus on property in the form of land. This is certainly where most of the current heat is generated, but the assault on property rights is not limited to real estate. Use of forfeitures is a broad and growing trend. The increasing willingness of the government to impose financial liabilities retroactively is deeply troubling. The issues surrounding the deregulation of telecommunications and utilities are intricate, but so far no indications have appeared that Congress is going to respect this property any more than it respects other types. The same is true of the Internet and intellectual property, though these forms of property have the growing power of the nerd classes behind them and may fare somewhat better in the long term. So far the government has shown little sensitivity to the needs to create intellectual property on the computer networks, as shown by its hostility to encryption technology. Even the denial of people's right to the disposition of their own bodily organs fits into the trend to disrespect the idea of property rights.

Because of this breadth of assault, we need some theories that are not linked so tightly to land. What else might be going on?

One productive line of inquiry is to focus on the political system. Conservative commentators point out that the nation has developed a special political class dependent on the government, particularly the federal government, for its income and status. This group includes not just the Congress and its bloated corps of minions, the executive branch, and the bevy of state and city employees. It sweeps in major elements of the press, consultants who batten on regulatory programs of all sorts, and businesses that furnish the goods and services mandated by the government.

To maintain itself, the political class must provide things to the electorate. This has led to a political race to the bottom, where the two parties compete to see who can pander in the most shameless and effective style, doling out subsidies, tax breaks, and other goodies. The problem with this strategy is that the budget well has run dry. Simply continuing to give out the same old benefits does not make the grade. After a few years, these are regarded as entitlements—as property, if you will—and paying them out earns no political points. New benefits are necessary, but the government has run out of money to give away to favored constituents. The solution is easy: give them other people's property. All you need is some airy language about the environment or community interests or former injustice, and a cover story about why the chosen donor is mean and evil, and you are on your way.

The political class is also seduced in a less cynical way. The bedrock faith of the Progressive Era, the New Deal, and the Great Society was that the wise guardians of the government would steer society to a New Eden by micromanaging everything, especially the private sector. Being a wise guardian makes you feel virtuous and useful. I know. I have been one. Unfortunately, the reality is more like the New York City factory zones. The guardians decree, and the only thing that prevents utter disaster is that people ignore them. But the myth that one is a wise guardian is hard to let go of. You will notice that the New York City Planning Commission does not respond to its failure by deciding to disband.

Unfortunately, the federal government has gotten too big, powerful, and occasionally vicious to ignore. People who persist in their dreams of being wise guardians despite all the evidence that it just isn't working, and who can deploy all the coercive power of the modern state in an effort to make it work, are downright dangerous. One of the amazing, and underremarked, phenomena of American life during the past few years is the explosive increase in the use of punitive measures of all kinds against the professional and managerial classes. Environmental protection, finance, government contracting, politics, employment relations: all are subject to massive criminal codes, plus fierce civil penalties and punitive damages. The newspaper story on New York City's factory zones quoted one urban designer as saying: "The city had one idea of how we were all supposed to live and function and it turned out to be a mismatch. Being practical, we don't obey." If the Army Corps of Engineers or the Environmental Protection Agency, combined with the U.S. Department of Justice, were in charge of enforcing New York's factory zone laws, these areas would now be ghost towns instead of thriving centers of new industries and stores, and that impudent urban designer who actually boasted about not obeying would be rotting in jail, along with many building owners.

The political class is increasingly composed of lawyers, and this is a marriage made in hell. Law school does not train anyone to function in the real world of producing goods for the market. Lawyers are taught to maneuver within a system of self-contained logic, and over the past half-century this system has come to consist largely of government controls over private activity. This empire of law has two needs. First, it constantly seeks new areas of conquest because there are fertile sources of money for lawyers. Once things get settled, people do not need lawyers to interpret for them. This leads into the second need, which is to keep the law in a state of uncertainty. An area that never gets settled is as lucrative as a brand-new one. It is greatly in the interests of the legal class that Superfund liability be based on a ten-part test of so-called equitable factors, or that the status of visual art as "work for hire" be determined by thirteen factors, each of which must be explored through intensive legal discovery, or that determining a taking requires a three-factor analysis that is total logical hash. In every instance, the outcome is unpredictable, which means that any given case can be settled only by a lawsuit, and the lawsuit itself will be expensive. The legal system is in the position of demanding perfect justice in the allocation of seats on every airline flight that takes off, no matter how long it delays the flight or how expensive the inquiry.

Almost all environmental statutes provide that private groups that sue the government can collect attorneys' fees for their trouble. This has made environmental litigation into a lucrative business. Since it is now almost impossible for the government to write an environmental impact statement that can satisfy every judge in America, environmental plaintiffs can look forward to long, publicly funded careers. Furthermore, the boards of the environmental groups, like the boards of the foundations that nourish them, are liberally spotted with representatives of the nation's big law firms. Look at the roster of the executive committee of the Natural Resources Defense Council, perhaps the most able and effective of the litigating environmental groups. NRDC is a leader in the fight against "wise use" Westerners. It also pioneered the use of media hype scare tactics in the Alar crisis of 1989, which cost Washington apple growers over $100 million. The organization was founded with a grant from the Ford Foundation and still collects goodly sums from Ford and other large foundations. The chair is F. A. O. Schwarz, Jr., of Cravath, Swaine & Moore; the founding chair is Stephen P. Duggan, of Simpson, Thacher & Bartlett; the chair emeritus is Adrian W. DeWind, from Paul, Weiss, Rifkind, Wharton & Garrison—all of them blue-chip New York City law firms. This situation is not atypical, as Jonathan Adler shows in his recent *Environmentalism at the Crossroads.*

The legal profession can feel virtuous for supporting the environmental groups, help write laws ensuring that taxpayers at large will pay a good chunk of the litigation bill, and then make millions defending corporations that are adversely affected by the environmentalists' actions. Hey, is this a great country, or what!

If you follow this line of reasoning, you have a new theory of what is undermining property rights. Property owners just happen to be in the way of the political class and the lawyers. Environmental crises and other justifications for control over property fit perfectly with the needs of these groups. Someone must be on the receiving end of regulation and control, and it is only logical to pick on a group whose relative political power has declined, such as nonsuburban landowners. You certainly do not kick the suburbanites; they are too powerful. But you have to pick on someone who has something to take.

None of these theories depends on any concept of a grand conspiracy. They all rest on the idea that large numbers of people pursuing their own basic self-interest can wind up as a strong political force and that people are good at devising intellectual rationales explaining why their self-interest is a moral imperative. The instincts are as strong as those driving the wolves and moose at Isle Royale.

More explicit theories of conspiracy can also be found. Some of the beleaguered landowners refer to environmentalists as "eco-socialists." Another common phrase is, "The green tree has red roots." The underlying theme is that the environmental movement is the inheritor of the Marxist ideologies of the last 150 years. The old dream of state ownership of the means of production, such as factories, utilities, and so on, is defunct, but the left still wants to socialize ownership of private property that takes the form of land and natural resources. In this view, expressions of concern about the environment are largely a cover for an economic agenda. The group is opposed to "capitalism," and uses environmentalism as a flag of convenience for its forays.

Which of these theories is right? Actually, all of them. All of these forces are at work, interacting with each other in convoluted ways. This is why property issues are so hard to sort out.

The question is what any of us can do about the destruction that these forces are wreaking on us, including those of us who are part of them. The old line from Pogo—"We have met the enemy and they are us"—is much overworked. But it is overused precisely because it is so often apt. We as a society have lost touch with our Lockean roots. We have forgotten that we evolved a system based on private property because experience proved that this is the only way to promote the values that we share as a community.

One of the strongest of these values is the desire to promote a growing economy. Unlike our ancestors, we need not spend seventeen years at hard labor with an axe to clear a 160-acre farm, and we like it that way. The wealth of our society is not little green pieces of paper called money, but time and opportunity. We can spend time with families, or enjoying the beauty of the West, or riding bicycles or motorbikes, or dipping into the great culture of our civilization only because our economic system generates a huge economic surplus over the subsistence level. This surplus is a heritage of our Lockean civilization, as the fate of the communist world demonstrated. The next time someone blathers about how we are all "too materialistic," ask politely if she wants to return to the preaudio days when the only people who heard great music were courtiers. (Curious. Everyone who thinks this way assumes they will be one of the courtiers, not one of the peasants.) Is my affection for the radio and the CD an example of my excess materialism? Or perhaps these antimaterialists wish to return to preautomobile days, when most people lived and died within twenty miles of their birthplaces. Maybe they want to do without antibiotics, or food packaging materials.

Also included on the list of community values is a dedication to nurturing individual development and autonomy. "Community" is not synonymous with "anthill." We want people to be able to act freely and creatively, inventing themselves and defining their own personhood, if you will. Control over property, whether it takes the form of land, computer hardware, or electric guitars, is a crucial part of this.

Respect for the environment is on our list of community values, and it is clearly rising. But it is equally clear that this value is also promoted by a respect for property and inhibited by disregard. The urban sprawl so hated by the press is the product of a lack of property rights, not an excess. Ditto for the crisis in the West. Destruction of potential species habitat and historic structures will be accelerated by the decline of property rights. The rising concern for the environment is making itself felt in the free market, but the market needs property rights or it cannot work. If things continue on their present course, we will also find that increasing chunks of the nation are "saved" environmentally at the cost of being rendered inaccessible to the people and subject to the whims of bureaucratic control and sound bite politics. This system is not sustainable. It will, in the not so long term, erode support for environmentalism. It will not outlast the next fad.

If we pull up our Lockean roots, we will find that we have pulled up all these community values, including environmentalism, along with them. Yet many of us seem intent on doing precisely this.

The question is what any of us can do about these terrifying trends. What do we do Monday morning? Vague pieties do not count. No calls for more altruism, a stronger sense of community, an increase in general intelligence, or an informed public. We are about as altruistic as we are going to get, we are not getting smarter, and ignorance is usually rational. We have to work with the tools we have in these areas as well.

The best prescription for reform is that we need to act on a heightened sense of self-interest. True selfishness is the ticket out of our imbroglio. To explain this, which you might not find convincing right out of the box, let me introduce one last building block of current political theory, the concept of prisoner's dilemma.

Prisoner's dilemma is, according to William Poundstone's entertaining book of this title, "one of the great ideas of the twentieth century, simple enough for anyone to grasp and of fundamental importance."[1] It describes situations in which people have much to gain by cooperation, but in which strong incentives exist that make cooperation unlikely. The name comes from the situation used to illustrate the problem. Two people suspected of a crime are separated for interrogation. The police have some evidence, but they would like to nail it down, and are willing to give a break to whichever of the two talks. The situation is: if both keep silent, the police will use the existing evidence to send both to prison for three years; if one talks and the other does not, the talker will go to prison for one year and the silent one will go up for ten years; if both talk, then both will spend five years in jail. Their dilemma is insoluble. Each is better off if he talks, no matter which choice the other makes. The ironclad result is that both will talk and do five years in jail even though both would clearly be better off if they both kept quiet.

The world is full of prisoner's dilemma situations, instances in which people are better off if they cooperate over time, but in which the short-term incentives to cheat are substantial. Two children trading toys have a prisoner's dilemma problem. How can either be sure that if she holds out her toy the other will not snatch it without releasing her own? A common solution is for each to put down her toy and move far enough away to make it impossible for either child to snatch both of them. Buying a house is a prisoner's dilemma problem. The buyer must deliver the money, the seller the deed. Each faces the possibility that the other will cheat, and then extract a price for doing what he was supposed to do in the first place. The solution is the escrow agent, who holds whichever comes in first, the deed or the money, until both are in hand. Anyone making a security deposit on an apartment, which is delivered to the landlord and not to an escrow agent, is failing to solve a prisoner's dilemma problem. Landlords, dollars in hand, have creative ideas about compensable damage.

In the real world, prisoner's dilemma gets pretty mushy. Fortunately for the future of human society, dealings are rarely limited to a single transaction. In real life, the two criminals have many opportunities to replay the game, and learn that over repeated plays of the game they are better off if both keep quiet. In experiments performed with money rewards, subjects learn to cooperate and rake in the cash, though the bargains are always shaky and often unstable. (After reading Poundstone, get David Axelrod's *The Evolution of Cooperation*.) Games are also multi-person rather than two-person, the numbers of plays are infinite, many games are going at once, and the payoffs are affected by concepts of religion, morality, and reputation. All of these complications create opportunities to escape the iron logic of the basic game. There are some variations in which cooperation is easier to achieve, and some in which it is harder. Nonetheless, prisoner's dilemma permeates our lives. Over and over, the basic question at issue is how to achieve long-term cooperation in the face of strong short-term incentives pushing in the other direction.

Much of our legal system is designed to solve prisoner's dilemma problems. For example, the state can serve the function of the escrow agent and guarantee performance. This is a function of contract law, which reassures the party who must act first that the other party will keep the bargain. The only alternative is to act like the children trading toys. Vaccination against disease is a prisoner's dilemma problem. The procedure carries some slight risk, so each individual would be best off if everyone else got vaccinated while he did not. So we make a rule, through the government, that everyone must participate. Otherwise, each will seek his own advantage, the system will collapse, no one will be protected, and the disease will rampage.

The constitutional dimension of the legal system is our way of solving serious, and potentially deadly, prisoner's dilemma issues. Start with an example far removed from property rights. If you believe strongly in a particular religion, you might have strong incentives to suppress a competing one, especially if you fear the competitor will try to suppress you. Or you might fear that the other religion will be made a favorite of the state supported by your tax revenues. The competitor, like the fellow criminal in the prisoner's dilemma, has the same fears and concerns about your church. Our solution as a nation is the "free exercise" and "no establishment" clauses of the First Amendment to the Constitution. These prevent both suppression or establishment. A threatened religion can enlist the full power of the society in its defense. But the society does not defend the particular religion. It defends the principle that we are all better off if no one is allowed to yield to the short-term temptation to suppress another religion. Because of these clauses, your church is no longer tempted to assault the competitor. You know this would not be allowed, and you also know that you are safe from assault and do not need to make a preemptive strike.

By now, you can tell where this line of argument is going. Protection of property rights is a solution to prisoner's dilemma problems. If you like wetlands, or historic preservation, or 3-acre zoning, your short-term incentive is to grab if you can. If you are allowed to indulge in this temptation, it sets up a destructive process. Other people with other short-term interests demand the same right to seize your property for *their* pet causes. An amazing aspect of the assault on property rights is how many sets of interests have organized themselves to join in and how quickly this has happened. The next step, of course, is that people who own property race to use it up before it can be taken—like the effort to spend money quickly during periods of runaway inflation. Once everyone understands that the basic bargains no longer hold, that we have stripped away our ancient solutions to the prisoner's dilemma, then it is Katy-bar-the-door.

In the end, the old civil liberties argument applies. The weapons you wield to take from others today will be turned against you tomorrow. The holders of the new property—financial assets, intellectual concepts, copyrights, suburban real estate—are all going to find that their legal protections are gone. The doctrines they use to seize endangered species habitat or wetlands or historic structures can now be turned against them by anyone politically stronger. The Introduction to this book posed some questions, such as how you would distinguish between a law seizing endangered species habitat and a law commandeering your vacation home to house the homeless, or a law demanding that you devote some percent of your time as a professional to causes stamped worthy by government regulation. Here is the answer: there is no distinction. You professionals and knowledge workers are growing dependent on raw power, not on law. You have been cutting down the forest of laws to get at the devil, and the winds are starting to blow.

Soon, for your own protection, you will want to reinstate the old rules that keep prisoner's dilemma problems from degenerating into a Hobbesian war of all against all. Where will you go for allies? To the westerners, whose communities and livelihoods got destroyed? Why should they help? To the natural resources companies—the producers of wood, paper, metals, oil, and so on? No. They are being pushed overseas and will have no interest in arguing about U.S. property rights. To the developers? No, again. They have learned not to inventory land. They have become builders, not land developers. Tell them where and they will build, but they are leaving the battle. To the churches, whose property is getting frozen into nonpastoral uses because people like to look at it, or to all the owners of wetlands whose net worth has been reduced to zero? Can you knowledge workers depend on your fellows? I doubt it. Why should those interested in copyrights defend financial assets when the basic links between these two things have been severed? Unless both are treated as "property," which can be defended in general—like the principle of freedom of religion—then defending financial assets does not help copyright holders fend off future threats to themselves.

No, whatever your type of property, you are now on your own, at the mercy of whatever coalition of political pirates thinks you look worth robbing. You can sugar-coat it by saying that you are being given the honor of collaborating with a coalition of enlightened fellow citizens who understand that a higher ethic (as defined by themselves) will be served by devoting your assets to its pursuit, but the result will be the same for you. Among the most important members of such coalitions is the political class. As economic historian John Powelson says, "The most disheartening conclusion of the book [*The Story of Land*] may be that whenever a reformer . . . has changed the land tenure system by fiat he, she, or it has retained a substantial portion of the rights instead of yielding them to the peasant. This observation applies universally, from the ancient world to the Third World today, in 'capitalist' and socialist countries alike."[2] There is no reason to think changing the term *land* to the more general *property* will change this conclusion.

So let us talk about enlightened self-interest. Perhaps there is still time to repent. Perhaps this bleak picture is like the Ghost of Christmas Yet to Come in *A Christmas Carol*. It is on the way, but Scrooge's fate is still malleable, and he can change it if he has the will. Some justices of the Supreme Court have a sense that the Court as an institution has gone seriously astray. Many lower court judges have a much better sense of the stakes. Congress is feeling heat from the increasing number of people hurt by current practices, and perhaps the political system can be moved to action.

The initial burden must fall on those who are dedicated to the great principle that the human right to property is crucial for Justice, Economic Efficiency, Political Freedom, and Personal Autonomy. This vanguard must devote itself to missionary work, especially with the media, but also with the public at large. The message must emphasize not only the importance of the right to property, but also the lack of conflict between this right and other values important in our society. To believe that people should pay for housing or food does not mean that you favor homelessness or starvation. Similarly, you can believe in the right to property and still support environmental protection, or historic preservation, or bicycle trails, or any of numerous other causes. The world is full of choices and trade-offs, and respect for property is the only way in which a society can let its members pursue their many diverse goals in a peaceful and efficient fashion. You should be able to call yourself an environmentalist even if you are not willing to become a thief. The pro-property forces should stand firmly where they belong, on the moral high ground.

The message must also promote the use of a better language. The basic analytic tools used in this book, such as rational ignorance, single-mission agencies, capture by special interests, pursuit of self-interest by government officials, the enduring power of greed, and prisoner's dilemma, are not novel. They are the coin of discourse among policy wonks, and they provide crucial insight into current controversies of many kinds, including disputes over the right to property. They are important aids to thought. Yet the concepts have little role in our national debates. They have not made their way into the mainstream media, or into the language of congressional debate, or into legal analyses of the administrative process. This is unfortunate, because the lack of a good language leaves public discussion afloat in a sea of buzzwords and vacuity. Injecting these terms, and the rich veins of thought underlying them, into this discussion would do much to improve its quality.

The forces of reform should realize that the most important barrier to change is ignorance, and the dynamics of this factor are changing. In the past, it has been rational for the average person to remain ignorant of the convolutions of wetlands, or endangered species, or land use, or the war on and in the West, but it has all gone too far. There are too many assaults, and the pattern has become too repetitive. Luckily for the cause of reform, the price of ignorance is rising. Ignorance about any of these topics individually remains rational, but ignorance about property matters in general is becoming highly irrational. The bargains that solved our collective prisoner's dilemma and let us each be secure in peaceful enjoyment of the types of property we value have broken down. It is important to all of us that they be reconstituted. In the end, reform will come if, and only if, enough of us make clear to our elected representatives that we understand that we have created a terrible prisoner's dilemma problem and that we expect them to solve it. If enough of us make this into a voting issue, then our public servants will act. So tell them you are on board this train. And tell them that you are not motivated by concern for abstract justice, or out of concern for the community, or by any other noble purpose. They are used to outwaiting such transitory emotions. Tell them you have decided that ignorance about property matters is no longer rational and that you are acting on the basis of the most reliable motives: greed, fear, and a clear understanding of your own long-term interests. That is a motive the political class can understand.

WASHINGTON, D.C., 1996

I go to the opening meeting of the Fly-In for Freedom, an annual event attended mostly by westerners who are involved in the use of natural resources. About two hundred people are there in a modest hotel on a Saturday morning in June. They have a couple of days of meetings and seminars, then visit Congress to lobby for property rights legislation. Women in Timber has lots of representatives. There are also ranchers, timber company people, some miners, and the Blue Ribbon coalition, which promotes trail use, including use by motorized vehicles. Attendees pay their own way, and for many of them it is not easy. Congressional staff members speak and tell them that legislation is not likely in 1996. Maybe 1997. Several listeners say they do not know if they can hold on another year. The logging bans are turning their towns into ghosts.

The opening session starts with individual introductions. Each person gets up and tells who he or she is and why he or she is there. I tell them I am writing a book on property matters. The group applauds loudly. I find this striking. This is the Wise Use Movement, the archvillain of the environmentalists. Practically everyone qualifies for *The Greenpeace Guide to Anti-Environmental Organizations*. Yet they all assume spontaneously that having a stranger present who announces his intent to publicize their discussions is a good thing. There are no dark cabals about ruining the land or stealing natural resources. There is mostly puzzlement over the twists that events have taken. The greatest frustration at the conference is over the ignorance of the rest of the country. Again and again people talk of the difficulty of explaining the realities of the effects of the programs in the face of feel-good sound bites. They are convinced that the more any visitor sees, hears, and explains the truth, the better it is for their cause, and the more likely it is that Congress will finally be moved to act.

I leave, hoping they are right.

Notes

Chapter 1: Stage Setting

1. "No Satisfaction," *Washington Post,* August 31, 1995, p. D3. (What they actually said was, "As far as this council is concerned, muck-spreading under normal circumstances is a bona fide agricultural pursuit.")
2. John J. DiIulio, Jr., "How Bureaucrats Rewrite Laws," *Wall Street Journal,* October 2, 1996, p. A18.
3. "'Angel' Cries over Lack of Lights in New Display," *Washington Times,* December 18, 1995, p. A7; "Scourge of Little Rock Becomes Bright Light at Disney," *Washington Post,* December 25, 1995, p. A21.
4. *Resource Sentinel,* passim.
5. Robert Bolt, *A Man for All Seasons,* p. 66.

Chapter 2: Some Stories

1. Earth Vision Institute, outtakes of full speech of Bruce Whiting, in *Forest Wars,* video-cassette.
2. ESA Coalition, press statement, July 14, 1994, quoted in Ike Sugg, *Rats, Lies, and the GAO,* p. 3.
3. Ibid.
4. The original Domenigoni statement can be obtained from the National Policy Forum at (202) 544-2900. It was part of the forum held on December 21, 1994. The GAO report is called *Endangered Species Act: Impact of Species Protection Efforts on the 1993 California Fire* (GAO-RCED-94-224), July 8, 1994. GAO gives away single copies of its reports to anyone who asks. Call (202) 512-6000 or fax (301) 258-4066. *Rats, Lies, and the GAO* was published by the Competitive Enterprise Institute, which can be reached at (202) 331-1010 (telephone) or fax (202) 331-0640. I side with the CEI, but this is one of those rare instances in which the documents are easily available and are not numbingly complex, so any interested reader is invited to form an opinion.
5. *Land Use Law and Zoning Digest* 48, no. 1 (January 1996): 20.
6. Maryland–National Capital Park and Planning Commission, *Staff Recommendations on Public Hearing (Preliminary) Draft Amendment to the Master Plan for Historic Preservation:*

Sunnyside, (February 2, 1994). This account also relies on personal communications with the owners.

7. Rick Henderson, "Preservation Acts"; James Bovard, *Lost Rights*, p. 35; personal communications.

8. United States v. Ellen 961, F.2d 462, 464 (4th Cir., 1992).

9. Statement of Thomas Rule before the House of Representatives, Committee on Resources, Task Force on Private Property, *Hearings*, July 17, 1995.

10. Agins v. City of Tiburon, 447 U.S. 255 (1980). Extra detail from William Fischel, *Regulatory Takings*, pp. 52–54.

11. Stephen J. L. Page, "'In My Former Life as a Seagull,'" *Wall Street Journal*, December 27, 1994, p. A16.

12. David W. Dunlap, "Buildings Department Says Fordham's Radio Tower Is Too Tall," *New York Times*, September 30, 1994, p. B3; Fordham University, fact sheet: The Fordham University Radio Antenna (n.d. [c. January 1996]); Fordham University, press release: State Supreme Court Upholds Fordham's Right to Complete Radio Tower on Rose Hill Campus, June 12, 1996; personal communications.

13. Ehrlich v. City of Culver City, 911 P.2d 429 (S. Ct. Cal. 1996).

14. Ali F. Sevin, Letter to the Editor, *Washington Times*, October 26, 1995, p. A22; personal communications.

15. Sam Kazman, "Home *Not* Alone: New York's War on Landlords," *Property Rights Reader* (January 1995): 33–35.

16. Catherine Toups, "Accused John Is Cleared but City Keeps His Car," *Washington Times*, November 6, 1992, p. A1; Leonard W. Levy, *A License to Steal*, p. 157.

17. Statement of David A. Smith before the House of Representatives, Committee on Resources, Task Force on Private Property, *Hearings*, June 13, 1995.

18. Defenders of Property Rights, *Property Rights Reporter* 2 (Fall 1995): 1.

19. Frank J. Murray, "Survivors May Now Sue over Theft of Body Parts," *Washington Times*, November 6, 1995, p. A1; Frank J. Murray, "Doctors Control Access to D.C. Dead Body Parts," *Washington Times*, November 6, 1995, p. A6.

Chapter 3: A Primer on Property

1. Terry Anderson, *Property Rights and Indian Economies*, passim.

2. John P. Powelson, *The Story of Land: A World History of Land Tenure and Agrarian Reform*.

3. Ibid., pp. 71–72.

4. Douglass C. North, *Structure and Change in Economic History*.

5. A. John Simmons, *The Lockean Theory of Rights*, p. 4. Simmons's "reasonably complete (but by no means exhaustive) list of prominent books and articles" (p. 13) on Locke and Lockean issues runs to over four hundred entries (pp. 355–376).

6. William A. Fischel, *Regulatory Takings*, p. 171.

7. Quoted in Gregory K. Dreicer (ed.), *Between Fences: National Building Museum Exhibition Catalog*, p. 13.

8. John Locke, *Two Treatises on Government*, bk. 2, sec. 49.

9. William M. Denevan, "The Pristine Myth: The Landscape of the Americas in 1492," p. 369.

10. Benjamin H. Hibbard, *A History of the Public Land Policies*, pp. 67–68; Clarence H. Danhof, "Farm-Making Costs and the 'Safety Valve': 1850–1860," *Journal of Political Econ-*

omy 49 (1941): 317–359, reprinted in Vernon Carstensen (ed.), *The Public Lands*, pp. 253–296.

11. North, *Structure and Change*, pp. 158–170.

12. The most elegant synopses of the economic arguments for property that I have found appear in Yale law professor Robert Ellickson's "Property in Land," and Professor Douglass C. North's *Structure and Change*. The next few pages draw heavily on their marshaling of the material. Enough embellishments have been added that you should not blame them for any errors, though.

13. North, *Structure and Change*, p. 111.

14. J. Bradford DeLong, *Slouching Towards Utopia?* pp. 62–69.

15. Douglas Farah, "Cuba Bucks the Past, Socialist Economy Shifts Gears When Workers Get Dollar Incentives," *Washington Post*, November 17, 1995, p. A35.

16. Terry L. Anderson and Dean Lueck, "Agricultural Development and Land Tenure in Indian Country," in Anderson (ed.), *Property Rights and Indian Economies*, pp. 147–166.

17. Michael Williams, *Americans and Their Forests*, pp. 426–430.

18. Columbus-America Discovery Group v. Atlantic Mutual Insurance Co., 974 F.2d 450 (4th Cir. 1992), *cert. denied*, 113 S. Ct. 1625 (1993) (CADG I); Columbus-America Discovery Group v. Atlantic Mutual Insurance Co., 56 F.2d 556 (4th Cir. 1995), *cert. denied*, 116 S. Ct. 352 (1995) (CADG II).

19. Fischel, *Regulatory Takings*, pp. 25–47.

20. Keystone Bituminous Cool Association v. DeBenedictis, 480 U.S. 470 (1987).

21. Garrett Mattingly, *The Armada*, pp. 61–62.

22. Julian L. Simon, "Origins of the Airline Oversales Auction System," p. 48, and personal communications.

23. Aged Hawaiians v. Hawaiian Homes Commission, 279 P.2d 279 (S. Ct. Hawaii, 1995).

Chapter 4: Complexities

1. Armstrong v. United States, 364 U.S. 40, 49 (1960).

2. William Fischel, *Regulatory Takings*, pp. 64–99.

3. Stephen C. Fehr, "Developer to Pay for Virginia Metro Station," *Washington Post*, November 16, 1995, p. A1.

4. Garrett Hardin, "The Tragedy of the Commons," in Garrett Hardin and John Baden (eds.), *Managing the Commons*, p. 16.

5. Richard E. Epstein, *Takings*, pp. 8–15.

6. Leef Smith, "Park May Limit Access to Popular Mountain," *Washington Post*, August 24, 1995, p. C3; Peter Finn, "Few Hikers Show at Old Rag as Permit System Starts," *Washington Post*, October 8, 1995, p. B7; Victoria Benning, "A Peak Peek from Old Rag Will Cost Hikers," *Washington Post*, December 12, 1995, p. E3.

7. Epstein, *Takings*, pp. 236–238.

8. Fischel, *Regulatory Takings*, pp. 253–269.

9. George Korngold, *Private Land Use Contracts*, p. 3.

10. Summarized in Fischel, *Regulatory Takings*, pp. 352–355.

11. Richards v. Washington Terminal Company, 233 U.S. 546 (1914).

12. Yvonne Chiu and Mike Mills, "High-Tech Means Trouble: The Cellular Industry Wants U.S. Protection as Communities Say No to a Towering 'Eyesore'," *Washington Post*, July 31, 1995, Washington Business section, p. 5; Lorraine Woellert and Doug Adams, "Cel-

lular Phone Poles Unwanted: The Skinny, Skyscraping Antennas for the New Technology Are Raising Cries of NIMBY," *Washington Times*, October 29, 1995, p. A1; Mike Allen, "Wireless Systems Put Out Their Antennas," *New York Times*, May 27, 1996, p. 29; John J. Keller, "Bad Reception: with Cellular Towers Sprouting All Over, Towns Begin to Rebel; City Hall Finds Red Tape Has Become Best Way to Thwart Phone Firms; 'Monster Across the Street'," *Wall Street Journal*, July 3, 1996, p. A1; Bill McAllister, "Runyon's Towering Inferno: Renting Postal Airspace Burns Some Neighbors," *Washington Post*, September 25, 1996, p. A21.

Chapter 5: Political Legitimacy

1. William P. Alford, *To Steal a Book Is an Elegant Offense*, p. 132.
2. R. Jeffrey Lyman, "Learning from Norman Williams," p. 8.
3. Steele v. FCC, 770 F.2d 1192, 1199 (D.C. Cir. 1985).
4. Statement of Nathan Deal at National Policy Forum, *Sane Environmental Enforcement: How Enforcement Went Wrong, and How to Correct It*, August 3, 1995.
5. U.S. v. Darby, 312 U.S. 100, 124 (1941).
6. Oliver Wendell Holmes, *The Common Law*, p. xx.
7. Ted Gup, "Appreciation: Woman of the Woods, Mollie Beatie, a Natural as Fish and Wildlife Chief," *Washington Post*, July 1, 1996, p. B1.
8. Bennis v. Michigan, 116 S. Ct. 994 (1996) (concurring opinion).
9. Douglas H. Ginsburg, "Delegation Running Riot," pp. 83, 84.

Chapter 6: Endangered Species

1. George T. Frampton, Assistant Secretary for Fish, Wildlife and Parks, Department of the Interior, before U.S. House of Representatives, House Resources Committee, Endangered Species Act Task Force, *Hearings on Endangered Species Act Reauthorization*, May 25, 1995, p. 3.
2. Jane Fritsch, "Nature Groups Say Foes Bear Friendly Names," *New York Times*, March 25, 1996, p. A1; Al Kamen, "Group Forced to Toss Back Logo," *Washington Post*, April 3, 1996, p. A17.
3. Statement of Benjamin Cone before the U.S. House of Representatives, House Resources Committee, Task Force on Private Property, *Hearings*, June 13, 1995; Lee Ann Welch, "Property Rights Conflict Under the Endangered Species Act: Protection of the Red-Cockaded Woodpecker," in Bruce Yandle (ed.), *Land Rights*, p. 151; Department of the Interior, Fish and Wildlife Service, "Availability of an Environmental Assessment and Receipt of an Application Submitted by Mr. Ben Cone, Jr., for an Incidental Take Permit for Red-Cockaded Woodpeckers in Association with Management Activities on his Property in Pender County, North Carolina," *Federal Register*, July 10, 1996.
4. "In the Forest, a Fight over Firewood: Environmental Suit Blocks Poor Villagers," *Washington Post*, January 14, 1996, p. A14.
5. Statement of Margaret Rector at National Policy Forum, *Private Property Rights*, pp. 35–37.
6. Statement of Mary Fattig before the U.S. House of Representatives, House Resources Committee, Task Force on Private Property, *Hearings*, June 13, 1995.
7. Brian Mannix, "The Origin of Endangered Species and the Descent of Man," pp. 56, 58.

8. Charles C. Mann and Mark L. Plummer, *Noah's Choice: The Future of Endangered Species*, p. 161.

9. 50 Code of Federal Regulations sec. 17.11, 17.12.

10. Statement of Ike Sugg before the U.S. House of Representatives, House Resources Committee, Task Force on Endangered Species Act, *Hearings on Endangered Species Act Reauthorization*, May 18, 1995, p. 8.

11. Babbitt v. Sweet Home Chapter of Communities for a Great Oregon, 115 S. Ct. 2407 (1996). The language quoted earlier in the paragraph is from Justice Scalia's dissenting opinion.

12. Barton H. Thompson, Jr., "The Endangered Species Act: A Case Study in Takings and Incentives," p. 5, n. 14.

13. Jonathan Adler, *Environmentalism at the Crossroads*, pp. 42–45.

14. Mann and Plummer, *Noah's Choice*, pp. 195–197.

15. Fish and Wildlife Service, Department of the Interior, "Endangered and Threatened Wildlife and Plants, Proposed Special Rule for the Conservation of the Northern Spotted Owl on Non-Federal Lands," *Federal Register*, February 17, 1995.

16. Sugg statement, May 18, 1995, p. 10.

17. Robert D. Thornton, "The Search for a Conservation Planning Paradigm: Section 10 of the ESA," pp. 21, 23.

18. Fish and Wildlife Service, Department of the Interior, "Endangered and Threatened Wildlife and Plants; Proposed Rule Exempting Certain Small Landowners and Low-Impact Activities From Endangered Species Act Requirements for Threatened Species," *Federal Register*, July 20, 1995.

19. Alan Cutler, "What Is a Species? Examining Biology's Most Contentious Concept," *Washington Post*, August 9, 1995, p. H1.

20. Avery, *Biodiversity*, p. 6.

21. Mann and Plummer, *Noah's Choice*, pp. 46–47.

22. Julian L. Simon and Aaron Wildavsky, *Assessing the Empirical Basis of the "Biodiversity Crisis,"* p. 6.

23. Mann and Plummer, *Noah's Choice*, p. 50.

24. Ibid., pp. 91–92.

25. Michael Williams, *Americans and Their Forests*, p. 433; *Statistical Abstract of the United States* (115th ed., 1995), Table 1148.

26. Simon and Wildavsky, *Assessing the Empirical Basis*, pp. 7–10.

27. Two fundamental works are George Sessions (ed.), *Deep Ecology for the 21st Century*, and Bill Devall and George Sessions (eds.), *Deep Ecology*. For recent technical work, see the Environmental Protection Agency, *Ecological Risk Assessment Issue Papers*. Mann and Plummer do an excellent job of presenting both sides in *Noah's Choice*. A readable, expert, and skeptical review of claims for biodiversity can be found in Stephen Budiansky's *Nature's Keepers*.

28. Rhonda L. Rundle, "Bats and Ticks Hold Clues to New Drugs," *Wall Street Journal*, April 17, 1996, p. B1.

29. Robert W. Hahn, "Thinking Clearly About Takings, Endangered Species and Economics: A Comment," (draft), at American Enterprise Institute Conference, *Economic and Constitutional Perspectives on Takings*.

30. "Record Maryland Deer Hunt," *Washington Post*, April 17, 1996, p. D6.

31. Mann and Plummer, *Noah's Choice*, pp. 183–186.

32. Fish and Wildlife Service, Department of the Interior, "Endangered and Threatened Wildlife and Plants, Final Rule to List the Mexican Spotted Owl as a Threatened Species," *Federal Register,* March 16, 1993; Fish and Wildlife Service, Department of the Interior, "Endangered and Threatened Wildlife and Plants, Determination of Threatened Status for the Northern Spotted Owl; Final Rule," *Federal Register,* June 26, 1990.

33. Robert H. Nelson, "Bruce Babbitt: Pipeline to the Almighty," *Weekly Standard,* June 24, 1996, p. 17.

34. Les Line, "In Long-Running Wolf-Moose Drama, Wolves Recover from Disaster," *New York Times,* March 19, 1996, p. C1.

35. Nelson, "Bruce Babbitt." See also Robert H. Nelson, "Unoriginal Sin: Judeo-Christian Roots of Ecotheology," in Competitive Enterprise Institute, *Proceedings from the Seminar on Ecology and Religion,* p. 73.

36. Oscar Wilde, *An Ideal Husband,* Act II (1895).

37. Attributed to Andy Stahl of the Sierra Club. Taken off the Internet: http://www.aloha.net.

38. Joan Biskupic, "High Court Hears Landowners Assert Rights Under Species Act; Justices to Rule Whether Economic Loss Gives Rise to Suit," *Washington Post,* November 14, 1996, p. A2.

39. Statement of David G. Cameron before the U.S. House of Representatives, House Resources Committee, Task Force on Private Property, *Hearings,* July 17, 1995.

40. Statement of Terri Moffet before the U.S. House of Representatives, House Resources Committee, Task Force on Private Property, *Hearings,* June 13, 1995.

Chapter 7: Wetlands

1. Defenders of Property Rights, *Property Rights Reporter,* 1, no. 4 (Fall 1994), 2, no. 3 (Summer 1995).

2. Leovy v. United States, 177 U.S. 621, 636 (1900).

3. Statement of Donald D. Etler before the Senate Committee on Agriculture, Nutrition, and Forestry, *Hearings on Conservation, Wetlands and Farm Policy,* pp. 1–2.

4. Winston Harrington, "Wildlife: Severe Decline and Partial Recovery," in Kenneth D. Frederick and Roger A. Sedjo (eds.), *America's Renewable Resources: Historical Trends and Current Challenges,* pp. 205, 207.

5. U.S. Department of the Interior, *The Impact of Federal Programs on Wetlands,* 1:1.

6. Ibid.

7. Ibid., 2:281.

8. Virginia S. Albrecht and Bernard N. Goode, "All Is Not Well with Section 404," *National Wetlands Newsletter* (March–April 1996): 14, 15.

9. National Research Council, Committee on Characterization of Wetlands, *Wetlands: Characteristics and Boundaries,* p. 253.

10. Robert Langreth, "Altered Weeds Eat Mercury Particles in Lab Experiments on Toxic Waste," *Wall Street Journal,* April 17, 1996, p. B7.

11. Statement of James S. Burling before the U.S. Senate, Committee on Public Works, *Hearings on S.851, The Wetlands Regulatory Reform Act of 1995,* November 1, 1995, pp. 9–11.

12. Craig E. Richardson and Geoff C. Ziebart, *Red Tape in America,* pp. 35–36.

13. National Research Council, *Wetlands,* pp. 243–255.

14. Robert J. Pierce, "Redefining Our Regulatory Goals," *National Wetlands Newsletter* (November–December 1991): 12.
15. Defenders of Property Rights, *Property Rights Reporter* 2, no. 4 (Fall 1995): 3.
16. Statement of Bernard N. Goode before the U.S. Senate, Committee on Environment and Public Works, Subcommittee on Clean Air, Wetlands, Private Property, and Nuclear Safety, *Hearings*, July 19, 1995, p. 4.
17. White House Office on Environmental Policy, *Protecting America's Wetlands: A Fair, Flexible, and Effective Approach*, p. 12.
18. Council on Environmental Quality, *Environmental Quality: Twenty-Fourth Annual Report (for the Year 1993)*, p. 102.
19. Margaret N. Strand, "Federal Wetlands Law," pp. 1, 82.
20. 33 Code of Federal Regulations Part 330 App. A.
21. Virginia S. Albrecht and Bernard N. Goode, *Wetland Regulation in the Real World*. See also their "All Is Not Well with Section 404," p. 14.
22. 40 Code of Federal Regulations 230.10(a)(2).
23. Jonathan Tolman, "A Sign of the Times," *Wall Street Journal*, September 20, 1994, p. A22.
24. Jonathan Tolman, *Gaining More Ground: Analysis of Wetlands Trends in the United States*, p. 3.
25. Ibid. The figures for 1995 were given to me by Tolman in a personal communication.
26. *Statistical Abstract of the United States* (115th ed., 1995), Table 1101.
27. Environmental Law Institute, *Wetlands Deskbook*, pp. 386–399.

Chapter 8: The National Commons

1. Michael Williams, *Americans and Their Forests*, pp. 396–397 (railroad story); Editorial, *Wall Street Journal*, January 24, 1996, p. A12 (quoting Majority Leader Robert Dole).
2. Richard L Stroup, "Hazardous Waste Policy: A Property Rights Perspective," pp. 868, 869.
3. Williams, *Americans and Their Forests*, pp. 114–115, 133–134.
4. John A. Lynn, "The History of Logistics and *Supplying War*," in John A. Lynn (ed.), *Feeding Mars*, pp. 9, 19.
5. Williams, *Americans and Their Forests*, p. 132.
6. Charles F. Wilkinson, *Crossing the Next Meridian: Land, Water, and the Future of the American West*, p. 91.
7. George Will, "What Price Liquor?" *Washington Post*, September 16, 1996, p. A29.
8. David Herbert Donald, *Lincoln*, pp. 154–155.
9. Vernon Carstensen (ed.), *The Public Lands*, pp. 122–181.
10. Alston Chase, *In a Dark Wood*, p. 20.

Chapter 9: Grass, Timber, Ore—and Backpackers

1. *Shane* (Paramount Pictures, 1953; screenplay by A. B. Guthrie). Novel by Jack Schaefer (Boston: Houghton Mifflin, 1949). (Note to trivia buffs: This dialogue is not in the novel. It must have been added to the movie version by the screenwriter, A. B. Guthrie, who wrote *The Big Sky* and other novels and is perhaps the finest depicter of the Old West.)
2. Bernard DeVoto, Introduction to Wallace Stegner, *Beyond the Hundredth Meridian*, pp. xv, xxi–xxii.
3. Stegner, *Beyond the Hundredth Meridian*, p. 220.

4. Karl Hess, Jr., *Visions upon the Land*, p. 58; Robert G. Athearn, *Union Pacific Country*, pp. 187–193.

5. Stegner, *Beyond the Hundredth Meridian*, p. 221.

6. Kirk Johnson, "Where a Zoning Law Failed, Seeds of a New York Revival," *New York Times*, April 21, 1996, p. A1.

7. The cost of fencing is analyzed in Clarence H. Danhof, "Farm-Making Costs and the 'Safety Valve'": 1850–1860, *Journal of Political Economy* 49 (1941): 317–359, reprinted in Vernon Carstensen (ed.), *The Public Lands*, pp. 253, 264–267.

8. Hess, *Visions upon the Land*, p. 61.

9. Hess, *Visions upon the Land*, p. 157.

10. *Evergreen Digest* 1, no. 1 (April 1996): 2.

11. "The Forest Products Industry and Idaho's Economics Base," *Evergreen Magazine* (March–April 1996): 16, 17.

12. Estimated from figures and maps in Michael Williams, *Americans and Their Forests*, pp. 433–440, and *Statistical Abstract* (115th ed., 1995), Table 1148.

13. Williams, *Americans and Their Forests*, p. 217.

14. Ibid., p. 418.

15. Professor Lewis Hendricks (University of Minnesota), quoted in William Souder, "30,000 Logs Under the Sea," *Washington Post*, August 14, 1996, pp. A1, A12.

16. Alston Chase, *In a Dark Wood*, pp. 13–24.

17. U.S. GAO, *Information on the Acreage, Management, and Use of Federal and Other Lands*.

18. Ian Fisher, "Clinton Says the Protection of Sterling Forest Is a Priority," *New York Times*, April 23, 1996, p. B5.

19. National Commission on Wildfire Disasters, *Report* pp. 10–12.

20. George Johnson, "In Sick, Crowded Ponderosa Forests of West, Seeds of Infernos Lie Ominously in Wait," *New York Times*, May 11, 1996, p. 7; Tom Kenworthy, "Wildfires Rekindle Debate on What's Best for Forests; Some See Flames as Restoring Equilibrium," *Washington Post*, September 2, 1996, p. A10; James Brooke, "Western Wildfires Near Record Season: Total Suppression Policy of 1960's Has Led to Big Buildup of Fuel," *New York Times*, October 24, 1996, p. A16.

21. Nancy Langston, *Forest Dreams, Forest Nightmares*, p. 39.

22. John L. Dobra, "Reform of the 1872 Mining Law: A Primer," Anderson, *Multiple Conflicts*, pp. 35, 40.

23. Richard Gordon, *Mining Law*.

24. Norris Hundley, Jr., *The Great Thirst: Californians and Water, 1770's–1990's*, pp. 76–77.

25. Mineral Policy Center, *Burden of Gilt*, p. 27.

26. Samuel Western, "A Man, a Mine, and a 29-Year Battle With Interior," *Wall Street Journal*, July 31, 1996, p. A15.

27. James Brooke, "Mining Companies Increasingly Look Abroad," *New York Times*, August 13, 1996, p. A10.

28. "This Land Is Your Land," *Popular Science* (December 1993): 9.

29. Donald L. Snyder et al., *Wilderness Designation in Utah: Issues and Potential Economics Impacts*, p. 76.

Chapter 10: Waterless World

1. Terry L. Anderson, "Water Options for the Blue Planet," in Ronald Bailey (ed.), *The True State of the Planet*, pp. 267, 283.
2. John D. Leshy, "Sharing Federal Multiple Use Lands," In Sterling Brubaker (ed.), *Rethinking the Federal Lands*, pp. 235, 258.
3. Marc Reisner, *Cadillac Desert*, p. 111.
4. Wallace Stegner, *Beyond the Hundredth Meridian*, pp. 322–323, 343.
5. Reisner, *Cadillac Desert*, pp. 240, 340.
6. Kenneth D. Frederick, "Water Resources: Increasing Demand and Scarce Supplies," in Kenneth D. Frederick and Roger A. Sedjo (eds.), *America's Renewable Resources: Historical Trends and Current Challenges*, pp. 23, 73; *Statistical Abstract of the United States* (1995), Table 1103.
7. Reisner, *Cadillac Desert*, pp. 324–328.
8. Ibid., p. 147.
9. Richard W. Wahl, *Markets for Federal Water: Subsidies, Property Rights, and the Bureau of Reclamation*, p. 38.
10. B. Delworth Gardner, *Plowing Ground in Washington*, p. 296.
11. Reisner, *Cadillac Desert*, p. 171.
12. Robert S. Devine, "The Trouble with Dams," pp. 66–68.
13. Ibid., pp. 64, 74.
14. Gardner, *Plowing Ground*, p. 298.
15. Anderson, "Water Options," p. 280.
16. This description is drawn from David Getches, Report to the Northwest Planning Council, and from various issues of the *Northwest Fishletter*, available at Internet http://www.newsdata.com.
17. David H. Getches, *Report to the Northwest Power Planning Council from the Workshop on Fish and Wildlife Governance*, p. 1.

Chapter 11: Sorting It Out

1. Donald R. Leal, "Making Money on Timber Sales: A Federal and State Comparison," in Terry L. Anderson, *Multiple Conflicts over Multiple Use*, pp. 17, 29.
2. Donald L. Snyder et al., *Wilderness Designation in Utah: Issues and Potential Economic Impacts*, pp. 71–88.
3. Marc Reisner, *Cadillac Desert*, p. 512.
4. Al Kamen, "Floodgate," *Washington Post*, March 8, 1996, p. A19.
5. See particularly the series of books edited by Terry Anderson that are listed in the Bibliography.
6. James Brooke, "Bird-Watchers Keep Eye on Politics," *New York Times*, April 5, 1996, p. A16.

Chapter 12: Land Use and Zoning

1. Richard F. Babcock and Charles L. Siemon, *The Zoning Game Revisited*, p. 256.
2. William A. Fischel, *Regulatory Takings*, p. 282.
3. Babcock and Siemon, *The Zoning Game Revisited*, p. 257.

4. Fischel, *Regulatory Takings*, p. 285.
5. Steve Twomey, "New Cause to Shutter," *Washington Post*, June 3, 1996, p. D1.
6. Kenneth Harney, "Home Buyers Want Modern Towns with Lots of Old-Fashioned Charm," *Washington Post*, June 1, 1996, p. F1.
7. Stephen C. Fehr, "Town House Debate Hits Many People Where They Live," *Washington Post*, February 18, 1996, p. A1.
8. Richard Babcock, *The Zoning Game*, p. 19.
9. Peter Pae, "Loudon to Study Extending Water, Sewer Lines to West," *Washington Post*, April 11, 1996, p. B1.
10. Todd Shields, "Calvert Board Curbs Development in South," *Washington Post*, August 24, 1996, p. C5; Jackie Spinner, "Calvert to Tighten Enforcement of Existing Regulations to Control Growth," *Washington Post*, March 17, 1996, p. B5.
11. Jackie Spinner, "Calvert County Stays Thrifty in Prosperity: Luck, Skill Underpin Healthy Cash Flow," *Washington Post*, March 10, 1996, p. B1; Todd Shields, "Nuclear Plant Warms Wallets, Surge in Work Force Is a Boon to Calvert," *Washington Post*, June 6, 1996, p. B1.
12. *Statistical Abstract of the United States* 1995 (115th ed.), Tables 355, 365.
13. Nollan v. California Costal Commission, 483 U.S. 825 (1987).
14. Dolan v. City of Tigard, 114 S. Ct. 2309 (1994).
15. Minutes of the Regular Meeting of the Marin Count Board of Supervisors Held Tuesday, January 23, 1996, at 9:02 A.M., available on the Internet; David Rolland, series of stories for the *Point Reyes Light*, available on the Internet.
16. Michael Janofsky, "Protesters Fight a Plan for Washington's Home," *New York Times*, March 13, 1996, p. A12; Jonathan Yardley, "Preservationists Are Barking Up the Wrong Cherry Tree," *Washington Post*, March 18, 1996, p. D2; Maryann Hagerty, "Stafford County Panel Rejects Wal-Mart Plan," *Washington Post*, April 2, 1996, p. E3; Maryann Hagerty, "Wal-Mart Retreats on Historic Site," *Washington Post*, July 2, 1996, p. C1.
17. Fischel, *Regulatory Takings*, p. 353.
18. Lucus v. South Carolina Coastal Council, 505 U.S. 1003 (1992).
19. Noritmitsu Onishi, "Sand and Surf, Unspoiled by Crowds: Parking Bans Keep Two Queens Beaches Clear of Outsiders," *New York Times*, August 24, 1996, p. 25.
20. Timothy Egan, "Jet Skis vs. Peace on Islands in Battle of San Juan County," *New York Times*, March 16, 1996, p. 6; Lesley Hazleton, "Weekend Getaways: Three by the Sea," *New York Times*, June 9, 1996, Sec. 5, p. 1; Michael J. McCarthy, "From Sea to Shining Sea, Water Bikes Make Big Waves with Safety Authorities," *Wall Street Journal*, June 21, 1996, p. B1; M. L. Lyke, "Islands of Calm; A Jet-Ski Ban Yields Silence, at Least for Now," *Washington Post*, June 22, 1996, p. A1.
21. Defenders of Property Rights, *Property Rights Reporter*, 3, no. 3 (May–June 1996): 1.
22. Stephen Fehr and Eric Lipton. "Area Leaders Frustrated by Anti-Growth Revival: Residents Adept at Stopping Big Projects," *Washington Post*, May 27, 1996, p. B1.
23. Bob Ortega, "Urban Mecca: Portland, Oregon, Shows Nation's City Planners How to Guide Growth; Crucial Factor in Its Success Is a Regional Approach, Especially to Land Use; Suburban Sprawl Lingers On," *Wall Street Journal*, December 26, 1995, p. A1.
24. Babcock, *The Zoning Game*, pp. 168–173.

25. Linda Wheeler, "Gardens, Bitter and Sweet, Tenants Lament Plot's Demise," *Washington Post*, April 18, 1996, District Weekly section, p. 1.

26. Herbert Inhaber, "A Market-Based Solution to the Problem of Nuclear and Toxic Waste Disposal," p. 808; James V. DeLong, *Privatizing Superfund: How to Clean Up Hazardous Waste*, pp. 37–51.

27. Editors of *Consumer Reports*, "If the Boots Fit . . . ," *Washington Post*, June 3, 1996, p. B5.

28. *Statistical Abstract of the United States* (115th ed., 1995), Table 398.

29. Ibid., Tables 398, 417.

30. Marc Reisner, *Cadillac Desert*, p. 510.

31. Valerie Reitman, "Designer Potholes: Japanese Gladly Pay for a Bumpy Ride," *Wall Street Journal*, September 5, 1995, p. A1.

Chapter 13: The Quick Tour

1. Robert V. Pambianco (ed.), *The National Trust for Historic Preservation*, p. 1.

2. William A. Fischel, *Regulatory Takings*, p. 51.

3. Paul W. Valentine, "Church-State Twist: Maryland City Fights to Save Old Monastery," *Washington Post*, April 9, 1996, p. D1; Paul W. Valentine, "Maryland City Wins Round in Battle to Block Razing of Monastery," *Washington Post*, June 14, 1996, p. B3; B. Drummond Ayres, Jr., "A Cathedral Controversy May Define Los Angeles," *New York Times*, June 17, 1996, p. A10; "Cathedral Reprieved by California Judge," *New York Times*, June 21, 1996, p. A16; Bruce Fein, "Religious Freedom vs. State Authority: Federalism Under Siege," *Washington Times*, October 22, 1996, p. A14.

4. Penn Central Transportation Co. v. New York City, 438 U.S. 104 (1978).

5. "In Chicago, Law Speeds the Saving of History," *New York Times*, May 26, 1996, p. 13.

6. Richard Bernstein, "Critics Say Details Entrap Landmarks Panel," *New York Times*, April 28, 1993, p. A1.

7. Quoted in Donald L. Snyder et al., *Wilderness Designation in Utah: Issues and Potential Economic Impacts*, p. 13 (no reference given).

8. Fischel, *Regulatory Takings*, p. 329.

9. Constance E. Beaumont, *How Superstore Sprawl Can Harm Communities (and What Citizens Can Do About It)*.

10. "A Rails-to-Trails Network for Hikers and Bikers Pumps Up Its Tourism Muscle," *Wall Street Journal*, March 14, 1996, p. A1.

11. "Real Estate Notes, Open Space Survey," *Washington Post*, August 12, 1996, p. E11.

12. Timothy Aeppel, "Angry Landowners Turn Public Paths into Unhappy Trails: Feuds over Former Railways Split Many Communities; Ride Around Cornfield," *Wall Street Journal*, October 16, 1995, p. A1.

13. Richard Welsh (NARPO), untitled paper on the Internet, January 1, 1996 http://www.halcyon.com/dick/row.html.

14. William Grimes, "Court Rejects Sculptors' Case," *New York Times*, December 2, 1995, p. 13.

15. "City as Canvas," *Washington Post*, September 26, 1996, District Weekly section, p. 1.

16. Martha Cooper and Henry Chalfant, *Subway Art*, p. 6.

17. Gary Younge, "The Pilgrimage of Paint: New York Draw Foreign Graffiti Artists," *Washington Post*, September 4, 1996, p. A3.

18. Terry L. Anderson and Dean Lueck, "Agricultural Development and Land Tenure in Indian Country," in Terry L. Anderson (ed.), *Property Rights and Indian Economics,* pp. 147, 163.
19. The California and Florida stories are documented extensively in Roger Pillon, "Can American Asset Forfeiture Law Be Justified?" pp. 317–318. The motel story was told to me by an observer. For more, see Leonard W. Levy, *A License to Steal.*
20. Linda A. Malone, *Environmental Regulation of Land Use,* pp. 3–15.
21. Eric Lipton, "A Man with a Grave Mission, Fairfax Librarian Tracks Down Forgotten Cemeteries," *Washington Post,* April 30, 1995, p. B1.
22. *Bartlett's Familiar Quotations* (15th ed., 1980), p. 703. I associate the addendum with the eminent historian Crane Brinton, who taught for many years at Harvard University, but I have never been able to pin this down.

Chapter 14: Legal Issues.

1. William A. Fischel, *Regulatory Takings,* p. 87.
2. Webbs Fabulous Pharmacies, Inc. v. Beckwith, 499 U.S. 155, 161 (1980), quoting Board of Regents v. Roth, 408 U.S. 564, 577 (1972).
3. PruneYard Shopping Center v. Robins, 447 U.S. 74, 82 n. 5 (1980), quoting United States v. General Motors, 323 U.S. 373, 377–378 (1945).
4. Nollan v. California Coastal Commission, 483 U.S. 825 (1987).
5. Jed Rubenfeld, "Usings," pp. 1077, 1082.
6. Pennsylvania Coal Co. v. Mahon, 260 U.S. 393 (1922).
7. Lynch v. Household Finance Corp., 405 U.S. 538, 552 (1972).
8. Penn Central Transportation Co. v. City of New York, 438 U.S. 104 (1978).
9. First English Evangelical Lutheran Church of Glendale v. County of Los Angeles, 482 U.S. 304 (1987); Nollan v. California Coastal Commission, 483 U.S. 825 (1987).
10. Fischel, *Regulatory Takings,* p. 318.
11. Lucas v. South Carolina Coastal Council, 505 U.S. 1003, (1992).
12. Kaiser Aetna v. United States, 444 U.S. 164 (1979); PruneYard Shopping Center v. Robins, 447 U.S. 74 (1980); Nollan v. California Coastal Commission, 483 U.S. 825 (1987); Dolan v. City of Tigard, 114 S. Ct. 2309 (1994).
13. Hage v. United States, No. 91–1470L (Court of Federal Claims, March 8, 1996).
14. This information was given to me by one of the participants.
15. Statement of David Lucas, in National Policy Forum, *Private Property Rights,* p. 24.
16. *The Federalist,* No. 51, p. 356.
17. Gideon Kanner, "Not with a Bang, But a Giggle: The Settlement of the Lucas Case," pp. 5–7.
18. Gregory Overstreet, "The Ripeness Doctrine of the Taking Clause: A Survey of Decisions Showing Just How Far Federal Courts Will Go to Avoid Adjudicating Land Use Cases," pp. 1, 3.
19. Peter Brunner, "Dolan v. Tigard Reaffirms Cynicism."
20. San Diego Gas & Electric v. City of San Diego, 450 U.S. 621, 656 n. 22 (1981) (Brennan, J., dissenting).
21. Fischel, *Regulatory Takings,* p. 233.
22. Hage v. United States, pp. 31–32.

23. American Resources, Summary of State Takings Legislation.

24. Loren Smith, Introduction to Roger Clegg et al., *Regulatory Takings: Restoring Private Property Rights*, pp. 1, 3.

Chapter 15: Matters of the Mind

1. Lisa Bannon, "The Birds May Sing, But Campers Can't Unless They Pay Up; ASCAP Warns the Girl Scouts That 'God Bless America' Can Hit Legal Sour Notes," *Wall Street Journal*, August 21, 1996, p. A1; Ken Ringle, "Campfire Churls; Publishing Group Seeks Royalties from Sing-Alongs," *Washington Post*, August 24, 1996, p. B1; Ken Ringle, "AS-CAP Changes Its Tune; Never Intended to Collect Fees for Scouts' Campfire Songs, Group Says," *Washington Post*, August 28, 1996, p. C3; ASCAP (advertisement), "Girl Scouts Threatened by ASCAP? Absurd!" *New York Times*, September 1, 1996, p. E9; ASCAP (advertisement), "Girl Scouts Threatened by ASCAP? Absurd!" *Washington Post*, September 4, 1996, p. A12.

2. Paul Goldstein, *Copyright's Highway*, pp. 162–164.

3. Steven Mufson, "In Fight for Intellectual Rights in China, Pirates Still Winning," *Washington Post*, February 18, 1996, p. A29; David E. Sanger, "Chinese Pirate Factories Have Roots Abroad, U.S. Study Says," *New York Times*, June 3, 1996, p. D1.

4. Barbara Carton, "Farmers Begin Harvesting Satellite Data to Boost Yields: GPS Technology Can Micromanage Fields Right Down to the Thistle Patch," *Wall Street Journal*, July 11, 1996, p. B4.

5. American Petroleum Institute, ATM Research and Industrial Enterprise Study (ARIES), press release and attachments, February 23, 1996.

6. See James P. Womack, Daniel T. Jones, and Daniel Roos, *The Machine That Changed the World*.

7. John Holusha, "Making the Shoe Fit, Perfectly: Custom Footwear by Computer at Off-the-Rack Prices," *New York Times*, March 20, 1996, p. D1.

8. Joel Mokyr, *The Lever of Riches*, pp. 33–36.

9. U.S. Information Infrastructure Task Force, *Intellectual Property and the National Information Infrastructure*, p. 160.

10. Baker v. Seldon, 101 U.S. 99 (1879).

11. Lotus Development Corp. v. Borland International, Inc., 49 F.3d 807 (1st Cir. 1995), *aff'd by an equally divided court*, 116 S. Ct. 804 (1996).

12. James Gleick, "I'll Take the Money, Thanks," *New York Times Magazine*, August 4, 1996, p. 16.

13. Michael Siconolfi, "The Outsider: Did Smith Barney Cheat a Stockbroker to Clinch a Merger? Mr. Inman Claims Firm Stole His Finance Ideas to Save Viacom-Paramount Deal," *Wall Street Journal*, August 8, 1996, p. A1.

14. Leslie Wayne, "Once Again, a Cozy Deal Leads to Court: Yet Another Corruption Trial Involving Municipal Bonds," *New York Times*, July 10, 1996, p. D1; Leslie Wayne, "Former Partner at Lazard Freres Is Guilty in Municipal Bond Case," *New York Times*, August 10, 1996, p. A1.

15. James Boyle, *Shamans, Software, and Spleens*, pp. 21–24.

16. Tamar Lewis, "Move to Patent Cancer Gene Touches Off Storm of Protest," *New York Times*, May 21, 1996, p. A14.

17. Eric Lipton, "Turning Point for Traffic Tie-Ups: Planners Have Some Newfangled Notions for the Area's Congested Intersections," *Washington Post*, November 26, 1995, p. B1.
18. Virginia Postrel, "On the Frontier: An Interview with Esther Dyson," *Reason* 28, no. 5 (October 1996): 28, 30.

Chapter 16: Confused Alarms

1. William Poundstone, *Prisoner's Dilemma*, p. 9.
2. John P. Powelson, *The Story of Land*, p. x.

Bibliography

BOOKS

Adler, Jonathan. *Environmentalism at the Crossroads*. Washington, DC: Capital Research Center, 1995.

Alford, William P. *To Steal a Book Is an Elegant Offense: Intellectual Property Law in Chinese Civilization*. Stanford: Stanford University Press, 1995.

Altshuler, Alan A., and José A. Gomez-Ibanez. *Regulation for Revenue*. Washington, DC: Brookings Institution, 1993.

American Indian Lawyer Training Program. *Indian Tribes as Sovereign Governments: A Sourcebook on Federal-Tribal History, Law, and Policy*. Oakland: American Indian Resources Institute Press, 1988.

Anderson, Terry L. (ed.). *Continental Water Marketing*. San Francisco: Pacific Research Institute, 1994.

———. *Multiple Conflicts over Multiple Uses*. Bozeman, MT: Political Economy Research Center, 1994.

———. *Property Rights and Indian Economies*. Lanham, MD: Rowman & Littlefield, 1992.

Anderson, Terry L., and Peter J. Hill (eds.). *The Political Economy of the American West*. Lanham, MD: Rowman & Littlefield, 1994.

———. *Wildlife in the Marketplace*, Lanham, MD: Rowman & Littlefield, 1995.

Anderson, Terry L, and Donald R. Leal. *Free Market Environmentalism*. San Francisco: Pacific Research Institute, 1991.

Anderson, Terry L., and Randy T. Simmons (eds.). *The Political Economy of Customs and Culture*. Lanham, MD: Rowman & Littlefield, 1993.

Athearn, Robert G. *Union Pacific Country*. Lincoln, NE: University of Nebraska Press, 1971.

Avery, Dennis T. *Saving the Planet with Pesticides and Plastic*. Indianapolis: Hudson Institute, 1995.

Axelrod, Robert. *The Evolution of Cooperation*. New York: Basic Books, 1984.

Babcock, Richard F. *The Zoning Game: Municipal Practices and Policies*. Madison: University of Wisconsin, 1966.

Babcock, Richard F., and Charles L. Siemon. *The Zoning Game Revisited*. Cambridge, MA: Lincoln Institute of Land Policy, 1985.

Bailey, Ronald. *Ecoscam: The False Prophets of Ecological Apocalypse.* New York: St. Martin's Press, 1993.

Bailey, Ronald (ed.). *The True State of the Planet.* New York: Free Press, 1995.

Beck, Warren A. and Ynez D. Haase. *Historical Atlas of the American West.* Norman, OK: University of Oklahoma Press, 1989.

Blackburn, Thomas C., and Kat Anderson. *Before the Wilderness: Environmental Management by Native Californians.* Menlo Park, CA: Ballena Press, 1993.

Bolt, Robert. *A Man for All Seasons.* New York: Vintage, 1990.

Bovard, James. *The Farm Fiasco.* San Francisco: ICS Press, 1991.

———. *Lost Rights: The Destruction of American Liberty.* New York: St. Martin's Press, 1994.

———. *Shakedown: How the Government Screws You from A to Z.* New York: Viking Press, 1995.

Boyle, James. *Shamans, Software, and Spleens: Law and the Construction of the Information Society.* Cambridge, MA: Harvard University Press, 1996.

Brenton, Tony. *The Greening of Machiavelli: The Evolution of International Environmental Policies.* London: Earthscan, 1994.

Brubaker, Elizabeth. *Property Rights in the Defense of Nature.* London: Earthscan, 1995.

Brubaker, Sterling (ed.). *Rethinking the Federal Lands.* Washington, DC: Resources for the Future, 1984.

Brush, Stephen B., and Doreen Stabinsky (eds.). *Valuing Local Knowledge: Indigenous People and Intellectual Property Rights.* Washington, DC: Island Press, 1996.

Budiansky, Stephen. *Nature's Keepers: The New Science of Nature Management.* New York: Free Press, 1995.

Cantor, Norman F. *The Civilization of the Middle Ages.* New York: HarperCollins, 1993.

Carstensen, Vernon (ed.). *The Public Lands: Studies in the History of the Public Domain.* Madison: University of Wisconsin Press, 1963.

Chase, Alston. *In a Dark Wood: The Fight over Forests and the Rising Tyranny of Ecology.* Boston: Houghton Mifflin, 1995.

———. *Playing God in Yellowstone: The Destruction of America's First National Park.* New York: Harcourt Brace, 1987.

Clawson, Marion. *The Federal Lands Revisited.* Washington, DC: Resources for the Future, 1983.

Coase, R. H. *The Firm, the Market, and the Law.* Chicago: University of Chicago Press, 1988.

Cooper, Martha, and Henry Chalfant. *Subway Art.* London: Thames & Hudson, 1984.

Council on Environmental Quality. *Environmental Quality: Twenty-Fourth Annual Report* [for 1993] Washington, DC: GPO, n.d.

Deal, Carl. *The Greenpeace Guide to Anti-Environmental Organizations.* Berkeley, CA: Odonian Press 1993.

DeLong, Brad. *4-Wheel Freedom: The Art of Off-Road Driving.* Boulder, CO: Palladin Press, 1996.

DeLong J. Bradford. "Slouching Towards Utopia? The Economic History of the 20th Century." Unpublished manuscript draft, September 1996.

Devall, Bill, and George Sessions. *Deep Ecology: Living as if Nature Mattered.* Salt Lake City: Peregrine Smith Books, 1985.

Diehl, Janet, and Thomas S. Barrett. *The Conservation Easement Handbook: Managing Land Conservation and Historic Preservation Easement Programs.* Cambridge, MA: Land Trust Alliance, 1988.

Donald, David Herbert. *Lincoln.* New York: Simon & Schuster, 1995.

Dorn, James A., and Henry G. Manne (eds.). *Economic Liberties and the Judiciary.* Fairfax, VA: George Mason University Press, 1987.

Dreicer, Gregory K. (ed.). *Between Fences: National Building Museum Exhibition Catalog.* Washington, DC, and New York: National Building Museum and Princeton Architectural Press, 1996.

Eagle, Steven J. *Regulatory Takings.* Charlottesville, VA: Mitchie, 1996.

Echeverria, John, and Raymond Booth Eby. *Let the People Judge: Wise Use and the Private Property Rights Movement.* Washington, DC: Island Press 1995.

Ely, James. W., Jr. *The Guardian of Every Other Right: A Constitutional History of Property Rights.* New York: Oxford University Press, 1992.

Endicott, Eve (ed.). *Land Conservation Through Public/Private Partnerships.* Washington, DC: Island Press, 1993.

Environmental Law Institute. *Wetlands Deskbook.* Washington, DC: Environmental Law Institute, 1993.

Epstein, Richard E. *Simple Rules for a Complex World.* Cambridge, MA: Harvard University Press, 1995.

———. *Takings: Private Property and the Power of Eminent Domain.* Cambridge, MA: Harvard University Press, 1985.

Farber, Daniel A., and Philip P. Frickey. *Law and Public Choice: A Critical Introduction.* Chicago: University of Chicago Press, 1991.

The Federalist Papers. Edited by B. Wright. 1961.

Fischel, William A. *Regulatory Takings: Law, Economics, and Politics.* Cambridge, MA: Harvard University Press, 1995.

Frederick, Kenneth D., and Roger A. Sedjo (eds). *America's Renewable Resources: Historical Trends and Current Challenges.* Washington, DC: Resources for the Future, 1991.

Friedman, Lawrence M. *History of American Law.* 2d ed. New York: Simon & Schuster, 1985.

Gardner, B. Delworth. *Plowing Ground in Washington: The Political Economy of U.S. Agriculture.* San Francisco: Pacific Research Institute, 1995.

Gassman, Lawrence. *Telecompetition: The Free Market Road to the Information Highway.* Washington, DC: Cato Institute, 1994.

George, Henry. *Progress and Poverty.* New York: Robert Schalkenbach Foundation, 1992 (orginally published in 1879).

Getches, David. *Water Law in a Nutshell.* 2d ed. Minneapolis: West Publishing Co., 1990.

Glendon, Mary Ann. *A Nation Under Lawyers: How the Crisis in the Legal Profession Is Transforming American Society.* Cambridge, MA: Harvard University Press, 1994.

Goldstein, Paul. *Copyright's Highway: The Law and Lore of Copyright from Gutenberg to the Celestial Jukebox.* New York: Hill & Wang, 1994.

Greater Yellowstone Coalition. *Sustaining Greater Yellowstone, a Blueprint for the Future.* Bozeman, MT: The Coalition, 1994.

Gwartney, James D., and Richard L Stroup. *What Everyone Should Know About Economics and Prosperity.* Bozeman: MT: Political Economy Research Center, 1993.

Hardin, Garrett, and John Baden (eds.). *Managing the Commons.* San Francisco: W. H. Freeman, 1977.

Heckel, Paul. *The Elements of Friendly Software Design.* 2d ed. San Francisco: Sybex, 1991.

Hess, Karl, Jr. *Visions upon the Land: Man and Nature on the Western Range.* Washington, DC: Island Press, 1995.

Hibbard, Benjamin H. *A History of the Public Land Policies.* New York: Peter Smith, 1939.

Holmes, Oliver Wendell, Jr. *The Common Law.* Boston: Little, Brown, 1963 (originally published in 1881).

Hundley, Norris, Jr. *The Great Thirst: Californians and Water, 1770's–1990's.* Berkeley: University of California Press, 1992.

Hyde, Henry. *Forfeiting Our Property Rights: Is Your Property Safe from Seizure?* Washington, DC: Cato Institute, 1995.

Jansen, Robert B. *Dams and Public Safety: A Water Resources Technical Publication.* Washington, DC: U.S. Department of the Interior, Bureau of Reclamation, 1983.

Ladd, Everett Carll, and Karlyn H. Bowman. *Attitudes Toward the Environment.* Washington, DC: American Enterprise Institute, 1995.

Langston, Nancy. *Forest Dreams, Forest Nightmares: The Paradox of Old Growth in the Inland West.* Seattle: University of Washington Press, 1995.

Levy, Leonard W. *License to Steal: The Forfeiture of Property.* Chapel Hill: University of North Carolina Press, 1996.

Locke, John. *Two Treatises of Government.* Edited by Peter Laslett. Cambridge: At the Press, 1960.

Ludlow, Peter (ed.). *High Noon on the Electronic Frontier: Conceptual Issues in Cyberspace.* Cambridge, MA: MIT Press, 1996.

Lynn, John A. (ed.). *Feeding Mars: Logistics in Western Warfare from the Middle Ages to the Present.* Boulder, CO: Westview Press, 1993.

Maczak, Antoni, and William N. Parker (eds.). *Natural Resources in European History: A Conference Report.* Washington DC: Resources for the Future, 1978.

Malone, Linda A. *Environmental Regulation of Land Use.* New York: Clark Boardman, 1991.

Mann, Charles C., and Mark L. Plummer. *Noah's Choice: The Future of Endangered Species.* New York: Knopf, 1995.

Martin, Albro. *Railroads Triumphant: The Growth, Rejection and Rebirth of Vital American Force.* New York: Oxford University Press, 1992.

McCallum, Henry D., and Frances T. McCallum. *The Wire That Fenced the West.* Norman, OK: University of Oklahoma Press, 1965.

Meiners, Roger E., and Bruce Yandle. *Taking the Environment Seriously.* Lanham, MD: Rowman & Littlefield, 1995.

Mokyr, Joel. *The Lever of Riches.* New York: Oxford University Press, 1990.

Nash, Gerald D. *The American West Transformed: The Impact of the Second World War.* Bloomington: Indiana University Press. 1985.

National Research Council, Committee on Characterization of Wetlands. *Wetlands: Characteristics and Boundaries.* Prepublication draft. Washington, DC: National Research Council, 1995.

Nedelsky, Jennifer. *Private Property and the Limits of American Constitutionalism.* Chicago: University of Chicago Press, 1990.

Nelson, Robert H. *Public Lands and Private Rights: The Failure of Scientific Management.* Lanham, MD: Rowman & Littlefield, 1995.

North, Douglass C. *Structure and Change in Economic History.* New York: Norton, 1981.

O'Laughlin, J., and P. S. Cook, with K. Rogers and T. Merrill. *Endangered Species Act at the Crossroads: New Directions from Idaho Case Studies.* Report 13, Policy Analysis Group.

Moscow, ID: College of Forestry, Wildlife and Range Sciences, University of Idaho, October 1995.

Pendley, William Perry. *It Takes a Hero: The Grassroots Battle Against Environmental Oppression*. Bellevue, WA: Free Enterprise Press, 1994.

————. *War on the West: Government Tyranny on America's Great Frontier*. Chicago: Regnery Publishing, 1995.

Pombo, Richard, and Joseph Farah. *This Land Is Our Land: How to End the War on Private Property*. New York: St. Martin's Press, 1996.

Poundstone, William. *Prisoner's Dilemma*. Garden City, NY: Doubleday, 1992.

Powelson, John P. *The Story of Land: A World History of Land Tenure and Agrarian Reform*. Cambridge, MA: Lincoln Institute of Land Policy, 1988.

Radin, Margaret Jane. *Reinterpreting Property*. Chicago: University of Chicago Press, 1993.

Reisner, Marc. *Cadillac Desert*. New York: Penguin, 1993.

Robinson, Nicholas A. *Environmental Regulation of Real Property*. New York: Law Journal Seminars-Press, 1994.

Rowley, Charles K. (ed.). *Property Rights and the Limits of Democracy*. Brookefield, VT: Edward Elgar, 1993.

Schama, Simon. *Landscape and Memory*. New York: Vintage Books, 1995.

Sessions, George (ed.). *Deep Ecology for the 21st Century: Readings on the Philosophy and Practice of the New Environmentalism*. Boston: Shambhala, 1995.

Siegan, Bernard H. *Economic Liberties and the Constitution*. Chicago: University of Chicago Press, 1980.

Simmons, A. John. *The Lockean Theory of Rights*. Princeton, NJ: Princeton University Press, 1992.

Snyder, Donald L., Christopher Fowson, E. Bruce Godfrey, and John Keith. *Wilderness Designation in Utah: Issues and Potential Impacts*. Research Report 51. Logan, UT: Utah Agricultural Experiment Station, Utah State University, January 1995.

Sreenivasan, Gopal. *The Limits of Lockean Rights to Property*. New York: Oxford University Press, 1995.

Stegner, Wallace. *Beyond the Hundredth Meridian: John Wesley Powell and the Second Opening of the West*. New York: Penguin, 1954.

Steinberg, Theodore. *Slide Mountain: On the Folly of Owning Nature*. Berkeley: University of California Press, 1995.

Thomas, Leri, and Alice Menks. *US vs NPS*. Privately printed by Alice Menks, P.O. Box 986, Madison, VA 22727, (703) 948-7165. n.d. (c. 1991).

Tucker, William. *Zoning, Rent Control and Affordable Housing*. Washington, DC: Cato Institute, 1991.

U.S. Department of Commerce, Bureau of the Census. *Historical Statistics of the United States: Colonial Times to 1970*. 2 vols. Washington, DC: GPO, 1975.

————. Bureau of the Census. *Statistical Abstract of the United States*, 115th ed. Published as *The American Almanac, 1995–1996*. Austin, TX: Reference Press, 1995.

U.S. Department of the Interior. *The Impact of Federal Programs on Wetlands*. 2 vols. Washington, DC: GPO, October 1988, March 1994.

U.S. Environmental Protection Agency, Office of Research and Development. *Ecological Risk Assessment Issue Papers*. EPA/630/R-94/009. Washington, DC: GPO, November 1994.

————. Office of Wastewater Management. *Constructed Wetlands for Wastewater Treatment and Wildlife Habitat: 17 Case Studies.* EPA832-R-93-005. Washington, DC: GPO, September 1993.

U.S. Information Infrastructure Task Force. *Intellectual Property and the National Information Infrastructure.* Report of the Working Group on Intellectual Property Rights. Washington, DC: GPO, September 1995.

Wahl, Richard W. *Markets for Federal Water: Subsidies, Property Rights, and the Bureau of Reclamation.* Washington, DC: Resources for the Future, 1989.

Walters, Timothy Robert. *Surviving the Second Civil War: The Land Rights Battle and How to Win it.* Safford, AZ: Rawhide Western Publishing, 1994.

Wildavsky, Aaron. *But Is It True? A Citizen's Guide to Environmental Health and Safety Issues.* Cambridge, MA: Harvard University Press, 1995.

Wilkinson, Charles F. *Crossing the Next Meridian: Land, Water, and the Future of the American West.* Washington, DC: Island Press, 1992.

Williams, Michael. *Americans and Their Forests: A Historical Geography.* Cambridge: At the Press, 1989.

Womack, James P., Daniel T. Jones, and Daniel Roos. *The Machine That Changed the World.* New York: Rawson Associates, 1990.

Wunderlich, Gene and W. L. Gibson, Jr. (eds.). *Perspectives of Property.* University Park, PA: Institute of Research on Land and Water Resources, Pennsylvania State University, 1972.

Yaffe, Steven Lewis. *The Wisdom of the Spotted Owl: Policy Lessons for a New Century.* Washington, DC: Island Press, 1994.

Yandle, Bruce (ed.). *Land Rights: The 1990's Property Rights Rebellion.* Lanham, MD: Rowman & Littlefield, 1995.

Zaslowsky, Dyan, and T. H. Watkins. *These American Lands: Parks, Wilderness, and the Public Lands.* Washington, DC: Island Press, 1994.

ARTICLES AND MONOGRAPHS

Adler, Jonathan. *Property Rights, Regulatory Takings, and Environmental Protection.* Washington, DC: Competitive Enterprise Institute, April 1996.

Albrecht, Virginia S., and Bernard N. Goode. *Wetland Regulation in the Real World.* Washington, DC: Privately printed by Beveridge & Diamond, 1994.

————. "All Is Not well with Section 404." *National Wetlands Newsletter* 18, no. 2 (March–April 1996): 14.

Altshuler, Alan. *The Governance of Urban Land: Critical Issues and Research Priorities.* Cambridge, MA: Lincoln Institute of Land Policy, 1994.

American Indian Digest. 1995 ed. *Contemporary Demographics of the American Indian.* Phoenix, AZ: Thunderbird Enterprises, 1994.

American Resources. *Summary of State Takings Legislation.* Internet: American Resources, April 23, 1996. (Internet www.arin.org/arin/state.html)

Andelson, Robert V., Robert A. Gilmour, and C. Lowell Harriss. *The Ethics of Land Use and the Ideas of Henry George.* Cambridge, MA: Lincoln Institute of Land Policy, 1994.

Anderson, Terry L. (ed.). *Reinventing Environmentalism in the New Era.* Bozeman, MT: Political Economy Research Center, February 1995.

Avery, Dennis T. *Biodiversity: Saving Species with Biotechnology.* Indianapolis, IN: Hudson Institute Executive Briefing, 1993.

Bator, Paul M. "What Is Wrong with the Supreme Court?" *University of Pittsburgh Law Review* 51 (1990): 673.

Bean, Michael J., and David S. Wilcove. "Ending the Impasse." *The Environmental Forum* 13, no. 4 (July–August 1996): 22.

Beaumont, Constance E. *How Superstore Sprawl Can Harm Communities (and What Citizens Can Do About It).* Washington, DC: National Trust for Historic Preservation, 1994.

Berger, Michael M. "News Flash: Property Owners Are Entitled to the Same Constitutional Protection as Nude Dancers and Draft Protestors." ABA meeting on Urban, State and Local Government Law, August 1994.

Bernard, Michael. *Transformation of Property Rights in the "Space Age."* Cambridge, MA: Lincoln Institute of Land Policy, 1994.

Bernstein, David. *Equal Protection for Economic Liberty: Is the Court Ready?* Policy Analysis 181. Washington, DC: Cato Institute, 1992.

Bordewich, Fergus M. "Revolution in Indian Country." *American Heritage* (August 1996): 34.

Bosselman, Fred. P. "Substantive Due Process and Regulatory Takings." ABA meeting on Urban, State and Local Government Law, August 1994.

Brinson, Mark M. *A Hydrogeomorphic Classification for Wetlands.* Washington, DC: U.S. Army Corps of Engineers, August 1993.

Brunner, Peter. "Dolan v. Tigard Reaffirms Cynicism." *The Gazette* 1996 (Internet http://www.opendoor.geez/Brunner)

Budiansky, Stephen. "Unpristine Nature." *American Enterprise* 6, no. 5 (September–October 1995): 64–67.

Burling, James S. "Property Rights, Endangered Species, Wetlands, and Other Critters—Is It Against Nature to Pay for a Taking?" *University of Wyoming College of Law, Land and Water Law Review* 27, no. 2 (1992): 312–362.

Burtraw, Dallas. "Compensating Losers When Cost-Effective Environmental Policies Are Adopted." *Resources* (Summer 1991): 1.

Call, David M. *Legislative Impairment of Contracts Between the State Water Project and Its Contractors.* San Francisco: Public Law Research Institute, Hastings College of Law, Fall 1994.

Callies, David. "'Rough Proportionality': Nexus Redux or Something Else?" ABA meeting on Urban, State and Local Government Law, August 1994.

Cato Policy Forum. "Property Rights and Environmental Protection." *Cato Policy Report* 14, no. 3 (May–June 1992): 6.

Clark, Lance R. and R. Neil Sampson. *Forest Ecosystem Health in the Inland West: A Science and Policy Reader.* Washington, DC: American Forests, 1995.

Clegg, Roger, Michael DeBow, Jerry Ellig, Nancie G. Marzulla, and Loren Smith. *Regulatory Takings: Restoring Private Property Rights.* Washington, DC: National Legal Center for the Public Interest, 1994.

Competitive Enterprise Institute. *Managing the Marine Commons: A Roundtable Discussion.* Washington, DC: Competitive Enterprise Institute, May 1995.

Conda, Cesar, and Mark D. LaRochelle. "The New Populism: The Rise of the Property Rights Movement." *Commonsense* 1 no. 4 (Fall 1994): 79.

————. *Property Rights Reader.* Washington, DC: Competitive Enterprise Institute, January 1995.

Dahl, T. E. *Wetlands Losses in United States, 1780's to 1980's.* Report to Congress. Washington, DC: U.S. Department of the Interior, Fish and Wildlife Service, 1990.

Dahl, T. E., and C. E. Johnson. *Status and Trends of Wetlands in the Coterminous United States, Mid-1970's to Mid-1980's.* Report to Congress. Washington, DC: U.S. Department of the Interior, Fish and Wildlife Service, 1991.

Davis, Andrew N., and Santo Longo. "Stigma Damages in Environmental Cases: Developing Issues and Implications for Industrial and Commercial Real Estate Transactions." *Environmental Law Reporter* 25 (1995): 10345.

Davis, Michael L. "A More Effective and Flexible Section 404." *National Wetlands Newsletter* 17 no. 4 (July–August 1995): 7.

DeAlessi, Michael. *Emerging Technologies and the Private Stewardship of Marine Resources.* Washington, DC: Competitive Enterprise Institute, January 1996.

DeLong, James V. *Privatizing Superfund: How to Clean Up Hazardous Waste.* Policy Analysis 247. Washington, DC: Cato Institute, December 18, 1995.

Denevan, William M. "The Pristine Myth: The Landscape of the Americas in 1492." *Annals of the Association of American Geographers* 82, no. 3 (September 1992): 369.

DeVault, John A. III. "Regulatory Takings: Can the Government Be Liable?" *Natural Resources and the Environment* (Summer 1991): 10.

Devine, Robert S. "The Trouble with Dams." *Atlantic* (August 1995): 64.

Dienstag, Joshua Doa. "Serving God and Mammon: The Lockean Sympathy in Early American Political Thought." *American Political Science Review* 90 (September 1996): 497.

Ellickson, Robert. "Property in Land." *Yale Law Journal* 102 (1993): 1315.

Elliott, Donald L. "Givings and Takings." *Land Use Law and Zoning Digest* 48, no. 1 (January 1996): 3.

Epstein, Richard A. "The Classical Legal Tradition." *Cornell Law Review* 73 (1988): 292.

————. "Covenants and Constitutions." *Cornell Law Review* 73 (1988): 906.

————. "The Harm Principle and How It Grew." *University of Toronto Law Journal* 45 (1995): 369.

————. "The Indivisibility of Liberty Under the Bill of Rights." *Harvard Journal of Law and Public Policy* 15 (1992): 35.

————. "International News Service v. Associated Press: Custom and Law as Sources of Property Rights in News." *Virginia Law Review* 78 (1992): 85.

————. "Justice Across the Generations." 67 *Texas Law Review* 67 (1989): 1465.

————. "Lucas v. South Carolina Coastal Council: A Tangled Web of Expectations." *Stanford Law Review* 45 (1993): 1411.

————. "Notice and Freedom of Contract in the Law of Servitudes." *Southern California Law Review* (1982): 1353.

————. *Organ Transplantation: Or, Altruism Run Amuck.* Occasional Paper 31. Chicago: University of Chicago Law School, 1993.

————. "The Path to the T. J. Hooper: The Theory and History of Custom in the Law of Tort." *Journal of Legal Studies* 21 (1992): 1.

————. "Possession as the Root of Title." *Georgia Law Review* 13 (1979): 1221.

————. "Property as a Fundamental Civil Right." *Cal-Western Law Review* 29 (1992): 187.

———. "Rent Control and the Theory of Efficient Regulation." *Brooklyn Law Review* 54 (1988): 741.

———. "Rent Control Revisited: One Reply to Seven Critics." *Brooklyn Law Review* 54 (1989): 1281.

———. "Takings: Of Private Property and Common." Washington, DC: American Enterprise Institute Conference, March 7, 1996.

———. "Two Fallacies in the Law of Joint Torts." *Georgetown Law Journal* 73 (1985): 1377.

———. "The Ubiquity of the Benefit Principle." *Southern California Review* 67 (1994): 1369.

———. "The Utilitarian Foundations of Natural Law." *Harvard Journal of Law and Public Policy* 12 (1989): 713.

———. "Why Restrain Alienation?" *Columbia Law Review* 85 (1985): 970.

Federal Geographic Data Committee. *Application of Satellite Data for Mapping and Monitoring Wetlands—Fact Finding Report*. Technical Report 1. Wetlands Subcommittee, FGDC. Washington, DC, 1992.

Firmin-Sellers, Kathryn. "The Politics of Property Rights." *American Political Science Review* 89, no. 4 (December 1995): 867.

Fischel, William A. *The Political Economy of Just Compensation: Lessons from the Military Draft for the Takings Issue*. Washington, DC: American Enterprise Institute Conference, March 7, 1996.

Gardner, Royal C. "Federal Wetland Mitigation Banking Guidance: Missed Opportunities." *Environmental Law Review* 26 (1996): 10075.

Getches, David H., and the Staff of the Northwest Power Planning Council. *Report to the Northwest Power Planning Council from the Workshop on Fish and Wildlife Governance*, February 12, 1996 (Internet: http://www.newsdata.com/enernet/fishnet/fishletter//fl2doc4.html).

Gidari, Albert. "The Endangered Species Act: Impact of Section 9 on Private Landowners." *Environmental Law* 24 (1994): 419.

Ginsberg, Beth S. "Babbitt v. Sweet Home Chapter of Communities for a Great Oregon: A Clarion Call for Property Rights Advocates." *Environmental Law Reporter* 24 (1995): 10478.

Ginsburg, Douglas H. "Delegation Running Riot." Book review. *Regulation* 1 (1995): 83.

Goklany, Indur M., and Merritt W. Sprague. *Sustaining Development and Biodiversity: Productivity, Efficiency, and Conservation*. Policy Analysis 175. Washington, DC: Cato Institute, August 6, 1992.

Goode, Bernard N. Statement before the U.S. Senate, Committee on Environment and Public Works, Subcommittee on Clean Air, Wetlands, Private Property and Nuclear Safety, July 19, 1995.

Gordon, Richard L. *Mining Law: The Last Public Land Battle*. Washington, DC: Cato Institute, forthcoming.

Hahn, Robert W. *Thinking Clearly About Takings, Endangered Species and Economics: A Comment*. Draft. Washington, DC: American Enterprise Institute Conference, March 7, 1996.

Henderson, Rick. "Preservation Acts." *Reason* (October 1994): 46.

Hess, Karl Jr. "Storm over the Rockies (The West at War with Itself)." *Reason* (June 1995): 18.

Hess, Karl Jr., and Jerry L. Holecheck. *Beyond the Grazing Fee: An Agenda for Rangeland Reform.* Policy Analysis 234. Washington, DC: Cato Institute, July 13, 1995.

Inhaber, Herbert. "A Market-Based Solution to the Problem of Nuclear and Toxic Waste Disposal." *Journal of the Air and Waste Management Association* 41, no. 6 (June 1991): 808.

Institute for Humane Studies. Symposium on Intellectual Property. *Harvard Journal of Law and Public Policy* 13 (Summer 1990): 757.

Kanner, Gideon. "Not with a Bang, But a Giggle: The Settlement of the Lucas Case." ABA Meeting on Urban, State and Local Government Law, August 1994.

Korngold, George. *Private Land Use Controls: Balancing Private Initiative and Public Interest in the Homeowners Association Context.* Cambridge, MA: Lincoln Institute of Land Policy, 1995.

Land Trust Alliance. *Conservation Options: A Landowner's Guide.* Washington, DC: Land Trust Alliance, 1993.

Lazarus, Richard J. "Putting the Correct 'Spin' on Lucas." *Stanford Law Review* 45 (1993): 1411.

Liebmann, George. "Modernization of Zoning: A Means to Reform." *Regulation* 2 (1996): 71.

Lyman, R. Jeffrey. "Learning from Norman Williams." *Land Use Law and Zoning Digest* 47, no. 10 (October 1995): 8.

Mannix, Brian. "The Origin of Endangered Species and the Descent of Man." *American Enterprise* (November–December 1992): 56.

Maryland–National Capital Park and Planning Commission. *Staff Recommendations on Public Hearing (Preliminary) Draft Amendment to the Master Plan for Historic Preservation: Sunnyside, Locational Atlas Resource #15/50.* February 2, 1994.

Marzulla, Roger J., and Nancie G. Marzulla. "Regulatory Takings in the U.S. Claims Court: Adjusting the Burdens That in Fairness and Equity Ought to be Borne by Society as a Whole." *Catholic Law Review* 40 (1991): 549.

McElfish, James M. Jr. "Property Rights, Property Roots: Rediscovering the Basis for Legal Protection of the Environment." *Environmental Law Reporter* 24 (1994): 10231.

McElfish, James M. Jr., Philip Warburg, and John Pendergrass. "Property: Past, Present, Future." *Environmental Forum* 13, no. 5 (September–October 1996): 20.

Mineral Policy Center. *Burden of Gilt.* Washington, DC: Mineral Policy Center, June 1993.

Mueller, Tara L. "The Salvage Timber Sales Law: A Serious Threat to Public Lands Management." *Environmental Law Review* 26 (1996): 10065.

Myers, Phyllis. *Lessons from the States: Strengthening Land Conservation Programs Through Grants to Nonprofit Land Trusts.* Washington, DC: Land Trust Alliance, 1992.

National Association of Homebuilders. *The Truth About America's Wetlands.* Washington, DC: The Association, n.d. (c. 1994).

———. *The Truth About America's Forests.* Washington, DC: The Association, n.d. (c. 1994).

National Commission on Wildlife Disasters. *Report.* Washington, DC: The Commission, March 24, 1994. Available from the American Forestry Association, Washington, DC.

National Trust for Historic Preservation. *Preliminary Program: 50th National Preservation Conference, October 16–20, 1996.* Washington, DC: The Trust, 1996.

National Trust for Historic Preservation and Land Trust Alliance. *Appraising Easements.* 2d ed. Washington, DC: The Trust and the Alliance, 1990.

Nelson, Robert H. "Bruce Babbitt, Pipeline to the Almighty." *Weekly Standard,* June 24, 1996, p. 17.

————. *How and Why to Transfer BLM Lands to the States.* Washington, DC: Competitive Enterprise Institute, January 1996.

Note. "Taking a Step Back: A Reconsideration of the Takings Test of Nollan v. California Coastal Commission." *Harvard Law Review* 102 (1988): 448.

Novak, Theodore, et al, "Landowners Need Defensive Strategies." *National Law Journal,* September 26, 1994, p. B10.

Oppenheimer, Todd. "The Rancher Subsidy." *Atlantic* (January 1996): 26.

O'Toole, Randall. *Run Them Like Businesses: Natural Resource Agencies in an Era of Federal Limits.* Research Paper 32. Oak Grove, OR: Thoreau Institute, March 1995.

Overstreet, Gregory. "The Ripeness Doctrine of the Taking Clause: A Survey of Decisions Showing Just How Far Federal Courts Will Go to Avoid Adjudicating Land Use Cases." *Journal of Land Use and Environmental Law* 10 (1994): 1.

Pambianco, Robert V. (ed.). *The National Trust for Historic Preservation: Organization Trends.* Washington, DC: Capital Research Center, July 1995.

Pierce, Robert J. "Redefining our Regulatory Goals." *National Wetlands Newsletter* 13, no. 6 (November–December 1991): 12.

Pillon, Roger. "Can American Asset Forfeiture Law Be Justified?" *New York University Law Review* 34 (1994): 311.

————. "Freedom, Responsibility, and the Constitution: On Recovering Our Founding Principles." *Notre Dame Law Review* 68 (1993): 507.

————. "Prodding the Court to Protect Property Rights." *Cato Policy Report* 16 (January–February 1994): 1.

Quarles, Steven P., John A. Macleod, and Thomas R. Lundquist. "Sweet Home and the Narrowing of Wildlife 'Take' Under Section 9 of the Endangered Species Act." *Environmental Law Reporter* 26 (1996): 10003.

Reed, Terrance G. *American Forfeiture Law: Property Owners Meet the Prosecutor.* Policy Analysis 179. Washington, DC: Cato Institute, September 29, 1992.

Richardson, Craig E., and Geoff C. Ziebart. *Red Tape in America: Stories from the Front Line.* Washington, DC: Heritage Foundation, 1995.

Roisman, Anthony Z., and Gary E. Mason. "Nuisance and the Recovery of 'Stigma' Damages: Eliminating the Confusion." *Environmental Law Review* 26 (1996): 10070.

Rose, Carol. "Property as the Keystone Right?" *Notre Dame Law Review* 71 (1996): 329.

————. Statement before the Senate Judiciary Committee Hearing on "The Right to Property," April 6, 1995.

Rose-Ackerman, Susan. "Inalienability and the Theory of Property Rights." *Columbia Law Review* 85 (1985): 931.

Rothbard, Murray. "Law, Property Rights, and Air Pollution." *Cato Journal* 2, no. 1 (Spring 1982): 55.

Rubenfeld, Jed. "Usings." *Yale Law Journal* 102 (1993): 1077.

Sax, Joseph L. "Property Rights and the Economy of Nature: Understanding Lucas v. South Carolina Coastal Council." *Stanford Law Review* 45 (1993): 1433.

Sedjo, Roger A. *The World's Forests: Conflicting Signals.* Washington, DC: Competitive Enterprise Institute, February 1995.

Sidak, J. Gregory, and Daniel F. Spulber. *Deregulatory Takings and the Regulatory Contract.* Washington, DC: American Enterprise Institute Conference, March 7, 1996.

Simon, Julian L. "Origins of the Airline Oversales Auction System." *Regulation* 2 (1994): 48.

Simon, Julian L., and Aaron Wildavsky. *Assessing the Empirical Basis of the "Biodiversity Crisis."* Washington, DC: Competitive Enterprise Institute, May 1993.

Sinclair, Robert S. "Preserving Paradise: With Critics on All Sides, the Nature Conservancy Must Be Doing Something Right." *Washingtonian* (February 1996): 37.

Smith, Robert J. "Resolving the Tragedy of the Commons by Creating Private Property Rights in Wildlife." *Cato Journal* 1, no. 2 (Fall 1991): 439.

———. "The Anti-Property Rights Crusade." *CEI Update* (January 1995): 6.

Strand, Margaret N. "Federal Wetlands Law." In Environmental Law Institute, *Wetlands Deskbook* (1993): 1.

———. "Recent Developments in Federal Wetlands Law: Part I." *Environmental Law Reporter* 26 (1996): 10283.

———. "Recent Developments in Federal Wetlands Law: Part II." *Environmental Law Reporter* 26 (1996): 10339.

———. "Recent Developments in Federal Wetlands Law: Part III." *Environmental Law Reporter* 26 (1996): 10399.

Stroup, Richard L. "Hazardous Waste Policy: A Property Rights Perspective." *Environmental Reporter,* September 22, 1989, p. 868.

Sugg, Ike C. "Caught in the Act: Evaluating the Endangered Species Act, Its Effects on Man and Prospects for Reform." *Cumberland Law Review* 24 (1993–1994): 1.

———. *Elephants and Ivory: Lessons from the Trade Ban.* London: Institute of Economic Affairs, 1994.

———. *Rats, Lies, and the GAO: A Critique of the General Accounting Office Report on the Role of the Endangered Species Act in the California Fire of 1993.* Washington, DC: Competitive Enterprise Institute, August 1994.

———. *Reforming the Endangered Species Act: The Property Rights Perspective.* Statement before the Endangered Species Act Task Force of the Committee on Resources, U.S. House of Representatives, May 18, 1995.

Thompson, Barton H., Jr. "Judicial Takings." *Virginia Law Review* 76 (1990): 1449.

———. *The Endangered Species Act: A Case Study in Takings and Incentives.* Washington, DC: American Enterprise Institute Conference, March 7, 1996.

Thornton, Robert D. "The Search for a Conservation Planning Paradigm: Section 10 of the ESA." *Natural Resources and Environment* 8, no. 1 (Summer 1993): 21.

Tolman, Jonathan. *Federal Agricultural Policy: A Harvest of Environmental Abuse.* Washington, DC: Competitive Enterprise Institute, August 1995.

———. *Gaining More Ground: Analysis of Wetlands Trends in the United States.* Washington, DC: Competitive Enterprise Institute, October 1994.

U.S. Department of Agriculture. Soil Conservation Service. *Summary Report 1992, National Resources Inventory.* July 1994.

U.S. Department of the Army. Corps of Engineers. "Final Program for Nationwide Permit Program Regulations and Issue, Reissue, and Modify Nationwide Permits." *Federal Register,* November 22, 1991.

U.S. Department of the Interior. Fish and Wildlife Service. "Endangered and Threatened Wildlife and Plants; Proposed Special Rule for the Conservation of the Northern Spotted Owl on Non-Federal Lands." *Federal Register,* February 17, 1995.

————. "Endangered and Threatened Wildlife and Plants; Proposed Rule Exempting Certain Small Landowners and Low-Impact Activities from Endangered Species Act Requirements for Threatened Species." *Federal Register,* July 20, 1995.

————. *Handbook for Habitat Conservation Planning and Incidental Take Permit Processing.* Preliminary draft. September 15, 1994.

————. *Recovery Program, Endangered and Threatened Species.* Report to Congress, 1994.

————. *National Wetlands Inventory.* November 1994.

————. *Photointerpretation Conventions for the National Wetlands Inventory.* January 1995.

————. *Wetlands Classification System.* Wetlands Conservation Part 660. 1993.

————. *Wetland Criteria/Indicators/Procedures.* N.d.

————. *Use of Aerial Photography for Mapping Wetlands in the United States: National Wetlands Inventory,* September 1994.

U.S. Department of the Interior. Office of the Inspector General. *Department of the Interior Land Acquisitions Conducted with the Assistance of Nonprofit Organizations.* Report 92-I-833. May 1992.

U.S. Department of Justice. Letter to Hon. Charles T. Canady, Chairman Subcommittee on the Constitution, House Committee on the Judiciary, September 20, 1995.

————. *Annual Report of the Department of Justice Asset Forfeiture Program Fiscal Year 1993.* 1994.

U.S. General Accounting Office. *Agricultural Conservation: Status of Programs That Provide Financial Incentives.* Letter report RCED-95-169. April 28, 1995.

————. *Animal Damage Control Program: Efforts to Protect Livestock from Predators.* GAO/RCED-96-3. October 1995.

————. *Bureau of Reclamation: Information on Allocation and Repayment of Costs of Constructing Water Projects.* GAO/RCED-96-109. July 1996.

————. *Clean Water Act: Private Property Takings Claims as a Result of the Section 404 Program.* GAO/RCED-93-176FS. August 1993.

————. *Cotton Program: Costly and Complex Government Program Needs to Be Reassessed.* GAO-RCED-95-107. June 1995.

————. *Ecosystem Management: Additional Actions Needed to Adequately Test a Promising Approach.* RCED-94-111. August 1994.

————. *Endangered Species Act: Impact of Species Protection Efforts on the 1993 California Fire.* RCED-94-224. July 1994.

————. *Endangered Species Act: Information on Species Protection on Nonfederal Lands.* Letter report RCED-95-16. December 1994.

————. *Endangered Species Recovery on Refuges.* RCED-95-7. November 1994.

————. *Federal Land Management: Streamlining and Reorganization Issues.* T-RCED-96-209. June 27, 1996.

————. *Federal Lands: Information on Land Owned and on Acreage with Conservation Restrictions.* GAO/RCED-95-73FS. January 1995.

————. *Federal Lands: Information on the Use and Impact of Off-Highway Vehicles.* GAO/RCED-95-209. August 1995.

————. *Forest Service: Distribution of Timber Sales Receipts Fiscal Years 1992–94.* GAO/RCED-95-237FS. September 1995.

————. *Forest Service: Issues Relating to Its Decisionmaking Process.* GAO/T-RCED-96-66. January 25, 1996.

————. *Forestry Functions: Unresolved Issues Affect Forest Service and BLM*. GAO/RCED-94-124. May 1994.

————. *Information on the Acreage, Management, and Use of Federal and Other Lands*. GAO/RCED-96-40. March 1996.

————. *Intellectual Property: Enhancements Needed in Computing and Reporting Patent Examination Statistics*. GAO/RCED-96-190. July 1996.

————. *Intellectual Property Rights: U.S. Companies Patent Experience in Japan*. GAO/GGD-93-126. July 1993.

————. *Mineral Resources: Federal Coal-Leasing Program Needs Strengthening*. RCED-94-10. September 1994.

————. *National Parks: Difficult Choices Need to Be Made About the Future of the Parks*. RCED-95-238. August 1995.

————. *Natural Resources: Defense and Interior Can Better Manage Land Withdrawn for Military Use*. NSIAD-94-87. April 1994.

————. *Public Pension Plans: Evaluation of Economically Targeted Investment Programs*. PEMD-95-13. March 1995.

————. *Public Timber: Federal and State Programs Differ Significantly in Pacific Northwest*. RCED-96-108. May 1996.

————. *U.S. Forest Service: Fee System for Rights-of-Way Program Needs Revision*. GAO/RCED-96-86. April 1996.

Wade, William W. "Economic Considerations of Regulatory Takings Reform: Judicial Precedent and Administrative Law vs. Legislative Intent." Bureau of National Affairs, *Environmental Law*, August 4, 1995, p. 676.

Warburg, Phillip, and James M. McElfish, Jr. "Property Rights and Responsibilities: Nuisance, Land-Use Regulation, and Sustainable Use." *Environmental Law Reporter* 24 (1994): 10520.

Welsh, Richard. Untitled paper. Internet: National Association of Reversionary Property Owners, January 1, 1996. [Internet: http://www.halcyon.com/dick/row.html]

White House Office on Environmental Policy. *Protecting America's Wetlands: A Fair, Flexible, and Effective Approach*. Washington, DC: Executive Office of the President, August 24, 1993.

Yandle, Bruce. *Regulatory Takings, Farmers, Ranchers and the Fifth Amendment*. Center for Policy Studies Property Rights Project, October 1994.

Young, Richard D., and T. E. Dahl. *Use of GIS in Assessing Areas of Rapid Wetland Change*, In *1994 GIS/LIS Conference Proceedings*, 851.

HEARINGS, CONFERENCES and COLLECTIONS

American Bar Association. *Conference on Urban, State and Local Government Law*. August 1994.

American Bar Association. Section of Natural Resources, Energy, and Environmental Law. "Endangered Species Protection." Symposium. Special issue of *Natural Resources & Environment* 8 no. 1 (Summer 1993).

American Enterprise Institute. *Conference on Economic and Constitutional Perspectives on Takings*. Washington, DC, March 7, 1996.

American Law Institute–American Bar Association. *Inverse Condemnation and Related Government Liability: Course of Study Materials*. San Francisco, May 4–6, 1995.

Competitive Enterprise Institute. *Proceedings from the Seminar on Ecology and Religion.* Washington, DC, April 30–May 1, 1993.

Federalist Society. *Conference on Takings and the Environment: The Constitutional Implications of Environmental Regulation and Supplemental Materials.* Washington, DC: Federalist Society, 1992.

Keystone Center. *Keystone Dialogue on Incentives to Protective Endangered Species on Private Lands: Final Report.* Symposium. Keystone, CO: The Center, July 25, 1995.

Land Economics. "Private Markets, Public Decisions: An Assessment of Local Land-Use Controls for the 1990s." Symposium. Special issue of *Land Economics* 66, no. 3 (August 1990).

National Policy Forum. *Private Property Rights: A Roundtable Discussion.* Washington, DC, December 21, 1994.

———. *The Endangered Species Act: Recovering Common Sense.* Washington, DC, June 13, 1995.

———. *Sane Environmental Enforcement: How Enforcement Went Wrong, and How to Correct It.* Washington, DC, August 3, 1995.

U.S. House of Representatives. Committee on the Judiciary. Subcommittee on the Constitution. *Hearings on Protecting Private Property Rights from Regulatory Takings,* February 10, 1995.

———. Committee on Resources. Task Force on Private Property. *Hearings.* May 17, June 3, 13, July 17, 1995.

———. Committee on Resources. Task Force on Endangered Species Act. *Hearings,* May 10, 18, 25, 1995.

U.S. Senate. Committee on Agriculture, Nutrition, and Forestry. *Hearings on Conservation, Wetlands and Farm Policy.* March 14, 1995.

———. Committee on the Judiciary. *Hearings on the Omnibus Property Rights Act of 1995 (S.605),* April 6, 1995.

PERIODICALS AND NEWSLETTERS

Alliance News. Alliance for America. P.O. Box 449, Caroga Lake, NY 12032. Tel.: (518) 835-6702; Fax: (518) 835-2527.

American Forests. American Forests. 1516 P St., NW, Washington, DC 20005. Tel.: (202) 667-3300.

Blue Ribbon Magazine. Blue Ribbon Coalition. 4990 Valenty Road, Pocatello, ID 83202. Tel.: (208) 237-1557; Fax: (208) 237-1566.

Cato Policy Report. Cato Institute. 1000 Massachusetts Ave., NW, Washington, DC 20001. Tel.: (202) 842-0200; Fax: (202) 842-3490.

CEI Update. Competitive Enterprise Institute. 1001 Connecticut Ave., NW, Suite 1250, Washington, DC 20036. Tel.: (202) 331-1010; Fax: (202) 331-0640.

CERA News. Citizens Equal Rights Alliance, Inc. P.O. Box 23205, Santa Fe, NM 87502. Tel.: (505) 466-0216.

Defender. Individual Rights Foundation. 9911 West Pico Blvd., Suite 1290, Los Angeles, CA 90035. Tel.: (800) 752-6562.

eco-logic. Environmental Conservation Organziation. P.O. Box 191. Hollow Rock, TN 38342. Tel.: (901) 986-0099.

Environmental Forum. Environmental Law Institute. 1616 P St., NW, Washington, DC 20036. Tel.: (202) 328-5150.

Evergreen Magazine and *Evergreen Digest.* Evergreen Foundation. 5000 Cirrus Drive, Suite 201, Medford, OR 97504. Tel.: (541) 773-2247; Fax: (541) 772-2882.

Exchange. Land Trust Alliance. 1319 F St., Suite 501, Washington, DC 20014. Tel.: (202) 638-4725; Fax: (202) 638-4730.

Insider. Heritage Foundation. 214 Massachusetts Ave., NE, Washington, DC 20002. Tel.: (202) 546-4400; Fax: (202) 544-6979.

Landlines. Lincoln Institute of Land Policy. 113 Brattle St., Cambridge, MA 02138. Tel.: (617) 661-3016.

Land Rights Letter. Land Rights Foundation, Inc., P.O. Box 1111, Gloversville, NY 12078. Tel.: (518) 725-1090; Fax: (518) 725-8239.

Land Use Law & Zoning Digest. American Planning Association. 122 S. Michigan Ave., Suite 1600, Chicago, IL 60603. Tel.: (312) 431-9100.

Multiple Land Use Review. American Land Rights Association/National Inholders Association. 30218 NE 82nd Ave., Battle Ground, WA 98604. Tel.: (360) 687-3087; Fax: (360) 687-2973.

National Parks. National Parks and Conservation Association. 1776 Massachusetts Ave., NW. Washington, DC 20036. Tel.: (202) 223-6722.

National Wetlands Newsletter. Environmental Law Institute. 1616 P St., NW, Washington, DC 20036. Tel.: (202) 328-5150.

New York Property Rights Clearing House. Property Rights Foundation of America. P.O. Box 75, Stony Creek, NY 12878. Tel.: (518) 696-5748.

News from the FLOC. Fairness to Land Owners Committee. 1730 Garden of Eden Road, Cambridge, MD 21613. Tel.: (410) 228-3822; Fax: (410) 228-3965.

NWI Resource. National Wilderness Institute. P.O. Box 25766, Georgetown Station, Washington, DC 20007. Tel.: (703) 836-7404; Fax: (703) 549-6889.

PERC Reports. Political Economy Research Center. 502 S. 19th Ave., Suite 211, Bozeman, MT 59715. Tel.: (406) 587-9591; Fax: (406) 586-7555.

Positions on Property. Property Rights Foundation of America. P.O. Box 75, Stony Creek, NY 12878. Tel.: (518) 696-5748.

Property Rights Reporter. Defenders of Property Rights. 6235 33rd St., NW, Washington, DC 20015. Tel.: (202) 686-4197; Fax: (202) 686-0240.

Resource Sentinel. Hunting & Angling Club. P.O. Box 3639, Minneapolis, MN 55403. Tel.: (612) 339-3564.

Resources. Resources for the Future. 1616 P St., NW, Washington, DC 20036. Tel.: (202) 328-5000; Fax: (202) 939-3460.

Sierra. Sierra Club. 85 Second St., San Francisco, CA 94105. Tel.: (415) 398-5384.

NEWSPAPERS

New York Times
Washington Post
Washington Times
Wall Street Journal

VIDEOTAPES

Earth Vision Institute. *Forest Wars*. Gypsum, CO: Summit Films, 1996. Available from Summit Films, Box 420, Gypsum, CO; (970) 524-9769, tel.; (907) 524-9708, fax.
————. Outtakes of full speech of Bruce Whiting.
Bruce Babbitt, "Debate on the Alaska National Wildlife Refuge." *MacNeil/Lehrer News Hour*, PBS, November 27, 1995.

LEGAL CASES

This is by no means a comprehensive listing of cases concerning takings. It represents only the major cases used in this book. The most comprehensive recent list is in Steven J. Eagle's *Regulatory Takings* (Charlottesville, VA: Mitchie, 1996).

Supreme Court (In chronological order)

Baker v. Seldon, 101 U.S. 99 (1879).
Chicago, Burlington & Quincy Railroad v. Chicago, 166 U.S. 226 (1897).
Hadacheck v. Sebastian, 239 U.S. 394 (1915).
Pennsylvania Coal Co. v. Mahon, 269 U.S. 393 (1922).
Village of Euclid v. Ambler Realty Co., 272 U.S. 365 (1926).
Miller v. Schoene, 276 U.S. 272 (1928).
Nectow v. Cambridge, 277 U.S. 183 (1928).
Lynch v. Household Finance Corp., 405 U.S. 538 (1972).
Penn Central Transportation Co. v. City of New York, 438 U.S. 104 (1978).
Kaiser Aetna v. United States, 444 U.S. 164 (1979).
Andrus v. Allard, 444 U.S. 51 (1979).
PruneYard Shopping Center v. Robins, 447 U.S. 74 (1980).
Agins v. City of Tiburon, 447 U.S. 255 (1980).
Webb's Fabulous Pharmacies, Inc. v. Beckwith, 449 U.S. 155 (1980).
San Diego Gas & Electric Co. v. City of San Diego, 450 U.S. 621 (1981).
Hodel v. Virginia Surface Mining & Reclamation Association, 452 U.S. 264 (1981).
Loretto v. Teleprompter Manhattan CATV Corp., 458 U.S. 419 (1982).
Kirby Forest Industries v. United States, 467 U.S. 1 (1984).
Hawaii Housing Authority v. Midkiff, 467 U.S. 229 (1984).
Ruckelshaus v. Monsanto Co., 467 U.S. 986 (1984).
United States v. Riverside Bayview Homes Inc., 474 U.S. 121 (1985).
Williamson County Regional Planning Commission v. Hamilton Bank, 473 U.S. 172 (1985).
Connolly v. Pension Benefit Guaranty Corp., 475 U.S. 211 (1986).
MacDonald, Sommer & Frates v. Yolo County, 477 U.S. 340 (1986).
Keystone Bituminous Coal Association v. DeBenedictis, 480 U.S. 470 (1987).
Hodel v. Irving, 481 U.S. 704 (1987).
First English Evangelical Lutheran Church of Glendale v. County of Los Angeles, 482 U.S. 304 (1987).
Nollan v. California Coastal Commission, 483 U.S. 825 (1987).
Pennell v. City of San Jose, 485 U.S. 1 (1988).
Presault v. Interstate Commerce Commission, 494 U.S. 1 (1990).

Yee v. City of Escondido, 503 U.S. 519 (1992).

Lucas v. South Carolina Coastal Council, 505 U.S. 1003 (1992).

Keene Corp. v. United States, 113 S. Ct. 2035 (1993).

Dolan v. City of Tigard, 114 S. Ct. 2309 (1994).

Babbitt v. Sweet Home Chapter of Communities for a Great Oregon, 115 S. Ct. 2407 (1995).

Bennis v. Michigan, 116 S. Ct. 994 (1996).

Other (In chronological order)

Hall v. City of Santa Barbara, 833 F.2d 1270 (9th Cir. 1987).

Whitney Benefits v. United States, 926 F.2d 1169 (Fed. Cir.), *cert. denied*, 502 U.S. 952 (1991).

United States v. Ellen, 961 F.2d 462, (4th Cir. 1992).

Reahard v. Lee County, 968 F.2d 1131 (11th Cir. 1992); 978 F.2d 1212 (11th Cir. 1992); 30 F.3d 1412 (11th Cir. 1994).

Southview Associates, Ltd., v. Bongartz, 980 F.2d 84 (2d Cir. 1992).

Florida Rock Industries v. United States, 8 Cl. Ct. 160 (1985), 791 F.2d 893 (Fed. Cir. 1986), *cert. denied*, 479 U.S. 1053 (1990); 21 Cl. Ct. 161 (1990), 18 F.3d 1560 (Fed. Cir. 1994), *cert. denied*, 115 S. Ct. 895 (1995).

Loveladies Harbor, Inc. v. United States, 15 Cl. Ct. 381 (1988), 21 Cl. Ct. 153 (1990), 28 F.3d 1171 (Fed. Cir. 1994).

Loveladies Harbor, Inc. v. United States, 27 F.3d 1545 (Fed. Cir. 1994) (procedural decision).

Aged Hawaiians v. Hawaiian Homes Commission, 279 P.2d 279 (S. Ct. Hawaii, 1995).

Ehrlich v. City of Culver City, 911 P.2d 429 (S. Ct. Cal. 1996).

Hage v. United States, No. 91–1470L (Fed. Cl. 1996).

Index

375